BOXING

the story of money, blood, sweat and tears

LOYISO MTYA

Copyright © Loyiso Mtya

Published by RedOystor Books; 2021
in association with *SILULO ULUTHO TECHNOLOGIES (Pty) Ltd*

All rights reserved. No part of this publication may be reproduced, stored in a retrieval system, or transmitted in any form or by any means, electronic, mechanical, photocopying, recording, or otherwise, be lent, re-sold, hired-out, or otherwise circulated without express written consent of the author.

Published by RedOystor Books
an imprint of RedOystor Media (Pty) Ltd
   visit www.redoystor.com/contact-us for more information.

www.redoystor.com/Boxing

www.instagram.com/redOystor
www.facebook.com/redOystor
www.twitter.com/redOystor

Book Cover Design: RedOystor Media
Book Cover Image: zedge.net/profile/6066ba20-a14d-32e7-9285-759ac4aee38d
Layout & formatting: RedOystor Media

Editing done by Zuko Blauw - EL Museum
Proofreading by Lisa Phiri and Malibongwe Tokwe

Also available on Amazon.com
Available on Kindle and other retail outlets

  ISBN: 978-1-991206-92-3 (Print)
              978-1-991206-93-0 (epub)

To Clive, you fought a good fight champ.

London | Johannesburg | New York

ULoyiso nguGqirha

This is a Xhosa poem written by Nceba Dladla, a former boxer who was trained and mentored by Loyiso Mtya - preserved in its original form.

Enenen' Loyiso kukuphumelela,
Bubuchule bukachwenen' ochul' ukunyathela.
Ukuchwayita nokucondob' okuchaz' ukuzenzela,
Luvuyo' oluvez' ukuvum' ukuvavanywa nokuvonywa-vonywa ngokuzinikela.

ULoyiso nguLwaz' olude oku kukakrwecizulu,
Ulwazi ngamandl' asetyenziiswa ngobuchul' obunzulu.
Uzalw' enxanelulwaz' unyana waseMaqadini,
Olo nxan' aluthobe ngamanz' agxojagxojw' emanqindini.

Mbonen' uLoyiso yingqang' emanqindini ' eneentsiba zayo,
Utshotsh' entla tshomi noko engena matshamba.
Yingqwayngqwayi negqalanqa kumagqal' eqonga lamanqindi,
Uchunge-chunge ichul' ekuchophel' imicimb' echanekiley' enqindini.

ULoyiso nguMtya nethung' ukusebenza nzima, ukuzimisela,
Ukuzimisel' usebenza nzim' ujong' empumelelweni.
Empumelelwen' ekuzibaluleni ngaphaya ezinkwenkwezini,
Ezinkwenkwezi kuyehlukwana phofu ebuqaqawulini.

Njengembethi-manqind' uLoyis' uqabel' eqongeni,
Njengomqeqesh' uLoyis' uliqabel' iqonga,
Njengomlawul' uLoyis' uqabel' eqongeni,
NjengoMqondis' uLoyis' uliqabel' iqonga.

ULoyis' ukhe wafundisa njengetitshala,
Akuphuma kwaNokholej' uMqad' ubeyititshala.
Okhe wayititshala kwakanye,
Wohlal' eyitshala nditsho Kanye.

Iimbethimanqindi zakh' uzixelele ngale mfundo,
Ezo ziphumelel' iintshinga Kwanezo Zingena ntshinga zinemfundo,
Uthe kuz' imfundo ngunozala wentlutha ye Sizwe,
Isizw' esinemfundo bubutyebi bezizukulwana.

Mvanje ngemisebenzi yakh' uLoyiso uwongiwe,
Uthwesiwe ngesidanga sobuGqirha mvanje.
Kuthwe kuy' utshotsh' entla mfo kaMqadi ngoku unguGqirha,
Siyavova iNkosi yoXol' ivumile ULoyiso nguGqirha!!!

Contents

FOREWORD	IX

THE MONEY — 1

I AM A BOXER FIRST AND FOREMOST	3
WHERE ARE THE BLACK HEAVYWEIGHTS?	21
BOXING DURING APARTHEID RULE	29
TOO MANY WORLD SANCTIONING BODIES.	39
WHAT SELLS TICKETS	47
CONTRACTUAL BOXING DYNAMICS	55
WHY BOXERS MIGRATE TO GAUTENG?	61
THE BUSINESS OF PROMOTERS	69
FIXING BOXING IN THE EASTERN CAPE	83
WE DON'T NEED BOXING MANAGERS	93
WHERE DOES ALL THE MONEY GO?	97

THE BLOOD — 109

CAN A BOXER TRAIN THEMSELVES	111
GIVE ME A COMPLETE FIGHTER	123
IS FIGHT-FIXING STILL A PRACTICE?	133
BORN IN AFRICA, MADE IN ENGLAND	139
TRANSKEI BOXING BACK WITH A BANG	155
THE MAKING OF THE BOXING MECCA	165
CALL IT SISA DUKASHE STADIUM	201
IF YOU CAN MAKE IT AT THE ORIENT THEATRE	213

SWEAT AND TEARS — 231

THE FUTURE OF BOXING IN THE EASTERN CAPE?	233
THE BIGGEST FIGHT THAT NEVER HAPPENED	249
SCHOOLS BOOST MECCA BOXING	257
WHEN DEATH MAKES NO SENSE	263
MDANTSANE GIRLS ROLL WITH THE PUNCHES	271
FOR THE LOVE OF BOXING	279
THE FOUNDING FATHERS OF THE BOXING MECCA	291
THE MEDIA	305
WITH A LITTLE HELP FROM FRIENDS	311
HISTORY-MAKERS IN THE MECCA	323
WHO SPOILED THE BUFFALO PARTY	337
CAN MIKE TYSON FLOAT LIKE A BUTTERFLY?	341
SO NEAR AND YET SO FAR	345
NEW IDEAS TO IMPROVE BOXING	351
THE HEADACHE OF SETTING THE RANKINGS.	363
UNIFYING AMATEUR BOXING	367
THE COVID-19 KNOCKOUT	375

About The Author	**387**
Bibliography & Notes	**389**
Glossary & Acronyms	**395**
Boxing Weight Divisions	**403**
Acknowledgements	**407**
Index & References	**409**

FOREWORD

Firstly, let me start by saying, I have never had the opportunity to be a boxer. I played other sports, but boxing was not one of them. However, as backgrounds would go, I am a student of sports.

The first thing I should say about Loyiso Mtya, boxing runs in his DNA. He lives and breathes boxing. Boxing is Loyiso and Loyiso is boxing. Secondly, the establishment of Boxing South Africa (BSA) was made possible in part because of the role that Loyiso Mtya played in bringing boxing to the forefront of sports in South Africa.

No one disputes the fact that boxing runs in the veins of Loyiso Mtya. He comes from a pedigree of a boxing family - big fans of the sport and very much involved in every way. The Mtya's are known to be avid promoters, supporters and partakers of boxing. Their passion is so deep you would be forgiven if you thought boxing was synonymous with the Mtya family. And I learnt to love boxing because of the Mtya family. I take up the challenge for anyone to prove me wrong, but I am convinced, and it is my firm belief that Loyiso Mtya is boxing South Africa, and boxing South Africa is Loyiso Mtya.

I will not go much into the detail of our personal relationship; however, it should be made clear that our professional relationship when I worked with him and Boxing South Africa - back when I served as the Minister of Sports, I saw a man with a passion and a vision for the sport. I experienced a very knowledgeable sports administrator. BSA is solid because of the passion and commitment of Loyiso Mtya and his team - he was the "Main Man".

Boxing in South Africa is not English. The home of boxing in South Africa is Mdantsane. And Mdantsane came alive with boxing because of this one man's passion. With this contribution to the book as it pertains to the history and development of boxing mainly in the Eastern Cape and partly in the rest of South Africa, I firmly believe boxing would not have been done the way it was done had it not been for the involvement and contributions of Loyiso Mtya. This is not to say there weren't others who contributed. It is my conviction that's Loyiso played a big role in making it all possible - is'starring se boxing.

When I worked with him, I appreciated his insight into boxing. He was and still is a phenomenon in boxing as much as he is a phenomenal person as a leader, guide and mentor.

When I entered the sporting movement, I didn't know much about boxing but Loyiso together with Dumile Mateza - the late broadcaster with a remarkable voice, and Mzi Mguni (also late) - legendary boxing manager, collectively made me fall in love with the noble art. They made me understand and appreciate what boxing was really about. This wasn't about me; I didn't know boxing; I knew other sports, but this trio shined the spotlight on boxing it became hard to ignore.

When the time came for the change in The South African Boxing Act 39 of 1954; myself, Loyiso, Dumile, Mzi Mnguni and many others, we created the only sporting federation that is governed by Parliament. This was made possible with the guidance of this trio, the MECs at that time - including Mondli Ngungubele, Nosimo Balindlela, Msebe from the Free State, Narend Singh - from the IFP; they made a huge contribution to the development and face of boxing as we know it today. And I believe we got it right.

Women boxing was encouraged and motivated personally by Loyiso Mtya. When it was introduced as a legal sport in South Africa it fell on his lap and he was the man to deal with it. He was keen to see how women would be part of this life-changing sport. The likes of Mama B, often pay tribute to Loyiso for leading the "Women in Boxing" agenda. He was galvanising all players within the sporting world to make room for women's boxing, using the groundbreaking development project Baby Champs to create a chance for women - and it worked. I would like to believe Loyiso played a critical role in ensuring it comes to life.

When I came back from being an Ambassador Designate in the USA after 5 years, the first person I met in the office – when I was appointed Chairman of BSA – was Loyiso Mtya and the team. While people thought I was there to get rid of Loyiso as the Boxing SA administrator, I understood how his passion and role was important to the development of boxing. I decided that if boxing was to survive the hardships it was experiencing at the time, Loyiso was the man to keep as the acting CEO of Boxing SA. Together we changed the administration and development of boxing and improved the audit of Boxing SA. The auditor's reports are there for all to see. After a year and a half of working together, I felt I had done what the Minister of Sports at the time, Fikile Mbalula had asked of me to do with Boxing SA.

After that, Loyiso left Boxing SA, because he was unhappy with developments within the organisation. Boxing was falling apart and not much was being done about it. I still believe his passion and experience were a loss to the organisation and boxing as a sport. For this reason, I could not get myself back into sports administration - but myself and Loyiso kept in touch till today.

I was pleased and excited when he told me he had written a book on the history and development of boxing. Finally, he would express his passion for the world to see, he would teach the youth and lead them from the streets that are full of ill-discipline, drugs and liquor. He would educate communities and lead them to a new world stage of self-awareness and self-confidence. And so I still maintain, Loyiso knows more about boxing than most people I know in the boxing world. That has been my journey with Loyiso.

I didn't get to read the full book, but the little that I got and my experience having worked with Loyiso Mtya, leaves me with no doubt in my mind that it is packed with well-meaning and well-resourced information about the world of boxing. Loyiso knows more about boxing than most people I know. Anything you want to know, want to have and want to achieve in boxing, Loyiso Mtya is the Man for the Job. This book has my blessing.

When he was approached to be awarded an Honorary Doctorate by Trinity International Bible University, I was the first person he shared it with and asked for my advice. He presented it to me because he believed I was his Senior and he needed to honour my contribution towards his achievement of the Honorary Doctorate. However, I believed otherwise, I told him he had earned it and that he deserved it, and this book is a testament to that - Loyiso Mtya is boxing and boxing is Loyiso Mtya.

Ngconde Balfour

Mr Ngconde Mathemba Balfour

Minister of Sport and Recreation (1999 – 2004) of the Republic of South, Minister of Correctional Services (2004 – 2009), Former Ambassador-Designate to the USA (2009 – 2014)

THE MONEY

LOYISO MTYA | 1

CHAPTER 1

I AM A BOXER FIRST AND FOREMOST

BOXING IS A UNIQUE sport.

It is romantic. It is addictive.

It is scientific. It is artistic.

It is dynamic. It is magnetic.

It is humane. It is sensitive.

It is thankless. It is jealous.

It is mysterious. It is appalling.

It is reverting. It is harsh, nasty, cruel.

It is dramatic. It is dangerous. It is violent.

It is sweet. It is sour. It is brutal.

It is graceful. It is demanding. It is compassionate.

It is personal. It is arguably all of these things put together, and more. I was born into it. I was born for it. And I believe it to be the noblest of arts. Having been involved and worked in the boxing game in every category all my life, I still find it as exciting and enticing as any drug one gets hooked on. Gradually as I've taken each step up within its ranks, I have also found it be also contradictory.

With its successes and misfortunes, it still makes boxer's dreams come true, as much as it breaks them with one punch. It brings fame and fortune. But the same fame and fortune can be a one-way ticket to self-destruction and despair. Once it mixes with your blood system, it never lets you go. It is chronic and compulsive.

When boxers start, their dreams are all the same. Everybody is going to be a world champion. A majority of boys from Mdantsane in the Eastern Cape, and recently even some girls, have at some stage worn boxing gloves and faced someone they were billed to fight. Sometimes even a friend or own brother or sister.

Many were given an absolute thrashing and never came back to fight. It doesn't take long to realise the road ahead and finding out that it is much harder to become a boxer in reality than is in one's dreams. Some decided to get involved in other categories of the game.

They preferred that rather than leave the game they were born into and had grown to love so much, they would do something else. They plunged their energies into officiating, analysis, writing, commentating, anything to keep them in the sport until they became legends of the game. Like boxing, people will always tell you, "Once the boxing bug stings, you stay stung."

I am one of the few, if not the only one, that did it all. And did it with massive success. Today as I pause to look back, I smile and take pride in not giving up and taking my attention elsewhere. Even though I realised that I was well equipped to reach the top of the mountain, I did not have the dedication it takes to produce the best of myself.

I count myself fortunate to have been competitive enough to gain a measure of success that has resulted in me winning titles, awards and other accolades in every category I have engaged in.

Those accomplishments include winning the South African Junior Middleweight championship when winning it was a mammoth task – the period roundly regarded as the Golden years of boxing. I retired from the ring with great satisfaction. Firstly, that I had taken the brave decision to be a boxer and secondly, that I had made my mark in the world of boxing. No one I know has ever claimed to have been forced to take up boxing.

That is a personal decision. Especially the decision of becoming a professional boxer. Boxers know the dangers which they expose themselves to. Temporary and permanent injuries. Even death. They cause it. They suffer it. They face it every day in the gym. They wrestle with it every time they step into the ring – the bravery of knowing the risk and challenging it head-on. Only the bravest can lay claim to such accomplishment. Boxers are some of the most courageous people one can meet.

I am proud to have been one of them. I am proud to have shared the boxing rings with them. And I love them with all my heart. I will always do. Boxing is my home. The boxing ring is my house. I'm not going anywhere. The journey I have taken in boxing has armed me with the knowledge and experience to write about the people I have met, the places I have been, the events, social, political and otherwise, that have influenced boxing in South Africa and the world.

As I fought my way through the amateur ranks, up the professional boxing ladder to winning the national title, I learned that hard work, keenness to learn, and paying attention are the recipe and ingredient for success in boxing. This line of work is not as simple and easy as one would think. Every day you choose, and some of these choices are about life or death. Or close enough to resemble life or death.

Boxing is no different. Skills, strength and power can be trained and developed. But desire has to come from within.

The boxing gym is a school on its own. One has to go, learn and get a good education. Boxing demands the capacity to go through all the physical and mental drills that push the body and mind to the edge. Boxing gives birth to courage and desire to achieve that ultimate victory, fame and fortune. We prepare our bodies to be so impenetrable, our minds to be so intense to denying pain, fear and fatigue.

Confidence and determination play a vital role. These are also requirements by which fans measure and accept their heroes. Boxers are not expected to doubt themselves. Going through my first three coaches, former boxers *Aycliff Stengile* and *Lungisa Dukashe*, as well as *Mthuthuzeli Baduza*, the school teacher allocated to train us, I soon learnt that fighters, as well as their trainers, are aware of the dangers they face.

I am aware that one punch can make the difference between life and death. I am also aware that the very same punch could make the difference between a life of poverty and one of fortune. Boxing is different from other sporting codes in that while the display of excellent boxing skills is of utmost importance, the shortest route to victory is a knockout. And that means the training and education for offensive boxing must be as necessary as the drills and awareness for defense.

Protect yourself at all times, is the daily danger awareness call by trainers. Our sport is brutal. We are all aware that the main aim is to injure and knock opponents senseless. Like all other boxers, I always heard about one casualty or another—even death. But I always felt like it would not happen to me.

This brutality of boxing and its sometimes fatal results may be the answer to why there is such a strong connection between boxing, boxers and faith. The constant reminder of the possibility of death is enough for fighters to come to terms with the imminent risks as they come face to face with death every time they walk into the ring.

Death is always a possibility. That is a reality every fighter has to come to terms with. Boxers know their abilities, and they realise they are mere mortals. They are also well aware that strengths are nowhere near enough to serve as complete proof protection against all the evil, injury or death. They have to grapple with that.

In all that, they seek some kind of divine intervention. No matter where these fighters come from, every boxer pins their hopes and asks for protection from the Supreme Being referred to in many different ways but is known and accepted as God the Creator.

As in all human behaviour, there are differences or diversity in the way people worship and seek protection. Boxers follow their activities of faith according to their geographical, social or cultural and traditional backgrounds. Such appeals to the Higher Being are in most cases made in prayer, vocal traditional expressions like praise, dance, song, and traditional medicine and smoke.

While most boxers adhere to only one religious practice, many fighters tend to subscribe to both Christian and African traditional religions. Such practices are often intertwined. Religious services and traditional rituals become constant practices on the days leading to the fight, right up to the time boxers have to take that all-important walk to the ring.

Gospel songs have become an integral part of the ring entrance for several boxers. In South Africa, Christianity is the leading religion. For that reason, it is more prevalent and visible when boxers seek divine protection in the ring.

We give thanks and praise to God after each victory. Regardless of one's views on such matters, the effects of such beliefs and practices seem so profound and undeniable they have been lifting the spirits, lending needed confidence and producing the expected results for the people for centuries. However, it is important to note as a matter of great importance that not all boxers believe nor adhere to the practices mentioned above. There are boxers one would regard as squeaky clean, believing in themselves and their abilities much more than they believe in the luck of the game. Often they credit powers they cannot prove for their skills and victories.

Finally, in 1981 I had to say goodbye to my active boxing days because I had developed high blood pressure, which needed to be controlled. At that time, I was already too involved and connected in the game to walk away.

There was certainly a lot I could plough back. I thought I had too much information. I could not be satisfied with walking away from the game without ploughing back all that I had gained from boxing. I thought I owed it to boxing and all those involved in it, especially the youngsters.

I had seen a lot of young and eager boys growing up in my gym. Boys I had grown to love and who loved me in return. I was like a father to a lot of them. I could not leave them like that. I made up my mind to manage and train these boys. I have now found myself having to change my mind frame. I was no longer a boxer but a man, father and leader who had to look after the welfare and careers boxers. I had to guide their careers concerning fights, as well as their training. I had to learn that looking after them as fighters was not enough. I had to manage their lives and lead them to the future as men and leaders of tomorrow.

This change in position meant that my duties were no longer about me but about the guys I was about to lead. Being their manager and trainer meant that I would also be a teacher and a disciplinarian – a mentor. I felt I had enough knowledge and experience to deliver on that promise. It was not easy. But I enjoyed it. I still do. I was to get into the terrain I regard as the most critical appendage in the boxer's life – the trainer. I would now be the person who is there before, during and after every training program. I would also have to be there for the planning sessions and fighting contests the boxer takes on. The trainer studies and analyses the overall fighting abilities like natural skills, learned moves, strengths and weaknesses, and the general attitude of both his boxers and opponents.

A knowledgeable and experienced trainer knows that personal attitude is the primary determinant of how far the boxer can go through the thick and thin in the boxing field of play. The trainer knows that nothing comes easy in boxing. As such, he has to possess all the information, knowledge, and ability to teach, guide, and mentor through the journey.

He has to be able to prepare, analyse and come out with the winning formula. It is the trainer who is closest to the boxer, exchanging words, blows and sweat. The trainer is the last one out of the ring after everybody leaves. He cannot exit the ring without the final touch, embrace or final words of caution and motivation—all in line with keeping the fighter's mind firmly in the fight and the fight strategy intact.

Such final rituals make the difference between winning and losing a fight. The boxer will catch his trainer's voice amid all the noise of voices, music and all sorts of other disturbances during the bout.

My reign as a trainer was going to be an amazing journey and a career on its own. It was to take me to countries and gyms across the globe. Such excursions resulted in working relations and learning opportunities from gyms and trainers in South Africa, the USA, UK, France, Canada and Russia.

I can remember perhaps the two most outstanding trainers of all time, namely Emmanuel Steward–at the famous *Kronk Gym* in Detroit, Massachusetts and *Eddie Futch* in Las Vegas, Nevada. They went to their final resting places, remembering this enthusiastic South African youngster who visited their gyms. It put me in the mix of unforgettable training sessions with all-time greats like *Evander Holyfield* and *Riddick Bowe*.

If one has to be a trainer, coach or boxing teacher, one must be worth one's salt. Such experiences and work relations are priceless and cannot be overstated. *Nick Durandt* would always tell of his fruitful visits to Angelo Dundee. A legendary trainer of the likes of Muhammad Ali and Sugar Ray Leonard. Colin Nathan always looks forward to his annual trips to the USA's trainer of champions, Freddie Roach.

Those are educational trips I would wish for any other trainer in search of knowledge and experience. Back home, right on my doorstep, were experiences I will treasure for the rest of my life. Training Nkosana Mgxaji, Welcome Ncita and Odwa Mdleleni. Guiding and mentoring the likes of Mxhosana Jongilanga, Mthobli Mhlope, Andrew Matyila and Khulile Makeba. Grooming and shadowing Mpush Makambi, Patrick Quka, Nkosinathi Joyi and Malcolm Klassen. I can only treasure my experiences with my brother and first champion Nyingi and now Zolani Tete and many other prospects. It is like the satisfying and gratifying sense of fulfilment that goes through a hunter's stomach when he looks at all the heads and horns of wild animals on his kill-trophy-wall.

Boxers are a rare breed. There is no skill, technique or exact science or experience to identify a boxer who will go all the way to the top. Maybe experience can do the trick. But I think it is mainly instinct.

Like any person born of a woman, every boxer has a unique set of strengths and weaknesses. You have to sit and observe how fighters of any category go through their daily routines of preparation. How they train, eat, drink and relax to get the body to pick condition.

You can then realise the amount of time and the exertion of mind that boxing takes from a person. It takes such responsibilities and sticking to such disciplinary demands that shape their personality. Some of those qualities never change even after retirement.

As a trainer, I was to learn to be a disciplinarian and to lead by example. Boxing takes kids from all social backgrounds and treats them the same. It instils in them a sense of discipline –toughness, deadliness and killer instinct. All of those attributes must be discharged with a positive attitude and manner. Boxing has a lot of taboos that begin with the trainer. I have always found it absurd that a trainer will discourage boxers from taking or abusing drugs and alcohol while he indulges himself from time to time.

I have also found it ironic and amusing how tough I am when driving my boxers to the most brutal training ends. I would push them to the limit. My demands are that they always give me the best of themselves – and nothing less.

I get them to do things that I was not prepared to do in my days as a boxer. I have to bring my psychological side to the fore every time I have to get them down to it, especially when they remind me how far I could have gone if I trained like them. My retort always goes to maybe I did not have a trainer like myself. I feel a sense of remorse for my trainers every time I say that. They tried their best.

I have learnt three things as a trainer. Firstly that you can only work with a boxer as much or as far as he allows you to train him; secondly, when comes the stage when the fighter tells the trainer how he should be trained, you can add one more loss or the first loss to his record. Thirdly, it takes strength of character and determination to build the capacity to adhere to the brutal and grinding training regime. With every encounter, I encourage them never to lose it.

It takes a special kind of person to stick to the game plan prepared during those long and painful hours in the gym. Pit that again against the physical and mental pressure brought about by the challenge for best physical shape. It takes an exceptional trainer to usher a boxer to that place and habitual space to accept that routine as a way of life.

My determination and drive are for hard work. When it comes to training boxers was strengthened once I realised that fighters in the Eastern Cape, where I have plied my boxing trade, are born in the game and have natural rhythm and talent. However, they shy away from strict discipline and hard work. They prefer rhythmic light and comfortable exercise to the demanding physical drills. What they don't realise is that they are needed for power, durability and stamina to compete effectively at the highest level. Their eating and drinking habits, as well as the hours they keep, are hardly what one would expect from world-class participants. They prefer to have around them people who tell them exactly what they like to hear. They do not want to learn new things, especially when people are watching. It is always like they know it all.

You can count in one hand boxers who are disciplined and faithful to their trade. Therefore, it is no wonder why once the going gets tough, they do not get going. They falter under intense pressure and constant pain. It is unfortunate that much later in their lives or careers, and too late, they learn that talent alone is not enough. It is at this late stage in their career that they finally find the need to learn. Unfortunately, at that stage, it is too late for the body to learn. And the mind is too brittle to adapt to the new practices. Remember the adage of the old dog and new tricks. My educational journey in boxing has taken me to a point where I have mastered the art of studying a boxer. I identify his strong and weak points. From there, I come up with a strategy to turn him around into a formidable force of talent and power. Boxers have flaws and tendencies that are often spotted and usurped by their opposition. Sometimes such habits are easily overlooked because the fighter is winning.

It takes a lot of discipline and modesty to recognise that one has flaws that need to be corrected and make him a better fighter. Some habits that turn out to be weaknesses are sometimes not the boxer's doing but are a result of the training program brought about by the trainer and technical team. As a trainer, I had to learn to be a teacher. I realised that the best gift you can give a youngster who dreams of being a world-class boxer is the knowledge and ability to negotiate his way in and out of a tough and challenging situation. These in-the-ring skills are vital to a successful boxing career.

If a fighter can handle any encounter brought about by their opponent in the deep ocean or dark forest of the boxing ring, they can take on life. Sometimes what we have come to know as the square jungle is actually the truth machine – a test of a boxer's will to survive the real world.

The boxing ring is where everything is laid bare – where all truth is told. I believe that knowledge of the game comes first and foremost. All the big posh spaces, all types of punching and speed bags, all sizes and types of fast and slow rings, they are meant to assist and make things much more manageable. Maybe my beliefs have to do with my humble beginnings. In my boxing experience, the best boxing gym would be in a classroom or somebody's garage with a candlelight. The sizes and numbers of the sand-filled punching bags were determined by the strength and toughness of the ceiling on which they were hung. One or two of the punching bags are already torn, and everyone shares the one size fit all boxing gloves. That is the boxing training we could boast about.

The sparring ring was formed with classroom chairs or a human chain by other boxers in garage gyms. Water was a commodity you enjoyed once you got back home. Made to measure equipment was always a dream for the excellent and very successful trainers and managers who guided our fortunes. The same situation was still in place with a lot of mentors of my time.

Such legends and producers included the likes of Spokes Witbooi, Mzi Mnguni, Menzi Nqodi, Boyboy Mpulampula, Galelekile Botha and Koko Qebeyi. Today's state of the art and electronic equipment and accessories make things easier. When the trainer has the knowledge and the ability to impart that understanding to the boxers, this equipment makes a world of difference. Against all odds, we had to learn to punch above ourselves and challenge the rest of the world. We would not be successful by embracing our shackles as the only way to success.

Knowledge remains the key to success. As a cornerman, I had to learn to keep my fighter's mind, focus, determination, confidence and discipline in the fight no matter the challenge from the opponent. It is true when they say that every boxer has a strategy until they get hit. It takes a lot of mental and physical training to maintain the presence and effect of your efforts in the ring. As a cornerman, you have to have presence, language and the plan to keep your fighter in the fight and turn any fight around. Once a boxer gets under pressure, all the old habits come back.

Habits are more incidental than hereditary. A lot of times, they are a result of peer pressure or role models. There was a time when many upcoming boxers in my region tended to slap when hitting because of one of the local heroes, the God of boxing at the time, *Nkosana Mgxaji*. He had a tendency to slap his punches. It took a lot of work for us trainers of that era to correct that and turn it around. We did that with great success. The results are there for all to see. There are no more *slappers* in our boxing. Bad habits can be corrected.

Adaptation and preparedness to learn and sometimes change to new styles make it easier to adapt and even adjust to challenges brought by opponents in the ring. Some camps have teams of specialists whose job is to study the opponent and come out with the strategy to take advantage of the weaknesses, compromise strengths, and then impose their boxer's skill and will in the fight.

Technology has made things so much easier by bringing everything to one's doorstep – even by slow motion over and over. It takes a lot of studying. It takes a lot of practice. Over and over again. I have learnt that the journey to the top of the boxing ladder allows no room for complacency and stubbornness.

I never really had a high work ethic as a boxer, but I made up for that with big talk and a show of confidence. I had lots of that, and later when I started training boxers, I tried as much as I could to rub it on them. And it always paid dividends. I cannot help but laugh out loud these days when my ex boxers remind me of things I used to tell them, just to get them in fight winning mode. It is a sense I learned from the game.

Boxing develops its special blend of confidence. Confidence in boxing simply means the willingness and courage to fight anyone under any circumstances without fear. Confidence allows no hesitation and has no room for half measures. It brings an urgency and intensity to take chances in situations where fear would have caused one to hesitate.

A confident, well trained and intelligent boxer will use all the slightest opportunity presented by a lapse of concentration in his opponent's armour. Something that a less confident fighter would rather not. The truth is, confident boxers are also human. They have a fear of defeat and use such fear to go all out and destroy. Moreover, boxing also instils adaptation and respect inside and outside the ring. That is of utmost importance as it wins over fans and friends whose support is much needed for career progress in boxing's long and arduous going.

Such values come much easier with kids who have grown up under strict parental guidance. They carry over such positive and basic outcomes from home to the gym. I found that character making the exercise of coaching and guiding boxers so much easier. I know it does for other trainers and coaches as well. In managing my boxers, I discovered this role as different in that the manager plays the leadership role in the gym. The manager looks after the general welfare of the fighter inside and outside the ring. That includes even the training itself. I learned that it becomes a tricky situation for those boxers and the people managing them to look and concentrate only on counting the money coming in and always forgetting about controlling, spending and investment obligations.

Many managers have been found wanting when it comes to the tax obligations of their fighters. Like many managers during my period, I found money management to be a big challenge. Such financial challenges are two-fold. They are firstly a consequence of little or no training on financial management on the manager's side. Secondly, the boxers themselves are to blame for the problems far more than the thought-to-be-enlightened managers. The boxer's reluctance to spend sparingly and save for a rainy day puts them in a bad financial state.

Once the boxer turns professional, they develop a different attitude. He knows that he is going to be paid for every fixture he shows up to. The kid who was once dedicated and prepared to do as he was told changes into a hard-nosed businessman. But the 'hard nose' effects are only as far as expecting a big pay, not investment. The manager's role gave me a clear perspective of how managers, promoters, media and even the fans treat boxers. Boxer dynamics and circumstances force the manager into a situation where he also has to play the role of psychologist, motivator and educator.

Boxing has many stories of deceit and backstabbing that cause a lot of unease and mistrust among the boxing teams. The game abounds with stories of liars, thugs and thieves who come into the game to make some quick buck. This makes boxers uncomfortable wherever they are, and they keep moving from stable to stable and manager to manager. Such inconsistencies give rise more often than not hurt the performance of the boxer.

It was also as a manager that I realised the powerful effect of the media in boxing. Many times I have ended up wondering what happened to the Ethics of Journalism. Boxers believe what they read, as do fans and everybody else. Many stories that the media feeds the fans is always far from the truth. Some media persons have no other intention than to advance the agenda of a particular promoter or manager for a few favours like free lunch, or in many instances in our boxing, trips overseas. It is favourable stories from such relations that the media entices the public by writing strategic articles to create and influence public opinion favouring the promoter, manager or boxers connected to them.

Fans fall in love with such a boxer based on what they read or hear about him. They make him something he is not. This usually results in the fighter and his people believing too much in the boxer's abilities and in their minds; they put him where he does not belong. Purse demands start to balloon, travelling teams tend to grow, and the fans, believing what they read, begin to demand better quality opposition.

When the pressure becomes too much, the promoter subsequently bows and makes the fight. The big bout finally happens, and the poor kid is found wanting – unprepared for what he would be facing. Once again, a promising career is nipped in the bud before it gets enough time to bloom.

Media can also boost a fighter's confidence and put him on fast forward with his career. It can praise him and put him on a pedestal that gives him a sense of invincibility. This sense of invincibility goes a long way towards getting a talented and dedicated boxer to do things he would not normally do with lesser self-confidence. Today there is social media, which was not there during our time. Today's manager finds himself having to deal with the new influences that social media imposes on the boxers.

For the boxer to deal or not to deal with social media becomes the big question. Sometimes social media develops to be a habit or an addiction that takes too much of the boxer's time. Weaker boxers can sometimes be harassed and humiliated to the point of destruction. I have seen boxers exchanging words and even swearing at members of social media. This happens when the media questions his fighting style or when fans and followers on social media seem to be siding with his opponent. I never had to deal with social media as a boxer, but as a manager and trainer, it has become a reality that one has to deal with every other day. And because boxing fans are on these platforms, you cannot ignore it. However, as with any public relations exercise, one has to handle the media and social media with care and caution. Careers have been made and destroyed by the very same media we court to showcase our sport. My advice to boxers on social media matter is that they should be their men and women and take their fighting personally and seriously. They should look to the people closest to them for support and encouragement.

Those people are their families, teams and close friends who have their interests at heart. They should take encouragement and motivation from the people that they know. Those are the people they should look up to rather than the faceless and unidentifiable people who keep throwing punches from the darkness. That's far more dangerous than the best opponent.

They have to be at their best mental and physical frame for the actual fight. While I was managing and training my boxers, I found my reputation growing far and wide, with approaches from radio and television to analyse and do commentary, while promoters were on my doorstep requesting that I do matchmaking for their tournaments. I found myself doing everything at the same time. I found myself having to manage, train, match and do the ring announcement and rush down to the side of the ring to do radio commentary at the same time. Later I would do commentary and boxing analysis for SABC TV on a full-time basis.

When I finally made my move as a matchmaker, I had already built close and fruitful relations with managers, trainers, boxers and stables all over the country. That made it easier to put suitable matches together. Matchmaking is an art that brings about excellent quality and entertaining fights without putting some boxers careers at risk. Such risks usually happen when one manager or camp is overprotective of their boxers to disallow any contact with an opponent who has the slightest chance of winning.

Such protected boxers end up fighting mismatched opponents that keep them winning but not learning. Developing a fighter is about keeping him winning in contests that get him to learn, improve and gain more experience. Only quality opposition can deliver that kind of education. Boxing fans pay for and expect excellent and entertaining fighting skills. But they demand that such qualities come from both sides of the ring. They demand blood and destruction, but the ultimate destroyer must have been through a formidable challenge to gain such victory. Fans pay to see something special in the form of massive skills, speed, strength, power, poise and control, all in one package.

They will come back and pay to see that kind of fighter. A good matchmaker identifies that kind of fighter and knows precisely how to match him, even before the fans realise what they have in front of them. At some point, I was forced to balance managing my boxers, training them while also having to match them effectively and gainfully.

My experience in managing boxers and matchmaking for every promoter in East London gave me enough leverage to settle as a promoter as soon as I started. Promoting boxing today is far different from promoting boxing twenty years ago. There is an evolution and revolution that one needs to adjust to. These dynamics sweeps across all facets of the game from administrators to boxers, managers, trainers, ring officials, promoters and even the fans. As a promoter, I found myself where I had to put my money first.

Boxer's purse money is just part of the process of organising a boxing tournament. The logistics take as much of the money as the purses themselves. In the end, all one has to make is a profit. It was the process of putting up the money and going through all the logistics of matching, signing up the boxers, organising transport and accommodation, venue, ring, doctors, hospitals, ambulances, and other requirements to the success of a fight. Marketing was mainly done through radio, print and placards. There was so much enthusiasm from the fans that sometimes marketing was done simply because one had to do it. It seemed like something one could do without. Fans checked out for themselves where and when fights would be held.

I sometimes think that this may be why we never walked that extra mile to learn and familiarise ourselves with marketing awareness and more sophisticated strategies as promoters in the region. There were no sponsors to assist in increasing the purses of boxers nor boost the profits. But that was made up for in attendance. Those days, the paying crowds came in droves and covered every expense, including the boxers' payments and the promoter's profits.

But that was soon to change with the introduction of television and sponsorship. This new phenomenon meant there were more marketing and more money that widened the negotiating fields. Negotiations for fights and purses to be paid by the promoters for boxing fixtures become daily life. And boxing becomes business. You hardly recognise the guy who used to be your kid, and you were the mentor. Fights are different in stature. So are the negotiations and agreements. It is much easier to put together small or development tournaments. It is much more challenging to put together national and international fights. The real-world level is something else. It is the reason that even now, the most prominent promoters in the world cover areas they are comfortable with when it gets to that level. But it's something that has to be done. At this point, experienced agents and consultants run the roost.

Boxing promoters need them more so in cases like those of purse bids where information and physical presents of a representative plays a massive role. It makes a difference between winning and losing the bid. I have sighed a breath of relief after finding lately that many of our new promoters have taken that extra step and forged working relations with overseas promoters and agents. I think we are growing. Significant fight negotiations at the highest level are not your typical day to day conversations like the purse money agreement for small fights. It is winning and wins at all costs. The psychological advantage becomes the forerunner. It wins fights. As a promoter, you have to understand each camp and know what to expect. Fight dates are just as important as the venue. Once the date for the bout and the venue has been agreed to, you are good to go. The tough negotiations and agreements then follow – the size of the ring, which is of standard as far as rules are concerned. But in some cases, one camp may not be comfortable with the standard size. They seek adjustments. The surface of the ring sometimes becomes a matter of significant concern.

Should it be hard and allow for quick movements? Should it be soft and slow down the movement of the fighters? What design of gloves should be used? Who comes first or who gets introduced first in public gatherings, including the ring entry and introductions? Lately, the negotiations start with agreements about who the A fighter among the two fighters is. That fighter takes the lion's share. The B fighter takes the rest. But it's not that easy.

The next step is to satisfy the requirements of the sanctioning bodies. Such conditions are expected to be considered and agreed to with specific time limits. If this requirement is not met, the promoter may lose money. Such requirements include sanctioning fees, belt payments, travel and accommodation guarantees for the boxing teams, officials and administrators.

While dealing with the sanctioning body on one side, the promoter has to deal with the other stakeholders like sponsors and television broadcasters on the other side. These logistics have brought about downfalls for many promoters. More was to come when I settled into the office of Boxing SA after I was appointed PRO and later Director of Operations.

I also had two stints as Acting CEO. This put me in a position where I had to work with and serve all the different facets of boxing. I was able to appreciate how boxers, teams, promoters and administrators here and abroad handle boxing matters. I am happy to say that there are promoters in South Africa that are so professional they could handle their boxing affairs without the national office. And boxing would go on. There are those who need to be assisted every step of the way. I found promoters who were so connected that they were somehow kept abreast of all daily activity and information in the BSA office.

But I also found that some people were in the highest boxing office working as proxies for promoters. Many of them were there to give an unfair advantage to one promoter over the other. And this would always happen to the exclusion or disadvantage of the other stakeholders within the sport.

All over the world, boxing works the same. It is just the levels and intensity that differs. There is a lot of money that changes hands daily. It goes over the table, under the table and even around the table. Those monies are known only to the people who deliver and receive. While they are about boxing and boxers, the boxers and another stakeholder in the broader boxing space never know about them. Some fights are avoided by hiding behind promotional contracts and sanctioning bodies. Other fights are avoided by faking injuries. And in almost all of them, some money has changed hands. Money to make the fight happen; money to keep the bout from happening; or money to make it look like there was never a fight in the first place. There is a big grain of truth that boxing as bad as it sounds. It is not the mafia. Even though sometimes it seems to operate like one. There are still a lot of good and honest people in the game. They are just hard to find.

I once got an offer to play myself as a trainer of the fighter who was the leading actor in the movie Knuckle City. Interestingly enough, it came out of the blue. I am not an actor and have never aspired to be one, but this experience was one I could learn from. They didn't give me a script. I just have to do and say whatever is relevant in boxing for such a situation. How many people ever get that in a game that they love? If one or a few can be named, I am one of them. But if you can't name anyone, then I'm the only one. You name anything about boxing; I've done it. Having gone through and participated in all facets of boxing, I have felt the need to have this story written. This story is not different or unique. But rather that a boxer has written it. A boxer who has also been a trainer and boxing administrator. It is by the hand of a boxer and boxing lover of note. From the heart of a boxer. Through the eyes of a fighter. As boxers, we are sometimes unable to speak, cry or express ourselves. We get so used to having things done for us by other people. They even talk on our behalf. We believe too much in that saying that ours is only to fight. We let other people tell our stories – how we feel, how we see the world and how we experience our world. What next are we going to do? Most of the time, this gives the view that we have no feelings.

I have travelled this journey with other boxers and all the events I have gone through, groups I have worked with, and people I have met on my trip around the ropes. It is about things I have done, seen and experienced. It is about the lessons I have learnt. That journey has empowered me with a lot of education to understand matters I would have gone through without noticing had I not been actively involved. I feel qualified to tell the story through the understanding of a boxer. Telling this story creates something for all people and groups involved in this journey to celebrate. It is not a trauma history. It is a history of triumph. A celebration of achievement against all odds. Especially for the fighters.

I believe I am a better person after going through this experience. It has been so fulfilling. I have lived through life with boxers whose lives and achievements have never been celebrated. Let alone acknowledged. I believe that some of the stories that come out of this celebration will arouse some feelings of excitement and awaken some memories long lost in their minds. Those memories may motivate such people and cause them to stand up and pat themselves on the shoulders and tell themselves how great they are.

Like all other boxers before and during my time, I have been so swallowed and lost in the deep ocean that is boxing. In all that, there is also the public opinion that I have forgotten to celebrate my strengths and achievements.

Perhaps people do not see success for celebration as I do as a fighter. They do not view success the way I do. To them, a boxer is as good as his last fight. But to me as a boxer, and I think to all other guys who have walked this route, I am as good as my performance, win or lose. They have their expectations as fans and supporters. As a boxer, I have my own. I feel comfort and satisfaction for going beyond four and six rounders without tiring down. That to me must be cause for celebration that I am approaching the championship league. Maybe non-celebratory mode is a consequence of the upbringing of modesty instilled in me as a child.

As boxers, we are not supposed to brag. This may be construed as brash and selfish. I have always felt obliged to be graceful and thank everybody. Yes, I should be grateful to everybody who has sacrificed energy, time and money for me to have gone this far. I have praised everybody but myself.

I have decided to prepare boxers for the future and arm them to meet this challenge head-on. This book is for all who celebrate with the boxers. Maybe boxers should start by recognising their obligation to carry themselves in a manner that upholds the dignity and discipline to present in boxing. Wild as it might sound, we must showcase boxing as a sport for all and sundry.

That might give rise to them gaining the recognition and acknowledgement that makes it easier to enforce the right to be treated respectably and professionally. For that to happen, they must be well informed of all aspects of the game, including finances. Maybe this story will arouse the tiger in ourselves as boxers. Hopefully, it will endow us with the kind of knowledge and information to identify the agents who mingle with us, only to discover too late that they are just nothing more than petty intermediaries engaging in the new and more sophisticated slave trade. And boxers all over the world will roar like lions.

Everybody who is within earshot will hear the noise. They will realise that boxers have decided to take up the task of fighting and celebrating their brand new being and telling their story. Direct from the boxer's mouths. By themselves. For themselves. If we, as boxers, can achieve that, then the blood, sweat and tears we shed will not be in vain as a collective.

CHAPTER 2

WHERE ARE THE BLACK HEAVYWEIGHTS?

ACCORDING TO BOXING historian Ron Jackson, the beginnings of South Africa's status concerning challenging for the National championship was mired in confusion. Titles were challenged, sanctioned and won without any qualification according to the residence. Foreign boxers could challenge and win South African championships and abandon them on departure from the country.

There were two champions per division—the black and white champion. Mixed boxing was barred until 1973. The introduction of the All-South Africa champion – The Supreme Champion, was a welcomed event in the history of South African boxing. It stood above the two black and white champions. Despite an earlier decision by the South African Boxing Board of Control to allow mixed boxing and have one champion, the intention by boxing officialdom to allow mixed boxing, which was supported by the Minister for Sports, *Dr Piet Koornhof* - was overruled by the South African Government.

It was only in 1979 that all mixed boxing was allowed in South Africa. For the first time in the country's history, the new regulation brought about the introduction of only one champion per division. The Supreme champions automatically became the South African champions.

The Heavyweight division, as in all matters relating to boxing, led the charge. It's funny that with all its talent and enthusiasm in the game, the Eastern Cape has not been in the mix when it comes to producing this valuable commodity, a Heavyweight contender. More so, what about a black Heavyweight at the highest level?

Heavyweight boxing is so important and so embraced by boxing fans worldwide such that when there is no dominant Heavyweight champion, boxing sought of dies a little bit. Boxing is generated and measured by the strength and excitement of the Heavyweight division. The Heavyweight champion of the world becomes one of the most, if not the most recognisable faces in boxing. The *baddest* man on the Planet. He even becomes better known and loved by the people than most state presidents and movie stars.

Boxing administrators, managers, trainers, fans, and all people involved in boxing one way or another are known for recognising the importance and impact of the Heavyweight division in boxing, to the point that many will declare or make statements like, "there is Heavyweight boxing, and there is boxing." Sometimes they go as so as saying – as Heavyweights go, so does boxing. South African Heavyweight boxing has never been left behind in this scenario. All South African Heavyweight champions have also carried this aura and charm and have been blasted out as poster boys in magazines, billboards and television shows. All for the purpose of selling the Heavyweight Championship. And also because of their appeal and subsequent popularity.

The period up to 1984 is significant in international boxing standards. The division's time can be arguably rated and recognised as having been at its highest levels ever in terms of visibility and performance. That period of boxing boasted, among others, the likes of George Foreman, Joe Frazier, Jerry Quarry, Larry Holmes, Ken Norton and Gerry Cooney – to name but a few. It also had Muhammad Ali, who is recognised mainly as The Greatest Heavyweight of all time and arguably the Greatest Sportsman ever.

In the South African context, the country was doing its fair share of competing for its seat among the greats of Heavyweight boxing. History was there for the taking, and South Africa was determined to make its eternal mark. The whole world was looking for a white Heavyweight to take over the world championship that had been tightly in the grip of black boxers for as long as they cared to remember – the search had been on for The Great White Hope for some time.

South Africa was working and hoping that such a saviour would come from this country. The South African Heavyweight division was also enjoying the best of its times and trying its utmost to entice the greats like Ali and Holmes to come and fight the South African challengers *Gerrie Coetzee, Kallie Knoetze* and *Mike Schutte*. Who themselves were no slouches and could count among themselves a string of American and European Heavyweight heads they had slain and hung on their walls. They certainly deserved the chance.

But the sanctions against South Africa that served as punishment by the international countries for its Apartheid Laws was having a tight grip on all things South African. The sports boycott was firmly in place, and doors for the international competition were closed. It was against such sanctions the country was stopping at nothing and using significant amounts of money and influence with the ultimate aim of producing a Heavyweight great.

South Africa's Great White Hopes were being bred by the dozen. All roads were leading to a showdown between a South African boxer and Muhammad Ali. And later Larry Holmes. South Africa boasted competent brawlers like Mike Schutte and Kallie Knoetze, but judging by their standards, they would never have made it against the all-time greats mentioned above.

Perhaps the best of the South African brigade who had a decent chance of putting up a worthy effort if the opportunity has arisen was Gerrie Coetzee. He passed the litmus test with a great show and immense qualities of greatness as he carved his way up the international Heavyweight ladder leaving bodies of fallen American and European Heavyweights in his wake. His performances convinced the big boxing hats that he was the real deal.

Gerrie Coetzee confirmed his ranking as the finest Heavyweight South Africa has produced with such victories in his wake. He was a massive figure with a killer of a right hand to match.

His reign as South African Heavyweight champion was significant in that it was first, during the best times of world Heavyweight boxing, ranging from the commands of Muhammad through to Larry Holmes and, secondly, during the height of sanctions and sports boycott against South Africa.

Such was the impact of the sports boycott that to fight; he had to voice his stance against Apartheid. Such was his determination to challenge the reigning greats of the time that he became the first white South African boxer to speak out against Apartheid.

Trained by experienced and well-connected trainer Willie Lock, Coetzee's skill, speed, rhythm and paralysing right-hand power ensured his meteoric rise to the top of the Heavyweight rungs. Equally influential were the connections of Coetzee's manager Hal Tucker who provided his upgrade to the championship turf by careful international matching as well as smooth negotiating skills.

The Coetzee, Locke and Tucker combination became the most successful combination in the country, especially for its success in a division whose standards all of boxing are measured.

Coetzee challenged the South African Heavyweight title, one of the most unforgettable fights in South Africa boxing history. However, because of dirty tactics that included low blows, eye gouges, head butts and knee knocks, Mike Schutte was disqualified after six rounds.

Coetzee then outpointed both Kallie Knoetze and Schutte successively over twelve rounds. Unfortunately, the two fights nearly cost him his career as he shattered his hands. Successful surgery saved his career, and he was to continue the rest of his career with a 'bionic right hand.'

Coetzee then moved to the US under the wing of South African expatriate Cedric Kushner, who had since made it big in America in boxing promotion and show business. He was then lured by the legendary Don King, arguably the greatest boxing promoter of all time, to join him in his stable. Though serving under the Don's wing, joining him was the surest way of fighting for the title if you had the talent. King he was practically in control of all of the boxing at the time and Coetzee had it all.

With the master of bling, drama and political survey that was Don King behind him, it was no surprise that Coetzee started making the right and relevant noises to please the anti-apartheid brigade. This was meant for him to have smooth sailing in his quest for the biggest prize in sport – THE HEAVYWEIGHT CHAMPIONSHIP OF THE WORLD.

Writing in his book, Dancing Shoes is Dead, Gavin Evans says Coetzee quickly worked out how to play King's game – making anti-apartheid noises, deriding his white fans and then announcing he was voting a liberal "NO" in the government's 1983 constitutional referendum. And his presence went unprotested in the US. His stance ensured that he was not put under any pressure like what happened to other sports boycott bashers like Kallie Knoetze. With King on his side, Gerrie could never go wrong.

All he had to do was prepare and be ready when the call came. South Africa was practically running the WBA at the time, and Don King was the deal maker with the power and influence over all the sanctioning bodies to make things happen. He could not make South African deals with the other organisations, especially the WBC, because of the body's stance against Apartheid.

The WBA was working hand in hand with the South Africa Government in promoting boxing beyond our boarders. The first time I heard about South Africa – WBA deal was from the former sports editor and analyst Bert Blewett. He told me that a lot of South African money was used to keep the WBA afloat when it was struggling financially.

Unknown to ordinary South Africans, the South African Boxing Board president, Judge H.W.O Kloppers, was able to get himself appointed president of the WBA, ably assisted by two South Africans.

Specially selected South African boxers, promoters and ring officials benefitted heavily from WBA. South African Boxing Board Secretary Stan Christodoulou had the most significant share of this benefit. He was appointed as the sole South African boxing official to acquire record-breaking opportunities to referee world title fights.

As would be expected, Don King delivered, and Coetzee was in the ring to challenge Michael Dokes for the WBA championship. It would be his third attempt at a world title after his two earlier efforts. One against Big John Tate, and the other against Mike Weaver. Both of which ended in defeats—one on points and the other by knockout.

With American trainer Jackie McCoy who King had roped in to prepare Coetzee for the fight, Gerrie never put a foot wrong as he masterfully walked Dokes down and knocked him out to win the Heavyweight championship.

A South African boxer had done it. The country had achieved what the First World countries could not do – produce the white Heavyweight champion of the world. What the whole white world had been longing for – the Great White Hope. From Apartheid South Africa of all places. Arguably the best performance by a South African boxer overseas and a great day in the history of sport in South Africa.

Don King has always been known for his love of money. To him, boxing has always been business, and he used politics to have things his way. No sooner had Gerrie won the world title than King had put himself high up in the Apartheid food chain. Attempts to match Coetzee with Larry Holmes had not succeeded. As the champion's promoter, he agreed for Coetzee to fight in Sun City, where he had initially vowed never to go in respect and support of the sports boycott.

He firstly secured his pocket from the sanctions-busting budget and then allowed the bout between Coetzee and Greg Page to take place in Sun City. Both boxers belonged to him, so whoever won assured that King was the winner. Greg Page knocked Coetzee out to win the WBA Heavyweight title. And with him, the exit of Don King from the South African boxing scene.

It is worth noting that with all the efforts it has made and all the successes it has achieved in the boxing world against all odds, Eastern Cape boxing has not produced a Heavyweight of note.

While many people are aware of the strides of boxing development in the Eastern Cape and the popularity thereof, few have the slightest clue of the impact and pioneering gains a Heavyweight boxer from rural Alice made nationally and internationally. That was well before the most ardent of boxing fans became aware that there was boxing in the Border region. Only Queenstown was boxing at that stage. This boxer discovered his talent and started boxing in Cape Town when there was still no boxing on his home turf. He competed as an amateur and turned professional in Cape Town.

Remmington Colorado King Dyantyi was identified by talent scouts and prepared to hit the big time in the most prestigious boxing division, perhaps of all sport in the world. One can only imagine if our man had made an impact and had his name mentioned with all-time greats like Muhammad Ali, Sonny Liston and Joe Frazier. He missed the chance of meeting Sonny Liston by a whisker. Remmington came from the rural village of Dikeni (Alice), started his professional career in Cape Town against Patterson Maputu in 1963. He had three more fights in Cape Town before heading closer home and engaging in his fifth fight in Port Elizabeth in 1965.

He was spotted by an overseas scout and flown to Italy to further his boxing career overseas. He had five fights before heading back home to challenge and win against Ezrom Ngcobo for the South African Heavyweight title. Interestingly one of his opponents in Italy was Leotis Martin, who would later beat Sonny Liston of the Muhammad Ali controversies.

So quiet and uncontroversial was Dyantyi's life that not even people in his own Alice home knew about his boxing history and his role in paving boxing success in this region. I was one of the speakers at his funeral held at his home village in 2018.

The people of his village were genuinely surprised when I relayed his history. Even when contributors, legends and heroes of the sport in the region are mentioned, Dyantyi's name is never there.

South African boxing has never produced an indisputable Heavyweight in size and ability. That has been the domain of the white fighters. In simple boxing terms, black boxers that have been campaigning as Heavyweights have been Cruiserweights. This truth became evident after racial barriers were banned. The reigning black Heavyweight, at the time, was James Mathatho, who found himself so small in front of white Heavyweight champion Gerrie Coetzee. When they met to unify the South African title, he was lost in the ring.

His boxing skills, which were some of the best at the time, could not make any difference; but the exception to this rule may have been former South African champion Orsborn Machimane.

Orsborn was the black Boxing Heavyweight from Limpopo Province who also had a stint in the Eastern Cape under the mentorship of legendary trainer Boyboy Mpulampula, hence his tremendous skills. He had all the tools needed to make it to the top of the Heavyweight ladder, irrespective of who was there.

Beyond skills to outdo any Heavyweight of his time in South Africa, Machimane had what was always lacking among black South African Heavyweights, size in length and breadth. He also had the power to match.

One of the best matches made in South Africa was when Machimane and Corrie Sanders met in the ring. To the surprise of all and sundry, Machimane not only took over the direction of the fight from the beginning, but he also ripped Sanders's ribs apart with a left. That damaging punch had Saunders gasping for air and not able to continue.

Another black Heavyweight who achieved international exposure before it became fashionable was Ezekiel King Kong Dlamini. Before black boxers were recognised within the South African borders, he made it on the international scene. Originally from KZN, then known as Natal, Dlamini made his mark in the footprints of boxing. His story is that of legends. Such was the aura, charm and controversy around the man that he has movies shot and books written about his extraordinary march through life.

The Internationally acclaimed movie King Kong is based on his life and times. Unfortunately, he did not live long enough to enjoy the benefits of such stories. His wildlife would not allow it.

At the time of this writing, there is little or nothing to be excited about when it comes to black Heavyweights. And this is true not only in the Eastern Cape now but in South Africa as a whole.

The Heavyweight division's ranking space meant to accommodate the ten best boxers can only go as far as five, simply because there is just no one to list. The National champion is Ruan Visser, who has no one to defend against. The only black Boxing Heavyweight, Justice Siliga, is rated at number four.

CHAPTER 3

BOXING DURING APARTHEID RULE

IT REMAINS A TRICKY question to answer whether South African boxing was at its best during the Apartheid era or not. But the truth glares as clearly as the day that South African boxing was never in shortage of funds or sponsors at that stage of its life.

The private sector was throwing money in the game like it would never stop. That was good when one looked at the situation from the point of development of the game. But looking at it from the other side, the money was going only in one direction.

Only white promoters and white boxers were benefitting. Anything that did not have the preferred skin colour was not considered for funding. It was as simple as that.

The only black beneficiaries were those with close relations with or managed by white promoters, managers and trainers. They might get crumbs that fall of the table. But they would never get a sizable share for their contribution to the sport—irrespective of the fact that a majority of the fan base would be black.

The administration of boxing was strictly and by law in the hands of white officials.

There was only one reason for this. South Africa was under pressure from the more significant part of the world because of its Apartheid Rule. Not to be outdone by other sports codes that were boycotting this country, boxing took its stand. World sanctioning bodies ruled out any competition with South African boxing inside and outside its borders.

This was the reason boxers like Brian Mitchell and Welcome Ncita were forced to pack their bags and travel overseas for their world championship contests. Brian Mitchel had always expressed his desire for a non-racial South Africa – both in the land and sport.

Welcome Ncita, a black boxer who got the chance because of his shrewd manager Mzi Mnguni's close working relations with white promoter Rodney Berman.

In a political move aimed at weakening the international sports and cultural boycott, South Africa decided to reinvent itself as an entertainment magnet. The aim was to attract the world's attention in the midst of segregation. In a way, the Powers-That-Be were enticing the world to overlook the political tensions and problem of that time and invite them to enjoy themselves in the country.

This massive project, negotiated and done with Homeland leader *Lucas Mangope*, was meant to entice overseas entertainment stars and sports champions to come and perform.

The South African government managed to convince the Homeland leader to build a gambling casino whose glitz and glamour and money became hard to resist by tourists, sports and music performers. It was incredibly enticing to those who were struggling to make a name in the world of entertainment and boxing. If there was money to be made, this was their chance.

Even those who were losing their international glamour could not pass out on this opportunity. They saw South Africa as a chance to redeem their careers and to make a quick buck. This bold venture gave birth to Sun City in the *Bophuthatswana* Homeland.

At that time in South Africa's history, gambling of any kind was illegal. However, because of the importance and delicacy of the matter, *Mangope* was advised to use the supposed sovereignty of his part of the country to legalise gambling.

This ground-breaking deal would go a long way towards making the *Bophuthatswana* homeland a tourist attraction. It brought much needed economic gains in marketing attention and job opportunities for his people. In this case, the sports, the boxing gains for South Africa, went and achieved measures well beyond their imaginations.

At the climax of its prowess Sun International was able to attract, amongst others, boxing greats like Big John Tate, Mike Weaver and Duane Bobick.

Such was the lore and taste of money that these sanctions busters visited the country much against the advice of struggle icons and other Civil rights activists in America, the United Kingdom and other countries. Headed by former boxer turned great boxing enthusiast and visionary businessman *Sol Kerzner*, South African boxing flew to dizzying international heights, flexing its power and influence on sanctioning bodies like the WBA and IBF.

According to Gavin Evans in his book titled 'Dancing Shoes is Dead', the only boxer of note who visited South Africa and voiced his dissent was WBA world-beater Dwight Muhammad Qawi. He had come to fight Piet Crous and won the WBA Cruiserweight title. He made a very profound announcement at the time that he would never revisit this country until Apartheid was scrapped.

Apartheid, for those who need to be reminded, is a time in South African history where the native people of the land lived under conditions that make one feel ashamed and depressed. He said, "I'm disgusted. I'm convinced that blacks in this country are repressed and not given the same treatment as whites."

Such was the influence and strength of propaganda by the government machinery, according to Gavin Evans, that when James 'Quick' Tillis went to Soweto to watch a soccer match, he was introduced to the crowds as the guy who was going to destroy the white man's hero. He was given a standing ovation by the black mass in attendance. He was not going to disappoint.

They took him to heart.

He was their man. He was their hero.

However, when he got into the ring, he hardly threw a single punch, choosing to float around the ring in a poor imitation of Muhammad Ali.

He was beaten.

Maurice Toweel, the promoter among the famous Toweel brothers, was the leading promoter in South Africa. With his Springbok Promotions, he developed such great draw-cards as former world Bantamweight champion Vic Toweel and later Charlie Weir among a long list. Springbok Promotions continued until a new promotion named Golden Gloves under the directorship of Rodney Berman took over.

As Golden Gloves grew and took on new heights, Toweel's company lost its grip on boxing promotions and soon disappeared. It was like there were never there. History had found a way to erase them from the books. But if you were in boxing at that, you would know, they were a force to be reckoned with.

With the help of Sun International and a long term contract with MNET that later turned its name and be called Supersports, Berman took over South African boxing and the cream of the country's boxing talent. This is where the region now called Buffalo City, in the Eastern Cape Province, finally got the opportunity to showcase its long-hidden talent. Their time had come, and it did not disappoint, producing its first world boxing champion, Welcome Ncita.

He won the IBF world title when he outpointed Fabrice Benichou for the Junior Featherweight title. The region has since produced a lot more National and world champions than any Province in South Africa. It is extensively recognised at the BOXING MECCA, at least here in South Africa or Africa as a whole. Berman formed a partnership with Cedric Kushner, a South African who moved to the United States and succeeded as a music promoter. That move was to take South African boxing into a mainstream activity, competition and recognition. The Berman-Kushner duo was promoted at the highest level of the game. Great names like Don King and Bob Arum, among others, ruled the playing fields. There were only three world sanctioning bodies at that time: WBA, WBC, and IBF.

A little later, there would be the WBO. Of these organisations, only the WBC under Jose Sulaiman was politically relevant. It stood firm against South Africa and refused its champions to enter the country nor allow South Africans to fight for its titles. The WBA, headed by Gilberto Mendoza of Venezuela, and IBF headed by American Bobby Lee, saw nothing wrong and continued sending fighters and officials into the country. Meantime the United Nations acknowledged the WBC's stance against Apartheid.

Kushner convinced the IBF that he had no political history, no political affiliations, and no political agenda. All he wanted was a fair and non-racial spread of opportunities to all those he worked within boxing, irrespective of colour or race.

He emphasised that the reason the majority of fighters he promoted were white was not his choice. Still, the unfortunate history of the country as black boxing had been wholly marginalised from its beginnings.

He argued that he was only working to make right those wrongs that were doing more harm than good to the sport. He emphasised that the sanctions were hurting the black boxers more than the whites. At that time, Golden Gloves was only working with one black promoter and manager, Mzi Mnguni, in East London, and one matchmaker Ruben Rasodi in Soweto, Gauteng. This association was to make Golden Gloves the biggest ever boxing promotional outfit in Africa. The East London – Mdantsane region, better known as the Boxing Mecca, would benefit significantly from this exclusive working relationship.

Welcome Ncita, one of the boxers who benefitted immensely from Kushner's deals with the world of international boxing, became the first Golden Gloves champion. He was the first black boxer from his Eastern Cape Province and the last South African world champion of the apartheid era. As a black boxer, his rise to the top was filled with political undertones and suspicions. The general feeling of politically conscious fans was that his choice and promotion were more of political scheming than merit. It was window-dressing meant to ease the sports and cultural boycott.

There were also theories and later charges and convictions for ratings' bribery against the IBF. It was ironic and gratifying to boxing followers that when Welcome reached the top of the boxing ladder and won the world championship, he proved his true worth in gold.

He was such a brilliant artist that the outside world watched in wonder and awe as he bamboozled his opponents with his swift and smooth moving style accompanied by lightning combinations that left their prospects stunned and bewildered. Comparisons in looks and style to the great Sugar Ray Leonard became commonplace. His boxing mad followers back in his East London – Mdantsane hometown soon forgot their misgivings and accepted him as a true great – their first world champion, a first world champion for Golden Gloves, their son–a legend.

Ncita's rise to the top had carried more controversies than ordinary boxing fans were aware of. His ascendancy to the top did not come easy. The political situation at the time played its hand in both positive and negative ways. Positive in that finally, the pressure to bear on South Africa to dismantle racial barriers in sport had triumphed.

A black kid was able to contest for a world title and win it. Negative in that boxing pressure group called South African National Boxing Coordinating Council) SANBCC were still unhappy with the country's political state of affairs and all arrangements that allowed Ncita and other selected boxers to campaign internationally. They wanted Ncita to discontinue his international campaign until sport in South Africa became normal. They were correct in some ways.

The free world widely recognised the National Sports Council (NSC) as the sports desk of the ANC. Its founding members included experienced political leaders like Rev Makhenkesi Stofile, Mluleki George and Smuts Ngonyama, and sports administrators Mthobi Tyamzashe and Zola Dunywa. The founders had crisscrossed the globe successfully persuading, and in other cases pressurising countries and international sports organisations to discontinue or have no sports relations with South Africa.

They had done a lot. And they were prepared to do just anything possible to effect total sanctions against South Africa until all political, social, economic, sports, arts, cultural and all other barriers were dismantled. There could be no normal sport in an abnormal society. They pinned their lives to it because, as anyone could tell, that seemed to be the only language the government would listen to.

The boxing arm of the NSC that represented boxing interests was the South African National Boxing Coordinating Council (SANBCC).

The SANBCC was led nationally by former rugby player turned successful businessman and political activist Khaya Ngqula. The Border (BBCC) leader was former professional boxer Khulile Radu, who would become chairman of the Border Boxing Board and later a board member of Boxing SA. The group was naturally much more robust in the Border region than in other parts of the country. This was partly because of the massive activity and awareness of boxing and their massive membership base. These big numbers and the differing views in the case of what was becoming a national controversy divided the group.

Political pressure had at this stage resulted in almost all boxing sanctioning bodies cutting all ties with South Africa. It was left out in the cold in both the amateur and professional codes, out of the African, Commonwealth, World and all other amateur competitions, including the Olympic Games. From its humble beginnings, the most prestigious world organisation in the professional ranks at the time, WBC had pronounced South Africa as a non-starter and denied it any working relations.

All organisations, countries, groups and individuals associated with the WBC were under strict instructions to cut all working relations with South Africa. However, WBA, which is the oldest of the current sanctioning bodies, and the IBF that was relatively new at the time, were prepared to accommodate South Africa.

Ncita had fought his way up the IBF ladder and was its world Junior Featherweight champion. BBCC wanted him to vacate the IBF title and rather than fight for the more politically vocal and hence relevant WBC. There were no guarantees for a WBC title fight. This was the stance that according to myself and many other licensees within the boxing spaces, we found to be a raw deal and unacceptable.

We felt it was wrong and unfair for Ncita and his camp to sacrifice and work hard for the better part of their lives, only to be recalled once they reached the top of the mountain. Moreover, there was no guarantee that the WBC would honour that promise.

We would later be proved so right as the WBC, save for a representative and endless promises for a top rating for our boxers on winning the countless and smaller regional titles, simply disappeared from the South African boxing scene. Port Elizabeth promoter *Monde Ndlaleni*, manager Peter Qamba Menzi Nqodi, and many other boxing participants from all categories were not happy with the handling this sensitive matter. Collectively they were not impressed, especially by the self-righteous attitudes of certain members.

We believed and made our views and intentions very clear that SANBCC's ideals, noble as they were, should not be used to deny our people the enjoyment of the fruits they had sacrificed so much sweat and blood to gain.

We argued that Ncita was just an ordinary township kid who found himself in a position where his fists - the only thing he could use that produced his God-given talent and discipline - was delivering for him and presenting him with a better life that all young black kids were striving to achieve.

We imagined how long it would take for him to fight his way back to the top and re-establish himself if the title he had fought so hard for was dropped. It could have been better had Ncita been stopped while he was still campaigning as a contender. To wait for him to be champion first and then have him drop the title he had fought so hard to win could only succeed in defeating the gains that local boxing had achieved against all odds. We would have nothing and have to start from scratch.

While we were not against sanctions on South Africa, we were still against self-destruction. To us, this was no longer about Ncita and Mnguni, but it was for our boxing community as a whole. We were proud of what we had achieved against all odds. And we were not prepared to lose it. Welcome Ncita was not the only one in a line of local boxers who had campaigned internationally.

The only difference had been that he had done what others before him had failed to do, win the world title. Perhaps the boxer who had engaged in more international fights than all other boxers was the maestro himself, *Nkosana Mgxaji*. But he had failed to clinch the most significant prize when Sam Serrano stopped him and denied him the status he had fought so hard to gain. *Welile Nkosinkulu* had lost to Puerto Rican Julian Solis in an elimination for the WBA Bantamweight title.

Mzukisi Skweyiya had started his international campaign by beating Zambian David Natta before leaving South Africa and going into exile. Several other boxers in all Provinces had done the same. Our question was why this pressure for Ncita to vacate an already won title as if he was the only one. We questioned the honesty of the campaign.

It is worth noting that although boxing had led and had been the foremost code in dismantling racial barriers as early as 1979, all sports, arts and cultural activities at the time were still ruled and regulated under strict Apartheid stipulations. The banning of racial laws in boxing had promptly resulted in the forging of close working relationships between black and white boxing stakeholders. Such activities as training, and sparring sessions that operated underground, had come out in the open.

Black boxing became an open secret. However, the fruits were not enjoyed by all for partaking in it. Our white counterparts were, and still are, enjoying the first and best of everything because of past and present advantages.

It was easy for our rivals to demean us as apartheid apologists. We were not concerned. We believed we were simply defending boxing and our gains from being destroyed in the guise of a political principle. To make our voice stronger, we decided to organise other like-minded members within the boxing fraternity and formed our organisation, calling ourselves the Border Boxing Movement (BBM).

I was elected chairman, and Qamba became secretary of the group. We presented our case to local and national members of the NSC in separate meetings. We had no intention of waging war but wished to engage with the relevant parties prepared to listen to us on Ncita's championship predicament. We even made it known publicly that we would disband once the Ncita matter was settled. Both regional and national offices of the NSC, Zola Dunywa and Mthobi Tyamzashe, were prepared to listen to our concerns. We found the NSC, which was now the mother body of all sports in South Africa more accommodating.

After a series of meetings and discussions between ourselves as the differing local boxing groups, it was decided on advice from the NSC to escalate the matter to the ANC. We had also engaged in meetings with both national members of SANBCC to ensure that all stakeholders were consulted. The NSC was also prepared to take up the duty of organising such a meeting, and that added weight to our cause. The meeting was set to discuss and settle the matter once and for all. As two different groups, we were advised to prepare for the presentation of their cases. We should, as per further request, invite as many of our members, especially the boxers, as possible – that was my thinking.

In a meeting held at the Mdantsane Hotel on 2nd December 1990, all interested political and social groups were represented. We had finally gathered to thrash out a boxing conundrum that would make boxing history.

The meeting was held under the chairmanship of then Minister of Sport Steve Tshwete, assisted by local leaders Adv Hintsa Siwisa and Papa Joe Mati. The meeting coincided with a tournament in which South African Junior Lightweight champion Ditau Molefyane was defending his title against local challenger Sidima Qina. The BBCC had campaigned for a boycott of the tournament promoted by Monwabisi Guwa's Real First Team Promotions. The two different groups presented their cases before the bench of members from both ANC and NSC. Khulile Radu as chairman of the BBCC, presented their case, and I raised our case as the chairman of the BBM.

Minister Tshwete also requested the boxers who had attended the meeting in big numbers to stand up and have their views heard. All boxers who stood up voiced their displeasure at being denied the chance to fight for international honours. They also wanted the fight of the day to be held at the legendary Orient Theatre peacefully and without any disturbance.

After all, was said and done, Minister Steve Tshwete stood up and addressed a quiet and tense meeting. He told us that he had found many more positives than negatives after listening to both groups' objectives and concerns. One main positive was the resolve of the local people like fans, trainers, managers to assist in developing their boxers to be the best they could be.

The other was the dedication and discipline of local boxers, especially the one in question, Welcome Ncita – to make sure that their talent was not left to the waste. He said that the ANC, as the leading organisation of the struggle against inequality and denial of opportunity for some, would not sleep well if it found itself being the very machine to deny people, especially the black kids, the opportunities meant for them.

He praised the local people and Welcome Ncita, as well as his team and supporters for a job well done. He went as far as declaring Welcome The People's champion. He urged the two groups to work together for the advancement of boxing. Everybody in the meeting should go out and tell people to attend the tournament that day because boxing was the sport by which the Eastern Cape Province stood tall.

People who participated in the meeting were encouraged to spread the word because boxing was known by the length and breadth of the world, and the time had come for the world to know our boxing greats. True to Tshwete's word, the tournament was a great success.

The two differing groups disbanded on the same day, and all started to work together again. For some time, all differences that gave birth to the two camps were forgotten. The Apartheid Rule is over. Boxing is going on now after the dawn of democracy. It has its democratic dynamics.

CHAPTER 4

TOO MANY WORLD SANCTIONING BODIES.

BOXING IS A SIMPLE SPORT to the casual observer – two competitors standing toe to toe in a ring, exchanging punches. One wins, and the other is knocked out. That might be true, but the world of boxing is vast and wide. When I walked into the exciting yet dangerous world of boxing, I discovered a world filled with many moving pieces. I had my first fight as a raw amateur back in 1968. At that time, I could name all the world champions off the top of my head.

There was only one world sanctioning body. Only one champion per division. It was that easy.

There was only the WBA, which was established in 1921 under the name of the National Boxing Association. Following a meeting at the Flatiron Building in New York, the was a need to establish a body or entity that would govern the professional sport of boxing.

At the time, the New York State Athletic Commission had a firm grip on most sports codes, including world championship boxing. The National Boxing Association (NBA) was specially formed to break that grip. Having succeeded to break free of the NYSAC, the new body, at its inauguration in August 1962, decided to change its name to the World Boxing Association

(WBA) under the presidency of Emile Bruneau. With a membership of 51 states and city boxing commissions at its inception, this body grew to represent boxing across the world. In 1963 a new body broke away from the WBA and started its sanctioning practices under the name of World Boxing Commission (WBC). From the onset, WBC made its strict political intentions very clear. It joined the international sports and cultural boycott against South Africa for its racial policies. It refused all its champions and officials from partaking in any competitions with or against South Africa. Its new introductions included the reduction of championship rounds from 15 to 12 for health reasons. These were the condition under which the WBC would operate.

The United Nations acknowledged it for its achievements. These and other worthy achievements made it the most recognised and relevant sanctioning body in the world. The next world sanctioning body was to be formed in 1982 as a result of American Bobby Lee's failure to be elected WBA president. Lee had presented his decision to contest the election because of the failure of the sanctioning body to recognise American interests. America being a powerful nation, they wanted the world to see them as the 'powerful nation' they claimed to be. They wanted that position.

Unfortunately, Bobby Lee was beaten to the presidential post by Venezuelan Gilberto Mendoza in a neck and neck race that was swayed to Mendoza's benefit by a strong South African contingent led by SA Board chairperson Justice H.W.0 Kloppers.

Kloppers and his delegation had managed to manoeuvre themselves to the highest executive positions in the WBA. And this did not sit well with Lee. Everything he had worked to achieve seemed to be going down the drain. Standing up and taking a political stance on boxing would now be reversed as a mere sham.

Bobby Lee, the African American, walked out with a group of his supporters and formed the United States Boxing Association, also known as the USBA-INTERNATIONAL. With this new entity, they would continue to pursue the goals of seeking social justice while promoting the beautiful sport of fists and punches. The USBA-INTERNATIONAL would later change its name to International Boxing Federation – or IBF.

When I think back to it, the establishment of the IBF added to an already complicated situation. Everyone was fighting to have control of the boxing world in their territory. The Americans wanted to be in control and be in charge, while the rest of the nations who took part in the sport were uncomfortable with this arrangement. No sooner had the IBF been formed than challenges of its own doing confronted it. Structure, politics and in-fighting. I like to believe that because its constitution made it clear from inception that only American people could hold executive positions.

Japan and a lot of other Asian countries banned the IBF. As much as it had 'International' to its name, these nations did not feel represented by the entity. Since then, much has changed, in part through negotiations. So much so that Japan is now one of the IBF's most preferred venues, making it near impossible for fighters from other countries to get a fair deal in Japan in an IBF fight.

Sensing new opportunities for its ventures, South Africa's own Golden Gloves Promotions started courting the new organisation. They were seeking alternative avenues other than the WBA and WBC to feed their growing stable of fighters. Fighters who had now begun to cast their promotional tentacles across the country.

Black boxers in the Eastern Cape, especially from Buffalo City under Mzi Mnguni, gained immensely from the opportunities that flowed from the IBF relationship. IBF world champions were produced in their numbers. South African boxing was growing, which was something to be celebrated at that time. A little known town of Baffalo City was making its mark on the boxing map.

At the WBA's 67th convention in Margarita, Panama, in 1988, a group of 27 members broke away and formed the WBO. This was, they maintained, in disgust at the WBA's total disregard of its constitutional guidance.

They claimed that they were forced to take this decision reluctantly after persistent approaches for reform and a call for a better way of handling matters were either ignored or, in some cases, rudely rebuked and blocked. From then, yet another boxing organisation was formed. They named it the World Boxing Organisation and elected Dominican Republic's Luis Batista as acting president. However, due to ill health, he was soon replaced by another Dominican Republican, Ramon Pina Acevedo.

South Africa was also to take advantage of this newcomer and add to its list of sanctioning bodies prepared to give it a chance. Not to be outdone, the WBU, and also thereabout, the IBO sprang. It was as though every other month or year, there would be a new body mushrooming and claiming to represent the needs and desires of the boxing fraternity. The wider the footprint of the sanctioning body, the more power it seemed to claim. Though the WBU was strong in the United Kingdom, it canvassed a lot of support in South Africa. Numerous promoters took it up, and more champions from South Africa were produced.

The IBO, though based in America, found its own country less welcoming and was soon seeking support elsewhere. The South African crowd was again welcoming. Buffalo City in the Eastern Cape, known as the Boxing Mecca, was taking advantage of the growing number of sanctioning bodies and produced world champions by the numbers.

This was followed by a long list of other boxing sanctioning bodies that sprang like wild mushrooms and took boxing by the scruff of the neck. The other sanctioning bodies are the WBF, IBA and IBC. However, unlike the IBA and IBC, who produced some world champions in South Africa, the WBF headed by South African Howard Goldberg took over the country like a raging bull. With the growing love for boxing, this particular boxing association made serious inroads into South African boxing.

Based and more visible in the Western Cape Province, it also ventured boldly into the Eastern Cape, producing many more champions as the South African championship itself. Suddenly South African boxing was a force to be reckoned with. We were recognised for the champions we produce—powerful talent with speed and agility the world could not ignore.

Sadly, at that time, anyone could start a boxing sanctioning body. People with a clear vision were soon running the show. And if you had a good sense of how the sport works and deep financial pockets to fund your operations, you were in for the long road. You would be milking it from all angles.

I don't know if it was the realisation that boxing has money not just as a sport but also for the gambling fanatic.

When we started boxing, it was for the love of the sport. Soon those with a keen sense of ambition suddenly realised there were other means of making money in boxing than fighting in the ring and getting battered and bruised or promoting boxing events with a chance of making little or sometimes no profit at all.

There was the opportunity of sanctioning and owning world championships. Since then, big business has come to boxing and snatched this opportunity. The sanctioning organisations, or the owners thereof, demand a condition for promoting or fighting for their titles, huge sanctioning fees from the promoters, and percentages of purse money from the boxers. That is why companies, individuals or families privately own the sanctioning bodies. According to *Frank Maloney*, boxing promoter and former manager of ex Undisputed World Heavyweight Champion Lennox Lewis, "If you can persuade enough managers, promoters and fighters to compete for your world titles and pay the sanctioning fees to do so, you're home and running."

The many sanctioning bodies have weakened the sport's credibility in recent years, and a lot of the public would be happier if there were a handful of champions. Some people do agree. But say that to all the managers, promoters and boxers who already hold the titles. They will tell you to jump. The present state of affairs in these sanctioning bodies presents them with opportunities to choose whom or not to unify the titles with. So many opportunities. So much money.

The positive or negative situation of having countless governing bodies depends on where one is standing. One sanctioning body indeed means only one champion, just as FIFA is the only world governing body of soccer.

One has to be damn good even to make the Top Ten of the Ring Magazine ratings. Having one champion means real competition and that the best man is the real deal. This scenario does wonders for the reputation of boxing.

Too many champions and titles weaken and demean boxing in the eyes of the paying customers—especially where boxing had to compete with other sports for attention. But consider the situation of poorer countries and weaker currencies. The proliferation of sanctioning bodies creates more opportunities for activity, visibility, and more chances to be champions and earn a better living for their youngsters. I know that for sure with my own country and, especially, my region.

This proliferation of sanctioning bodies has changed many lives and resulted in many youngsters putting food on the table for their parents and siblings. It is a reality that would have remained a dream if circumstances were different. This side of boxing shows the unfairness of the boxing game.

According to the many conclusions reached by recognisable boxing analysts and contributors, the boxing lot is greedy, ungrateful and backstabbing. Howard Goldberg, from Cape Town, a former world-class referee and judge, echoes such views with a sense of disappointment and disgust. Having been elected as the fourth president of the WBF, Goldberg accepted the position with the ambitious intention of making a difference at home and creating opportunities for boxers, officials and promoters that were not getting anywhere else. He was the first and only South African to be elected president of any sanctioning body. He sets as examples the cases of the WBC and the WBA, who are well recognised and embraced in South Africa but have done next to nothing for this country's boxing despite making many promises.

He claims that the WBC used its well-known stance against the Apartheid Government to meet former President Nelson Mandela after his release from prison but did not deliver on its promises. While on the other side, the WBA, a well-known Apartheid boxing supporter, has been using only Stan Christodoulou to the exclusion of every other local official who deserves a chance. He says, "The IBF to its credit has used Deon Dwarte in overseas fights. But only Dwarte."

The WBF has gone beyond ring support and went as far as the gyms, donating equipment worth R20 000 each in six gymnasiums in Khayelitsha, Cape Town. The WBF, he notes with dismay, besides giving more opportunities and producing more champions, both male and female and ring officials, does not receive the respect and acceptance it deserves.

Without the WBF as one of the sanctioning bodies in this country, boxing here would be worse for wear. For years now, the leading and most credible organisations are the WBC, WBA, IBF and WBO. Fighting for a world title of at least one of these bodies is the ultimate dream for every boxer, irrespective of capabilities. Managers and promoters have sleepless nights trying to have their fighters rated by one or two, if not all of these leading world bodies. All roads lead to the champions of each division.

Activity, visibility and records against credible opponents will lead any boxers to get rated and get a crack at the title for any of the bodies. Considering all the above, Buffalo City and its people can be proud of its boxing product which has risen to international recognition against all odds.

EASTERN CAPE BOXERS WHO HAVE WON WORLD TITLES

» Welcome Ncita - Beat Fabrice Benichou on points for the IBF J/Featherweight title – 10 March 1990

» Vuyani Bungu – Beat Kennedy Mckinney on points for the IBF title J/ Featherweight title– 20 August 1994

» Mbulelo Botile – Beat Harold Mestre by KO 2nd round for the IBF Bantamweight title – 29 April 1995

» Sakhumzi Magxwalisa – Beat Choasing Charlemsi by KO 2nd round for the WBU J/Bantamweight– 15 June 1996

» Mzukisi Sikali – Nungdiew Sakcharuporn on points for the WBU J/Flyweight title – 8 November 1996, beat Luigi Castglione by KO 8 for the WBU J/ Bantamweight – 1 August 1998

» Patrick Quka – Beat Giamaria Petriccioli by KO 11 for the WBU Bantamweight title – 2 August 1997

» Zolani Petelo – Beat Ratanapol Sor Vorapin by KO 4 for the IBF Mini flyweight – 27 November 1997

» Mpush Makambi – Beat Adrien Dodson by ko11 for the IBO Middleweight title – 8 September 1998

» Lindi Memani – Beat Juan Herrera on points for the WBU mini Flyweight title – 12 September 1998

» Hawk Makepula – Beat Rafael Torres by 5th round Tech. Dec. for the WBU J/Flyweight – 22 September 1998. Makepula would later unify the WBU and WBO titles in beating Jake Matlala.

» Wele Maqolo – Beat Fahsung Pongsawang on points for the WBF MiniFlyweight title – 25 September 1999

» Zolile Mbityi – Beat Dimitar Alipiev on points for the IBO Flyweight title – 22 October 1999

» Mhikiza Myekeni – Beat Jose Garcia Bernal for IBO LightFlyweight title – 17-04-2002

» Nkosinathi Joyi – Armando La Cruz by KO for IBO Minimumweight title – 04-11-2006

- » Zolani Marali – Beat Jean-Marie Godet on points for WBF SuperBantamweight title – 08-09-2006

- » Simphiwe Vetyeka – Won the IBO Bantamweight title – July 2009, IBO Featherweight title in April 2013, WBA Featherweight title on 6 December 2013.

- » Noni Tenge – Beat Gritty Amanua Ankrah for WBF female Welterweight title – 12-08 2009, Beat Daniella Smith for IBF Welterweight title on 11-06-2011

- » Siphiwe Nonqayi- Beat Juan Alberto Rosas on points for IBF Junior Bantam title – 31 – 07 – 2010'

- » Unathi Myekeni – Beat Renata Szebeledi on points for WBF SuperBantmaweight title – 12 09 2010

- » Thabo Sonjica – Beat Sylvester Lopez for IBO SuperBantamweight title – 06-97-2013

- » Lwandile Sityatha – Siphosethu Mvula on points for the WBF SuperFlyweight title – 31-05 2014

- » Ali Funeka – Beat Roman Bilaev by TD for IBO Welterweight title - 15-11-2014

- » Zolani Tete – Beat Teiru Kinoshita on points for IBF Junior Bantamweight title 18-07-2015, beat Arthur Villanueva on points for WBO Bantamweight title - 22-04-2017

- » Xolisani Ndongeni – Abram Ndauendapp on points for the WBF Lightweight title – 08-04-2018

CHAPTER 5
WHAT SELLS TICKETS

IT HAS BEEN MORE than forty years since Muhammad Ali, the three-time world heavyweight boxing champion who helped define his turbulent times as the most charismatic and controversial sports figure of the 20th century.

He is generally accepted as the greatest Heavyweight boxer, arguably one of the best boxers. Certainly, one of the best athletes of all time introduced boxing to million-dollar purses. Since then, a year hardly passes without a boxer making it as one of the top money-makers. Floyd Mayweather Jr has taken the earning powers of boxing to levels never seen before in any sport by leading the payment line for five years in succession.

This proves that boxing is certainly a big-money sport.

It may be argued that inflation always rears its ugly head and affects the value of all currencies such that the value of the Rand was much higher or stronger than it is today. But all adjustments one can come up with to compare the different boxers earning power, today's fighters take home much higher earners than their counterparts of the past.

The sheer numbers of Rands and Dollars paid today are mesmerising, to say the least. Boxers' earnings in countries like the USA and UK have skyrocketed because of the introduction of new marketing techniques.

The viewership is no longer limited to the crowd in the boxing venue but is spread around the country and the rest of the world, in homes and paying venues through closed-circuit television, satellite transmission and pay per view TV. Such innovations have significantly increased viewing audiences. Boxers are now able to be paid earnings following the returns of such buys.

In the South African context, boxers are mostly paid according to their drawing powers. At least, that is what happens in the main bout – usually a title fight. Sometimes in the main supporting bout and main *prelim* will also generate revenue for the boxers as well.

The rest of the boxers in the bill are usually paid standard purses per round. The big earners are the draw-cards—the big name boxers who have a significant local and national following to fill the venues. The marketing of upcoming tournaments or boxers varies from promoter to promoter based on budget but is merely based on TV, radio, newspapers and handbill appearances. Of late, social media has also worked its way into the marketing space. Casinos have also paid a big part in the earnings of especially the white South African boxers.

The Casinos have been known to assist in the marketing and lending logistical and financial support in tournaments staged in their venues. Obviously, when people are at the casino venue, spillage will spend money on the tables and gambling machines. Casinos know this, so they don't mind spending a little to get people to the venue.

Their financial and marketing clout was also used to attract the big-time international boxers, hence busting the international sanctions against South Africa when the whole world discourages them from participating or against fighters coming from this country.

South African boxers who have benefited from their drawing powers range from township draw-cards like Nkosana '*Happy boy*' Mgxaji in Mdantsane to Anthony '*Blue Jaguar*' Morodi. Levy '*Golden boy*' Madi and Enoch '*Schoolboy*' Nhlapo in Soweto also had the crowd-pulling power of a truly successful boxer.

These boxers were known to pull between 20 000 and 25000 fans for their fights at Sisa Dukashe stadium and Orlando stadium. Their purses were based on crowd attendances as there were no sponsorships to assist in promoting the fights. Promoters made massive investments into these bouts. They were putting their money upfront and hoping to profit on the gate takings. More often than not, they made more profit than they imagined.

Among the white boxers Charlie 'Silver Asassin' Weir, Gerrie Coetzee 'the Boksburg' Blits, and Kallie Knoetzee 'Die Bek' van Boomstraat have been known as the biggest drawcards among the white crowds. The crowd attendance for Knoetze's WBA World title fight with Big John Tate was announced at 50 000.

Qualities like charisma and flamboyance boost the personal magnetism of boxers and have been identified as strengths for drawing the crowds up to universal. Giant marketing strategies increase the magnetism of these boxers to dizzying heights. In the process of writing this book, I sent the question to boxing fans around the country to check their views. The responses were as diverse as boxing styles. But they were interesting. Please note that this is by no means a professional debate but rather an exchange of views from the people who work on boxing one way or another daily.

My survey was based on whether economics play a part in the drawing power of the boxers. I also wanted to understand or at least disprove my notion of what makes them big crowd pullers – does it differ by race, area or location and financial backing.

South Africa's unfortunate historical situation premised on its racial laws that affected how each racial group's lives would develop from birth to death. As a result of these laws, one will find better social development within the white race. They often have money to spare for entertainment events like boxing, which may not be the case among black people and other races in South Africa.

Race and inequality tend to play a significant role in who can afford to go where, why and how. Does that mean that white boxers draw bigger crowds than their black counterparts? Does drawing power have to do with talent or race? Is it a talent that attracts the people, or is it a racial phenomenon? What makes a draw-card? I believe the answer there lies in representation by population. One population is just so much more affluent than others. Each population naturally knows its own and supports its own more than it does others. Andile Sidinile is a former amateur boxer, a current boxing promoter and an analyst. He is based in East London. He says, "I think talent sells tickets."

Talent in promoting the fight is to have a perfect plan, a perfect promotional plan. Talent also in terms of who is fighting. Any boxer with talent will have a loyal fan base. Allow boxing tournaments to have an entertainment feature. Let it be an outing to even the casual boxing fan. Mbenge and Mchunu were topping the bill at Emperors, and it was a full house. It's rubbish and pure political ignorance to argue along with crowd racial profiling. When last did we see a full house at Orient Theater? It is only an 1150 capacity venue. Is it because we do not have white fighters. Why are black fans not filling it?

The truth is nowadays you have very few promoters but more wannabes who I call boxing event management companies. A boxing promoter would have a unique business model and sell tickets according to such. An event manager would always complain about the race and favouritism of others. Economics is supply and demand. It's not about haves and have nots. That's a pure simplistic definition in this debate.

The economics, in this case, can be a factor only when you feature mediocre boxers. They can be a factor also when you use small venues. These are choices made by the promoter. The middle class is shrinking in South Africa. People are currently reprioritising between a need and a want. This is not done based on colour, but it's a class and affordability issue. Coming back to the debate, any customer would sacrifice for a good product.

Boxing is a product that must be enhanced with good entertainment, talent and incremental plans. Hardcore and casual boxing fans should be aware of the career or journey of the promoting boxers.

Allow them to be part of that journey. They should know the plans. That is a product you are selling. If, for example, a soccer team is constantly losing, they sell fewer tickets. But, if they are winning and have high prospects of winning the league, they have a full house consistently. The economics become secondary, and race factors become nil.

Simphiwe Sinyabi is a former boxing coach and a current promoter. He is based in East London. He says, "This question is very much relevant, and the answer on that is, yes. The element of discrimination is the order of the day. Even in Gauteng, when you look at sponsorship, even at EMPERORS PALACE, only Golden Gloves and not a single other promoter are allowed to promote there." White people are selective in who they are supporting at the boxing venues, but they come in big numbers when it's a white boxer. Here in East London, they regard boxing as a sport for black people. It is rare to see white people attending boxing tournaments in the Mecca of boxing, but they come out in big numbers when it is a white boxer. Even then, you see them in one particular spot, and they leave after the white fighter is finished.

Gary Murray is a former world-class boxer. He stays in Cape Town. He says, "Support is given to any boxer with talent no matter what colour people support great fighters end of the story."

Mlungisi Dube is a promoter who lives In Durban. He says, "In Durban, Indian boxers sell better." Louw Passons is a long time boxing fan. He lives in Gauteng. He says, "To me, there is no colour in boxing. You support the talent that represents South Africa. I am a boxing supporter for the last 45 years when I started at the age of 16. Since then, I followed boxers like Kosie Smith, Pierre Fourie, Elijah Makhathini, Baby Jake Matlala, Dingaan Thobela, Brian Mitchell and many others."

Mava Malla is a former professional boxer. He replaced *Stanley Christodoulou* as CEO of SA boxing, thus becoming the first ex-boxer to be CEO of Boxing SA. He says, "White boxers sell more tickets. Colour is the factor. Who attends June 16? Watch any sport all over the world and look at the audience. It is white people because we still have black and white. But look around the world, it is people with a fair complexion who feel the big arenas."

Mzoli Dabane Ka Tempi is a boxing fan. He lives in Cape Town.

He says, "We can go around in circles as much as we want—economics and politics influence sales. I have seen people in tournaments who know nothing about the game coming to support their kind. I have also seen people sponsoring tournaments because they are organised on their own. So the economics play a role. White boxers, good or bad, will bring more to the organisers."

Welile Mguli is a boxing fan and researcher. He lives in Gauteng.

He says, "All the aspects mentioned like economy and sponsors constitute racism. White fans attend because they have money based on their colour. It is the preferential treatment since the Colour Bar Act. Blacks would go to all games if they had money. Its economics."

Anton Gilmore is a former world-class boxer. He is now a trainer. He says, "Location, quality of fights and who is promoting, that always makes the difference."

Coenie Bekker is an ex-boxer who lives in Cape Town. He is a former opponent of mine. We share a fight apiece. He says, "Truth be told, more whites support any colour in the sport worldwide."

Michael Pawson is a former manager. He lives in Gauteng. He says, "Surprisingly, the race issue has been transcended in boxing as far back as I can remember there has never been a black-white thing. Even blacks in the Apartheid era loved Gerrie Coetzee and Charlie Weir. But yes, it is an economic thing and very little racism. THANK GOD for that."

Droeks Malan is a renowned boxing writer and analyst. He lives in Gauteng. He says, "If the boxer has an exciting crossover style and personality, and can speak English, then colour does not matter. Many white people loved Dingaan Thobela and Baby Jake Matlala just as Tommy Oosthuizen and Brian Mitchell had a lot of black support."

Tsepo Tshehla is an ex-South African Featherweight champion. He lives in Witbank. He says, "We must not run away from the fact that one of the crucial determinants of the sale of tickets relates to the disposable income. Let us be fair that you cannot expect someone who earns less than R2000 a month to afford entertainment tickets. The scenario looks worse when more than 70 per cent of black people are forced to earn less than R2000 a month."

The majority of black people receive slave wage and spend too much time at work doing overtime to offset the deficit. Therefore they either don't have a surplus after addressing their needs or time to attend boxing.

Have you investigated how a highly unequal distribution of income affects economic development, which depends on factors such as spending? Don't you think a highly unequal distribution of income skews the playing field, thus disadvantaging mostly black boxers since the 1884-5 Berlin Conference resolutions?

Sello 'King Lion' Taunyane is a boxing fan who lives in Gauteng. His opinion is that, it's a problem of transportation as big fights are only in Suburbs in Emperors, and Carnival City, no more boxing near the townships.

Lesley Flavell is a boxing gym owner and sponsor. She lives in Gauteng. She says, "I think the price of tickets sometimes makes it less accessible to the general boxing public, but I think there is an equal love of boxing on both sides. Tando Jafta is a businessman and a boxing fan from East London. He says, "Problem starts with us black business not supporting boxing events, and that leaves promoters and government to pay for everything."

Whites support each other and have proper venues. Jack Chaney is a boxing fan. He lives in Gauteng. He says, "The biggest ticket sellers are boxers linked with a football team."

Andre Thysse is a former SA Junior Middle Weight champion. He lives in Gauteng. He says, "In the boxing world, it depends on the boxer, not what colour he is. In South Africa, it depends on what province or area your box in. In Johannesburg, white boxers sell better, and in EL, black boxers sell better."

Daniel Faku Canham is a boxing fan. He lives in Port Elizabeth. He says, "A well decorated and the marketed athlete will sell tickets. A good example is Mayweather. On a national scale, it depends on the area the boxer is based. Athlete attitude and behaviour attracts people irrespective of race or colour."

Vuyani Mbinda is an ex-boxer and founder member of Ubuntu Boxing Fraternity. He lives in Mdantsane. He says, "I am not sure if the question of who sells more tickets can be answered properly because, in our situation as black people, the Theatre can be full, but 30 to 40 per cent of the crowd are in without paying because of their connection or privilege. The most paying customers in boxing are black people. Most paying customers in almost all sports codes are black people. It is not a question of black or white but who likes most, and in this case, blacks come out tops."

Brian Wysonke is a businessman and boxing sponsor. He lives in Gauteng. He says, "Difficult question to answer, and it should not be answered on racial lines but rather look at the geographical area. You hardly have a white boxer in EC, so black boxers will naturally bring more fans into the venue in areas like EL. Bear in mind that the marketing of the show plays a major role. Have a show with no stars, and you battle to fill the venue. Have a show with household names, and you fill the venue. Nothing to do with colour."

In summing up my view on this matter, crowd attendance is affected by historical, political and socio-economic factors that most people from all walks of life, irrespective of their personal beliefs and social backgrounds, find very hard to fathom. People simply can neither qualify nor measure the quality of what they have never heard of nor ever seen. Why? Because it is easier to see, appreciate and support the people in front of us than to open our minds and explore what is either far or is around us. Most people only look straight ahead and at the surface. And sadly, in human beings, the surface is the colour of the skin.

Boxing is still going on as usual here and around the globe, oblivious of all factors and influences over, under, ahead and around it. But the question of whether crowd attendance in boxing or any other sport, for that matter, is a racial phenomenon or not still has to be addressed thoroughly, honestly. And answered satisfactorily.

CHAPTER 5

CONTRACTUAL BOXING DYNAMICS

AT THE BEGINNING of the decade, Boxing South Africa – otherwise known as Boxing SA, as mandated by the Boxing Act 11 0f 2001 introduced a standard contract to allow boxers to be contracted to promoters and managers for two-year renewal terms.

The two most important terms of the contract, which always pose as the main bone of contention are the first year of the contract where the promoter must give the boxer a minimum of four fights a year, and secondly, that the boxer must not take any fight by another promoter without consent from the contracted promoter.

In layman's terms, a contract brings together two parties in a voluntary agreement to deliver on agreed expectations. The intention, especially reduced to writing creates a legal obligation to both parties to honour the agreement.

The BSA contract was meant for boxers to train in full comfort, knowing that they had a guaranteed line up of fights. The promoter or manager could plan to make his or her investment a reality without having to deal with other competitors for the boxer's services.

BSA would regulate the terms of the contract.

The terms and conditions of the relationship between the boxer, the manager and the promoters would be outlined in detail. To level the playing field, these terms would be standardised in every contract.

Where necessary, Boxing SA would intervene. Or step in to resolve issues that seemed exploitative to any of the parties involved in the agreement. After the invention of the new contract and its optimistic expectations, new dynamics emerged and forced Boxing SA to have a closer look at the new scenario.

As you would have it with any developing field of sport, controversies have followed one after the other. Boxers in particular felt blind-sided after having signed contracts and then left to idle without fights with periods of inactivity equal to the term of the contract itself – two years.

The main dynamic was the simple reason that everybody who had a promising boxer or could lay their hands on good quality talent. With a litany of would-be promoters lined up to sign up every young soul eager enough to through a punch, a majority of these promoters could not deliver.

They either did not have the necessary resources to make the fights happen nor did they have the connections to bring together the right combination to pit their eager boxers toe to toe in the ring.

Major role players in the world of boxing whose business has always to be minded are boxers, managers, trainers and promoters. But the terms of agreements, wherever you go, here and abroad have one common discrepancy in that they are seldom, if ever conducive to a free and fair working relationship among the signatories. The people who usually get the shortest and roughest end of the deal are the boxers.

The ones who take the punches, feel the pains and strain their body to take on whatever their opponents dish out. Ultimately, they are the ones left out in the cold. They are the reason the is money on the table, yet when everyone has taken their share, very little is left for them to enjoy of nurse their bruised faces. This effectively means that the contract is unfair to the boxers.

The scenario with these agreements did not end there. It brought about the second dynamic – that even promoters and managers who are held in high esteem, and on whom BSA, boxers, managers and the boxing fans could rely on to deliver the fights and facilitate the upward movement of the boxers failed more than they succeeded.

Boxers could not get the number of fights as agreed to in the contracts. And being a boxer who has no fights to contest or defend does not make you a champion. It makes you a trained fighter with no prospects of glory.

Many boxing champions were stripped of their titles as they could not defend the titles within the regulated time limits. When you lose something you have not defended, it is far worse than losing something you put up your fists for. I am a boxer, and I know that.

What is even sad is that a lot of those champions had joined these new promotional outfits after becoming more successful and visible, and hence more marketable commodities. They expected much more. But all they become was a nice trophy sign-up on paper with nothing to show in the ring.

Another reality for boxers came in the form of the inability of managers to make good on the signed guarantees. It emerged that the managers just signed the boxers to stay firmly in their gyms under their guidance without any hope of producing the means for upward movement other than relying on the promoters to deliver.

This puts the boxer firmly in the position of a perpetual beggar. One who is always prepared to do anything to please the promoters. When there is no money to feed your family or to take care of your personal needs anything that shines will attract you. It has become very clear over time that the real manager of the boxers were the promoters themselves.

The managers themselves were nothing more than glorified entourage who are there to the flowing cash and promised glory should their boxer ever get to fight. And so it is true, the heavier dependency lay more with the promoters than the managers.

This shaky situation has had the Buffalo City boxing community arguing, complaining and squabbling among themselves and other boxing stakeholders.

Besides having to deal with the movement of boxer among themselves, they have always had to deal with a much bigger problem – the exodus of boxers from the region to Gauteng where they have joined the more affluent white counterparts who are better placed to deliver on the contracts. The cream of boxers migrates in big numbers to Gauteng year after year. The common pain brings them together. You must, however, not be misled by the above scenario. The achievements by the collective of boxers, managers, trainers in Buffalo City since professional boxing started here in 1965s has been nothing short of amazing. It has been too good, especially if one has to consider the region's economic situation.

If it was not for the love, enthusiasm and involvement of the people in the development of boxing, this region would have been so much poorer. The Government has also played a big role in putting aside sizable funds to sponsor boxing development and tournaments.

Buffalo City Municipality is situated in the most southern tip of Africa. Far-flung from Gauteng Province which is the economic and sports hub of the country, as well as the giant economies of the United States and Europe where all the big events are happening. And where boxers have to draw opponents for quality competition and international recognition.

It is also one of the poorest Provinces in South Africa. As a result, it becomes a heavy financial burden and logistical nightmare for boxers for the Eastern Cape and their teams to travel up North or across the seas for contests that make the difference in visibility and achievements. As a boxer, you want to be seen. You want to showcase your skills in the ring.

You want to hear the jeering voices of your fans. That is what boxing is about. So when you come from the furthest tip of the African continent, it is near impossible to bring boxers from these places with their big entourages to fight in places where the money flows with great abundance.

Moreover, the Rand status against the Dollar is a king-size headache. Our achievements are buoyed even more by the fact that they are gained despite the economic slump that has been ravaging the country for about some time. While BCM has produced world champions in almost all the sanctioning bodies like WBA, WBO, IBF, WBF, IBF and IBO, new dynamics have left the boxers crying more than ululating. It brought BSA to a point where the regulatory body of South African boxing had to rethink the delivery of this contractual mandate. It had to change its stance for the sake of the boxers. It had become clear that there was more to the situation than meets the eye. The boxers, who are the core and the nucleus of the game became the beggars and the biggest losers. It was felt that there was a need to give them space to talk and make deals with the highest bidders.

Faced with the daunting task of levelling the playing fields among all its stakeholders, BSA decided to tackle the matter aggressively and effectively. The contracts were temporarily suspended while the task of replacing them got underway.

The roadshow of 2012 became a two-fold project. Firstly, the introduction of the new board members as well as the promotion of interaction between associations of boxers, managers, trainers and promoters and ring officials. In the subsequent dialogues across the country, boxers complained bitterly about the ill-treatment they were subjected to after signing the contracts.

They echoed their situation of having no say whatsoever on the amounts they were to fight for as they were bound by contracts. This situation made it impossible for them to listen to other promoters offering better purses or opportunities. It resulted in the successes of a few but the failure of a whole lot more.

Boxing SA reiterated that there was a crisis in boxing that needed urgent attention. It was due to the mandate vested in it to review the contracts – how it is usurped, what achievements or failure can be attributed to it and, finally what changes, updates, extensions or cancellations could be made to so that it could be relevant to the ever-changing landscape, dynamics and attitudes that accompany boxing.

Bad and undesirable practices had to be eliminated.

The first step was to suspend the renewal of existing licenses, review the Boxing Act and see if, especially where it came to contracts, it was still relevant to current affairs. Time frames for fights would be attached periodically. Minimum payments per fight would be introduced.

There would be penalties for failure to honour the guarantees made and expected in the contract. If need be, the whole long term contracts concept would be banned.

This, it was envisaged, would go a long way towards reaching the desired quest of empowering boxers and placing them in their rightful place as the main players, while simultaneously recognising and acknowledging the role of promoters as business people. This would further enhance the promoters' positions and understanding by all concerned that contraction of boxers was rather for business and investment purposes than selfish interests.

An analysis of this new dispensation gave rise to a lot of views. Some of the new considerations looked and sounded well enough. Others could be kicked out of court if challenged. If or when contracts were reintroduced two aspects could not be denied.

Firstly people or boxers would look into the boxing agreements and sign the contracts with a better understanding. And secondly, people without capacity would not rush to sign boxers. Thirdly boxers would make some research and ask questions before signing and fourthly maybe BSA would make certain requirements for people to pass before allowing them to put pen to paper. There are a lot of options. But boxing must go on.

CHAPTER 6

WHY BOXERS MIGRATE TO GAUTENG?

AMONG THE BIGGEST challenges facing the community in the Eastern Cape Province generally, and Buffalo City, in particular, has been the constant migration of its best talent to Gauteng Province.

The lost skills have included people from all walks of life, ranging from academic, political or sports skills. All have left the region because of the lack of resources back home. They heed the beckoning of plenty of opportunities in the wealthiest Province in the country.

The Eastern Cape is endowed with talent in most if not all sporting codes. But it is boxing which possesses the best and most successful sportsmen and women. The academic sector has referred to this exodus as the brain drain. In boxing, we call it brand or talent drain.

Our brightest stars are all going up north looking for better economic opportunities. It is true, they could enhance the brand of the Province within the Province, but they are lost to the attraction of good money in the land of gold and money. They migrate to Gauteng for personal improvement and empowerment. Local boxing has been suffering knockout after knockout from this syndrome. In the last two decades, Buffalo City has seen itself being creamed off its best boxers.

Most of the exceptional boxing talent groomed in Buffalo City, they have left these shores to search for money and gold. The biggest beneficiaries of such migration has mostly been the white managers and trainers in the Gauteng Province. The talent that has left these shores has been so brilliant and successful that it has made great trainers of everybody who has had the fortune of landing talent from Buffalo City.

It has been no secret for any trainer who wants quality and ready-made talent; Buffalo City is the place to scout and poach from. Good boxers are ten a penny. The new trainers do not have to teach anything new. They take on the young men who have been sharpened to the core. Their fighting skills are brilliant, and they are hungry to make it in the big city.

These boxers are ready-made in the desk rings in classrooms where their talents are honed. All the new trainers and managers do is provide the means. And the boys do what comes naturally and add what they have been taught back home – they box. While some regard it as hypothetical and naïve to complain or protest about the mass exodus of fighters from one person to another, nothing mirrors human nature quite so emphatically as losing out of the bigger picture of one created and natured from the beginning.

The same goes for one who finds finished goods landing on his lap. Such is the rush for the Buffalo City brand of boxers that Gauteng managers and trainers have known to hire agents within the region to lore fighters. Text messages, conversations in hushed tones, and air tickets have been the order of the day. There are so many reasons why eloping boxers have been as different as night and day. The arguments supporting fighters leaving the southern shores have been as strong as those arguing vehemently against it. These arguments are so good and hold so much water; you, as a person listening, are bound to believe the person arguing one case until you meet the next one arguing against it. It certainly depends on who you are talking to at a particular time.

Boxing has been widely known to attract kids coming from the most impoverished backgrounds. It has been known as the sport where it is much easier to advance with very little or no financial base. This scenario does not lie only with the boxers but also with the older folks who take it upon themselves to assist one way or another where they find this talent struggling to make ends meet. Those people are usually a family friend, the guy leaving up the street, or the one who has set up this semi or non equipped structure where the kid's train. The structure is usually a car garage, an unused local building or a classroom. The more lucky ones get to use the local community hall.

This situation has a string of true and living stories. As the youngster grows within the sport, so do the natural demands of the game and nature in general. When you are doing well in any situation, you will want more of your benefits. Which always means wanting more of the finer things in life.

There are different role players in a boxers life: the manager, the promoter, the trainer and many others. However, with a limitation of the available people and resources, the one person who assumes the role of trainer and manager finds himself occupying another position, that of being a funder as well. The youngster's activities inside and outside of boxing need funding to keep them going, and so this position is vital while it is also demanding.

As the only source of income for many of these boxers, the manager must often step in for some of their most basic needs. He sometimes has to pay school fees for the children or siblings of the fighters out of his pocket until the next paying gig for the boxers. In cases where the biological fathers are not there for one reason or another, he finds himself having to oversee the youngster's personal growth and development. Like when the time comes for him to go for his customary circumcision rituals when he comes of age. They become like father and son. Most of our managers do not run boxing as a business. That's the starting point.

The father-son relationship is good as far as keeping relations of respect, and good communication are concerned. Still, the manager/client relationship should be at the forefront for business purposes. The practice of ignoring business skills and personal improvement keep them ignorant and unaware of changes around them.

Again the practice of looking for sponsorship by word of mouth without providing a CV is another no-no. Potential sponsors can see no value return to their investment. Perhaps if gyms could be registered as Non-Profit Organisations (NPO's) and run along strict business practices like many gyms do in Gauteng, things could improve a bit. It would attract the much-needed confidence that is the requirement for long and trusting relationships. That is the difference between black-owned and white-owned gyms. White managers invest in the boxers in terms of sponsors and accommodation. Many Eastern Cape boxing managers who have lost many boxers feel that the practice is itself oppression in disguise. But one that is very difficult for the boxers to notice at that stage because of hunger. They argue the boxers still come back empty-handed and needy after retirement. The same way they do with black trainers. One would have thought that with the skills and experience they have, white managers or trainers would be able to impact some of such skills to their investments. But they don't. To them, it's business as usual.

This bond among the black managed or trained boxers naturally give rise to expectations. As the fighter grows within the game's rungs and wins more meaningful fights, there develops this expectation that they will be together for as long as it takes. A strong bond develops as the boxer gains more popularity and starts earning more money in more prominent bouts. Sometimes, to the point where the fighter and his manager agree that they will be together until the end of the boxer's career. A marriage of minds, vision and purpose becomes the foundation of their relationship.

At least that seems to be valid until the poaching begins. The poaching eagles start to circle in on the relationship to find weakness when the signs are there that this is a champion in the making. It is then that a boxer starts receiving phone calls, text messages and even personal visits showing the brighter side of life. For many black boxers, money is the weakness. When they have to choose between feeding and taking care of their families, and their loyalties to their training manager, the choice is too hard to bear. Before they know it, they are signed up to a gym in the city of Gold and money.

These are professional poachers – they know what they are doing. They do their research well. Their agents feed them all the information they need – information about the boxer's well-being, family and financial status, and anything they may use to lure them to the big city. A lot of the boxers still stay at home with their parents. Others remain in *shacks* within the yard or away from home. And when the opportunity to escape that part of their lives, they grab it with both hands. Sadly, a lot of them even leave home for the gym without eating, not knowing what they will eat when they come back. It is no surprise that a promise of a furnished flat and a small job accompanied by no less than three fights a year is a life changer, a dream come true.

This is a predicament whose solutions cannot be thumb sucked. It is an all-encompassing challenge starting from the homes to the managers, trainers and even the promoters. It is far from the general belief that only struggling managers and trainers must deal and permanently lose to this challenge. It shows how tough managing a boxer is in an environment characterised by poverty, unemployment, and squalor. Even the managers we think highly of are not doing as well as we believe they are doing. It's a dog eat dog world, where only the brave survive. And brave means only one thing – money, or the ability to make money happen.

Why do you think there are so few tournaments in our area? Why do the few promoters use the same boxers over and over again? Why are our few world champions finding it difficult to defend their titles at home? The promoters here do not spread their wings and promote boxers from all stables. The practice of billing the same fighters from the same stables over and over to the exclusion of all others is killing the game. These promotional habits arise from boxers' monopoly by the promoters who can contract the boxers to long-term contracts. They obtain this muscle from the power they have over the Government funds. And they flex the muscle selfishly and unashamedly. Well, it is called business, but the irony of this business in our case is that our promoters do not use their own money to promote tournaments. Nor do they have sponsorship from private businesses.

The business practice called OPM (other people's money) has always been alive and well in boxing. This, I think, has strictly meant using cash from other business people who gain millage and subsequent marketing leverage from the promotional ventures, especially when fights have TV coverage.

This is the opportunity Gauteng managers are taking advantage of. They give the EC boxers everything they do not get back home. The sponsors get opportunities to advertise on the boxer's attire. They also get a well-timed mention every time the boxer is on the public podium.

They also enjoy added advantage and promotional leverage over their counterparts in other Provinces. This business punch comes in the form of Golden Gloves Promotions. The biggest boxing promotion in Africa in the last 40 years has the monopoly of all Casinos in the country. Its tight hold on South African boxing even stretches over to television. It has the lion's share of TV coverage by *SuperSport*. It ensures that all the fighters who join managers and trainers aligned to its promotion are kept as busy as possible and are pushed to world title fights. At the time of this writing, only one outfit, only the relatively new Last Born Promotions, has been able to source private funding for the tournaments it has promoted since its inception.

Mlandeli Thengimfene is a co-founder of Last Born Promotions and the manager of World Bantamweight champion Zolani Tete, whose nickname the promotions have been named. Since winning the world championship, Tete has acquired several sponsorships, something that has always only been connected with white boxers and, to a slight extent, black boxers who have white managers.

But is this enough to withstand the flow of approaches and courting coming from up North? No, it is not enough. It will take more than one promotion, one manager and one boxer to stop the significant numbers of fighters from migrating every year. This scouting is not the only resident at the professional level.

Agents and scouts attend all the amateur championships and pick up the cream of the crop. They then claim that the boxers have been with them from the beginning. Money is the name of the game.

Few local people, if any, want to be involved and use their time and money when the boxer is still struggling, and the bright future on the horizon is not yet clear. There are business people and a lot of others who possess academic qualifications. They could lend some advice in the advancement of the boxers around them. The majority of them are boxing fans by birth.

They are born into boxing, just as most of their peers in Gauteng are born into soccer. Certain boxing managers and trainers who have taken that route and approached some professionals to assist have been rudely awakened to the fact that not all are honest in this business.

Some have been flatly turned back while the boxers have been taken away, especially where the approached person is a boxing licensee. Under more ideal circumstances, this would be the perfect answer for any stable.

What can be done to curb this constant outflow that has weakened the BCM for such a long period? Do the local mentors have to look into themselves to find the solutions, or is it much bigger than themselves and can only be solved by people in higher places?

The Eastern Cape boxing community needs to look into themselves and concentrate on improving performance, particularly on training and mentoring. In any sporting code, the way raw talent is identified, groomed, and made to blossom is the best investment before focusing on the return on such investment, which is the biggest challenge.

Local mentors tend to concentrate on the harvest rather than on what they plant. That is why there are so many licensees but very scarce action or meaningful input. This looks like the same challenge facing the Province from the roots. The historical poverty of this widespread, largely rural region.

As long as the EC is Province is unable to create means to sustain and retain its talent, there is no stopping this flow. Maybe a leaf can be taken from the same beneficiary of this movement.

In or around 2005, the Gauteng Province introduced an outreach program meant to attract sportsmen and women from other Provinces to what they aptly called the home of champions.

It was such a marvellous and far-reaching idea. It attracted sports prospects of all sports codes from around the country. Even sportsmen and women from outside the South African borders heeded the call. It is a project along those lines that the Eastern Cape Government should adopt to intervene and save its gold, silver and diamonds that are their boxers.

Boxing in the Eastern Cape region has always been a success story. Our boxers have won every championship there is to win in National and World boxing, except for the WBC championship. No other sporting code nor social activity has come close to emulating or equalling what boxing has achieved for this Province.

Maybe the only exception could be Politics, courtesy of producing struggle giants that include Nelson Mandela, OR Tambo, Thabo Mbeki, Walter Sisulu, Winnie Madikizela Mandela, and Steve Tshwete – to name but a few.

The list is long, and so it was no surprise that one of its sons, the legendary Hawk Makepula, was selected to carry the South African flag and lead TEAM SOUTH AFRICA in the 1996 Olympic Games in Atlanta, Georgia.

South African boxing is ruled and regulated under the South African Boxing Act 11 of 2001. This effectively makes boxing the only sports code regulated by an Act of Parliament in South Africa. In the absence of private sponsorship, the Eastern Cape Government has been carrying boxing in this region. Annual funds are allocated to assist in promoting small, National and International tournaments.

This gesture has kept boxing alive to some point. But is not enough to keep everybody happy. For starters, there are far too many promoters than the budget can satisfy or accommodate. It results in internal squabbling and mudslinging that only succeed in slowing down and hurting the game than facilitating and developing it. The smaller promoters whose licenses allow them to promote what is referred to as development tournaments are not pleased with the heavy budgets that amount to millions of rands and are allocated to the fewer promoters. These few are licensed to organise world title fights.

The world and international fights are usually promoted to coincide and celebrate Political events. Here, they only use boxers contracted to them. The rest are left to idle and suffer in the doldrums. Perhaps The Eastern Cape Government could make good on this funding by using its political muscle to form partnerships with the private sector.

It could persuade the financial giants to use some of their funds to sponsor boxers, boxing clubs, tournaments and all events meant to upgrade boxing in the region. Boxing has done well enough without such massive muscle.

One can only imagine how far it would go with the local financial giants pushing it. Such successful marriage would have succeeded where the boxing gurus and officialdom have failed.

The EC Government has already played the part of mothering its boxing kid and carried it on its back all the way, conquering the world in the process. It could go a step further by not only funding boxing tournaments and events. It could register and regulate all boxing clubs in the Province and make them solvent enough to sustain and retain their boxers.

That would empower the local managers and trainers of the gyms and enable them to contract boxers to the clubs just as they do in other sports codes. Local boxing would be so much bigger and more successful by putting its local boxing on the same par with other sporting codes like Soccer, Rugby and Cricket. After all, it has already been doing so much better than all of them combined.

CHAPTER 7

THE BUSINESS OF PROMOTERS

PROMOTERS IN BOXING are the people who organise fights for boxers. They put tournaments together and get the boxers to fight for a fee. Under normal circumstances, and except for a few exceptions, they decide who fights whom, when and where. They decide how much and who gets paid. They organise and arrange all the money to be available upfront to make sure that all boxers contesting in the tournament are paid.

They have to put their money first as a guarantee.

Contestants in a tournament have to be paid whether money has been made afterwards made or not. In some cases, one or more boxers must be paid even without physically participating in the tournament.

Promoters sometimes make a lot of money. Other times, they lose a lot of money. But more often than not, they make more money than they lose. Especially those whose tentacles are well spread and are in command of big sponsorship with television rights. I call these promoters, *ring smart*.

To the *ring smart* promoter, boxing is more than a sport. Boxing is business. And their business is acknowledged and protected even by The South African Boxing Act 11 of 2001. The Act recognises that the ultimate aim of the boxing business is to make maximum profit. The *ring smart* promoter will always go out to make the most out of every fight, if not most of his fights. Accordingly, the promoters reserve the right to object and may even sue people who are found to be advertising a competitor's brand in their promotions, including the boxes clothing.

For the promoter to do good business, they have to sell their product very well. In this case, the boxers and the tournaments need to have the widest public reach and exposure.

Promoters who are good at marketing their boxing events have prominent profiles. Their projects become more visible, attracting better boxers and paying fans, thereby bringing in the much sought after revenue for all parties involved and the people working within the promotion, including the boxers.

Television and sponsors will naturally follow the crowd. Where boxing fans come in their number, the more profits for the promoter. This enhances the stability of the one promoter against the smaller ones who find themselves unable to compete. I like this process because it weeds out the fluff. And the boxing world is full of fluff.

There are always issues between promoters and managers when running the careers and business of boxing. It is a point of continuous disagreement, especially when discussing and making decisions for the boxers. Managers are known to look after the best interest of the boxers, while promoters have their sponsors to look after.

In many other cases, there will be disagreements on who represents the best interests of the boxers when it comes to representation to the national or international sanctioning bodies.

This situation makes running the business of boxing very difficult. Boxers need exposure to fights. Promoters want fighters who pull enough crowd to appease their sponsors. Often the decision on who takes priority in all this wrangling becomes a tough one to make.

What then are the real issues? Is it the nature of maximising profits like in any business? Are the promoters so scared of the managers that they try to push them as far away from the business as possible? Is it the managers who are just comfortable collecting percentages without really working? Or are they just failing to understand even the very matters that work to their advantage?

Unless you have lived much of your life practising boxing one way or another, it is difficult to grasp the little secrets and smarts that go on in the game. Having money to spare and an ego big enough to outdo everybody does not automatically make you a successful promoter. You have to walk the long road of learning the trade over time to know how boxing works.

Boxing is not child's play. You will be battered and bruised for entertainment. As someone once said to me, if you want to make money in boxing, don't follow in the footsteps of Mike Tyson or Lennox Lewis. The money is made in promotions and not taking knocks to the face.

Besides being business-wise, you have to be able to spot good boxing talent from a tender age. You want to nurture your potential to full growth, finding yourself a boxer who will go all the way and return your investment.

In a sport where there are no long-lasting friends and loyalties, you still also have to have trustworthy managers and trainers to be successful. This makes the promoters the most powerful people in boxing.

Bucket loads of cash go over the table, under the table and around the table in the process. It is all to ensure success in putting together all the deals to build long-term relations with the boxers, manager, and funders.

Promoters are not everybody's toast when it comes to trust. Without them, however, chances are that there would be far less or no boxing at all. Even the most talented, best known and most successful boxers past and present would be living in obscurity. Every generation has its darling and most trusted boxer. This phenomenon resides in every boxing country the world over. Their success or lack thereof depends on their organisational skills and expertise. They come from different backgrounds. The environment in which one grows up hones and plays a significant role in how one operates later in life.

While there is always everybody's darling, there is also always everybody's villain, the most mistrusted. To ensure that they maximise profits, promoters must possess the skills to convince everybody. They must persuade the boxers through their managers or agents to accept the most minimum of payments even though these payments are not enough to sustain the livelihoods of fighters who take the beating in the ring. It is always the promoter's way or the highway, in more ways than one.

History tells that the most famous and most trusted promoter of all time was American Tex Rickard. He staged the first tournament to gross more than a million dollars at the gate in 1921. Jack Dempsey and Georges Carpentier headlined the tournament. In recent times the two most successful promoters of their era, Americans Don King and Bob Arum, have also been suspected of dubious business deals. Though they have never been successfully charged and convicted of any wrongdoing, their actions have attracted the FBI's investigative eye, and they have had their businesses scrutinised.

Boxing always has to deal with the murmurs of corrupt activities. Promoters have been accused of anything and everything, from stealing money from boxers to the looting of sponsors and TV funds. In the real world, these are serious crimes; in boxing, they are part of day-to-day business.

The more heinous crimes would be fight-fixing, money laundering from promoters with undue influence and tight grips on the sanctioning bodies, managers, and the media. The boxing fraternity does not forgive these.

Rumours of these crimes perpetuated have subsequently raised fears that boxing is not as clean as one would like to believe. Well, if you come to think about it, boxing has never been clean. When money is involved, chances are you will find someone with sticky fingers or dirty hands.

Ideally, we would love the sport to be clean of any corruption and crime. However, as a boxer who has been a promoter and an administrator, we tend to fight the battles we want to win, and those that required the most from us, we prepare ourselves and live to fight another day.

While the general feeling is that the way things are done in boxing arouses many suspicions, the participants themselves, especially the promoters, see nothing wrong with their activities. For them, they make the fights happen, whatever means required. They believe this is the way to get things going – you step on a couple of toes. You grease one or two sticky palms. It creates good relations and strengthens friendships. To them, far from being villains, it is business as usual.

Don King, widely recognised as the greatest promoter ever lived, has been sued by no less than seven world-renowned boxers, including Muhammad Ali, Lennox Lewis, and Mike Tyson. King made out of court settlements with and paid all of them.

Knowing that promoters can get away with out-of-court settlements naturally raises the question of whether boxers need promoters, especially if these promoters seem only to be looking out for their own survival.

Can't they just take care of business themselves?

Many boxing followers and experts believe that no boxer can successfully promote himself and still be in a position to stand their ground in the ring. The mental and physical work of getting ready for the fight itself is enough. Adding the frustrations of dealing with the moving pieces of promotions, marketing, getting the right sponsors, and all the other requirement is more than one punch can take out.

One should not add more complications. Promotion involves spending money and accounting for it. Multi-tasking for the sake of maximum profit can end up minimising the fighter's mental and physical focus, consequently resulting in a drop in performance.

His earning capacity, which was his very reason for forcing himself into everything, may suffer. His earnings will either dive or never get off the ground. Once the fighter becomes part of or wants to do everything, he spreads himself too thin. The demands are sometimes too much and frustrating. The successes stories of Floyd Mayweather Jr and Oscar De La Hoya are excellent examples and are encouraging. But also very rare – once in a blue moon kind of situations. Boxers need a good and expert support base. They should not be hands-on. This allows them to focus on what they are good at while their team promotes them to the levels they deserve to be.

Mayweather had Al Haymon. De La Hoya had Richard Schaefer. Tried and tested masters of the game. They had them do all the work. The two boxers were well represented. In setting up his Golden Boy Promotions, former world boxing champion and superstar Oscar De La Hoya realised that his success as a promoter lay in gaining the services of someone who had boxing expertise.

He understood that he needed someone with boxing knowledge to take his promotion to the highest echelons. He had to gain the respect of the best boxers and the ability to challenge the most prominent promoters of the time. He hired Richard Schaefer, an experienced financial expert. Richard had cut his teeth in the banking sector, and managing money was his game. Their association gave birth to the largely successful GOLDEN BOY PROMOTIONS to boxing's fortune.

Floyd Mayweather Jr is the biggest money earner ever in all of sport. Also, depending on whom you are talking to, he is the best boxer or greatest boxer ever.

He calls himself The Best Ever, even changing his ring name to the now well known "MONEY" Mayweather. He hired Al Haymon, a well known and successful manager and advisor of boxers. Haymon is a mystery of a man who is seldom, if ever, seen. He is not known to grant interviews or photos to the media. He is just known to those who closely work with him. He used his worth to buy television time from the most prominent broadcasters.

On the other hand, he signed many worthy boxers whose services were much sought after by the promoters and fans. He used such leverage to get promoters to sign his boxers for fights and pay him for TV time while also receiving payment for adverts and his signed boxers' fees. Mayweather was one of those boxers Haymon signed. When Mayweather retired, who else to guide his promotional empire than Al Haymon, this was a groundbreaking business move in boxing, which many successful boxers will surely adopt.

In the South African context, Rodney Berman, Director of internationally recognised Golden Gloves Promotions, has been monopolising the promotional use of MNET, which was later changed to Super Sport on DSTV, for more than 40 years. This promotional grip comes courtesy of a long term contract signed with the giant broadcast channel. He has ruled the African market, picking the best boxers, making his through the International scene with one or two handpicked black promoters to work alongside him for political convenience.

His excellent business acumen and solid financial backing ensured his immense power and strong international connections. As would be expected, Berman naturally acquired the cream of South African boxers. They needed him. No one in South African boxing had ever wielded such immense power in world boxing outside of ring official and administrator Stan Christodoulou. This affected boxers' easy pickings because they needed Berman and were prepared to embrace wherever they had a working relationship with him as a career saviour. If a boxer had the talent and the will, Berman was the man to call. The only grain of concern even among boxing participants and supporters, his admirers included, was that the Golden Gloves Promotion did not do much in terms of developing the entire system of South African boxing, or as another would call it, other categories of the game.

As is always the story with boxing and a case between promoters and their business deals with boxers, Golden Gloves also had their hands full, dealing with allegations of shortchanging their fighters.

The majority of world title fights were promoted overseas. As would be the case, such tournaments had to be co-promoted with overseas promoters. They raised some serious allegations that, though never confirmed by the boxers, were strong enough to gain the attention of certain boxing administrators and politicians.

Dumile Mateza and Mava Malla, Boxing administrators during that period, even took the matter to Sports Minister Steve Tshwete for his attention. Tshwete could not act because nothing came out of the boxers themselves, people who were supposed to be the victims. The allegations could not be investigated and proved true or false that purse agreements with overseas promoters believed to be contracted in the powerful American currency, the dollars, were presented and paid to the South African boxers in South African Rand.

There was no official complaint from the boxers to follow any illegal practices of creaming off the dollar's value, which would mean that the fighters were paid much less value than initially agreed.

All such allegations could never be proved. And so the matter disappeared like dust in the wind. Good boxers could not join and fight under the Golden Gloves banner with their managers and trainers. The Golden Gloves Promotional outfit had its own specially selected promoters, managers and trainers. These lot were mainly tasked to deliver the talent – that was their work. They found good raw talent. Trained it and made it great.

That success and visibility from such a robust base made the few selected Golden Gloves managers and trainers the toasts of South African boxing. They were said to be the best, though not necessarily that perception was not valid. The main competition among them developed to be two-fold in who could poach the best boxers from East London in the Eastern Cape and Limpopo. Also, one of their crucial master plays was who was the most capable among them to take the readily-made boxers further. Perhaps no black person in South Africa gained from the Golden Gloves association than Eastern Cape boxing businessman Mzi Mnguni.

Armed with his business acumen and natural ability to spot and develop talent, Mzi, as he is affectionately known, took full advantage and monopoly of his relationship with Berman. He made massive inroads and fruitful achievements in management and promotion on a scale never seen before in his Province. He became a legend in his lifetime. As expected, through Golden Gloves, he produced the first world champion from the Eastern Cape in Welcome Ncita, Vuyani Bungu, Zolani Petelo and Mbulelo Botile. This was all done through the International Boxing Federation (IBF), the world sanctioning body over which Berman and South African partner, American based Cedric Kushner, had an immense influence. Branco Milenkovic of Branco Sports, a Serbian national who gained South African citizenship and stayed in the country, secured a wrestler's and later a boxing promoter's license. He became immensely successful.

He won a big pie of the South African boxing industry when he surprisingly gained his slice of monopoly on SABC TV. When he signed a contract with SABC to be the sole promoter to stage South African, International and World title fights in this country, he made a mark for himself. This was a massive coup indeed. The circumstances of which were very mysterious and suspicious.

The fact that a multitude of local promoters who had been struggling to gain the opportunity to stage such fights was left out in the cold made it scandalous at best. The majority of such promoters were the long-struggling black promoters staying and promoting in the townships and rural areas where the majority of boxers lived. It was regarded as a coup d'etat on his side. The history of South African boxing would never be the same. He made this binding agreement with a public entity with a government mandate to serve all South Africans.

Yet here he was, a newcomer to the country cutting out other people and gaining a monopoly where there had been South Africans before him who had been promoting and sharing the SABC slot for years. There was a huge hue and cry of racism that went on until it was evident that action had to be taken. This deal made Branco Milenkovic the most prolific boxing personality in the country and Africa as a whole.

Among the black folk, who was most affected by the deal. Milenkovic challenged Golden Gloves on the International front and became the second most significant South African producer of world champions. But unlike Berman's Golden Gloves, who had a string of sponsors from the private sector, Branco had no private sponsors to back him. Like the black promoters before him and during his time, he relied on Government funds and SABC TV to fund his tournaments. And fund his tournaments they did, much to the disappointment of other promoters.

The Gauteng Government became his biggest financial backer, closing out all other promoters. In this regard, as was the case with the SABC, he was gaining where the black promoters who should also be part of the Province's opportunities were shut out. Many of them could only observe the shenanigans from the sidelines – looking through the windows with the hope that someone might throw them a bone.

Even in other Provinces, and unlike the case with the black promoters, funds were more considerable and more readily available for Branco, a white promoter. Only in the OLD South Africa will you find this acceptable. The fact that it was happening post-apartheid is unforgivable.

As Boxing SA Director of Operations and later Acting CEO between 2012 and 2013, I had inherited this unfair and unacceptable state of affairs between the national broadcaster and a single promoter. At this time, there were robust debates among licensees and other stakeholders about whether TV broadcast rights belonged to BSA or the fight promoter. But this was also misleading as BSA had never demanded the broadcast rights.

It was just a piece of blown-up fake news to take promoters attention away from the actual facts. All that BSA requested was access to all agreements made between SABC and the promoter. For the regulatory body to demand its sanctioning and administrative fees from an informed position, these details needed to be made available to the public or at least the key stakeholders.

In 2012 I led a team of ten promoters representing all Provinces to present and argue the plight of boxing and the state in which it found itself after SABC decided to close out everybody else to the benefit of only one promoter. The crucial meeting took place at the Headquarters in Kempton Park, Gauteng.

This large and anxious group of promoters included Provincial chairperson and representing. Among them were the influential Mzi Mnguni, the Eastern Cape Promoters Association chairman, and Xoli Gumende of Gauteng Promoters Association.

We had no choice but to challenge the SABC to account for its regrettable decision. BSA paid for the expenses of all promoters and representatives travelling from other Provinces. On discussion was the Branco TV monopoly, as well as the complex matter of TV broadcast rights. Much to the dismay of other promoters, the position of Branco being the only contracted promoter of SABC televised tournaments put him in the sole position of negotiating for broadcast rights with whoever was involved in producing boxing events. This complicated matter of broadcast rights would spill over and be debated later in the 2013 boxing convention. The challenge on the monopoly was based on the political reality that the SABC was a public entity and could not be usurped by a single individual to the exclusion of all other deserving competitors.

The Competition Act in South Africa allows competitors to fight monopoly and bullying in business transactions. Much of the anger arose from the reality that the poorer competitors from whom Branco had snatched the SABC broadcast pie were that. Like his poorer challengers, he could boast of no sponsorship or any other funding source other than SABC and Government sources. The two giant government entities teamed up together and endowed him with immense power to call all the shots in local boxing activities.

His influence spread far and wide across the corridors of a good number of administrative Government offices, the international sanctioning body IBF, members of the media, as well as boxing. Staff members reported and kept him privy to every move within Government and BSA offices. He was informed of every single proposal or plan presented by competing promoters. And curiously enough, he was benefitting massively from all positive media coverage he was getting at the cost of the taxpayer's coffers. SABC representatives in the meeting went out of their way to assure the boxing representatives of the national broadcaster's commitment to the development and upliftment of the sport of boxing through its broadcast.

They explained that in committing and signing the groundbreaking agreement with Branco Sports Productions, their actions were honest and based only on ensuring that SA boxing was taken to the highest levels. Branco had presented to them an agreement with the International Boxing Federation(s) that the sanctioning body would only recognise fights promoted by Branco Sports in South Africa.

Out of ignorance, they were made to believe that IBF stood as a representative of the collective world sanctioning bodies like WBA, WBC and IBO. Unbeknown to them, the IBF acronym does not have the "s" at the tail end, as was presented to them. They did not know that.

They believed that this was the national broadcaster's way of keeping

South African boxing as visible and marketable as possible. Soon after that meeting, Branco Milenkovic disappeared from the boxing scene.

He never promoted another boxing event again. However, much to the dismay of all boxing participants and stakeholders, it became curious to note that Branco Milenkovic's exit as a promoter and strong player in the game coincided with the withdrawal of the SABC and its broadcast of boxing. A lot of different reasons, depending on where one stands, have been put forward for the broadcaster's flight from the game. The reasons put forward range from corruption, unprofessionalism, and lack of sponsorship from the SABC funds. Whatever the reasons, what is clear is that all of the boxing has to look into itself and see how it can work itself out of this quagmire.

The 2013 Boxing *Indaba* would pursue broadcast rights and resolve that SABC must negotiate broadcast rights directly with the promoters. However, such negotiations should be kept transparent and presented to BSA, wherein the regulatory body would take up its sanctioning, and supervisory duties of tournaments agreed.

BSA would be paid 10% of the gross broadcast fee agreed upon between SABC and the promoter. Such resolutions came to nothing as there was already no live boxing broadcast at that time. Even the assurances by SABC during the promoters' workshop in Kempton Park in 2017 could not change the situation as boxing had still not come back. The struggle to bring live boxing back to the TV screens continues.

While every boxer needs to be promoted, the truth is that not every fighter needs a promoter. Promoting a boxer is an ongoing project. It does not start and end only with a fight. There are several ways in which a boxer can be both boxer and promoter in his fights. One way is to put up all the money for the event and hire a promoter on a flat fee to run with all the activities. The logistics of putting the fight together should be entrusted to a vendor tasked with rendering such services—someone or a company that will not be in the grips of one particular promoter.

The promoter should be paid a flat fee, and the boxers take a comfortable amount after all expenses are paid. This, however, can only happen with a boxer who is already financially set and has the money to pay upfront or use as collateral. Coming from how payments are made in boxing, it is only fair that all activities should be transparent and open for all to scrutinise. Such payment processes differ from country to country and, in the case of television, from channel to channel. The various sources of funds include sponsors, donations and loans.

Gate takings and television pay per view recourses can only be projected based on fight marketability and appeal to the public. They are the last to come and be counted. They can not be used as collateral or guarantees. In most cases, the promoter has to be financially strong to put together a boxing tournament. He has to advance such guarantees or pay upfront money to cover boxers' purses, travel, accommodation and sanctioning fees. That is usually well before the funders open their pockets.

Funders must first make sure and be satisfied that they will eventually get returns from their investment before committing to making out payments. This is where beginners or boxers who are still struggling financially find it hard to initiate and manage their promotions. If, for example, the total amount, usually called the pot, collected from all the funders, including sponsors and television, is projected to be R5m, it would be safe to assume that such amount would be divided as purse money among the boxers. However, this is not true. Pot money, should in principle, be shared with those who participated in the tournament after all fight expenses have been paid. Unfortunately, the current practice is that the promoter or promoters will take anything from 30 to 50 percent of that original loot before deciding how much everyone else will be paid. It is called business as usual.

Consider for a moment how much the promoting boxer would make if there were no promotional intermediaries. This is how boxers like Sugar Ray Leonard, Oscar De La Hoya and Floyd Mayweather Jr wriggled themselves out of the promoters' grip and made their millions. It is easy to envision such amounts. But In the real world, there is reality. Not every boxer can be a promoter nor be in charge of his promotion.

He has to be something special to achieve such status and capabilities. The boxer has to be exceptional in talent and have such worldwide command and inter-racial appeal to achieve massive global returns from all around the boxing world. He also has to have the business intellect and the suitable support structures to see his vision through. That kind of person comes once in a blue moon. The wonder boy.

Promotion goes far beyond organising the tournament. It is discovery, development and marketing of the talent that is of utmost importance towards realising the dream of promoting a *megastar*. That in itself needs time and working around the clock with a team or teams of devoted experts. It's called investment. Every boxer needs to be well trained, well fed and well-matched to be the final product and success everybody dreams of.

That is sacrifice. The promoter will have to take the risk of keeping that boxer active even after a loss. Fighters with promoters have that benefit. They have somebody to look after them and keep them afloat with benefits and activities that keep them going outside of boxing – product endorsements, appearance fees and other income-generating activities.

Fighters without promoters have to do all that by themselves or members of their teams who sometimes do not have the talent for that, to do it for them. It is difficult to come out with a specific answer in this matter as there have been successes both ways. Boxing promoters have been doing it for as long as the life of boxing itself. Not much seems to be changing. Lately, the few boxers that have done it successfully have finally shown that perhaps there is life in it.

Another question is whether it can be done in the South African context. I made my first attempt to be a promoter when I was an active boxer. My application was turned down because the laws of the country would not allow it. I received and responded in kind to the same requests during my time as Director of Operations and later Acting CEO of Boxing SA.

The enquiries for promotional licenses by boxers came from Isaac Hlatswayo, Hawk Makepula and Philip Ndou. They wanted to promote their fights. I had to explain to them the legal stand of the South African Boxing Act that disallows participants to hold two licences, making it impossible for boxers to box and promote at the same time.

Steadily but surely, boxers worldwide are becoming more aware of the business of boxing, its logistics and how money is made. Sometimes, somewhere, somehow, some great local boxer with the capacity to promote will break free and make his mark. And South African boxing history will be made.

CHAPTER 8

FIXING BOXING IN THE EASTERN CAPE

BOXING IN BUFFALO CITY Metropolitan Municipality (BCM) has enjoyed as much success as it has endured poverty, unprofessionalism and division. You could say, "It's the best of both worlds," but that should not be the case.

There has always been this unanswered question of how such a small region is arguably the poorest Province in the country, notwithstanding the challenges mentioned, being able to perform at the highest level of boxing in the world. How is it that people who shine in the boxing world return to this place without much to show for it after showcasing prolific boxing careers? Why would it be that we still cannot develop the community, the city, and Buffalo City's people even though we have some of the best boxing talent? How is Buffalo City celebrated for success after success without ever growing or improving its brand image. Although many categories are active in the game, starting from boxing administration and down to the manager, trainers, ring officials, and boxers, the biggest blame for this appealing and degenerating state of the game has been put squarely on the game doorstep of the local promoters. Almost everybody I have talked to, besides my own experiences, echoes the same sentiments.

Outside promoters and especially white promoters, have taken advantage of the local promoters' weaknesses, social and economic conditions. There was especially one white promoter who took advantage of the situation and made the region his diamond field. He was known to boast, "they are my children. I feed them."

Promoters have been accused of, among others, greed, jealousy, backstabbing, lying, thieving and thuggery. It adds to the historic challenge that has been fingered as endemic in this beautiful game – the lack of professionalism.

This state of affairs has caused dissatisfaction and subsequent factionalism among the stables, managers and especially the promoters. And as one would know, a divided house never wins. Many reasons have been put forward for this sad state of affairs. But none have been identified as much as the scarcity or lack of resources. The overload of numbers scrambling for such limited opportunities means there are many mouths to feed but very little to go around the table.

The Province has always struggled to attract the public sector to support the development, success and legacy that is the embodiment of boxing in this region. In the short period after the withdrawal of big-time sponsors like Ellerines, King Korn, Old Buck and lately Vodacom, local boxing has struggled to make ends meet. Without the support of corporate and Government, boxing in the region finds itself lagging.

Though the companies mentioned above were not sponsoring all categories of boxing, as in boxers, clubs and amateur boxing, their financial clout was strong enough to fund whole tournaments. However limited they might be, when you have funds coming in, you find a way to make progress.

There was enough money to pay for boxers' purses, travel, accommodation, ring officials, and all other logistics with corporate sponsorship. Boxing became the life and blood of Buffalo City. The sport benefited, and the sponsors also benefited. It was a win-win situation.

Television coverage was the main attraction, even though some tournaments without television coverage were big or good enough to warrant a financial boost in the local administration's opinion.

Lately, our promoters have been divided into two warring factions; those who have vehemently refused to have any working relationships and those who are open to working with whoever supports the growth of boxing in buffalo City.

Brought about by the availability to some and unavailability to others of Government and Municipality funds, boxing promoters find themselves at each other's throats. When there is no other source of financial assistance or funds, those who need funding will inevitably fight each other to get whatever is made available.

Without Government funding, and thank God for it, boxing in the BCM region would have succumbed and died a long time ago. It has become an awkward situation.

The Government funds have not been evenly spread among them, though. Promoters are invited to apply. Government dispenses the money according to set requirements, supposedly the most important of which is the capability of the promoter and the size or quality of the tournament. Dissatisfaction originates, and the fights begin when some promoters seem to be getting more than their fair share. The less financed promoters do not accept the rationale given for such significant differences in funds allocated.

Courts have even found themselves being overworked and overcrowded as promoters have challenged Government grants. And these challenges have meant that less and less funding comes to the sport. However, I would think that the promoters have reason to question the disparities in fund allocation, especially when some promoters are known to be cosy with the government officials tasked with deciding who gets funded.

The government and municipality funds have resulted in boxing promoters being at each other's throats all the time. A sense of entitlement is so massive that one cannot think to seek financial assistance from anywhere other than the public sector.

Funding grants, for what was known as development tournaments, were even suspended by the Eastern Cape Government after the promoters took the matter to court — leaving the boxers and other stakeholders high and dry without any form of support. Only the promoters who organise significant events have been able to continue with their promotions. And there are only three in the Province. This has led to boxers employing shuffling plus bobbing and weaving moves between promoters in a bid to secure fights – and thus more court battles among promoters.

One needs to ask how boxing got to the point. How did a sport with so much clout find itself depending on Government funding for promotion? Is it the lack of creativity that has seen many begging at Government coffers?

Or is it a matter of the Government being the only player in the industry that is open to supporting boxing dreams. If that is the case, it is unfortunate that political connections have become the unwritten requirement to receive funds. Without such relationships, promoters will have no funding resources available to them.

Boxing seems to have been captured by politicians using the influence they have to dictate terms that benefit their own choice of promoters. Gone are the days when boxing was a social obligation to people working inside and outside of it. People are in this game for their gains.

Granted, one should benefit from working and adding value to the game. However, this should not be to the detriment of the sportsmen who make the sport come to life. Without boxers, boxing is not a sport. Without trainers and managers, boxers will not develop nor get the exposure they need.

It is near impossible to source money from Government and not expect politics to creeping in. Eastern Cape boxing has learnt the hard way. They have also learned that where there is politics, there is bound to be factionalism and division.

This dependence on Provincial and Local Government money has resulted in promoters rushing from office to office in government buildings when they hear that someone has received something. If one gets something, so should others. It is there that factions begin.

There develops the association of haves, and the have nots. Many of them have no idea of how the business of boxing is run. However, they want money because Government is giving away money. With the right connections, some will get the money they do not deserve without knowing what boxing promotion is all about – if it is to be a success.

Theirs is to get government funding and cut as much from it as possible to make a sizable personal amount before attending to boxers' purse monies and event logistics. The victims here are the boxers. They get confused with all the stories and approaches they get from promoters. Other times, they are courted by promoter agents, who make matters even worse by taking a chunk of what would generally be their boxing fee.

As the faction associated with the '*haves*' has grown in promotional strength, they use their acquired financial muscle to poach boxers from the association of have nots – thereby creating a recipe for conflict.

Managers find themselves listening to how often boxers from other stables are fighting, while they just train to no avail. This situation forces the managers to tow promotional lines. Something that under different circumstances would be foreign to them. Recently Boxing SA sent a team of its longest-serving and most experienced board members to try and resolve the long-standing impasse between the rival promoters. This after the two groups refused to recognise each other, both claiming to be the legitimate leadership of promoters in the Eastern Cape.

One side was led by the chairman of the Eastern Cape Promoters Association [ECBPA], Ayanda Matiti. As would be the case if all was well, it claims to be the legitimate leadership of promoters in the Province. It is the group that has been leading the promoters in the Province before the separation.

As a result of this long history of disagreements, a rival group was formed by those opposed to the current leadership. The new group led by Tando Zonke have, on realising the large numbers in their fold, took the bold and confident step of conducting their elections and announcing their leaders as the true representatives of boxing promoters in the Eastern Cape.

This is the challenging situation that the BSA team encountered when they landed in the Province. When it became evident that it was impossible to house the two warring factions under one roof, the BSA contingent led by Chairman Peter Ngatane, CEO Tsholofelo Lejaka and board members Thando Jack and Khulile Radu decided to hold two separate meetings on two different days.

A joint meeting was finally held in one room while in another room of the same Hotel, Provincial manager Phakamile Jacobs conducted the weigh-in for the following day's tournament. Spectators who had come to witness the weigh got a taste of what they would pay for the next day.

The opposing camps got into a scuffle but were separated before engaging in a full physical toe to toe *slugfest*.

The BSA leadership left without announcing a clear resolution regarding which camp governing body would recognise. At the time of this writing, signs are pointing to the new Tando Zonke structure that had already done its elections and appointed its leadership as being the recognised structure to represent promoters in the Province.

Perhaps it is not wrong for promoters to approach the Government in the absence of private sector sponsorship. After all, boxing remains the only sports code in the country still run by an act of parliament. Without such essential financial backing, boxing, especially the Eastern Cape, would be dead by now. On the contrary, it has been highly successful. If one considers the belts, trophies and awards in both the professional and amateur ranks, it has been nothing short of phenomenal. Maybe it is time to change the mindsets and make a direct approach inviting the private sector for guidance. But the first question that comes to mind is if there is any glimpse of a chance that a company or group of business can pump and invest their money in a code as fragmented as our boxing is now.

This division does not only affect professional boxing but has manifested itself in both professional and amateur bodies. The reason being that the amateur body, as where all of the boxing begins, is where the promoters scout for talent on whom to invest. The ongoing infighting negatively tainted the game to a point where even its people have been forced to leave and look for greener pastures. It does not cast a positive view for sponsors who may be keen to come to the party. Companies think about their image and their brand alignment. As a matter of fact, white promoters don't get Government funding, but they have more tournaments because of private sector sponsorship. But then, doesn't that have to do with racism?

Many people will say no. But it remains a big question why it's only white people who get financial assistance. The private sector is, after all, a white domain. Besides the divisions and factionalism, there is also a lack of business acumen or unity among the local boxing people. Such negative factors solidify and give credence to those who believe that racism is not the reason for the lack of sponsorship or financial assistance among black-owned promotions, gyms or boxers. Nor is it a fact of black areas being too risky to align with.

One sure reason given by people I have had conversations with is that the people of boxing in the Eastern Cape and especially Buffalo City are not doing justice to the game. They have not reached a point of running their promotional companies and gyms along pure business lines.

They are not success orientated go-getters who will work in unison and support one another all the way, stopping at nothing to gain what they deserve. They are much happier and more comfortable working alone. When in a position of power or gain, they will rather hold the hand of a stranger, especially a person of a different race or nationality, than assist one of their own. The jealousy and backstabbing among them are so deeply rooted that they think nothing of plotting the downfall of another. Their attitude has weakened their status and inter-dependence. They have become victims of being used by their very enemies against one another–hence the migration of their boxers to white managers and promoters in Gauteng. You would be surprised at how many of them have been used as agents to poach boxers from the Province to pursue their careers somewhere else. All the above inputs and questions are meant to turn around the fortunes and delete this destabilising poison. This is a sport that has seen and achieved massive successes against established competitors and countries, against all odds. The first step would be to take an honest look into ourselves and decide whether our practices, attitudes, and habits make for an acceptable and professional outfit that attracts good relations from other sectors of life, be they business, religious, political and economic.

Such introspection would enlighten us, advise us and introduce us to who we are. And what the rest of humanity see when they look at us. My view is that such a mirror would reflect a people endowed with pure and unadulterated talent. People with an uncanny ability to adapt and practise all sorts of boxing requirements needed to take us to the top.

Fighting talent flows in our veins. We can learn where we lack in training capabilities from others, adapt and improve. We have been keen promoters and organisers but lack in skills. We need guidance in management practices. We do not need to be asked about our love for the game. With our limited skills and fewer facilities, we have managed to take our boxing to the stars. I think we would find out that we need professional skills. It is interesting how many views and solutions have been brought forward. But they have all pointed to the same direction and destination. Living examples from inside and outside the country have been sighted.

My view is that a Public and Private partnership would be the most effective turnaround strategy for our game. It echoes sentiments that formulate the common input from many boxing contributors and analysts.

It is common knowledge that our challenges are premised on little or lack of skills or professionalism in a province that is brimming with boxing talent, enthusiasm and involvement. The skills we can develop and learn, and professionalism would be the offspring of a developing culture that seeks to put the business of boxing ahead of personal need. Such overwhelming qualities weigh heavily and negatively on the historically low economy of the region. How then, can this partnership be formed. And how can it save boxing after the damage boxing has done by shooting itself on the foot? It needs the will from all parties to work to make it happen. If the Eastern Cape Government is willing, which I think it has already shown, it can deliver the private sector to the boxing fraternity and its activities. It can achieve that feat by using its powerful position and influence to entice or attract more business partnerships by putting incentives that benefit business, the community and sports in general.

The Government possesses the clout to entice business with the benefits that profit-making companies are always looking for. They would join forces to assist in the development of skills and fight promotions in boxing. This would be favourable for all of the boxing if the whole country would be involved in such a venture – without wiping off the entire South African Boxing Act and privatising boxing.

Maybe a business major funder of boxing would demand complete control of the vital financial positions. The private funder would appoint such positions as CEO and CFO. Such appointed staff would report directly to the employer. That strategic business arrangement would serve as a guarantee and confidence booster. It would ensure that its personnel controlled funds flowing from the private partner. Boxing SA would then run the daily operations of boxing under its appointed COO.

Such a partnership would undoubtedly impact the South African Boxing Act 11 of 2001. As an Act of Parliament, it places all regulation on the Government's table. A careful step by step review of the rules and regulations would result in the amendment and change of the face of the Act.

These changes would bring about a new relationship whose influence would permeate down to the lowest rungs of boxing licensees. The benefits would reach the farthest and widest rural locations where boxing is already embedded and running – all be it with great talent but very little or nothing in life skills. In the early 2000's public media giant Vodacom became a significant funder of boxing. Vodacom had confidence and comfort in knowing that its CEO, Mtobi Tyamzashe, was, strategically, chairman of BSA at the time.

Tyamzashe was well equipped in both the academic qualifications to lead such a gigantic business as Vodacom and the extreme experience in all levels of sports administration and boxing. He grew up in the boxing gyms of Ginsberg, Eastern Cape, and would later become one of the leading figures of boxing at Fort Hare University in the early 1970s. Tyamzashe was, however, overlooked for the BSA board by Sports Minister Makhenkesi Stofile in 2006, opting to instead replace him with an experienced administrator and successful lawyer and ex-amateur boxer Adv. Dali Mpofu. When Tyamzashe did not return, so did Vodacom.

It would be the last time after an era of successful funding that South African boxing would have a giant sponsor as a funder. Maybe until further notice. Tyamzashe departed without realising his dream – he was preparing to introduce and unpack to boxing stakeholders and hopefully implement a new project that would promote boxing as a franchise.

Vodacom was the last funder after such giant sponsors, including Old Buck, King Korn, Ellerines, and boxing funders during the Apartheid era. It is important to note that all the above boxing investors before Vodacom were happy to invest and operate in boxing within the Rules and Regulations set out in The South African Boxing Act 39 of 1954. And so was Vodacom under the new South African Boxing Act 11 of 2001.

The prevailing conditions during Vodacom's period were far different from that prevalent at the time of its predecessors. They were, especially before Vodacom and 1994, as different as chock and cheese, or more specifically, as black and white. The same goes for this present period. Administrative, political, as well as economic playing fields have taken drastic changes. So have the challenges, the attitudes and the needs. And so should boxing if it is to be in line and relevant to the new landscape.

Former South African Flyweight champion Andrew 'Last Born' Matyila is emphatic that it is time for a change. The change must happen from top to bottom. He believes the time has come for Boxing SA to have a competitor. He is adamant that within the boxing spectrum with sufficient capabilities if one has to judge by interested contributors that constantly volunteer information every day.

He is convinced that lawyers, teachers, current and ex-officials from all sectors of life, including sports, have enough skills and depth of information to make a big difference and take boxing to higher levels. Boxing SA is a Schedule 3 Public Entity under the executive authority of Sport and Recreation. This situation effectively makes BSA a non-profit organisation without a strategic marketing or communications arm that speaks the language and provides for the corporate world's expectations.

Added to that is the seemingly irrelevant state of the South African Boxing Act 11 of 2001 in the ever-developing and evolving world of boxing. Suggestions to have it reviewed have been thrown around for as long as one can remember but never implemented. The daily changing environment and attitudes make it ineffective and unable to execute its mandate in line with current expectations, especially those of the Rainbow Generation.

But there is some light at the end of the tunnel. When writing this piece, the Eastern Cape Department of Sports Arts And Culture had taken the bold move of getting together its promoters to iron out the divisions. The department on whose shoulders the burden of funding local boxing has solely lied for the last 10 to 15 years made it their goal to get the private sector more involved in boxing in the region. The squabbles that have been the order of the day in local boxing circles and activities for far too long may soon be a thing of the past. With that behind. Boxing can move on to greater heights/

Such a move, if successful, will be the much-needed solution that can undoubtedly bring about a better future for the youth of this highly committed and talented but deeply divided community. The Government's involvement makes the task more appetising in that Government is the surest vehicle to negotiate, entice and bring back the private sector. It is also hopeful that such a trend that begins in the Eastern Cape will spread to other Provinces.

"We are either the masters or the victims of our attitudes. It is a matter of personal choice. Who we are today is the result of the choices we made yesterday. Tomorrow we will become what we choose today. To change means to choose to change," writes John C Maxwell, where he teaches about what each leader needs to know.

One could interpret this statement as putting the blame squarely on the boxing people for the situation boxing finds itself in today – far lower standards than expected from a sports code that has always carried the dreams and aspirations of the Eastern Cape community. This scourge has impacted all categories from the top echelons of administration down to the ring capabilities of the boxers. Maybe, just maybe, change will come.

CHAPTER 9

WE DON'T NEED BOXING MANAGERS

IN HIS BOOK TITLED The Holyfield Way, James J Thomas writes, "Unfortunately, I saw too many situations in which the manager appeared to be more concerned with his relationship with the promoter than with the interests of the fighter." I have managed boxers and gained experiences that taught me that managing a fighter needs a special breed of person altogether. The nature of boxing calls for fighters to seek someone to look after their interests. Such interests do not only end in the ring and boxing activities.

They can venture into the daily life of the boxer and sometimes his family. They are the managers. Undoubtedly the most important and most influential figures in a professional boxer's career.

The manager is the person in charge of all business and activities surrounding the boxer. He is the guide. He makes the final decisions. It is the manager's task to call the shots. It is the manager's role to negotiate anything involving the fighter, from who, where, and how much he fights for.

He has to look after the general well-being of the boxer. That is including the negotiation of his fight contracts, investments and taxes. His duties also cover overseeing the boxer's training and preparation for a contest. Managers are as old as boxing itself.

During the days of the bare-knuckle fighting, the best pugilists had patrons, agents or minders who looked after them and their financial interests. However, as the sport began to lose favour, boxers turned to hiring professionals who not only took care of financial matters but were also wise in the ways of the ring and knew the ropes well enough to select suitable opposition.

A good manager will nurse a protégé carefully towards the top, and his reward for doing a good job will be to take a percentage of the boxer's earnings. The rates range from 25 to 30 and sometimes as much as 40 percent management fee. For the manager to receive up to 40 percent, he sometimes has to pay a huge amount as a signing fee or pay the boxer a stipend until the fighter starts to get some decent purses.

The practice of paying signing fees, however, does not happen in the South African boxing scene. In South Africa, the boxer pays out 25 per cent of his purse to the entire team. It becomes the duty of the manager to pay out the members of the team as per agreement. The managers take off the 15 percent and pay themselves, while the remaining 10 percent is divided amongst everybody else in the team.

The manager also has to solicit sponsorship or appoint someone who will secure sponsors and endorsement deals for the boxer. It is not uncommon to find the manager and promoter clinching a sponsorship deal without the fighter knowing.

In fair circumstances, and where the private sector is also involved and funding the game, sponsorship should be paying for all team players and activities around the boxers. That would include the manager, trainer, cut man, strength and conditioner, kit man and all other people's percentages.

Or, in the case of cut men, kit men and conditioners, it would be agreed upon flat fees. That way, a boxer could pocket his whole purse money. But the South African boxing economy does not create room to allow for such ambitions. It is that tight economically.

Some managers' attributes have often made them so audible and visible that they have become more famous than the boxers. They have become legends. But with time, the role of the manager has met with some serious challenges, especially from the boxers themselves. Some managers have tended to be more loyal to the promoters than to the boxers they are supposed to guide.

Such a disjointed loyalty to the promoter naturally compromises their determination to negotiate a good deal for their boxers. Once a manager becomes a lackey or fan of the promoter, he tends to see things through the promoter's eye, forgetting the interest of the boxer.

There have been situations where managers have been simply useless. Sometimes to the point of just being there as parcels or passengers, and all the moves and decisions rested so much on the promoter's shoulder. Such situations have sometimes resulted in the boxers being so frustrated that they have taken it upon themselves to manage their career and team.

When this happens, it usually develops into such a loss of trust and confidence that some boxing clubs have floundered. The appealing matter of managers with no clue about their duties and obligations has been found to be resident in South Africa and around the rest of the world. Sadly many of them have no clue about the reality and their obligation to understand the terms they deal with daily, even the most straightforward terms of a fight contract. Decisions that should be made by both promoter and manager are only made by the promoter. Yet, the contract is unambiguous on the duties and obligations of each licensee.

The Boxing Act specifies all categories of boxing and all duties, rights and obligations for each party. The New South African Boxing Act, 11 of 2001, ensures that professional boxing is run as a business. It follows, therefore, that the rights of promoters as business people is acknowledged. But it seems that many times nobody knows who should do what.

Maybe it is only the promoters who should know and run with the business. After all, they are usually the ones who have the money. But that, according to the rules and regulations of boxing, should not be the case.

Boxers have since come with some bold ideas to take control of their careers. For better or for worse. Nowhere was this view stronger and more vehement than during the time of former WBO Super Middleweight champion Chris Eubank. He instilled a sense of independence and self-assurance in the boxers, telling them that, unlike the general belief, the fighters themselves are the bosses, not the other way round.

According to the boxers, especially the more experienced and successful ones, boxers employ managers to negotiate fights and everything else within the business of boxing for them. Boxers then pay the managers amounts depending on which country they reside.

These bolds sentiments, which also emerged in a meeting of boxing stakeholders, including South Africa's Department of Sports Arts and Culture in Johannesburg in 2004, looked like taking boxing over and changing the local boxing landscape for some time. They have since died down, and managers are still as strong as ever. Maybe until further notice.

CHAPTER 10

WHERE DOES ALL THE MONEY GO?

THE RAGS-TO-RICHES story is about as old as boxing itself. In South Africa, the riches-to-rags story seems all too common, it's hard to miss. When great men of the ring rise to the top, the expectation is, when shall they fall. Boxers around the world have been known to make bucket loads of money as they boxed and charmed their way into the hearts of boxing fans. Throwing blinding combinations and delivering paralysing punches to dizzy and perplexed opponents. They have left fans in states of hysteria, screaming, hooked and asking for more. As fate would have it, these boxers have become cult heroes with every fight they win.

In, comes the money, the cars and the lifestyle that goes with it. After taking a couple of punches to the face, the spoils are all worth it. After all, life is too short to live in a ring of frugality. You only live once. And once is usually more than enough to live the way you want. The drive during their heydays is regarded as proof of wealth and evidence of the good life boxing provides. People could then be forgiven for thinking these boxers will show this wealth well after their boxing days are over. They would invest these lump sums wisely and retire comfortably and set for life. But the reverse becomes true. Some have fallen hard, many have taken self-exile, while others are hard to recognise.

Bongani Fuzile is an award-winning journalist who, like all youth born and raised in Buffalo City, has tasted his fair share of the boxing activity. And like all products of the sport, he did not stay long in the game to be hooked. His mind keeps going back to peruse over the state of the game. He worries over his heroes who made some respectable income in boxing but have nothing to show after their boxing days are over.

He used his journalistic skills to dig deeper in a bid to find out the real reasons and possible solutions to this disappointing situation in a sport that runs in the veins of the people of this region. "Like so many other people recognising this disappointing state of affairs, he cannot help but still celebrate the achievement of these legends as he thinks of their unmatchable skills as they dominated the world stage. But today, truth be told, none of them show any signs of monetary wealth," notes Fuzile.

He goes further to analyse their value and what they have to offer in their lives outside of boxing. "If they could be auctioned they would show no value," concludes Fuzile.

This leaves many questions. Many of them unanswered. Who is to blame? Who was responsible to make sure their wealth was protected. Who was responsible for their investments? Were they trained financially? Do they know their rights? Are they involved in determining their worth in the ring?

These are some of the questions boxing followers have asked when these champions are falling from grace into 'nonentities', reduced into spectators, not even sports commentators. These boxers have been successful in the sport and have fought and beaten great boxers in the world. They have travelled the world thanks to the sport. But there are no properties today worth reasonable values that are known to be owned by those boxers in their towns of birth.

In football and other sports codes, players have become overnight successes and command wealth in properties, movable or otherwise. Many boxers have nothing to show for their success in the sport. Maybe some of the reasons stem from the way the game is run or the way their managers handle the finances for them. It would seem that the money that finally comes to the boxers cannot change their lives or the lives of their families.

A lot of boxers and some people connected to boxers say the money is only negotiated, seen or touched by their owners or so-called managers. Fights also come in dribs and drabs. And those who have won international and world titles end up losing those titles without defending them in the ring, as there is not enough value in the money to promote the big fights for them to defend the titles.

Boxing also demands a wide range of commitments and sacrifices that cannot be satisfied without proper funds. When a fight has been organised and is a certainty, boxers start committing to a pattern of training that includes strict diets. This forces them to borrow money to buy food to raise their preparation to levels that assure tip-top condition. But sadly they have to pay back once they receive their meager earnings. But if this is true, where does the money they can show off come from?

They drive expensive cars, fly first class, and sleep in high-class hotels. They do not drive sponsored cars. So they pay for themselves. Surely some handsome amounts land in their hands after all calculations and payments are made. And this is not about one fight, but several fights spread over years. The question people ask is what happens to all the money?

Many promoters and have benefitted tremendously from the boxers. But that is the manner of business. But it gets tainted when some of them get accused of taking advantage of the boxers' ignorance. They have been known to deduct from the boxers or pay themselves much more than the actual acceptable share due to them as the boxers' representatives.

It is not a secret that the majority of the boxing talent is either illiterate or is not up to scratch with the financial jargon that runs boxing. Some managers have also been blamed for colluding with promoters to rob the unsuspecting boxers of heavy sums of money. This practice has been reportedly rampant where fights have been promoted overseas. In such cases, local promoters have been accused of playing the roles of managers or agents. They have then proceeded to use those positions to cream off the dollars while presenting the purses to the boxers in rands.

These accusations have, however, ended being just that – accusations. They have never been tested and proved. Different views have been exchanged tremendously for the eradication of this plight so that boxers lives can be improved. Some of the views have from time to time been implemented by BSA as life skills projects.

Boxers have been accommodated at some of the South African Universities for periods ranging from three weeks to a month at a time. In other similar ventures, BSA has hired financial and tax experts to tour the country and teach boxers these necessary skills. Some boxers have certificates of attendance after attending such courses. These ambitious projects have unfortunately yielded no successful or clear results. Maybe it is the implementation strategy that needs improvement.

The reason for this lack of financial management can be traced to the backgrounds of each boxer where there are few people or none whatsoever in the homestead who are working. The purse money of the boxers comes as manna from heaven. It attracts even distant relatives who come over with the expectation of some financial relief from the child they assisted in bringing up.

This becomes an added challenge for the young kid who has his dreams to chase. To an untrained kid growing up among other equally financially untrained people, the first dream is ownership of a posh car. This is where the opportunity for education comes.

A concerted effort by a private group or public entity would go a long way towards getting the fighters to know what they are up against, what is expected of them, as well as how they can go about doing it. Maybe a public/private partnership would start by identifying, through the office of Boxing SA, groups of ex-licensee who could be trained in life skills. Such trained and qualified people or groups would, after qualification, be dispatched to all areas near or around them to train the young professional boxers from the initial stages of their careers.

The education would have to strictly base on financial management, contracts, taxes and all other matters that have to do with their boxing careers and money.

Despite their lack of education at times or so-called poor background, a big number of the boxers are capable of understanding when taken through the basics of financial management by experts. The banks could select special members from their staff and allocate them to coach, teach and then advise the boxers to invest their money with them.

Such a venture could be done in association with Government and Boxing SA. The boxers could then have something to fall back on after their boxing days are over. Talking to Bongani Fuzile about his boxing career Xola Sifama, a successful professional boxer has seen no value in the money that boxers earn after their fights.

He says, "This boxing thing is to keep us away from crime and keep us fit and when you are lucky like me, you will go on and win world titles. But the honest truth is, there is no monetary value in these." He may have a point here but boxing should not be about staying away from crime. It should be part of the bigger picture; and the bigger picture is life itself.

In the conversations I have had with boxing people, it has become one of the views that maybe financial education should not be for the boxers alone, but their managers as well. The managers should be able to keep the momentum even in the gyms as they are mainly in charge of the boxers' finances. They should be able to carry the charge over to the usage and investment of the money. Boxers should have such an understanding that even talking the financial language with lawyers should not be a problem. Such knowledge and understanding would also put them in good stead when they are approached by seemingly sympathetic advisers in sheepskins who only want to reap them off. Fights also come in dribs and drabs and those who have won international titles end up losing these titles without defending them because there are no promoters with enough money to organise the defences.

When there is a fight coming boxers borrow money to finance their training. Those loans have to be paid back. What then needs to be done? This question has been asked so many times. I also know that Boxing SA has tried so many times and so many ways to attend to this appalling situation. Dismally of course. Some boxers have from time to time been sent to different universities and other financial institutions in this country.

The periods have ranged from three weeks to a month. Even tax experts have been sent to the different boxing towns in the country to address this matter. All these projects have been unsuccessful. Maybe the whole failure of the concept lies with implementation.

The consensus view is that there should be Boxing Academies in all boxing towns or cities in the country. I know that boxing activists like *Andile Sinile, Siphatho Handi* and *Vuyani Mbinda* have on different occasions, and independent of one another, approached Government for the erection of such Academies or Museums to initiate the education of boxers, as well as keep the legacy of all achievements for years to come. All those endeavours have come to nothing. While it is true that academies could change boxers lives, it seems that the only people who do not understand that are the ones who make the decisions – the Politicians.

Vuyani Mbinda and *Zuko Blauw* came very close to realising this dream. In 2006 they succeeded to hold a meeting with the Executive Mayor of Buffalo City Municipality and all members of the council when it was decided that an amount of R20m should be set aside for this historic project.

That dream still has to be fulfilled.

Boxing academies must be compulsory in each Province and former boxers should be hands-on in the development of boxing.

Loyiso Mtya at training session with Zolani 'Last Born' Tete who was preparing for his fight to become a dual world champion in the bantamweight division. Image: Mark Adrews (Daily Dispatch)

1992: Former world champion Dingaan Thobela in Hillbrow, Johannesburg. He was dubbed 'The Rose of Soweto' in his boxing days. (Photograph by Gallo Images/ Gisele Wulfsohn)

Bushy Bester, Willie Lock, Peter Mathebula, Stan Chrstodoulou and Joe Gumede attending the SA Boxing World Awards. (Image supplied by African Ring)

The late Tsietsi Maretloane will always have a special place in South African boxing history.

Nelson Mandela, activist against Apartheid, when he was a boxer in the early 50's

The dynamics of boxing as a sport in a time when there was a difference in privilege between black boxers and white fighters. (Image credit: DispatchLIVE)

The late Muhammad Ali, who rose above poverty and racism to become a world boxing icon with his promoter and manager Don King and fellow boxer Mike Tyson.

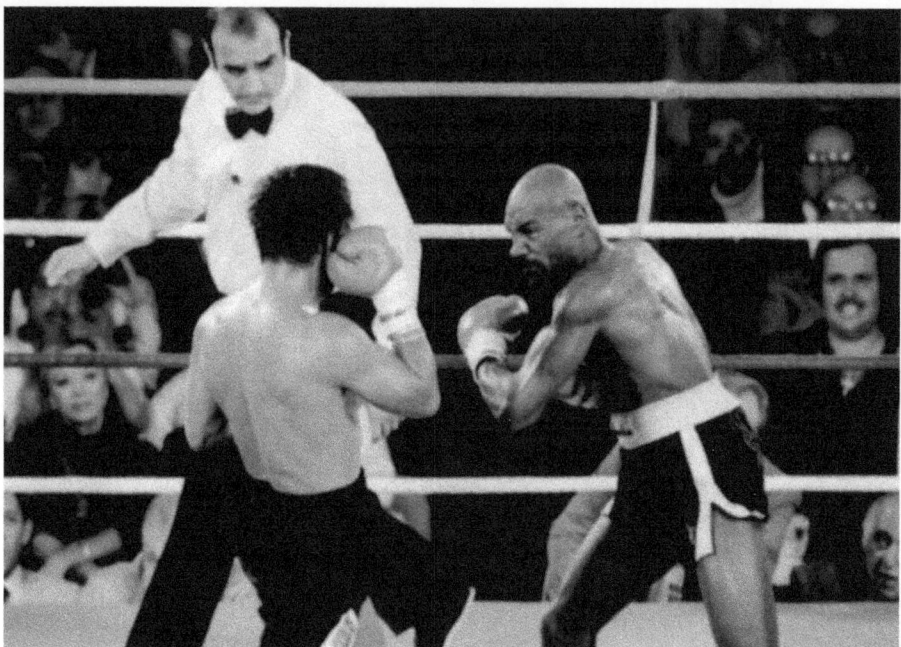

Referee Stanley Christodoulou looks on during the IBF, WBA and WBC World Middleweight Title fight at Caesars Palace on November 10, 1983 in Las Vegas, United States. Hagler won by a unanimous decision after 15 rounds.

In Apartheid-Era, South Africa wanted a 1979 heavyweight bout between John Tate, left, and Gerrie Coetzee so badly it allowed blacks and whites to sit together. Credit: Associated Press

TAKING TIME: Johannes Miya kneels as referee Lulama Mtya administered the count after being knocked down by Fraser Ndzandze. (Image credit: Sowetan Live)

IBF flyweight champion Moruti 'Baby Face' Mthalane. Image: ANTONIO MUCHAVE.

The late Bert Blewett, the former doyen of South African boxing journalism who served in many roles, from TV commentator and magazine editor to sport administrator.

Ricky Hatton, Loyiso Mtya and Brian Mitchell during a press conference at Emperors Palace on September 10, 2009 in Johannesburg, South Africa. (Photo by Lefty Shivambu/Gallo Images/Getty Images)

Former Golden Gloves Champion Welcome Ncita after winning the IBF Junior Featherweight Champion

Vuyani 'The Beast' Bungu IBF Junior Featherweight Champion

THE BLOOD

CHAPTER 11

CAN A BOXER TRAIN THEMSELVES

HAVING TRAINED BOXERS for a large part of my life, I have come across fighters and managers, or even families looking for someone to teach and train their youngsters. I have always regarded myself more as a boxing teacher than a trainer or coach. Boxers and their managers always look for a trainer who will produce the best out of the boxer and take him to the highest levels possible. After they have made their shortlist of candidates, they look at every one of the trainers. They check their track record, what fighters they have worked with and the kind of results they have produced. They compare them and measure against the performances and successes of those boxers. They then imagine how far they can go with each trainer before the final choice is made.

Few people realise the task and importance of a trainer to a boxer's make-up and success. He is in charge of getting the fighter in the best condition and must have a say in the boxer from what he does, what he eats, down to what he says. He can neither allow self-doubt nor complacency to creep in. The trainer is the control centre of everything around the boxer's career.

He has to take part in deciding opponents from fight to fight. He knows at what stage his fighter is in and what kind of style and pressure the fighter can handle. He has to have a say and take control of what the fighter does or where the boxer goes. Therefore, a trainer is a teacher, a conditioner, a dietitian, a psychologist, and everything else that produces the best out of the boxer.

One of the foremost characteristics of a trainer is discipline. That goes a long way towards shaping the character that he needs to instill into the boxers he trains to make them be a successful competitor. His character goes a long way towards keeping the gym and the boxers in check, especially in camp. There is the old saying that a trainer is as good as his boxer. The results of his boxers will determine his stature and rating among other trainers.

To get the best out of each boxer, the trainer must always be in the gym in time. He must work his boxers hard. But not only hard, but he must also work them well and work them smartly. He must design good and effective working programs that ensure pick conditions for each boxer and sound strategies that win fights against the very best.

Looking at another trainer's working methods and critiquing whatever they do is never going to take any trainer anywhere in the noble art. Nor any other game for that matter. One trainer can always learn something from another. Picking other people's mistakes is the easiest thing to do. However, the main thing is what you can do and how much more you can excel by watching, listening and learning from others. Remember that trainers are also human beings. They learn and practise the trade like anybody else. Experience, in the end, counts a lot. So they have to be always a step ahead of the other trainer and the corner.

Being a good trainer has nothing to do with one being perfect. No human being is perfect, as is natural with a good trainer. Getting the best out of the boxer through teaching, advice, and discipline is what counts most. A good trainer will go out of his way to get as much information about the opponent and his team as possible. But, in the end, he must be the embodiment of his program that sets him apart from the others.

A good trainer may look and learn from all the skills training and technique on TV cameras and realise that many of those drills and all other sorts you see there are just generic. It is just practised and done for the camera. Real boxing trainers and coaches work on the real stuff in their gyms or other secluded places off camera. A good trainer has to be a tactical strategist and psychologist. So many people can easily get you through all the roughs and tumbles of training, whip up a body to be in the best shape. They know boxing in and out but cannot give the boxer the actual fight. There's a difference. There are many guys like that. They know boxing well, and they can get you through a fight, but they aren't great at teaching you the moves. They often have very little clue how and when to apply such moves in the actual fight. To beat the world, through the boxers of cause, the trainer has to be in the top echelons when it comes to such attributes.

Great trainers can win fights for their boxers from the corner. Great boxing writer and analyst Bert Blewitt had this to say about trainers, "Training and trainers are an essential part of a boxer's make up."

There was a time when both were considered irrelevant and unimportant. Incredibly when boxing arrived in England in the seventeenth century, training was badly neglected and virtually ignored for nearly a hundred years. When boxers started taking up training more seriously, training in a country retreat became fashionable, mainly because of a recommendation by Professor Mike Donovan, an ex-Middleweight boxing champion, the man who made punching a ball in training a popular exercise.

Strength, conditioning and dieting personnel are everyday things in boxing. Some boxing trainers use strength and conditioners in their camps. Others do not need them at all. They feel that they only succeed in confusing the whole system. Some trainers use them to take off some of the load, especially when they have many boxers to train. A few of them are good, adding some unique value to the overall training program and the boxer. Others are overrated. Some of them do not add anything except extra muscles that make the boxer slow and sluggish.

Proper dieting is also another necessity that needs special care. Some trainers do it themselves, while in other cases, the boxers themselves or family members take that upon themselves. Unfortunately, many fighters leave that aspect to their mothers or wives. In reality, dieting is about managing food and liquid intake. It is about what the boxer eats, how much and when. All issues that matter to the eventual performance of the boxers have a lot to do with his intake. Dieting determines the boxer's weight management, strength, endurance and balance. All sorts of boxing training, be it skills, conditioning, strength or dieting, comes down to the boxer's discipline and intelligence. If he has to pay for everybody to do everything for him and still not abide by all the rules that will guide him to victory and success, then the whole exercise is a sure trip to futility.

HOW DO CHAMPS TREAT THEIR TEAMS?

In my long journey around the ropes, I have seen average boxers successfully performing at the top of their game and achieving great rewards. However, I have also seen fighters who had all the talent and never reached their full potential because they lacked the discipline or lacked the proper training support.

I have since discovered that success or lack thereof is a result of, mainly, the teams around the boxers. The people around the boxer can make or break the career of any fighter. Every boxer needs a good and capable team around him to make him realise his dreams. Boxers need not worry about anything else other than fighting. A great team ensures and allows a fighter just that – the freedom to do what they do best.

To perform to the best of his abilities without worrying about anything else. Fighters are usually drained and exhausted. They take punches for a living. They hone their bodies to endure and triumph over the harshest of punishment, pain and pressure. The fights may be long or short; they may be dreadful and straining. But the body must be prepared to stay in-form and perform – whatever it takes. The process of conditioning the body and mind while having to lose weight, and gain weight; and again lose and gain weight at the same time can be draining even among the toughest.

A complete team comprises a manager or advisor, trainer, one or two assistant trainers, a cut-man and a kit-man. Some teams even secure the services of psychologists who sometimes also play the role of motivator. There is no value in having a bunch of people who lend no real value to the betterment or advancement of the boxer.

In the South African scope, the boxer's team are paid 25% of the boxers payout. Specially secured people like psychologists, physicians and in other cases, the cut-men are paid fixed negotiated amounts. So in a perfect situation, the South African boxer should take home 75%. But that is not the case because many boxers owe money to a lot of people. In some cases, they owe money to the manager. Family members, friends and mentors in the neighbourhood have sometimes played significant roles in a fighter's upward movement. These families have formed structures that comprise mentor or trainer, or managed by members of the family or a close working friend.

Such structures have professionally and successfully brought up some fighters. Others are brought strictly by neighbourhood friends. They have found strong, trustworthy and resourceful guidance from these structures. Some fighters have decided to go it alone. But to be successful, those fighters have to belong to that special breed, which I have learned comes once in three generations.

Taking care of the team is of utmost importance for the ultimate success of the boxer. There is the question of how fighters treat their team members. Fighters who treat their team members well and are willing to invest themselves are typically the most successful. Some boxers treat their teams like dirt. Sometimes, there is the misleading belief that being with the boxer, travelling nationally and internationally, and appearances on the big venues is the ultimate treatment. Team members soon notice such shoddy treatment and do not give their best when it comes to their services. In the end, the fighter hits himself, and the results show in the performance.

A good manager or advisor, as the leader of the team, and in most cases the decision-maker should be more loyal to the fighter and the team more than they are to the promoter. A manager who is loyal to the promoter cannot negotiate in good faith on the fighter and team's behalf. The trainer and assistants play a very unique role in the boxer's make-up. Their energies complement each other, and their thinking and action are always about one goal – how to turn great fighting talent into big winning boxers.

A good trainer-fighter relationship depends on trust and respect. Without respect between the fighter and trainer, not much can be achieved. It has to be mutual, and the fighter has to listen and follow whatever instruction they are getting from the trainer. But, on the other hand, the trainer has to positively get under the boxer's skin and sense the boxer's inner feelings during preparation and the actual fight.

The life and future accomplishments of the fighters are in the trainer's hands more than anybody else. Travel arrangements are also negotiated settlements depending on the size and nature of the fight. They can become very sensitive as the stature of the boxer grows. For preliminary fighters, the promoter usually allows 3 or 4 people to travel. That usually includes the fighter. It is usually the fighter, the trainer, and the assistant trainer. As the fighter progresses, the promoter may allow 4 or 5 to travel out of his budget. That usually includes the cut man unless the team makes use of a local cut man, as is the case sometimes. The promoter's account becomes more open as the boxer progresses. Of course, that goes to include wives, girlfriends, or even family members. As far as who should travel should be in the order of importance. If a boxer needs more than the expected people, the expectation is, he will pay for them to travel.

In Africa, we are a people of family, unity and community. Our weddings are big; our funerals are big; everything we do, we want to go big. And so it is to be expected that a boxer coming from this way of life would like a big entourage. This is usually where the chaos starts. I have seen cases where the fighters ask their boxing team to share rooms with their family and friends who don't serve any purpose in the fighting event. I've seen cases where team members are asked to room together. This is never fair to the team. That has been known to break some of the strongest teams. The trainer, assistant trainer and cut man should not share facilities like rooms or bathrooms. Sometimes they agree just for the sake of keeping the peace, but among themselves, they talk about it.

IS IT REALLY NECESSARY TO TRAIN?

I rank boxing as the toughest and most challenging sport of all. While other sports codes base their competition on chasing, holding, pulling, pushing selected targets, objects and distances, boxing is all about the man in front of you. Boxing is a one on one. In boxing, it's about doing unto others more or before they do unto you. How much punishment you can take from your opponent, and how much punishment you can dish out before victory can be achieved.

In his book titled The A-Z OF WORLD BOXING, renowned boxing analyst Bert Blewitt informs that "Training was badly neglected and virtually ignored for a hundred years." That is until England revived boxing in the seventeenth century. One is left to wonder why. Preparation is the foundation of success in anything you do. Boxing is not different. Not training one's body for the gruelling punches is like asking for punishment. It begs the question, why would any boxer drop training. Why would a fighter and his trainer, for that matter, get into the ring without preparation. Training is as old as boxing itself. It is commendable that the English saw fit to recognise the importance of training and preparing mind and body for the rigour of what is globally referred to as a game. It a very dangerous to the well-being and life of the competitors.

Some fighters have not survived the multiple knockouts they have endured in the ring. In part because they skimped on training and getting their mind and bodies conditioned to the gruesome experience of facing an opponent toe to toe. It goes without saying, training is the most important part of any fighter's routine. It readies the mind and body for all the mental and physical abuse it will endure in the actual fight. The body has to be there, dishing out blows in strides. While at it, the boxer must mentally be in a space to do all sorts of manoeuvring to defend itself against the opponent's punishment.

The fighter has to stay strong both physically and mentally and be there for as long as it takes. The final product for a well-prepared boxer is a concoction of power, speed and endurance. Those specially acquired elements must be retained under the most demanding and most challenging circumstances in the ring. The ring is generally known as the Truth Machine because it has a way of exposing what and how much you prepared. Therefore, you need to build and develop the energy over a long period. Energy, energy and energy.

It takes much discipline to gather your mind and body to endure the pain of punishing that body and whipping it into shape. It takes even more discipline to push it and keep pushing while enduring the pain against the fighting machine that is the opponent.

It takes long and short distances of running, countless strengthening and stretching exercises, daily routines of skipping with and without the rope, attacking the pads and doing vicious assaults on the punching bag. Then rounds and rounds of shadow boxing and doing the same thing or same move over and over to learn and polish up on skills. And finally, you begin to spar. While sparring is usually an essential and direct addition to the fighter's preparation for war, it is also the most direct confrontational routine, the closest thing to the actual fight that you can do. Fighters have been known to get knocked down or out in sparring while preparing for contests.

Many trainers often overlook shadowboxing. But it must never be undermined. On the contrary, it is the best teacher of boxing. It can be effectively utilised for technique, concentration, balance, leg strength and stamina. It can be separated into different categories and must be closely monitored to produce the desired results.

Boxing with yourself without an opponent in front of you is the first step to fighter training. This is where one learns the fundamentals of boxing. The basics are the fighting stance, the positioning of the hands, the leg movements, and the basic punches of boxing – the jab, the straight punch, the cross, the hook and the uppercut. Combination punching flows from mastering those basics. Then there is what is usually called hand sparring. A routine is very popular in the Eastern Cape and has worked wonders in getting kids and even adults familiarised with boxing skills. Even those that are not going to be boxers. They have gone through their hand sparring in the streets and even at home.

When I opened my gym in 1979, I decided to take this kind of sparring a step further. First, I used it as a means of teaching the beginners their first steps at fundamental boxing. Then, I would identify boxers from the old and more seasoned fighters and line them up. I would then take from the new ones that we're still learning and line them up facing the more seasoned ones according to what I thought was the style the new one comer would follow. I would have the more experienced boxers box while the beginners had to follow all the moves and combinations the leaders were throwing.

The second mode of boxing is actual sparring. But light sparring. This mode can be affected even among non-boxers. It is best meant for beginners. They learn from it the practical part of boxing with your opponent right before them and fighting back. With advanced boxers, his kind of sparring is good when the boxers are either not of the same weight or have the same fighting ability. This suits the boxers perfectly in terms of gaining rounds to learn and gain experience. It also allows amateurs and other low ability fighters to spar with real good and hard punchers.

It serves as an excellent teaching and confidence building routine for beginners. The third mode is live sparring. The fighter has to prepare and be in good condition to start engaging in live sparring. This kind of sparring gets a boxer ready for the actual fight. It has to be intense and highly competitive. It needs real focus. It requires the fighter to have energy. It does not matter at this stage whether the sparring partners share the same build, size or style of the opponent. What is needed here is the work. Loads and loads of work. This kind of sparring has to be monitored. A fighter cannot afford to be in tough competitive mode every day. It kills the fighting spirit. The fourth mode of sparring is perhaps the most important in a fighter preparing for a fight. It is the fight specific sparring. This is where sparring partners must have the same style as the opponent, or at least be able to mimic it to the latter. There are also professional sparring partners who can mimic any style. Managers go all out of their way to look for and even hire these special sparring partners. They are always fit and ready to roll, always on standby to travel and do their job. Wherever you go, you find out that the everyday training usually consists of 2 to 3 training sessions. Sometimes, there is running, depending on the camp, trainer or boxer, mixed with swimming. Whichever way it is done, it should be early in the morning or in the evening. These times are most suitable for the cool fresh air that is good for the lungs. It also gives the boxer enough time to recover from the day sessions. Resting should be emphasised. It is good for quick recovery.

Trainers vary their approach with regard to strength work. Strength work develops the fighter's intensity and hardening of the punch. Some will do it after the run or swim, while others prefer to do it after the boxing skills workout. Other trainers put so much emphasis on strength workouts that they prefer a separate time for it. However, a fighter should do different daily routines to develop or improve the category of his armoury.

The changing of training routines assists in not concentrating on some strengths and weaknesses while leaving others behind. Boxers should not go full steam work. They risk burning themselves out before the contest. There must be off days for recovery. An expert's eye can see if the fighter is tired or overworked.

A great trainer can also spot a sharp fighter who is in the mood and still craves for more. Such conditions show themselves in training. Training should be eased and slowed down as the fight approaches. This allows for mental and muscle relaxation while also readying the boxer for combat.

THE TOUGH EFFORT OF MAKING WEIGHT

Making weight is a process used by weight-class athletes to lose weight to compete in certain weight classifications. The sports codes include boxing, lightweight rowing, weightlifting, wrestling and judo. Patterns of weight fluctuations vary among athletes. Some athletes constantly maintain a low body weight, where others lose weight for the competitive season or an upcoming fight in the case of boxers. It is the means or tendencies boxers prefer to use in losing weight, and the times they take to do so invariably have a negative or positive effect on their performances. The most common and most dangerous pattern is rapid weight loss, where there is a tendency to balloon between fights and leave weight making right up to the last few weeks to the contest. Such methods vary and include severe dieting or starvation methods such as fluid restriction, sweat suits, sauna baths, medical substances and even self-induced vomiting. Water is one of the essential ingredients in the human body, in fact, up to 60% of the human adult is water. Fluid restriction, especially when done by way of water restriction, which is usually the most practised method of weight reduction by boxers, may be hazardous to the boxers health. If you think about it, the brain and heart being composed of 73% water, surely the consumption of water must be vital when the boxer is in intense training.

Water restriction, as a weight reduction method makes it difficult for the human system to function, it results in tardiness, muscle cramps and severe brain injuries. Smooth and seamless circulation through the body cannot be overstated, especially when the body is in intense exercise. The human body will die if it does not receive a constant supply of water. Every cell in the body requires water. Imagine a boxer going through rigorous training with very little water circulating through the body. That would put the boxer's health at great risk.

Water is responsible for distributing oxygen, which is the regulator of all bodily activities. All such activities are initiated by the brain, which controls the whole body. There is general knowledge among the boxing community that there should be no water shortage around the brain. It protects the brain from crashing around the skull when hit during a fight from the apparent pressure of punches received from sparring and training sessions. Due to high water concentration in the brain, concussions are likely when the body is dehydrated. Without water and subsequent oxygen, the body will not produce energy and body organs will stop functioning, resulting in death.

The average body requires a certain amount of energy to function at healthy levels. Therefore, it goes without saying that a body training at the highest levels and competing against stubborn challenges will require double doses of oxygen. Or face fatality. These rapid weight making techniques are highly discouraged by medical advisors and knowledgeable and experienced boxing trainers and coaches. The dangers of such rapid weight loss include malnutrition which is caused by inadequate intake of nutrients, and dehydration, which is the most dangerous, caused by excessive loss of water from the body.

When rapid weight loss techniques are used, it is primarily water and lean body mass that is lost, not fat. Muscle carbohydrate stores and muscle water are decreased. This impairs muscular temperature regulation and cardiovascular function. A rapid weight reduction will affect strength and endurance capacity and ultimately impact performance. It may also result in psychological changes that may influence performance negatively.

Regular food intake is as important as the other ingredients. The right and relevant nutrition enhance the opportunities to acquire health, power, strength, overall conditioning and quick recovery. Moreover, it improves the chances of excellent performance and winning against when it matter most. The reverse can be said about junk or non-nutritious food. Fruit is essential as a form of diet. So is vegetables. But fruit and vegetables alone do not have all the necessary nutrients the body needs to endure a strenuous training regimen and subsequent encounter.

It is the primary nutrients like carbohydrates, proteins, vitamins and minerals that the body needs through its training and competition. Managing the consumption of such nutrients and water through the preparation period becomes of utmost importance. The need for exercise in the process of readying the body for the upcoming challenge is immense. There is roadwork, skipping, strength and conditioning programs and sparring. When all such activities are programmed and well managed in an adequately watered, roundly oxidised and sufficiently nourished body, the results cannot be short of amazing. Weight loss should mainly concentrate on the reduction of fat or fat loss. Not fluid or muscle loss.

The safest and healthiest way to lose weight in a controlled and planned way spread over a prolonged time allows for proper training, good nutritional practices and hydration. It also needs proper monitoring by knowledgeable and well-experienced advisers, as well as the boxer himself. Cutting weight then rehydrating back up to a functional weight to fight is probably the most critical and delicate thing in boxing. Most boxers come so far in weight that food and liquid intake after the weigh-in is the most important thing in the 36 hours before fight time. It sometimes becomes a desperate exercise.

Fighters have to get back to a functional weight or won't be as strong or as durable as necessary for the gruelling encounters they will be facing fight time. As a result, the boxer's stamina becomes the direst casualty, as does their punch and pressure resistance. Professional and intelligent fighters have it planned down to a science. They know how important it is to get nutrients into their systems. They also know when to stop. The experienced eye can see them a mile away. Just watch them at the weigh-in. Watch how they eat and then watch them on fight night.

If you walk around 75kg and rehydrate to say 67kg, you will compromise your performance simply because your best is not used to functioning low in weight. Speed, timing and stamina are always the most significant setbacks under such situations. Sparring weight in good condition is usually the right fighting weight after rehydration. No matter how much a fighter has to drop and rehydrate, even the strongest ones get only 90 per cent of their strength back. Many tried and tested tricks are used by experienced boxers and trainers that work as far as weight cutting is concerned. Sometimes these tricks are legal - other times, not so legal. Fighters use steam rooms, hot baths, food supplements, and occasionally unlawful PED's to cut weight. It depends on the fighter and his team. PED use or non-use bases on honesty and integrity.

Suppose you can build yourself up to the extremely strong 10 to 15 kilograms above your weight division and still be extremely strong and keep your stamina, then hats off to you because you're a winner in boxing. You've got it all figured out. Usually, there's a genetic thing or a resource thing. If you cut about 15 kilograms, but you're not drinking the proper amount of water or taking the appropriate amount of nutrients, and all you wear is a sweatsuit and run or sit in a steam room, it's a con job, and you will eventually lose and lose badly. That fighter is cutting into muscle and resistance, and that's not good. Water, fish and plant-based foods are the easiest things to burn off. There is food you can eat that is easier to burn off. Then some foods are nearly impossible to burn. Once you reach a certain weight, then the extra size slows you down.

Boxers have to know what they have to do. People don't realise how much longer the mind lasts than the body. Boxers with knowledge, experience and intelligence learn how to take care of themselves. They not only know what to do but how to do it. So a boxer who knows his story and is dedicated to it will understand and stick to what he has to eat and drink for recovery each day after training. Massaging is also essential to remove the lactic acid and loosen the muscles. Boxers have to find the motivation to train, eat, drink and generally do the right things. Discipline cannot be overstated.

CHAPTER 12

GIVE ME A COMPLETE FIGHTER

WHAT MAKES A complete fighter?

Every trainer looks for that fighter. The perfect fighter. The dream fighter. Some trainers have produced unbeaten fighters. Finding that kind of fighter complete with all the skills and credentials is very rare. Trainers and managers know it takes work to build a complete fighter. The question you would want to know about a boxing worth moulding. Were they unbeatable? Or did they come at the right time to beat everyone put in front of them?

Some of the best boxers are *'called'* into boxing because they either run away from something or run towards something. The youngster with anger issues because he was bullied as a child. For the kid who endured abuse from a parent or guardian, boxing is an escape into a world they control and take out their frustration.

So you would further ask the question:

Did they beat everybody? Or were they sometimes beneficiaries of unfair decisions? Again I would ask, "Is there a complete fighter?"

How many times have you heard the expression, "He is unbeatable" or "He is so good I don't know what it will take to beat him." Yes, you have, and you are still going to hear it. For as long as there are boxers in the ring and the timekeeper still says, "Seconds out, round number 1," they will always be that one fighter who stands head and shoulders above the rest.

Of course, some fighters do one or two things so well. They win fights without having to change to the next gear. And look unbeatable. They sometimes usurp their strong gifts so effectively, and they overwhelm their opponents so convincingly that we forget there may be some critical attributes they lack. Until the day they are challenged in all departments.

Think of deadly punchers who lack basic defensive skills. Think of skillful movers and quick combination overall boxers with no power but with brick-wall jaws. Then you find solid fighters because they are averagely gifted with all the skills and attributes of boxing.

Think of all these guys moving up the boxing ladder and winning, raising the roof—all the way. Until one day, they are challenged and taken in all departments. And the 27 – 0 (25 knockouts), 21 knockouts coming in the first round exposed for what it was – a paper record. And him a fake. So what is it that makes the Perfect Fighter?

Is it one all-conquering attribute that nullifies everything else others can bring to the table? Are two attributes enough? Or is it a set of possessions and skills that provide all the answers and challenges opponents can bring to the table? To dissect and inspect this experiment, I decided to list some of the things I think are tried and proven strengths. I am a trainer. And like every other trainer, I have been working to have that fighter.

The fighter that adapts to any kind of style and pressure put in front of him. The boxer that convincingly beats handles and beats any challenge put in front of him. The Dream Fighter.

So here we go. There are talents or qualities that a fighter is born with. The first God-given gifts that come to mind are speed and power. There are strengths like fight tactics, punch combinations and footwork that need to be learned. But all such attributes, whether God-given or acquired, require a certain level of development to perform at their utmost best. I have listed these attributes in no particular or special order.

They may not be enough but maybe the beginning of the answer in the quest to find boxing's wonder boy, the unbeatable fighter, The G.O.A.T – (Greatest Fighter of All Time).

BODY BUILD

He would have to be an athlete and also look like one. He would not have to be built like the mythical Adonis but would have to possess the good looking but menacing body. Opponents would have to see the abdominal muscles to assure them that their most brutal body attacks would be withstood.

The boxer's upper body and biceps would have to look like they had been chiselled by a master of the art – strong, loose and elastic. Such attributes would not be there only for envy. They would have to be real and effective. The body would have to be tough and durable. Prepared to take and do whatever it had to do – whatever the challenge.

TOUGHNESS

Physical toughness comes first in my mind. A boxer has to have a high level of toughness to endure the challenges brought to bear by opponents. Such situations will test not only the body but also the mind.

A less than tough boxer may have all the attributes that make him great. But he folds when pressure and pain are exerted on him; then he will fail to deliver his armoury. Boxing is about imposing your will against your opponent and get the fight to be on your terms.

PUNCHING POWER

The boxer's rugged and bruising come forward style of fighting would have to be accompanied by immense power. They would exploit the tendency of boxers flinching when they feel the power. That would be the style meeting opponents at the centre of the ring and daring them to exchange.

He would be prepared to fight through blood, sweat and tears to get his win no matter what, challenging his opponents to the limit. His fights would have fans coming back for more each time his name was mentioned.

PHYSICAL STRENGTH

Like rugby, boxing has its way of scrummaging. It has its tactics and techniques to achieve maximum effect and excellence. This is where boxers are locked inside or toe to toe exchanging blows. It's also known as fighting in the pocket. Punches are blocked or taken on the shoulders. Legs are used to push the opponent to the ropes or into the corners. A strong fighter who can push and manoeuvre his opponents to positions of his choice, especially where they are less comfortable, is better suited even to outwork better punchers than himself.

FIGHTING SKILLS

Skill has taken boxers to the top of the range. It varies from natural to man-made. It is an enabling factor in any category of the game. Be it power, strength, or speed, fighting skill is needed to deliver effective blows. Skills begin with the legs because the strength and speed of the legs are vital for a boxer's manoeuvres. The legs are the vehicle to dart in and out of the war zone as quick as possible. They are also the anchor for any delivery you can think of. The speed of the legs is God-given. However, they can be developed to be stronger and faster. In addition, other skills are learnt and practised.

SPEED

If you ever saw Nkosana Mgxaji and Welcome Ncita, you would surely realise what they mean by blinding speed. This duo could certainly pace it up with the best in the world. While Mgxaji was a slick and shifting performer with the kind of style that made fans go crazy, Welcome was a speedy and entertaining brawler when he started. He threw no less than a hundred punches per round but ended his career as a mover who threw fewer punches but never lost his speed. This kind of fighter is athletic and very difficult to keep up with.

CHIN

Sometimes it is called an iron chin. Others call it a granite wall; others have known it as the ability to take a punch flush on any part of the head and still come out fighting. It may generally be referred to as the chin, but the punch may land anywhere from the forehead to the nose and the jaw.

It holds up, and the owner keeps pouring on the heat without buckling nor losing rhythm. Some boxers have average qualities and abilities but are good enough to win big fights, even titles, because of their strong chins. They keep fighting back, taking the best shots until the opponent tires out.

Such shots are absorbed by the best and most accurate punchers of their generation. Opponents who are better than them in attributes like speed, strength, and even power make no difference. But imagine if they were equipped and well-rounded with all the other qualities.

DEFENSE

The first boxer that comes to mind is Zolani Tete. Certainly, the most important quality for any boxer is to have a long and healthy career. The boxer keeps his cool and composure, holding up against all his opponent's attacks where other boxers would panic and make all the wrong moves. It is held in such high esteem in the game. Such boxers have been known to win rounds without throwing a single punch.

An average boxer can get away with just displaying defensive skills like blocking, parrying, slipping, ducking, riding and rolling with the punches. It falls in the category known as Ring Generalship. When accompanied by quick thinking, able reflexes and nimble legs – that make for an even better fighter, and it scores points. It enables boxers to go from fight to fight without getting nailed by a good shot or a combination of punches. Defensive fighters can control the terms of the fight and perform longer distances under extremely challenging circumstances.

STAMINA

The fighter has got to have loads and loads of stamina. A long, tough fight needs a body that will stay there and fight back for as long as it lasts. A body that deteriorates or crumbles along in the fight will not make it to the end, especially if the going is tough. Boxers start fighting over three rounds as amateurs, four rounds as professionals and then develop long-distance with time as experience builds. This means that stamina is built over time; likewise, the boxer will find their staying power over time.

TOUGH LEGS

Tough legs is another basic requirement or foundation for a boxer's durability. The legs are the power base as well as a vehicle for movement. No matter how good a fighter may be, that boxer will not make it without good strong legs. Great boxers are built on a good foundation. The foundation of boxing is not always the punching power.

Punching power without strong legs is like having a tree with solid branches but shallow roots. That tree is bound to fall over easily. There have been boxers with less fighting skills who climbed up the ladder of world boxing and won fights against the best opponents, all because they had strong and quick legs.

WORKRATE

The high work ethic always makes for countless uncomfortable moments for the best boxers. On the other hand, some good boxers and punchers have been known to fold under the pressure of volumes of punches. How much a boxer can take outside the ring indicates how much they can take in the ring.

One does not have to be a big puncher for work rate. A balance of punches, footwork and head movement gives an average boxer a reasonable work rate. Effectively doing a lot in the ring can win many fights. The punches have to rain from all quarters.

VERSATILITY

A versatile boxer is gifted with a full bouquet of qualities – good fighting skills, decent punching power, strong legs, excellent work rate and more.

It can be intimidating and exhausting fighting someone who won't stop coming forward. Many fighters fold under these circumstances. As a boxer, if you want to last long in the ring, you must learn to take on the different fighting styles of your opponents. A boxer with versatility will be so equipped as to be able to push and pressurise tactical boxers. He will change style and be a smart boxer against come forward fighters. He withstands toe to toe and exchanges with the best if he has to. He will fight fire with water but will still fight fire with fire if it comes to that.

RECUPERATIVE POWERS

This boxer will be quick to recover without losing his mind or rhythm. As you would know, boxing is an explosive sport, and therefore a fighter with recuperative power masters their ability to recover quickly and get their strength and agility to keep fighting! As it will happen in boxing, a fighter will meet equally good boxers who will nail him, corner him or hurt him. But the boxer's recuperative powers will be so strong that they will recover within a split second and be back in the fight before they can take advantage of the damage they have caused.

CONFIDENCE

Boxing is so much more than fighting or typical boxing; it is both a mental and physical battle. Fighters who can win the mental fight can easily dominate the physical. Winning the mental battle is about having self-confidence in bucket loads. Boxers with loads of confidence are scared of no one and turn back from nothing. They win fights just by being confident and showing it. They like to challenge the boxers that are said to be untouchable and deliver performances few from positions of the underdog. They do not allow fear to make them hesitant. All opportunities created by lapses in focus by the opponent are taken and used effectively.

DEXTERITY OR PUNCH TECHNIQUE

Punch selection and numbers are also important assets for a boxer to gain recognition and acknowledgement. One of the first lessons a boxer gets taught in the gym is to be able to throw punches without losing balance.

Acquiring such a technique is not easy, mainly due to the difference in body mechanics. There is, for example, the belief that southpaws cannot throw more than three punches without losing balance. Another is that the taller boxer, the more difficult it gets to throw more punches. Such deficiencies can be gained with good basic teaching. It starts with the legs. A fighter who has learnt to put different punches together in combinations is difficult to beat and a joy to watch.

KILLER PUNCH

A boxer who can starch your lights out with one well-put punch wins the fight. The most common objective boxers have in every fight is to score a knockout. It's the quickest, most effective way to end a fight in victory.

It's always said that punching is about speed and timing. I tend to agree with that. However, I also think the same about a whole lot of other aspects of the game. A boxer with a combination of speed and timing, plus a killer punch, is most likely to cause a knockout during a fight. Clean and accurate punchers usually have longer careers than most. They work less and save a lot of energy. They take less punishment because many of their fights are very short. Once they have an opponent figured out, it is usually the end of the road.

HIGH IQ

Boxing needs a thinking fighter—a fighter who can think on his feet and through his hands. Split-second thinking and decision making may decide one's fate in the immediate fight. Or even the rest of his career. Do you make the right moves at the right time? Do you punch when you should have shifted? Do you throw three punches when you should have thrown one? Do you zig when you should have zagged? That makes a life decision in boxing. A boxer with a high I.Q. will make the right decisions at the right time.

ADAPTATION

Adaptation to new different personal styles and ideas is a significant plus in a boxer's war room. Opponents bring new challenges based on whatever they have learnt and can use as weapons in the fight. It takes a great deal of character to adapt, especially in today's boxing, where every single move a boxer makes is dissected, analysed and then used as a weapon to destroy.

Adapting to what one has learned and applying it against the opponent makes for a great boxer. But, unfortunately, there is so much studying and learning at the top level that it becomes nearly impossible to escape punishment for your mistakes. What with the new technology at everybody's fingerprints. It has taken the preparation and application of boxing to a level not humanely imaginable a few years ago.

SELF ADJUSTMENT

You need a fighter who can set the pace or the positions and conditions of engagement to suit his abilities or physical requirements. The case of former South African and IBO Middleweight champion Mpush Makambi IBO was a fast and graceful mover when he started his career. He had to change his style and slow down the pace of his fights with a ramrod jab and killer southpaw left-hand after a bullet ravaged his leg. Former South African champion Andrew Matyila could only throw an overarm with his right hand, courtesy of an injury to his thumb. Even hand wrapping had to be done in a certain way. This was done to protect the thumb. He had to set certain positions and angles for himself and his opponent to make maximum use of his left hand and throw the overarm. It takes some self-adjustment to go all the way to beat the best of the country and become champion.

DISCIPLINE

A boxer can have all the best attributes in the world – God-given, natural talent, developed and personally learnt. But without discipline, all of those qualities can be rendered useless. Discipline does not come in half measures. It is wholesome.

It has to be in all aspects of personal and general life. There are no short-cuts. Boxers who are known to be disciplined but lack direction in certain areas of their life or career are always caught out under the hard grind. At some points during their careers, especially during preparation for fights, boxers will have their resolve challenged about the training program, food and water intake, and sexual indulgence.

At a particular time, some well-needed things like food and water have to be taken in lesser amounts. While treats like sex have to be wholly abstained from. Rest is also of utmost importance.

CHARACTER

There is no character better suited for boxing than respect. It goes beyond just respecting one's parents or elders. A test of personal character goes to bear on the people the boxer works with daily.

How a boxer interacts and treats his manager, trainer, and club-mates, including his sparring partners, says a lot about his personality. This goes down even to the youngest and newest members of the gym. That is your role model.

CHAPTER 13

IS FIGHT-FIXING STILL A PRACTICE?

BOXING HAS HAD MORE than its fair share of controversy and scandal, possibly more than any other sport in history. So much so that many boxing fans across the world have this notion that some fights are fixed. The truth in these views depends on whom you speak to.

As a vicious sport known for its highway robberies, underhanded dealings and potentially fatal methods of cheating fighters, boxing is a hard business – not for the weak of heart. And this perception is brought about in many ways by the results of some fights, whether by judges' decisions or stoppages by referees.

In many cases, it has been boxers themselves doing what is generally known as diving. Is there something like fight fixing? Can ring officials be fully trusted for being honest and above board in making their decisions? If such cases exist, are there ways and means to alleviate this unacceptable situation? Some decisions have been so ludicrous and scandalous that many questions have been asked about the credibility and accountability of boxing officials.

Unfortunately, this awful situation is endemic in many parts of the world, including South Africa. For instance, boxers from the Buffalo City in the Eastern Cape have been accused of taking part in match-fixing for as long as I can remember. Eastern Cape crews have, themselves, blamed harsh treatment and robbery a lot of the times they have gone beyond their borders to fight in the neighbouring Provinces, especially Gauteng.

In earlier years, this practice was always associated with the mafia mobs where deals for boxers to take dives were made and punishable for failure to deliver. One well-known mob-controlled champion was the Italian giant Primo Carnera of the 1930s. Primo was known to be cumbersome, slow, and without rhythm, but that did not stop him from going all the way and winning the biggest prize in the sport. Such deals were responsible for making him a Heavyweight champion of the world. But the most famous suspected fix of all time, though never explained to satisfaction, was that of Muhammad Ali knocking out the fierce and menacing Sonny Liston for the world's Heavyweight championship.

Liston went down in the first minute of the fight from a punch that even movie replays could not catch in that fight. Though not denying Ali his place as The Greatest of all time, this saga certainly put a dent in his image and that of the noble art for some time. Who would have foreseen the taking over of boxing from the sinister mobs by the promoters? But, unfortunately, after the stranglehold on boxing was loosened from the mafia mobs, the game was not necessarily free from manipulation as promoters took over with more decent under the table deals than threats and brutality.

Don King came out of prison, maybe having been schooled inside the university of thieving and thuggery, in the ways of manipulation and scheming. He developed his brand to dizzying heights with the brilliance of Muhammad Ali, the boxer he promoted and gained global recognition as the best boxing promoter of all time. His name seemed to always prop up in conversations and reports about the fixing of fights. Though not all the time, boxing promoters have always borne the brunt of accusations because they create winners and subsequent draw-cards for their benefit. As the business people in the trade, it would only make sense that they would be seen as the front line culprits of any unscrupulous behaviour.

Boxing promoters have been known to go all the way to influence sanctioning, refereeing, judging and even the boxers' performance to get their favourable result. The money they toss around makes sure that they get what they want.

The stories of International promoter Don King and his ownership of the WBC have been making the news decade after decade while back home in South Africa, the hold and influence of Branco Milenkovic over the IBF is no secret.

The boxers themselves have been accused of being the villains in fight fixing. However, rumours have always surfaced in South African boxing about how this country managed to crack into the limelight of world boxing and become one of the leading producers of Heavyweight boxers.

Secret deals are said to have been made with a lot on the imported Heavyweights to take dives in their fights against the country's white prospects. A practice that was especially rampant during the period when the African-American Heavyweights like Muhammad Ali and Larry Holmes were ruling the roost.

The world was looking for a white Heavyweight to break the stranglehold of the black boxers on the biggest prize in boxing. So who else than an Apartheid white wonder kid to deliver the killing blow.

In his book titled 'No Punches Pulled South African', boxing analyst and writer Terry Pettifer quotes former Featherweight contender Tony Lombard about serious fight-fixing allegations. He alleges that South Africa's first world champion, Vic Toweel, won over Manuel Ortiz for the World Bantamweight championship in 1950, which Toweel won, as having been bought.

While all those claims were never proved to be correct or accurate, they certainly threw some doubts on the authenticity of boxing and its promoters and its ring officials. The welfare of boxers and boxing itself lies on their shoulders. The referee in a boxing match has tremendous power and authority. They must exercise that power fairly, quickly and effectively. The decisions are subject to rules which must be interpreted swiftly and effectively. The referee is the sole arbiter of a fight.

In implementing regulations, grey areas exist, and the officials have to use their discretion. They must call upon knowledge, expertise, experience and sound judgement to make quick decisions. Two important factors are called upon, impartiality and honesty. However, it's here that many officials are found wanting.

Promoters are in the business of boxing for profit. They contract boxers and make money for themselves. They will use whatever influence they have to protect their investments. They identify those in positions of power and keep them close. They prefer safe officials and pay them in kind. They will not talk to the officials directly, but somebody else will do the dirty job. A whisper here and a strategic remark there dropped is hint enough. Boxing analyst and writer Gaynor Noyce says, "do not believe any promoter who says he has no say in the allocation of ring officials." Their influence stretches far and wide.

Boxing promoters are known to pay for ring officials' licenses to work in the most recognised sanctioning bodies, influencing the sanctioning bodies on which they influence to give their preferred ring officials work and getting them trips overseas. These are some of the perks bandied about in boxing.

Such generous offers are sometimes known as greasing the palms or scratching backs. And this practice has put promoters in positions where their influence stretches far and wide. They gain leverage from the official in charge of allocations in the office and the officials working as referees or judges in the ring. A compromised referee who knows his job knows exactly what to do and does it with all the zeal and zest of confidence. They know whom to protect and how to dispense their power in the ring to keep the protected fighter as safe as possible. By using expertise and experience, they seize safe and relevant moments for pre-conceived agendas.

On the rings' sides are judges armed with the same years of training, experience and expertise. But, unfortunately, their pre-conceived agendas result in them scoring the fight based on what they want rather than what they see.

At that point, impartiality is neutralised, and each official acts based on what is expected of him. They don't care that in the process, a boxer's career is shattered, and boxing suffers another black eye. The more they win the confidence of the promoter, the better for them. And boxing suffers another black eye. Unlike the boxers and everybody else, promoters take the big risk of losing by putting their money upfront. On the other hand, the fighters risk putting a dent on their records, and perhaps a brighter future. Boxers never lose money to organise a tournament.

Their purses are guaranteed win or lose. Promoters put up the purses, travel and accommodation expenses along with advertising, sanctioning fees and money outside contracts in the name of welfare and good relations. Promoters even go to the extent of loaning boxers, managers and some officials money. In most cases, those loans are generally not refundable. To the promoters, it is a question of putting their ducks in a row. That, unfortunately, is the nature of the beast. It is called business. On the one hand, it's a sometimes cruel, slimy, thankless dog eat dog business where only the greediest survive. But, on the other hand, it's equivalent to a game of chess where intelligence, vision, diplomacy, and sound business acumen, accomplished organisational skills are demonstrated by people with few or no academic qualifications. The boxing game is unpredictable. It has its agenda. But above all, it gives the underdog a chance. Boxing dreams have been broken and shattered by inept and unprofessional judges' decisions.

Judges are supposed to be well-groomed, self-sufficient and confident people of high personal standing. Their emotions have to be controlled, their judgement impeccable and honest. Promoters are also able to have their way even inside the ring – through the referee. This is where the referee uses his experience and skills to disallow in-fighting to ease the situation of the preferred fighter who is uncomfortable fighting inside, or vice versa.

Sometimes the referee will disallow clean shots to the body by the other boxer because he is damaging the other fighter. Sometimes points are deducted for minor or no fouls at all. Sometimes, the most apparent scenario to the fans is when a fight is stopped prematurely, giving the house-fighter a win at all costs. This also puts into question the role sometimes played by some members of the media. Years back, the famous Ring Magazine, sometimes known as the Bible of Boxing, found itself in a scandal involving some of its boxing writers in the rating portfolio. Suspicions have always flown around here in South Africa of promoters who have certain members of the media in their pockets.

They are known to fly them, put them into high-class hotels, wine and dine them; all of this for the sake of having a good story or preferential reporting on the promoter, his tournaments and results of fights questionable fights given to the promoter's fighter. I am not sure whether to also list the art of matchmaking as fight fixing or not. But if it is not, I am inclined to list it as certainly a close cousin. A good matchmaker knows how to give the house or preferred fighter all the advantages to give him an edge in the fight.

The casual boxing fan may not know or recognise such fixing, but it is there. Those are the advantages Sugar Ray Leonard made sure he had in agreeing to fight Marvelous Marvin Hagler in their epic battle that Leonard won. Such advantages did not help Oscar De La Hoya against Floyd

Mayweather Jr Jr. Managers or trainers of fighters who are unaware of such dimensions in boxing and find themselves unwittingly assisting in getting their fighters to lose against the house fighters. A good matchmaker keeps the house fighters winning by ensuring they have an advantage on a 60 to 40 basis on all fight winning possessions like skill, speed, power and endurance. Sometimes it goes to cover small areas that can be regarded as small matters to many people.

Matters like height and reach, especially when it comes to punching style and punch skill, make a big difference. They determine the direction the fight will take. House fighters know three months before the fight, while the others have three weeks to prepare. For this reason, serious boxers keep themselves in good shape all the time. In big fights, negotiations and deals are not only based on dates, venues and purses as happens in smaller events.

The promoter or matchmaker will go all the way to give his fighter every edge he can achieve to sway the fight to his favour. Binding contractual agreements are made on things like the design and size of the gloves to be used. Some boxers prefer a particular type and size of the glove, and their demand should be met. The padding of the glove determines the effect on the opponent on landing. They will go all the way to make sure they get the glove to enhance their punching prowess and strengthen the chances of scoring a knockout. The size of the ring is also of utmost importance. Opposing camps will even grapple with whether to use a soft or hard ring. Leonard wanted a big hard ring and got his win slipping and sliding around, throwing punches in bunches. Mayweather gave De La Hoya all the advantages he demanded to fix the fight to his favour as much as he could. And still, beat him.

Up until around 1994, white South African boxing officials used their authority over their less powerful black counterparts by making sure to allocate two white judges and one black judge for every fight featuring a white and a black boxer. They sometimes took it a step further in the bigger fights where there were possibilities of knockouts by also having a white referee.

No wonder white boxers were always beneficiaries of questionable stoppages and split decisions. That was fighting fixing at its best.

CHAPTER 14

BORN IN AFRICA, MADE IN ENGLAND

GROWING UP AMID THE EDUCATION, culture and influence of the English occupation that started in 1795, it was no surprise that, in my initial opinion, everything regarded as good and everlasting amongst mankind was made in England. Unbeknown to me, the world is vast and wide; however, this did not stop the formulation of such a notion.

So it was that my education and understanding of boxing was that it started in England.

No surprise here, the occupation of the English came with it a deep indoctrination of world perceptions. As the only country in the world to call themselves 'Great Britain', you can only expect great things to come from there. I was to learn later that this understanding was not wholly but partly correct.

While South Africa, and most parts of the world, did gain and learned modern and safer boxing from the English occupation, boxing started in Africa. Then, however, it was exported through the whole world by a mixture of military might, political prowess, economic power and social influence.

Until today, attributes ensure the balance of power and confirm who or which country controls boxing at a certain point in time.

At the time of writing this opinion that power, influence and control of boxing resided in the United States of America. As things look at this present time and the foreseeable future, boxing superiority will stay in the USA for some time.

Judging by the tight grip it has on all facets of the game, boxing attention, and its influence on opinion and decision making, it will take something close to divine intervention to change the situation.

The earliest depictions of boxing come from a Sumerian relief in Iraq from the 3rd millennium BCE. Other reports of boxing or anything that resembled boxing in the 2nd millennium are found in reserves from the Mesopotamian nations of Assyria and Babylonia and Hittite art in Asia Manor. These depictions mainly place the earliest evidence of actual bare fist fighting around the mountains and valleys of Ethiopia.

While boxing, whether in the bare or covered fist, is mostly believed to have started around 6500 BC and 8000 BC, available archaeological evidence on Minion Crete and Sardinia produce visual scenes of actual fist fighting between 1650 and 1400 BCE.

This goes a long way to agree or prove evidence of the theory or conviction that fist fighting is as old as humanity itself. We have been punching each other in the faces for as long as we have been alive. If anything, I am tempted to think Cain and Abel had a little bit of their own tussle that resembled our boxing today.

ROOTED ON THE AFRICAN SOIL

Boxing began as a pastime, men circling and hitting one another with bare fists mainly aimed at the head. It later became more serious and competitive with some sort of covering on both hands, as it graduated and gained recognition as a full-contact game.

Known and recorded bare-knuckle boxing lasted about two years before it died down as contestants found reasons to cover their knuckles. And so began the process to ensure the spreading of boxing across the world and its control. When the Egyptians invaded the Nubian region in 4500 BC, they found out that people here had already been practising this form of contact sport for some time. Their soldiers learned the art of boxing from the locals and naturally carried such newly gained physical and tactical abilities to Egypt.

They practised and passed it on to others, especially the youth. As a result, boxing became very popular in Egypt to the point that even Egyptian Pharaohs are said to have attended the contests in specially erected venues.

From Egypt, it spread to other countries in the region, including Greece, eastwards to Mesopotamia – today it is known as Iraq, capital of Baghdad – where a lot of archaeological evidence can still be found. Boxing as a contact sport would later spread northwards to Rome, where the emperors entertained themselves and the jeering crowd to the slaves who fought each other in the arenas.

The Greeks took boxing to heart and introduced some form of organisation to lessen injuries, casualties and fatalities. In Ancient Rome, fighting became a popular spectator sport. Contests were held at Roman Amphitheatres. Theirs was bloodthirsty. Their matches were fought to the death to appease the spectators. While covering was allowed in other countries, Romans made it more dangerous and deadly by covering their hands with sharp and pointed metals meant to stab and maim.

Competitors were literally fighting for their lives. There was no form of defence whatsoever. They just attacked relentlessly with little concern for what was coming. Defence tactics of any sought were frowned upon. However, as time went on, slaves became very valuable commodities.

They were bought, fed and then used for combat. Circles marked on the ground were used as the fighting area. This is where the term ring came from. Gambling became a big business, and lots of money was made through betting. That brutal practice was abolished due to excessive violence and died with the fall of the Roman Empire.

In Ancient Greece, boxing became a well-developed sport and enjoyed consistent popularity. Although the majority of fights were contested with bare fists, there is also evidence in museums of Greek gladiators with their hands bound with leather thongs. There were no rounds.

They brawled and hurt each other until one could not go on anymore because they were knocked out or rendered senseless. In other cases, they just gave up. Of course, they hurt their knuckles in the process. Boxing was growing in leaps and bounds. It was then that they started to invent ways to protect their fists from being there for as long as the contest lasted, rather than give up as a result of broken wrists and bruised knuckles. They subsequently bound their hands with cloth or leather. Such binding was allowed only on the condition that it was purely meant to protect the hands of the fighter, not to hurt, injure or maim the opponent. Other than that, there were no sets of rules to adhere to as there were no structures set to monitor such regulations. So instead, they relied on traditional codes of honour and were looked down on as cowardly and unsportsmanlike behaviour. Thus, all sorts of running, holding, wrestling and head butting were considered to be against the expected behaviour of sportsmanship.

There were no defined rings other than circles made by spectators who could move away anytime to avoid stray punches when the action got too close. Punches to any part of the body were allowed. Other than blocking and the occasional ducking, there was no ring-craft in the form of jabbing, footwork, bobbing and weaving, parrying, slipping and sliding. Weight categories were not used, which meant that Heavyweights tended to dominate.

The style of boxing practised typically featured an advanced left leg stance, with the left arm semi-extended as a guard, in addition to being used for striking, and with the right arm drawn back ready to strike. With left-handed people or southpaws as they are called in boxing, the stance was the other way round.

It was the head of the opponent that was primarily targeted, and there is very little evidence to suggest that targeting the body was common. Such tactics would be introduced later by the English as a new, improved and safer art form of boxing – the noble art of self-defence or the sweet science.

GONE WITH THE WIND

During the Dark Ages, all forms of boxing disappeared from the radar. It is not clear whether they were still being practised underground or not. But whatever the case, boxing resurfaced in England in the seventeenth century.

The English introduced the first set of a comprehensive set of Rules of Boxing. Jack Broughton devised these rules in 1743. It thus became the foundation from which all the rules of boxing would be developed with time. Thus started the process of making boxing safer and more accountable. These new rules were then introduced throughout the world through invasions and occupation.

The first recorded bare-knuckle fight was in the 17th century. That period also saw the emergence of Englishman James Figg, a local boxer of note who is widely credited for the rebirth of boxing. He promoted his ambitious achievements by proclaiming himself as the first champion of England and went as far as declaring and gaining widespread acceptance and recognition as one who taught boxing. He built his Amphitheatre in the West End of London, from which he fought, taught and promoted all aspects of boxing. He retired unbeaten in 1734.

On Figg's retirement, one of his pupils, George Taylor, assumed the title of the champion until he was beaten and relieved of his championship status in 1740 by Jack Broughton; who, on gaining the champion status, began making strides to improve the art of boxing. He started building his Amphitheatre and introducing a set of rules to transform the game. He subsequently gained recognition after publishing his new rules and is widely accepted as The Father Of Boxing.

Boxing in the United States began among the slaves of the southern states early in the 19th century and spread gradually northwards. Bare fist boxing was not taken seriously in America. However, it started to enjoy some sought of recognition when the English Rules of Boxing controlling the game were tightening up. The first fight on record between white men occurred in 1816. Then, in the 1850s, boxing in the United States began to gain public acceptance and support. As the boxing bug continued its bite far and wide across the world, so was the king-size headache that was pounding Politicians and Legislators. This sport was going on without any sought of Government blessing and sanction. Incidents of injuries and casualties were making headlines. There was very little or no control during the contests. Organisers were not answerable nor accountable to any set structure. They operated as groups or individuals and were laws upon themselves.

The slightest approach or sign of intervention by legal authorities was enough to send the organisers and contestants underground. There were fears that the more underground boxing went, the more dangerous it would be. This scenario, regarded as barbaric by certain sectors of society, gave rise to the question of whether to allow boxing to go on unsupervised by the Government or to legalise it for Government to gain some measure of control. Arguments started to flare up, ranging from unorganised gatherings in busses and trains to workplaces, and finally, to parliamentary debates. The heat was on. Something had to give.

There were strong factual arguments for and against the legalisation of boxing. The presenters of the cases on both sides were just as gritty and determined. But the most gruesome verbal wars were fought at the highest law-making level in Parliaments. Here arguments were interrogating the legal, medical and political implications of giving boxing the legal go-ahead. There were suggestions that some countries took the route to use force to stop all perpetrators be brought.

However, it was argued that when the force had been used to suppress boxing in European countries like France and Germany, the practice had gone underground. A sprinkling of fights was recorded between 1854 and 1935 in Denmark, Belgium, Sweden and Switzerland. It, however, was to stay dormant in other European countries until it re-emerged after the First World War. Equally, many fly-by-night groups presenting themselves as regulatory, controlling, or promotional bodies were mushrooming worldwide where there was some semblance of boxing. They took advantage of any loophole available to apply or force themselves on Governments for recognition and entitlement to take charge of boxing. They were equally determined and relentless. There was very little or no stopping them.

Until today Britain and the United States, front runners in the fields of control, development, improvement and marketing of boxing, have not found answers and solutions to this plight. Boxing is at its highest levels in Britain but has never been legalised. It can, however, be sanctioned on a technicality. 'Fighting' is illegal in Britain. A very good reason why they cannot legalise boxing. But a 'contest' is legal.

Sir James Vaughan opened the flood gates to the triumph and joy of boxing people in 1897 when, in his judgement of a charge of manslaughter, he ruled that there was a thin partition 'between what is termed a 'fight 'and a 'contest'. Another judgement of a case in 1901 confirmed Vaughan's ruling. He ruled that the two gentlemen in the ill-fated fight between Jimmy Barry and Walter Croot, in which Croot lost his life, had been engaged in a 'contest'. Boxing was on its way. There was no turning back.

THE BRITISH INFLUENCE

The British judgement and all subsequent activities after that were going to have much influence in the course of boxing across the globe. Countries that were already embracing or were toying with the idea of allowing boxing, one way or another, under their jurisdictions, were finding a reason to accept boxing as an acceptable sport. Such countries primarily included Europe, Asia, the USA and South Africa.

The United Kingdom had, from its conception and adoption of the Rules of Boxing in 1743, thus led the way for the world to follow. It had thus paved the way to ensure safety measures in the game. More amendments and changes for safety have since been made since Britain again introduced more sweeping changes in the now globally accepted Marquis of Queensbury Rules.

Meanwhile, in South Africa, the argument of legalising boxing and putting it under state control was taking shape. However, it was not without its challenges. It had its fair share of fights that had gained momentum in the Kimberly mines, the military bases, and other spaces where people would gather and start engaging in such illegal fights.

Boxing had now stretched far and wide across the whole country and growing in great strides. Opposition to the legalisation of boxing was against letting Government allow people to injure and maim one another but still be protected by law. They listed and published all reports and statistics of injuries and fatalities from across the world to drive their point home.

The South African Government had gained some small measure of success in putting a stranglehold on traditional stick fighting practices in places like the Cape Colony. However, the locals were picking up boxing instead.

Moreover, in the Transvaal, especially in the north, now known as Limpopo, the local Venda tribe practised bare-fist fighting in open spaces as a tradition. Boxing remained illegal in South Africa until Ludwig Japhet, a lawyer who practised in Johannesburg and had a passion for boxing, was persuaded to take up the cause of boxing and strive for its legalisation.

With friends' aid, he drafted a bill and persuaded George Miller, the Member of Parliament for Germiston, to introduce the bill to Parliament in 1923. Backers of the proposal for the legalisation of boxing were sighting as motivation for their stance, the discipline that the game could instil among the youth, and the confidence and balance they could gain with self-defence. They pleaded for boxing to be legalised and put under Government control. State-appointed officials could monitor it and ensure its safety.

Opposition to it pointed out that boxing was barbaric, violent and deadly – the only game known where the intention was to injure and destroy. They painted a grotesque picture of boxers with broken noses, cut eyes and lips, cauliflower ears, punch drunk and dead fighters in detail. Indeed, they contended, South African Government could not legalise murder.

The pro boxing group had some measure of comfort in parliamentary discussions because the house was wholly divided. The debates were not based on political affiliations but according to the convictions for or against boxing. Political party affiliations counted for nothing. Members of the same political parties were in opposing corners. There were strong and vocal backers across all parties.

At the end of one parliamentary debate, the pro boxing crew seemed to be on course to a points defeat. Many who report on debate described it as a toe to toe slugging match, which could be likened to two well-conditioned brawlers having a go at each other with no quarter asked and none was given. But a Sunday punch turned the fight around – and saved the day.

The following day, there were screaming reports, especially by the Cape Times and The Argus Newspapers, of a girl having been raped and her boyfriend beaten up the night after the debate. This incident seemed to have scored the knockout punch as all opposition to boxing just melted.

John X Merriman was able to convince the majority of opposition to agree that perhaps had the young man had a knowledge of self-defence, the situation may have been different. He may have been able to turn the tables on the attackers and save his girlfriend from being raped.

The opposition gave in, and there was general agreement that legalising boxing would lead to more young men taking up interest and joining the sport – which was now being freely referred to as 'the noble art of self-defence.' Boxing was the winner.

Professional boxing in South Africa was finally legalised under the newly established Boxing Control Act in South Africa in 1923. This new promulgation also meant that Parliament would run boxing in South Africa, the only sport in the country to be ruled and regulated under an Act of Parliament. It was later run according to The South African Boxing and Wrestling Control Act 39 of 1954 under The South African National Boxing Board of Control.

GOVERNING OUR PUNCHES

Currently, in South Africa, the Ministry of Sport and Recreation governs boxing through the South African Boxing Act 11 of 2001. As established and mandated by the Parliament, Boxing South Africa (BOXING SA) regulates all boxing in this country. The United States of America comprises many State Commissions who make up and are overseen by The Association of Boxing Commissions. These associations are governed by the Professional Boxing Safety Act of 1996 as amended by the Muhammad Ali Boxing Reform Act. The US Federal Government controls all of boxing.

In Great Britain, the sport is governed by the Ministry of Sport. The British Boxing Board of Control, which was established in 1929 overseas boxing in the country. It is a Limited Liability Company which Stewards represent with no financial interest in the sport.

Before the proper and recordable realisation of the exact time or place where and when it started, bare-knuckle boxing was in South Africa. It is not clear if the British occupation introduced bare-knuckle boxing in this country, but what leaves no doubt is the control and safety measures they brought along in introducing London Prize Ring Rules. I am inclined to go with the fact that there was some semblance of bare fist fighting even before they came to these shores. Fighting, after all, is as old as the human race.

It is difficult to tell when and where the first fight in South Africa was held, but what is clear is that it did go on under the radar for some time in different parts of the country before some of these bare-knuckle brawls were reported. According to boxing historian Ron Jackson, the earliest reports or references to fights happening came from Cape Town in the 1860s, of two guys only known as Japie and Mahmood, respectively. As was the case with many other fights before and after it, there was an intervention, and the Police made subsequent arrests.

According to Jackson, there were reports around the early 1860s of public bare-knuckle fights in King William's Town. These brawls were between soldiers guarding the Cape Colony frontier. These reports were usually a few lines written and published by some disapproving editor of some newspaper. Ron Jackson is of the view that editors at that time were against this practice. Their coverage was merely meant to expose the undesirable practice to the Police.

There has always been the traditional bare-knuckle fist-fighting practised and very popular among the Venda tribes in the African context. This kind of bare-knuckle fist fighting, known as Musangwa, started more than 200 years ago, in the early 19th century. It is still being practised today.

Musangwa has never endeavoured to form part of conventional boxing. It is not clear whether it was there before or after what evolved to be the commonly accepted and regulated boxing in the rest of the country today. But it is still practised very strongly, even featuring the well known and famous conventional boxers when they return home from other Provinces for annual holidays. Some historians have reported sights of bare-knuckle fighting even earlier than the 18th century. One such authority is late ex-boxer, writer and trainer Theo Mthembu of the famous Dube Boxing Club in Soweto. This could mean that the 18th century and later times can be regarded as the period when actual reports of some of such brawls exist, were reported and can be traced. According to Mthembu, bare-knuckle boxing was being practised in many parts of what was then known as the Cape Colony, especially along the territory now known as the Border/Kei region of the Eastern Cape, in the traditional strongholds of kwaNdlambe, kwaNgqika and kwaGcaleka. The history of politics has changed places from being named after Kings, Chiefs and Princesses pre-colonisation. These places were named Transkei and Ciskei, respectively, during the homeland rule. The locations across the Kei River known as Transkei were *kwelabaThembu*, *kwelamaMpondo*, *kwelamaMpondomise* and *kwelamaBhaca*.

A big chunk of modern boxing in that area now resides mainly in the region presently known as OR Tambo Municipality. However, a later developer than its counterparts across the Kei, Boxing in these parts is growing rapidly and has already produced National and world champions in Simphiwe Khonkco, Athenkosi Dumezweni and Xolisani Ndongeni.

Administrator Sakhiwe Sodo has served in the amateur wing SANABO and as a board member of BOXING SA. A lot of other officials are currently serving in different positions. On the other side of the Kei, the place that would be known as Ciskei during the homeland rule, the practice was mainly in *kwelamaNdlambe*, *kwelamaGqunukhwebe* and *kwelamaRharhabe*. A big chunk of those areas is now incorporated in what is known as the Buffalo City Metro Municipality. The BCMM remains the biggest producer of champion boxers in modern boxing in South Africa. It has also produced many world champions and world-class trainers, promoters, managers, ring officials and administrators. As a result, it is now widely recognised as the Mecca of Boxing.

This awareness and practice of bare-knuckle fights can be traced back to job seekers who grew up engaging in traditional sticks fighting back home. This, to them, was a way of life.

They came from these rural parts of the country and landed in Kimberly and other mining areas to work in the mines as migrant labourers. Their skills, primitive as they were, used to be so entertaining to their white masters that they were called upon to engage without the sticks but their bare fists as a form of entertainment.

These contests graduated in time from ones among the same mine fighters to inter-mine championships. They are still prevalent in the much improved and highly regulated modern boxing. Racism was rife, and as such, black versus white contests were not allowed. Such engagements were a crime in the country and were punishable by law. Such fights were held in strict secrecy underground, and because of such racism and segregation, no records of such bare-knuckle fights exist.

In the last major bare-knuckle fights known worldwide, one fight that was recognised and stayed in the record books as one of the longest bare-knuckle fights happened in the Kimberly fights in South Africa between Barney Malone and Jan Silberbauer. It lasted five hours and two minutes.

Legend has it that, not to be out outdone by their subjects and to indulge in their form of entertainment to impress their wives, the white masters were not averse to settling their scores with fists once a few glasses of their brandy elevated their spirits and levels of bravery. So everybody always looked forward to the weekend.

While boxing was happening across the world, it was also growing in numbers of engagement. Its awareness and practice were now not solely in the Cape Colony, but it was introduced across the broader South Africa. Its presence was being felt mainly due to the growing numbers of the British occupation and stories of soldiers of the Dutch East India Company. They were said to engage in fist fighting among themselves.

THE WAY WE WERE

While bare-knuckle boxing was hitting the world, special fighting as a pastime or game was not new to South African black people, especially *amaXhosa* in the rural villages of the regions duly mentioned in the Cape Colony. Other than the spear and the shield used mainly for wars, stick fighting was a way of life. So if bare-knuckle boxing was going to take over, it would have to go through stick fighting - and would have to be very convincing.

This was the Xhosa way of life from the beginning of time. Before undergoing the customary initiation ritual of graduating boys to manhood (*ukwaluka*}, boys used to engage in stick fighting. They were then graded according to their prowess in the contests and knew precisely where they belonged in the rungs of seniority among boys. This practice was not forced upon anybody, but it was expected as a symbol of honour and recognition among boys and the community. Some boys were known to come home from school, drop their school wear and books, then rush out to look for other boys. They knew exactly what they were going to do there.

Girls also engaged in street fighting among themselves. Both boys and girls teams travelled from village to village across their regions to compete against opposition far and wide. As was referred to boys of the highest standing in warfare, achieving that feat of being an *inkunzi, ingwenya* or *ooxholovane* [champions] was a big honour recognised and respected by Kings and Queens, Chiefs and Chieftains – by all and sundry.

Grown men also settled their disagreements with sticks. Because there were no gender prohibitions, girls travelled far and wide with boys as cheerleaders and contestants. Times were allocated according to schedules so there could be no clash of times. There were separate times for boys' as well as time for girls' contests. Some girls have been known to be so good as to take on boys and beat them.

Sticks fighting is an art in itself. Like all other contests, it has its forms of tactics that need immense skills and long practice. In addition, its form of rhythm has got to be in tune with footwork, blocking, parrying and countering. One only needs two sticks, one on each hand. A combatant leads with one foot forward. Orthodox or right-handed fighters lead with the left foot, while southpaw or left-handed fighters lead with the right foot.

Good balance and nimbleness of foot are of importance in darting in and out and sideways, as well as fainting. The leading hand is used for defence. The stick is held in the middle part, and the hand on that part is wrapped with a piece of cloth. This is used mainly to protect the hand against injury. Both ends of the leading stick are used to parry the attacker's aside and counter. The middle of the stick that is held by the wrapped hand is used for blocking. There is no other form of protection. The second stick is for the attack. It is held high up over the head and is used for landing on the opponent's head, chest, waist or leg. Sticks fighting has its flare and stylists. It has got brawlers and movers.

It has its crowd pullers. Fighters come in all sizes and shapes. There are no scales and measures. Some small fighters who could weigh and be classified as Flyweights and Bantamweights in modern boxing have been known to be *iinkunzi, iingwenya, iinjinga* or *ooxholovane* (champions). This after besting opponents the size of Middleweights and Heavyweights boxers.

Like in bare-knuckle boxing, there were no rounds or referees. And very few rules. Contests were controlled according to a code of honour. For instance, one could not hit with the leading stick but only used it for protection. Likewise, one could not hit an opponent when they were down.

A fallen opponent had to be given a chance to stand back up. If an opponent needed some reprieve to sort out something hindering their focus of the fight, all they had to do was say *mhela* (wait a bit), and the opponent would step back. Contestants dare not break those codes, or they risked being ostracised in one form or another. Some of those punishments went as far as one being fined a sheep that was to be donated by the family.

Learning and preparing for contests constituted many *ukucweya* or *ukugqwakaza*, which in boxing is called sparring. *Ukugqwakaza* is borrowed from oxen where bulls do their form of play fighting by locking horns. Preparing or learning the fighting skills alone or *ukubeth úmoya* was also practised as it is done in boxing and is called shadowboxing.

Other than finding time to learn and practice during playtime, there were no special training manuals. Physical fitness and power were gained by natural means. Manual work at home, especially away from home, tilling the fields, and chopping wood made sure they achieved proper conditioning.

They travelled long distances on foot in errands for their chiefs, Kings or village leaders. They also walked to the events in other faraway villages. Distances travelled to the fights were not recognised as having any bearing on the performances. Contestants could not claim fatigue caused by travelling.

Steadily but surely, the colonial authorities were taking steps to stop the practice of stick fighting. They regarded it as a violent and brutal pastime. So they used their influence in churches and schools to convince the people to stop the practice.

There came a time when it became punishable at some schools. Boys who were found out to have attended or engaged in such contests during the weekend got lashes from the teachers.

By the time the Apartheid Government took over, sticks fighting was all over in rural villages close to towns. It was non – existent in the locations (*lokshins*) that were closely connected to cities. For example, in such close to town locations as Duncan Village near East London, Ginsberg near King William's Town, and Nonesi near Queenstown, sticks fighting was a bizarre practice. Such situations would come to bear on children as the youth born nearer town differed in looks, dressing style, walks and even the way they talked, from those born in far rural areas. The town fellows were so much smoother and cleverer in the ways of the world than the rural guys. This smart town fellow's style with so much difference to village lifestyle used to make any village boy dream of going to these areas – and change his life.

This new influence spreading among the youth close to towns was also brought in part by the emergence of local cinemas where boys watched cowboy fist fighting.

Boys started practising the new craze. Scenes of boys playing around throwing punches to one another or in the air, with fists wrapped in cloth or small cardboard or milk cartons, became a very familiar sight. This kind of fighting was fast becoming a way of life. Matters of misunderstanding were also settled with fists. Boxing was taking these areas, especially East London, by storm.

FIGHTING GHOSTS FROM OUR PAST

My father, affectionately known in East London circles as Bill, never boxed. He had quite a good reputation as a street fighter. He was there when boxing started in the East London area. He had already outgrown the stage of boxing himself. However, he was on hand when amateur boxing became competent enough to engage in tournaments and was then the obvious choice with his van for travelling.

He developed a deep knowledge, understanding and love of the game, never missed a tournament and knew all boxers. He analysed all their styles and was seldom wrong in predicting winners. He became my source of information. He also gave much credit to the East London Harbour for introducing boxing in this area, now known as BCM. He used to tell me stories of drunken brawls by the sailors on weekends. The fights were sometimes over local girls who visited the quarters for business. He used to tell me that, as a result of that, some sailors left sons and daughters behind.

Youth from around Duncan Village, Mekeni and Tsolo locations (*loxions*) used to go to the harbour on weekend afternoons, hoping for a fist-fight they could watch. They were seldom disappointed. They used to watch and marvel at the raw power and finesse of drunk but very strong sailors.

It was such a treat – men from overseas – of all races – having a go at one another with bare fists. Racism was very rife – and cruel to them. The Group Areas Act (1950), which had seen the country's partitioning into different areas according to racial groups, made sure that they were at the wrong place. They were not supposed to be there as, according to the segregation laws at the time, those areas were for whites only.

There were places where they could only be there at certain prescribed times or per special permission. They often had to fend themselves from white boys who took it upon themselves to force them out. Other times a police van would come blowing its horn, and they would have to scatter away. However, they were never deterred and would come back the following weekend. The kids would go back home or to their playing spaces and streets – practice what they had seen.

Their fighting skills improved with time. So much so that sport-minded people started to realise that other than rugby, there was another angle of taking kids away from the streets. But then, rugby was prevalent and was somewhat the only or one of the few sports among black people at the time. And this was also one important form of discipline and self-defence.

Surprisingly, East London and surrounding areas are the last places to take up traditional boxing in South Africa. Even later than Queenstown and neighbouring King William's Town. When it finally did take up the sport, it took it by storm, bringing along a style, rhythm and atmosphere unprecedented in South Africa. In less than ten years of taking up the sport and participating competitively, it was already leading the country as the boxing city – the home of thrills and excitement – the gathering place of boxing.

Thanks to the emergence of one bright wonder kid named Nkosana Mgxaji, better known by his moniker 'Happy Boy,' and many other people and events, it later gained the name. It got widely recognised as The Boxing Mecca. It is also no wonder that when modern boxing finally began in East London, who else could come and teach the youngsters the pro and cons of boxing than an Englishman who was a social worker at the East London Harbour. Showing the local would-be trainers and boxers how to box and how to train for boxing required a man of skill and knowledge of the sport. My father did not know where this gentleman came from. No one knows when he finally left South Africa to sail back home to England. Enquiries to local veterans who were there when he came to offer his services say he was known only as Dugan.

Boxers like Lawrence Ndzondo, one of the first professional boxers in East London and Simon Sali, administrators like Gilbert Gidana, trainer/managers like Mzoli Madyaka, as well as youngsters who were there and have a deep knowledge of the game like *Sheshe Dunjwa* could deliver no more information on the man.

Not surprisingly, a social worker introduced a white youngster to the youth who took up boxing in the township. Edgar Miya was a resident of Duncan Village who also got stung by the bug that was boxing.

As a Social worker with offices in the Duncan Village Community Hall, his job made it easy for him to mingle with white rugby and cricket players. It was there that he came across one young player by the name of Les Muller.

They stuck up a friendship that led to Miya introducing Muller to boxing guys in the township. The rest is the history that this book is trying to unravel. And so began a reign, a craze and involvement in a sport that was to take the region that is now known and recognised as the Mecca of Boxing to every corner of the world.

Every household and every person, be it, child, mother, father, grandmother or grandfather, has a story to tell about the noble art of boxing. Somewhere in the family, there is a father, brother and late sister or relative who is playing some role in boxing.

Initially, boxing here was about Duncan Village. But due to expansion brought about by political segregation, it spread to Mdantsane Township and surrounding areas that today also include rural villages. As a result, the rural areas are now producing National and world champions.

CHAPTER 15

TRANSKEI BOXING BACK WITH A BANG

MY JOURNEY IN THIS GAME has made me realise that contrary to popular belief, the love of boxing and all the talent it produces does not only exist in the East London and Mdantsane area. It is resident and visible in the whole area known as Buffalo City Metro and many other parts of the Eastern Cape Province, especially Transkei.

What makes Buffalo City different is the positive commitment of the boxers and the highly endearing involvement of fans. There is also an understanding of the game and its politics among the local population that keeps them relevant to any kind of revolution or evolution in the game.

These factors certainly set this region apart from the rest.

The Black Homelands Citizenship Act (1970) resulted in all people living in the homelands losing their South African Citizenship, which meant that boxers living in the homelands could no longer fight for South African titles. But lucky enough, boxing was still given a choice.

The homelands could choose to have their Homeland Act or stay with the South African Boxing Act. Understanding the intricacies of boxing in the region is why this area was saved from curtailing the gains it had made or destroying itself.

After consulting with the local boxing structures and Les Muller, who was running boxing in the Border or Kei region at the time, chose for Ciskei boxing to remain under the regulation of the South African Boxing Act. However, much of the influence came from Ciskei's then strongman General Xhanti Charles Sebe, a founder member of boxing in King William's Town and a big boxing supporter, who refused to accept the Ciskei Boxing Act.

At exactly the introduction and beginning of professional boxing in Transkei in 1977, the Transkei homeland made the political decision to run its own boxing affairs outside and independently of South Africa. It scripted and adopted the Transkei Boxing Act of 1977. This political move excluded Transkei boxers from the rest of South Africa, thus denying them all rights and opportunities to compete in any South African boxing activities.

This move had the dilapidating and deadly effect of denying Transkei promoters and managers not only the capacity to organise reasonably big and recognisable tournaments, but it also denied them the space for securing valuable and quality opponents for their boxers from outside its borders.

They could only match their boxers against the less than quality and mostly fight starved opposition that was prepared to venture into the independent homeland and fight their fighters at more than their average purses in South Africa. But none of those fights could be staged for the Cape Province and consequently the South African titles.

The choice to manage their boxing affairs internally meant that the Transkei was forced to create and develop their rankings and compete among themselves for their championships. Transkei boxers had to compete among themselves, hoping that one day one of them would go high enough to challenge and win a world title.

On winning the Transkei championship, new champions were not awarded the normal championship belt like the rest of the world was and is still doing. Instead, they received trophies for titles. The long and short term effects of this political practice were disastrous, hitting the homeland heavily as their champions and prospects proved to be very talented and competitive contestants good enough to take on the best of South Africa and found themselves in limbo.

Petros Gonya, along with Sakhiwe Sodo, Conert Dunjwa, Sheshe Dunjwa, and many others, were some of the initial developers of boxing in

Transkei at the time. They could rightly be referred to as the Founding Fathers of boxing in Transkei. Gonya was working at the Transkei Department of sport at the time. He was working under the leadership of Peter Madasa, the Director-General for Sport in the Transkei Government led by President Kaizer Matanzima.

Even before it adopted the Transkei Act, the region had already produced boxers who had their mark in South African boxing and were already in the rankings as prospective challengers for SA titles in the different divisions. These boxers included Thabo Seoka, Mxolisi Mpama, Mxolisi Nohenda and Ntuthuzelo Mazwana.

The Transkei region was beginning to have a strong boxing contingent. Their talent pool included the likes of My Boy Beya, Nkosinathi Silolo, Skhumbuzo Majeke, Joe Jongile and Ace Dingiswayo. Other prospects were paving their way up and making a showing in the boxing fraternity.

NEW BEGINNINGS

Boxing in Transkei became so stagnant that professional boxers like Khaya Tshaka, Kholekile Krexe, Lisethi Dinte, Nyaniso Dunjwa, Mongezi Nondabula, Yongama Ngqakayi, Phila Mzamo, Nxeko Mtirara, and Peter Mpikashe had a choice of either leaving the region or retire from boxing.

The then Border region, as it was referred to then, especially the part that includes the East London and Mdantsane townships, part of which is now Buffalo City and Natal, which is now KwaZulu Natal, became the biggest beneficiaries of such talent.

To prove their point, boxers like Yongama Ngqakayi, who left for East London, and Peter Mpikashe, who went to Durban, won the Cape Province and Natal Lightweight titles, respectively. They were to be followed by the brilliant beginners, Nkqubela Gwazela, Khaya Zibaya and Sinethemba Mncane.

Mncane was later to significantly impact the successful Baby Champs project aimed at developing young talent. Nkqubela Gwazela won the South African Flyweight title and acquired legendary status as one of the best pressure fighters of his time. These achievements were gained outside their region, where they could have made a more significant impact and been role models for development among their youth.

The promoters at the time had their hands full, trying to feed and satisfy the demand as boxing was, and still is, one of the leading and most productive activities in the homeland. Leading the charge against intense competition from across the Kei River were businessmen *Buyisile Noholoza, Anthony Bam, Visa Monakali* and *Mgedezi*.

They kept the boxing fires burning with tournaments in Mthatha, where there was a big demand from the University of Transkei and Butterworth. The University was also used as a venue for their bigger tournaments. To the people of Transkei, the Transkei Independence stadium was to them what Sisa Dukashe stadium was to the Mdantsane boxing fans. Legendary boxers and former champions Nkosana Mgxaji and Mxhosana Jongilanga fought at this stadium. Gauteng boxer Thomas Sithebe fought twice in the stadium against the Eastern Cape's Nkosana Mgxaji and Mxhosana Jongilanga.

Sithebe remains one of the SA champions who made two ventures into the homeland. He may have lost both fights against the two greats from Mecca, but their names will always remain etched in the archives of the Ciskei Homeland for generations to come.

It is also worth noting that Transkei has historically been the feeder of the nation when it comes to the human numbers involved in the development of all facets of life outside of its region. Its large and sprawling but poor landscape has given birth to the talent of all social nature from politics to labour and sports. Thus, despite its recognition as the most impoverished region in the country, its natural human product has always been unmatched.

In the political spectrum, names like Nelson Mandela, Oliver Tambo, Walter Sisulu, Chris Hani and Bantu Holomisa spring to mind. It is no surprise that many big names that have made great strides across the country in boxing have their roots in the Transkei.

They include the likes of Nkosana Mgxaji, the man recognised as having popularised boxing in the Eastern Cape, former National Middleweight champion Sydney Hoho, a world acknowledged referee and judge Alfred Buqwana, Gauteng Boxing Provincial Manager Archie Nyingwa and all-time South African great Mzonke Fana. All of this even before the Transkei Boxing Act came into effect. One can only wonder how rich the region could have been had it developed and retained its talent.

Mzonke Fana is one of the most successful and decorated boxers in the history of South African boxing. He is from Qumbu but grew up in Cape

Town after his parents moved there for economic reasons. But the family never severed the original roots. One of Fana's last fights was specially promoted in Qumbu to recognise his boxing achievements and enhance his status as a world conquerer at home. Mamali Promotions organised the fight event in partnership with KSD Local Municipality. Fana's achievements include two South African Junior Lightweight titles, two WBF Intercontinental titles, a WBO African title, a WBC International title, a WBA Pan African title, and two IBF world titles. Add to that list the Order of Ikamanga.

We can only wonder what could happen with the local boxing if all the champions mentioned above and Mzonke Fana prepared and achieved such status without leaving home. Tata Nelson Rholihlahla Mandela also did a bit of boxing in Johannesburg.

With the dismantling of the Homelands and the return of the Transkei back into the South African political fold, the region has proven its mettle by coming right back and competing at the highest level of National and International boxing. Its boxers are doing what they know best – fighting and winning titles.

MAKING UP FOR LOST TIME

Its trainers include Madoda 'One More Time' Dyonashe of Khulani Boxing Club and Mthethunzima Dumezweni of Villains Boxing Cub, who have produced world champions Siphiwe Khonco and Athenkosi Dumezweni, respectively. In addition, they share a list of other stars that have come out of Transkei. Yandisa Madikane is still very active at the amateur level, while Phindile Rhabe has been strongly associated with boxing at school. These trainers have been effective in producing competitive national and international champions in both amateur and professional ranks. They are counted among the best in the country.

At the time of writing this story, Transkei boasts of some of the best boxers currently in Simphiwe Khonkco (IBO World mini flyweight champion), Athenkosi Dumezweni (WBC International Super Flyweight champion), Siphamandla Baleni, world rated Xolisani Ndongeni and former IBO world Welterweight champion Thulani Mbenge.

While it can be said that Ndongeni, Khonkco, Dumezweni and a large number of other boxers are based in Gauteng, their way to the top was paved while they were still in Transkei.

South African Junior Lightweight champion *Xolani Mcotheli* of Mthatha is based in East London, while *Kholosa Ndobayini* of Qumbu is based in Gauteng. Being based in Gauteng is for economic reasons. Part of the boxer migration hitting the Eastern Cape is because boxers find better economic opportunities in Gauteng and the other more developed provinces.

Lately, lately local committees that have included such boxing development gurus as *Sakhiwe Sodo* have been pulling all stops to establish a boxing office in the Transkei. This has resulted from a feeling that the region is being neglected when spreading the resources meant to develop the game. In addition, they believe that the Eastern Cape Province is vast and predominantly rural, making it impossible for the single BSA official based in Transkei to service the region satisfactorily. "The gap needs to be closed for the good of boxing in the Transkei, in the Eastern Cape and South Africa in general," says Sodo.

It is felt that the Eastern Cape Province can be zoned into three areas, viz, the Transkei, the Eastern Province and the Border Region. Each of these regions should not only have a BSA office but should also have a BSA representative. Experienced Government administrator from Transkei, *Moffat Qithi*, served for a short period as CEO of Boxing SA. He did the costing on the South African Boxing Act 11 of 2001 and transferred it into rands and cents, but his exercise never saw the light of day as he left before presenting it to the BSA board.

He also left BSA before he could settle long enough to address the Transkei request for representation which had been on the table since 2005 during the period BSA was under the management of experienced lawyer Krish Naidoo.

Judging by the leaps and bounds by which boxing in this area is growing, the need for self-presentation and determination in the region is more significant than ever before—and becoming more urgent by the day. It is now doing much better than some Provinces that have self-presentation. There is far more activity in all categories of boxing than ever before. Soccer administrator and club owner Sturu Pasiya spread his wings to boxing and promoted several tournaments to keep the flame burning. A new breed of fighting professionals

The new surge in activity is now being facilitated by the efforts of Ntsikayezwe Sigcau, who has used his Sakhisizwe Promotions outfit and promoted almost all the latest upcoming professional boxers and shown them out to the fans and promoters outside Transkei. There is also far more remarkable achievements. Things become even more difficult for them during the licensing period. Sometimes they have to travel more than three hundred kilometres only to turn back because for one reason or another they have not been served.

While this Political quagmire had Transkei boxing handcuffed to a standstill, just across the River Kei that separates the two 'countries', Ciskei boxing was growing by leaps and bounds. This growth can be attributed to the far-reaching decision that General Charles Sebe made in consultation with legendary boxing pioneer Les Muller.

While the Ciskei demarcation lines were sometimes blurred and difficult to read and understand within the homeland's sovereignty, what remained crystal clear was that the two boxing mad townships Mdantsane and Zwelitsha were firmly within the governing tentacles of the Ciskei Government. Their growing development, especially Mdantsane, meant that they would soon become the powerhouse of boxing in South Africa. Sebe's decision was final – whether one liked it or not.

In Spokes Witbooi's words, "At that time nothing was impossible to bra Charles. He was influential and well respected." Within the discharge of those powers, Xhanti Sebe ruled that Ciskei boxing would stay within the South African Boxing Act. That groundbreaking decision was made against the ruling, or none thereof, made by the neighbouring Transkei. That made sure that boxing within the Ciskei Homeland would not have to go astray. Its boxers would still compete for the South African titles.

When the Ciskei assumed 'independent' status under the leadership of his brother Ciskei President Lennox Wongama Sebe, it did not need to guess how to decide who the leader of all Ciskei security and armed forces would be. General Xhanti Charles Sebe was a well trained Apartheid policeman who moved up the ranks of the South African Police. Sebe rose to the rank of General and became, aside from his brother Lennox, the most powerful man in Ciskei. Charles Sebe loved boxing. And he knew it.

Among other names like Stanley Baleni, Ngqabe and Busa, he was one of the founding members of boxing in King William's Town and its districts. He became a trainer of the first boxers in Zwelitsha. The fighters included Aycliff Stengile, my first boxing teacher, Abishai Sibhene, Zacharia Pule,

Sandu Khwaza, Amos Vangqa and Elliot Bolani. He also trained formidable contender Aubrey Peta in Uitenhage for some time while stationed in Port Elizabeth. Despite his busy police schedule, he never missed a day in the gym. Clad in a different tracksuit every day, he would lead training using all the exercises he learnt in the police training regimen.

He was also known to approach school Principals and request them to allocate space for boxing in their schools. At this time, he would fall in love with two prospects who would go all the way and make good names for themselves in South African boxing. The two boxers were Spokes Witbooi and Ruben Matewu.

Sebe's bond with Spokes was so strong that there were jokes among the boxers that Spokes was Charles's biological son. Even his wife Nomafakathi knew that. Elder boxers went as far as comparing their facial features and remarked much how they looked alike. So it was only proper that Sebe's understanding of the game would save the region and send it on its path to achieving the status of Boxing Mecca. After the 1976 school riots, things changed drastically for General Sebe.

The Political landscape was taking a new face. The country was imploding. There was resistance like never before, especially from the youth. There were riots all over. The whole country was turned hot and grey by fire and tyre smoke. The streets were burning. Buildings were falling from the fierce force of stones and petrol bombs. People, old and young, were dying from a combination of police violence and mob justice. Students were uncontrollable. Communities in townships and villages were up in arms. Unbridled violence was the order of the day. The fight for a free and liberated South Africa had reached its climax.

The long struggle for freedom from Apartheid Rule was gaining strength. The frustration and pressure that had been bubbling underneath for so long and been burst open by the National Party Government's decision to enforce Afrikaans as a medium of education at schools. The Homeland Police, in all Provinces including General Sebe's own Ciskei, found themselves in the middle of the turmoil, having to defend the Apartheid structures within their borders –in many cases as the General himself was soon to find out, against their own families and friends. The period from 1976 up to 1988 saw South Africa and its 'independent homelands' facing the fiercest resistance. The people had grown weary of waiting on speaking peace and non-violence to a government that only responded in violence. This period and its deadly situation led to the declaration of two states of emergency. The new state of emergency developments saw the South African Police (SAP) and the South African Defence Force (SADF) being granted broad powers that ensured their immunity to prosecution for atrocities committed against anyone raising their indignation against the state.

To the ordinary eye, this meant that the constitution of the time had been temporarily suspended, without any clear indication of how long 'temporary' would be. The escalating situation put Sebe in an unenviable position among his boxers, some of whom were students deeply involved in the student movement. At this point, Sebe had long broken away from the Zwelitsha Boxing Club and opened his gym in his Tshatshu Village. But, unfortunately, political power challenges within his circles were also not making life any easier.

Community pressures and the political awareness of the boxing youth that Sebe was training were forcing changes of attitude towards him. They realised that the prevailing matters were beyond just boxing as a sport. The situation was now a matter of principle. Their relationship with him had now become a matter of political life or death. Simultaneously, another situation, which was to make bitterly hated in the East London and Mdantsane circles, was taking place. Welile Nkosinkulu, a brilliant speedster and knockout specialist from Mdantsane who had a cult figure following, had left his Mdantsane stable under his long time and highly regarded trainer Ntaba Welcome Mtyongwe.

He was now under the management of high ranking Policeman Willie Ncoko. The two Policemen Ncoko and Sebe were now in charge of Nkosinkulu's affairs. Sebe was the trainer. Nkosinkulu, at this stage, was a charismatic loudmouth who correctly predicted rounds in which he would knock out his opponents. But he was politically ignorant.

To him, the presence of police around him and driving expensive cars meant his status was of the highest level. Yet, curiously the political situation never bothered him. Not even when his lifetime manager and trainer Mtyongwe suddenly found himself being transferred to Peddie, allegedly on the instructions of General Charles Sebe.

With Peddie being about 90 kilometres from East London, this unexpected transfer meant that he was far away from his boxers and the world of boxing in general. The rumour mill was rife that Sebe had used his political power and influence to have Mtyongwe taken as far away from Nkosinkulu as possible. To add further fire to an already boiling pot, it was also at this stage that play and movie writer Ben Nomoyi saved local idol Nkosana Mgxaji from signing a long term promotional contract with Sebe and local promoter Wridge Qeqe. It is said he had driven at breakneck speed to King William's Town, where Nkosana Mgxaji was apparently being forced to sign the deal.

Needless to say, the boxer's boxing career took a tumble, and he started to lose fights against fighters who would never have been good enough to be his sparring partners. Mdantsane and East London boxing people never forgave General Sebe for that. It came as no surprise under the then political climate, and General Charles Sebe found himself being summoned to a meeting by his boxers. However, when he arrived, he may have been surprised to find that the gathering included all his boxers like Aycliff Stengile, Spokes Witbooi, Ruben Matewu, Elliot Bolani, his nephew Toni Sebe, Thamsanqa Mazaleni, other amateur boxers and club officials. He was informed of the prevailing political and social conditions that made it impossible for them to work with him. He was respectfully requested to leave the gym and allow them to look for somebody else to lead them. It was a sad day for all the boxers in the gym, as well as many members of the community.

To them, Sebe had served boxing selflessly and had changed the lives of a number of their kids. Moreover, he had paved the way for the region's people to do what they liked most and be among the best in the world.

Spokes Witbooi remembers that day and Sebe himself vividly as he said, 'It's fine boys, I'm doing my job, and unfortunately not even boxing that is in my heart can separate me from my job. So it's sad, but we can't help it. Go do your job perfectly, and may you get good people to guide you. Good luck, boys. And with that, he left and never came back. General Sebe was later killed by a bullet allegedly from a soldier of the Ciskei Defence Force. It is alleged that he was lured into an ambush operation orchestrated by the South African security forces in 1991, under the rule of new Ciskei Ruler General Oupa Gqozo.

CHAPTER 16

THE MAKING OF THE BOXING MECCA

DUNCAN VILLAGE is situated close to East London. Close by is West Bank. In 1913 parliament had introduced the Natives Land Act, which set aside about eight but no more than 13 percent of land in South Africa to be occupied by the black peoples of the country. Whites would occupy the remaining 90 percent. Black people were evicted from farms and other areas where they were staying and forced to stay in overcrowded and arid lands or into the cities. These areas have been historically used as labour reservoirs for the town and the white suburbs.

Duncan Village is close to East London as a reservoir of the white occupied suburbs. Within close proximity is West Bank. It comprised smaller townships that included Tsolo, Ndende, Moriva, Thulandivile, Emaxambeni, Gomoro and Site B. All these areas were so close to town people could walk to and from work every day. But others, like domestic workers, they lived in their masters' homes, and some were allowed to see their kids on weekends while others could only do so at the end month. A lot of fathers worked as garden boys while mothers worked as kitchen girls. There was, however, little or no communication with their kids. That brought about the situation where children grew up without the care of their parents.

When they got home, they came to a familiar situation consistent with black residential zones. The towns occupied by black people in South Africa bore the same resemblance of living conditions below what is generally described as poverty level. There were very few people that lived in what could be recognised as houses.

For the most part, people lived in small tin matchbox structures at the back of the yards of the few more affluent people, as tenants or as extended family. In summer, the houses were unbearably hot. In winter, the roofs and ceilings could not hold up to the cold conditions. There was no electricity. People depended on candlelight—the luckier ones afforded to buy paraffin lamps. There was only one community tap for water serving the whole street. It was the same with public toilets – *oomasijongane* – where one community toilet with several seats for people to line up and relieve themselves simultaneously. The numbers were growing every day as crowds of new people moved from the rural villages and flocked into the townships, searching for work and what they thought would be a better life.

Bread or homemade fat cakes, what locals know as *vetkoeks*, and tea were the daily meal until the end of the week. To others, it would be only at the end of the month when parents came back from work. The parents would then bring back with them some better food that included meat and vegetables. There was always not enough food to cater for the large numbers of people that, one way or another, always found themselves there and suddenly became part of the family.

Living conditions taught people to share whatever they had. The living conditions developed the values of UBUNTU. Values that originated and are based on the roots of interdependence – I am because you are.

Some people tried to make ends meet by selling sweets, fruit and fat cakes. Others went as far as selling *umqombothi*, which is also known as African beer. Police would come and arrest the owner as well as all people in attendance for illegal gatherings. They referred to the beer by the derogatory name *kaffir* beer, which had then been banned and carried a jail sentence if you were found to be in possession of it.

Weekends were always the time to look forward to. Gatherings that were pepped up by off the cuff traditional arts like music, dancing and off the cuff praise-singing were the main entertainment. Traditional songs that grow to be national and international hits were composed in such loose organisations. A lot of talent was discovered from these gatherings. Some were even picked up by agents from Johannesburg and had their natural gifts honed and exposed. Johannesburg was and still is the place to be if your talent is showcased for your benefit. It is the magnet of South African social life. Later, shebeens would spring up all over the place and take over the weekend lives of the people. This new phenomenon that was initially used as a watering hole for people soon became a place where other than drinking, people started discussing and debating many issues and challenges of life.

These conversations included politics, economics, religion and sports. *Shebeen* life started attracting teachers, preachers, politicians and sports people. It was also here that boxing took its position among other sports like rugby, cricket and athletics, as a topic for discussion.

AN UNEDUCATED PEOPLE

Education, initially introduced by the missionaries so that black people could read the bible and be converted to Christianity, had now evolved. For black people, it was strictly delivered through the Bantu Education system, which was specifically designed to ensure that whatever skills they learned meant they could only see and appreciate things through white man's eyes, speak good English and Afrikaans to serve whites the best way they could.

When Bantu Education was introduced, many black teachers resigned in disgust. One of those teachers happened to be Thamie Nomvete, a founding father of boxing in East London.

The school was, therefore, for this and other reasons not something everybody looked up to, and as such, a lot of kids would start attending, only to drop out within a few months. The streets were so cruel and dangerous there were tales of brutality, casualties and fatalities every weekend. There was so much smoking and alcohol abuse, especially among the youth, that venturing out in the evenings was at one's own risk. Parents always prayed and hoped that their kids would find something to occupy them and keep them away from the streets.

The danger that always loomed in the streets gave rise to street wisdom. From a young age, boys had to learn to look after themselves and their sisters and any family member or friend in need of protection. They had to be armed and prepared whenever they went out. The streets were abuzz with young boys who were going around looking for trouble.

There were knife experts who became bosses in their areas because they could win knife fights and could stab people in the blink of an eye. This led to street or area gang fights. Such conflicts were caused by disagreements that ranged from home turfs where boys from one area could not operate on another or disagreements about having girlfriends in the opposing area. When such gang wars raged, the different groups would use all sorts of opportunities to waylay one another, especially when one would be alone. They would be attacked and brutally stoned, and even stabbed to death on their way to or from school, relatives or cinema.

At the very same time, there was another kind of youngster growing up. These were street fighters who could fight expertly against the most brutal of thugs or criminals with their bare fists. They were not part of the criminal or uncontrollable elements, but they knew all the tricks. They then used their fighting prowess to protect their areas against criminals. They were bosses of their areas or townships.

Everybody knew who they were. The *tsotsis* avoided them at all costs. They could not mess with them or anybody connected to them. The names of these bosses that stood out when I came to East London were Ryan Manuel, Brics Gunuza and Boy Mandla. But the greatest of them all was Boysana, otherwise known as *Ouh*.

This type of life naturally led to petty crime as young boys developed from the lives of stealing small change at home to being full-time expert pickpockets and bag snatchers. To them, crime became a daily practice. And a way to make ends meet. During that period in the life of black people, landing in jail for a black man was something that could happen anywhere, anytime, anyhow. So being arrested for stealing from a white man carried no stigma.

Black people could only be in town during certain specified hours. The guys utilised the time allowed for black people in town to steal as much loot as possible from old white men and women. They became masters at opening the wallet and taking off the money while it was still in full possession of the owner. That exercise was executed with such impeccable speed and timing that the owner felt nothing amiss until it was time to pay at the shop, or when they got home.

Pick-pocketing and bag snatching became an art form that was mastered by only a few, the smartest on the streets. Some guys worked in groups and used their numbers to detract the victim. The numbers were also used to deter would-be pursuers in the event of being chased. Others, especially the smartest thieves, preferred to work with their girlfriends. There were also the special guys who wanted to do it alone. This style was their version of the politically originated one man one vote. As would be expected, a lot of them, however, ended up in jail.

The Apartheid authorities at the time regarded pickpocketing as a minor offence, especially where there had been no physical attacks, injuries nor damage to property. Such prisoners did not spend a lot of time in jail. They were hired out to boere farmers in mainly, the Orange Free State. After the duration of sentences, the jail authorities drove them back home to be released where they had been sentenced. But a lot of things also happened that resulted in many of them never returning home.

FINDING OUR IDENTITY IN BOXING CLUBS

Legend has it in the local boxing community of a gentleman who approached the Border Boxing Team that was competing in the South African championships in the late 1960s. The story has it that he greeted them in the well known greeting term among AmaXhosa when they meet in other Provinces – *molweni bakhaya*, which means hello homeboys.

He then proceeded to tell them of how he was arrested and, on beginning his jail sentence, he and other guys were transferred to the Orange Free State. From there they would be driven by truck to potato and other farms between Kimberly and Orange Free State where they worked as labours.

He said some of them had died, killed by the farmers for not doing a proper job. Others were still kept in the farms even after the sentence because they were very productive. He was one of those released still in good health and was sent back home where on arrival he found out that the whole family had been moved to Mdantsane. So rather than go looking for them he got a lift in a truck to Bloemfontein and found himself a job there. He now had a family and maybe he would go back to the Eastern Cape – one day.

A lot of boys lost their limbs and lives in gang warfares. There were always serious reports of domestic violence. Notwithstanding the paltry and deadly conditions, the people were organising themselves into street units and working on fostering solidarity among both the youth and elderly.

The gatherings included school teachers, musicians, teachers, preachers, politicians as well as sports people. It was such progressive interaction that resulted in some youth seeing the world through new better-informed eyes and ears. Political scouts from mainly the ANC and PAC, before and after they were banned continued to strengthen their underground political education especially among the youth.

The meetings were not official nor formal, but rather loose gatherings where every discussed issue was part of a conversation. They won over a lot of young and elderly recruits through their political teachings that were generally known or covertly referred to as umrhabulo. Sporting codes like rugby, netball and cricket gained recruits, while boxing, would be expected of a new sport that was winning the hearts of the people especially the youth, duly won a number of the young boys.

All over the world boxing has been known to come much easier to the poorer sections of society. It has been proved over time that it can produce world-class performers with less training equipment and less to no healthy nutrition. It was because of their less expensive requirements at the entry point that boxing and rugby became the main sports codes that appealed to these prominently black and to a lesser extent, coloured youngsters in these areas.

They started using every open space and later occupied empty or unused buildings in their areas or streets to start practising boxing. They would soon be venturing to halls and classrooms as the campaign for the game grew stronger. These groupings and structures were becoming boxing clubs. The attending members were becoming fully-fledged boxers.

They used empty milk cans or wrapped their hands with any soft material they could lay their hands on to protect themselves. Candles were used in the evenings for light. Punching bags were made from bags filled with soil, sand or sawdust. Elder people who got interested and volunteered to help the kids started organising leadership positions of manager, trainer or kit-man.

Challenges were sent to the neighbouring clubs for inter-club tournaments. The communities were becoming aware of the new sport, and parents noticed the new commitment that was taking over their sons. The boxing bug had stung, and things were never going to be the same. Surprisingly Queenstown had already been boxing for more than 30 years when East

London was formally introduced to the game and started practising. It came as no surprise then that the first set of boxing gloves was received when Sax Manuel, a musician from Queenstown moved to East London with his own set of gloves. He had done some little boxing in Queenstown and would only spend his stay in East London concentrating on music. He donated his gloves to the first boxing club he encountered – The International Boxing Club. The International Boxing Club, sometimes referred to as Peacock as it was quartered in Peacock Hall, was formed around 1960 and is credited as the first fully-fledged boxing club in East London. It was formed in what was called Tsolo Location and would lead the way in the development and awareness of boxing until the second club, Duncan Village Boxing Club was formed in neighbouring Mekeni Location. They became very strong and formidable rivals.

The success of the two clubs gave rise to a new challenge. There was such public enthusiasm and involvement that the cream of the crop among the boxers started looking beyond the amateur ranks into the professional spectrum.

The news abounded about professional boxers in other Provinces like Natal (now KZN), Transvaal (now Gauteng, Limpopo, Northwest, Free State, Eastern Province and Western Province.) The new crop of amateur stars had to turn professional. There was no official or legal structure in the area to carry professional boxing processes or duties. In the process of putting the game together, the boxing people had been introduced to a young white man who played Provincial cricket and rugby.

He inexplicably clicked well with the black folks at a time when it was unfashionable and dangerous. He was drawn easily enough into boxing and started assisting in the finer points like understanding the rules, drawing scorecards and organising transport, among other things. Soon he was a full member sharing everything with the newly found black friends as if there was no law against it.

Among the founders and organisers was school teacher Thamie Nomvete who became the first manager of the club while Sherlock Ngcobo became a trainer. Madyaka was later succeeded by businessman Mzoli Madyaka who would become the obvious choice as the manager of International Boxing Club's new professional boxers. Madyaka thus became the first manager and producer of Nkosana Mgxaji when the future legend turned professional.

It came to rest on Madyaka's shoulders to help turn the boxers professional. This process needs a fully-fledged boxing board with all the powers vested in it by, at that time The South African Boxing Act 11 of 1954. The payment of the actual license to fight as a professional is the last step after assessment to assure the fitness of the boxers to turn professional, as well as their physical and mental health. Madyaka drove the first four boxers in his car at his own expense to Durban where they went through and satisfied all the standard requirements to be allowed to turn professional. The boxers who made this history as the first professional boxers were Lawrence 'Slow Poison' Ndzondo, Cornet 'Bisto Kid' Dunjwa, Stanley Toni and Alesta Mahashe.

The stage was set for history to be made. Missing out on this history were three boxers who could not make the trip for different reasons. Stanford Ngoma died due to unexplained causes, while Samuel Tokwe also missed out and did not continue boxing. Gideon Vakala missed the trip as he had left the country for exile for political reasons. Vakala is now back home in retirement. After his return from exile worked a spell as an administrator in the Eastern Cape Premier's office.

Now it was time to organise the first tournament for the boxers to fight. Madyaka, Muller and all other officials at the time who included Thamie Nomvete, David Tshaka, Gilbert Gidana and Andrew Nkone decided it was time for the region to have its boxing board run its tournaments and officiate its fights rather than hire officials from other Provinces.

Among them were also youngsters like Peter Goodman, who engaged in one fight as a professional and retired, and Mahlubi Dunga who was not a boxer. They were keen to develop the sport and were always ready to organise and run amateur tournaments.

The laws of segregation that were devised to cover every aspect of the life of any human being residing in South Africa did not make things easy. Firstly the boxing people, except for Les Muller, were black.

South African laws did not allow for black people to hold positions of power or officiate in certain public events like boxing. It meant that they could neither form a board nor officiate as referees and judges in professional tournaments.

Secondly, there was only one white man available. As was in line with South African laws, the Border Boxing Board of Control, as it would be called had to consist of a white chairman who could be appointed only from the Judiciary, a white secretary and several white officials who would act as referees and judges for the new boxing area. It would include boxing places like East London, King William's Town and Queenstown, which were also already active in boxing towns and would be fielding their professional boxers in the not so far future. This was in line with the South African laws.

Thirdly Les Muller who was the obvious choice to lead boxing could not be chairman as he was not from the Military, Police nor Judiciary. He could only be secretary. And so he did, becoming the first secretary of professional boxing in the Border region. It was also left up to him to organise like-minded white friends to come and join him and help develop boxing in the region.

Muller delivered on his promise and in no time white officials Swanie Swanepoel, Piet Kruger, Piet Jacoby Snr, Piet Oberholster and the Van Zyl brothers became constant visitors in the township to referee and judge fights. Meantime in town boxing was also emerging. White boxers like Keith Kyle, Louis Olivier, Pietie Jacoby who had earlier been secretly training and sparring with black boxers in the township were regular visitors as they also prepared to turn professional.

The Border Boxing Control was finally given government recognition under the chairmanship of government-appointed Judge Kritzinger. It is now safe to say that when racial barriers were finally dismantled in South African boxing, the Border region had already been at it for years.

It is still ironic that BCM boxing has still not been able to attract white fans. There were a number of them coming by *kombis* and busses when fights were still held at Sisa Dukashe stadium in the 1970s. But the numbers died down after the Mgxaji reign when tournaments were taken to the smaller Orient Theater. Maybe it was the Mgxaji effect.

Olivier and Jacoby were good enough and were winning fights at Mdantsane, Zwelitsha and Ginsberg halls, but the white fans were not coming as would be expected. Some hopes were raised when a white female boxer came onto the scene with a combination of pressure and power punches that are usually what appeals to white fans. Such hopes were raised when another white boxer Giovanni Bushby who was managed by his father Giovanni Snr and strategically trained by the legendary fighter Vuyani Bungu, came onto the scene.

Bushby possessed a jab, smooth movement and rhythm seldom seen among white boxers. But it was soon noticeable that the white fans left after the white fighters fights. This made the promoters come up with a plan of delaying the white fighters' bouts until before the main fight. This strategy worked well until the fighters started to lose.

White fans did not come back – except for one.

Joyce Greyvenstein is the only white boxing fan who has been with boxing through thick and thin. Greyvenstein came into the scene just as Les Muller was disappearing due to ill health. Joyce has been a fight fan through and through without any interest in taking any part as an official. She attends all tournaments in Mdantsane, Duncan Village without fail, and has subsequently won the 2008 BSA Fan of the Year Award. But Buffalo City still does not have a white boxing fan base that it can boast of.

MUSHROOMING BOXING CLUBS

The two clubs in East London would reign around representing the Border region for years. The pounding of the bags, the clap of the gloves and the boxing rhythm reverberated far and wide. Extra-ordinarily there were already boxing clubs in Queenstown and Zwelitsha but the vibe reached fever pitch when East London joined and started trading blows. The emergence of Mdantsane took local boxing to International levels. There were more competition and boxing was growing.

The Duncan Village Community Centre and Zwelitsha Communal Hall became the main boxing venues for club fights as well as Provincial and National championships.

The venues became popular and would also automatically be the venues for professional boxing-that is until the emergence of Sisa Dukashe stadium and the Orient Theatre in East London.

The first boxers in that time who are recognised as the true pioneers included, but were not limited to Lawrence Ndzondo, Alesta Mahashe, Cornet Dunjwa, Stanley Toni, Lungisa Dukashe, Enoch Sigcawu and Jake Sikhundla. Simon Sali and Monde Mbangxa who turned professional later than the first five would arguably be the stars and first draw-cards of that era.

They would later be joined by Cyril Adams, the first boxer to win a National amateur championship from the area, Nkosana Mgxaji the star who is credited with popularising boxing in the Mecca. Not in any order of seniority, as some were still very junior, Isaac Boqwana, Andile Tywabi, Kotikoti Sophila, Thabo Moloko, Sheshe Dunjwa, Xolani Lwana, Sparara Qelile, Mzwandile Magadlela, Enoch Sigcawu, Howard Tikana, Mxolisi Mgidi, Start Matinjwa and a lot of others also put the boxing mecca on the map. They were now products of several clubs that had mushroomed in the Duncan Village location.

In later years, around 1970 two clubs would emerge from this now boxing mad town. Nompumelelo Boxing Club was formed by boxer Cornet Dunjwa. It became very successful and commanded a horde of new fans. New youngsters there included Phakamile Makepula who was to give birth to former triple world champion Hawk, Mzwandile Biyana, Tony Batala, Vuyani Holliday and the Majaja brothers. After Cornet left for Transkei the club was run by David Qotile as manager and Sheshe Dunjwa as a trainer.

The clubs would engage in what then were East London championships, Mdantsane championships and Border championships. And in or around 1972 the arrival of former world light heavyweight champion boosted local boxing. Such a welcome visit improved the training programs and skills development of the boxers and trainers. Archie Moore visited East London clubs and conducted boxing clinics.

Perhaps the club that gained the biggest boost from Moore's visit was a new one called ABC 'Any-Body-Can'. The phrase comes from Archie Moore life story in a book *"Any Boy Can"*, which later turned into a the slogan *"Anybody can."*

It was also the influence of and perseverance of David Tshaka that little clubs that started with two or three boys would grow and produce respectable boxers. Such clubs would develop and produce other splinter clubs mushroomed in all corners of Duncan Village.

This development produced amateur and professional star performers that played a big role in boosting the fortunes of East London and its districts. Among that group of stars in that era, Mzukisi Skweyiya and Tsietsi Maretloane would reach for the stars, winning National and International honours.

Highly regarded competitors that included the likes of Phakamile Makepula, Mxolisi Sodinga, Lulama Mthoba, Ntsethu Sikobi, Dick Pirie, Mongezi Nondabula, Thamie Spampool, Lundi Majangaza, Sam Somgxada,

Pinki Dyantyi, Lulama Lwana, Vuyo Nomvethe, Thembile Ganya, Luvuyo Vabaza, Pretty Petela, Joe Menziwa, Joe Gunuza, Nceba Nkinkqa, Sandisile Gocongo, Boy Peter, Thandi Hlobo, Mthobeli Jack and Lundi Skepu would also emerge across both old and new clubs.

That chain of events led to the discovery and production of later champions like legends Mzwandile Biyana, Ndoda Mayende, Tony Batala, Mbulelo Botile, Toto Mokorotlo, Gabula Vabaza, and future triple world champion Simphiwe Vetyeka. It was at this stage that perhaps the biggest drawcard among the amateur boxers emerged. His name was Papa Njova. He was not very gifted in terms of skills but was so entertaining his entertaining pranks and charm gained the attention of young and old who would flock to the venues to see him perform.

He won some and lost some. But they always came back for more. But among the boxers that emerged during that era, Mzwandile Biyana remains in my opinion, the most underrated BCM boxer I know.

This is also the period that produced the hardworking Mbeki brothers, David and Mpumelelo. After they moved from Nompumelelo, they formed the David Qotile Boxing Club, named after elder brother David before their surname changed to Mbeki. The formation of this club and its efforts started a string of prospects in this talent-laden township. Such a product included the likes of former IBF world Bantamweight champion Mbulelo Botile.

The highly popular Nompumelelo Boxing Club is also a result of that spiral of new clubs. Its results did not only centre on ring performances but also the administration of the game. It would go on and influence new club leaders and administrators like Lungelo Ngcaba, Mongezi Smith, Mongameli Goci, Small Menziwa, Mahlulo Ntamo, Mncedisi Mcilongo, and a whole lot of others.

Top class trainers like Koko Qebeyi, Mapetla Mzamo, Ben Mtyaliseko, Joe Menziwa, Mzamo Njekanye and Mlamli Nkonkobe are also products of this drive. Khaya Majeke is an accredited physical trainer who has added a lot of input to SASCOC's scientific training programs for all sports codes. Mongameli Goci, Mahlulo Ntamo, Small Menziwa and a whole lot of others are well-respected administrators in both professional and amateur codes.

Siya Vabaza Booi, the first South African woman to gain International recognition and officiate in international fights was a product of this powerful Duncan boxing drive. She is now among the best and most influential female drivers of boxing in the world. Her influence would also result in the production of her nephew, former world champion Gabula Vabaza who ruled the Bantamweight division here and abroad until an untimely sickness put paid to the dream.

It is also important to note that all these clubs were training with little or no boxing equipment. The best they could manage was candlelight, punching bags made of sand, old and always torn boxing gloves, as well as makeshift boxing rings made of the classroom desks where they used to train. The floor was always of cement. They were lucky if the roof had a ceiling.

The first world rated boxer Nkosana 'Happy Boy' Mgxaji who had his first boxing lessons at the Peacock Boxing Club was training at Dalukukhanya Primary School in Mdantsane at the time of the biggest and best conquests in his career. No one was more surprised by Mgxaji's training quarters than his opponent Panamian Antonio Amaya.

He was coming out of a loss against all-time great Roberto Duran for the world Lightweight championship. After visiting Mgxaji's training quarters he felt more confident that he would never lose to a boxer who did more cabaret training than boxing training. Imagine his surprise when Happy Boy completely out-boxed and outfoxed him. American Sammy Goss also got the same treatment and lost.

It was the same for our first world champion Welcome {Hawk}Ncita and Vuyani Bungu who trained at Bulumko Primary School for their fights under candlelight in rings made of chairs. Mbulelo Botile and Zolani Petelo would soon win the IBF Mini Flyweight and Junior Featherweight titles respectively.

Vuyani 'The beast' Bungu would later break the record of world title defences by a South African when he made thirteen defences of the IBF Junior Featherweight title. This is what made their achievements so special. As long as there were boys and milk cartons or cloth to wrap the hands there was boxing. It became the topic wherever two people or more gathered. They talked about boxing at work. Preachers in churches referred to boxing during their sermons. They discussed boxing in taverns. They debated boxing in schools. Girls ululated about and sang boxing songs even when playing netball. Cultural and traditional musicians sang boxing. Boys in the rural villages threw away their sticks and started boxing. There was boxing in the air. The Boxing Mecca was born.

MDANTSANE, THE BOXING MECCA

The period around 1955 is very significant to the people of Buffalo City because unknown and unforeseen to them a new identity and culture were beckoning in the form of boxing. Apartheid Rule's long term plans had suddenly intensified and would, unwittingly create space and location for a new challenge. Such independence brought about a wholesome change in their lives and the birth of special pride, courtesy of the growth and ultimate recognition of Mdantsane as one of the best known and most celebrated locations in the boxing world. The National Party was shifting from the initial approach of master and servant rule between its white people and their black counterparts that had been set by the Colonisers, to what they envisaged as a more diplomatic and acceptable way of segregation and domination.

The major part of the 13 percent of the land allocated to black people in the country would be divided into 10 homelands. Black people would be allocated to those areas according to mainly their tribal orientations. They would then be given some kind of authority and token sovereignty to run their affairs. This, they said, would lead to their independence.

Mdantsane Township, situated 15 kilometres from East London, 37 kilometres from King William's Town, happened to fall under what would be called the Ciskei homeland. The other side of the mainly Xhosa region across the Kei River, called Transkei was given its authority. The name Mdantsane is derived from the stream that runs from Nahoon River down to the Buffalo River. Some believe the stream was called Dozane.

In 1960 people were removed from the Duncan Village areas to Mdantsane. This political exodus was done through the Apartheid Laws of the Group Areas Act where blacks were now being moved as far away from their white counterparts as possible. By 1963 about 12 500 families were already moved and settled at NU1.

UNITED BOXING, the first formal boxing club in Mdantsanne was formed at Mzimkhulu Primary School in NU 1 by a group of young boxers like Christopher 'Gaw'leshiya' Xokolo and Putye. They named it United Boxing Club. They included Mqotyana and Alfred Sizani, who would respectively become two of the most prominent amateur and professional ring officials in the country. The aim was to introduce boxing to Mdantsane and spread it far and wide. The club United Boxing Club immediately produced star amateurs like Solomon 'Axe Killer' Nojanga, Guy 'Dirty Boy' Ratazayo,

Mxolisi Madushela, Boy Putye and a young Daluxolo 'Smallboy' Tyekana, Dolly Bangiso and Balisa 'Sugar Basin' Molao. Thembisile Gacula, who later changed his surname to Ngumbela, also a product of this gym was to develop and be a pioneer of amateur boxing in the region, along with other amateur administrators like Andile Mofu, Boyboy Mpulampula and Vuyolwethu Mtekwana, they played an important role in changing the political direction of South African amateur boxing, now referred to as Olympic style or Open boxing. Gacula became the first product of the Eastern Cape to qualify as an international referee.

United is also well known as the club that nearly destroyed the great career of Welile Nkosinkulu from the beginning. This after one of its prospects Nkosana Tolbert was chosen as Nkosinkulu's debut opponent. Tolbert scored one of the biggest upsets in BCM when he pole-axed Nkosinkulu with a deadly haymaker in the first round.

Nkosinkulu would return later and carve his name as one of the most popular boxers this country has ever seen. Tolbert never retained that form. He retired a few years later with a good story to tell.

YAKUZA BOXING CLUB would be formed later by Guy Ratazayo. He had decided to move away and create more space. With him were bright young amateurs like Mbulelo Katywa who became the club's first professionals. Mandlenkosi Jakavu became one of the initial trainers of the gym before he became part of the formation of boxing against crime and later Xaba Boxing Club.

RISING STARS BOXING CLUB was another offspring of United BC. It was veteran professional Kotikoti Sophila, Luyanda Kana and Small Boy Tyekana who decided to make the move. They settled at Nkululeko Higher Primary where the club became a big local drawcard with popular amateurs like Luyanda Kana and Phopho Mejane.

Kana would later receive a Presidential pardon and walk out of jail free man. He is now a well respected and BSA award-winning Matchmaker, while also still holding a special interest in following the lives of ex-offenders and helping where he can. He works under the motto Asimanga siguqula ubomi.

INTERNATIONAL BOXING CLUB - As Mdantsane grew bigger and bigger, so did the formation of new boxing clubs as they started mushrooming from unit to unit. Some members of the Peacock Boxing club who had moved to Mdantsane from Tsolo Location formed the new International Boxing Club at Primary School in NU3. Its first boxers under trainer Welcome Mtyongwe were the great Nkosana 'Happy boy' Mgxaji, tall Bantamweight Thabo Moloko, Junior Lightweight Joseph Mnyabiso and promising Lindile Gangala.

Wongalethu High School Deputy Principal Makhunga Mvalo became a very vocal and respected manager of the club. Also with Mgxaji, was Mahlubi Dunga. Wherever there was Nkosana Mgxaji there was always Dunga working underground. He never really had a noted position but was very influential in Mgxaji's affairs. Some people called him a Project Manager. In no time the club produced star performers like Joseph Mnyabiso, Welile 'Ali' Nkosinkulu, Zweli 'Sugarcane' Ngcongolo, Cosmo Ziqu, Mlungwana Mgxaji, Lindile Gangala, Fikile Ngubelanga, Jacko Qabaka and Victor Fata. Nkosinkulu and Ngcongolo developed to be two of the best known knockout specialists in the country.

They both had long spells ruling the Bantamweight and Junior Featherweight divisions until they were forced by public demand to meet. At that time they were no longer club-mates as Nkosinkulu had moved from the International Boxing Club. Ngcongolo knocked Nkosinkulu out

GOLDEN GLOVES BOXING CLUB was formed by members of the old Duncan Village Boxing Club a few months later in Dumisa Primary School nearby. It was formed by ex-boxer Monde Mbangxa and trainer Shellock Ngcobo with a group of boxers that included Andile 'Jumbo Jet' Tywabi and Sithethi Mlombo. The first manager was school teacher Mr Marawu who would also lead the growth and development of amateur boxing in the region. Lennox 'Boyboy' Mpulampula, a star amateur was later to inherit the club and lead it to International status. It would go on to produce star performers like Mzukisi Skweyiya, Mlulameli Caleni, Monde Mpulampula, Zola Lawuse, Mava Malla, Khulile Radu, Elliot Zondi and Mabhuti Gwavu.

I joined the club after I was recruited by Boyboy and I turned pro under the management of former boxing star Monde Mbangxa who was already managing the career of Mzukisi Skweyiya. Later I moved to join the African Youth Boxing Club under Mzoli Madyaka. Skweyiya and I later met and trained together at Fort Hare University. We won the South African titles. Skweyiya won the Bantamweight while I won the Junior Middleweight title. On leaving Fort Hare after the 1976 schools boycott we decided to form our separate clubs. Meantime in Golden Gloves hard-working Boyboy developed to be a star trainer in both amateur and professional ranks. He became the first black trainer of TEAM SOUTH AFRICA in the 1996 Olympic Games. Among his proteges, as a leader in amateur boxing, are stars that included Ludumo Galada who soon won the Baby Champs and South African Featherweight titles as a professional before his untimely death.

Also among such stars was Phumzile Matyila who also won the SA Bantamweight title. Matyila is now a successful trainer of boxers and together with Mhikiza Myekeni and Zolile Tete, we are trainers at the All Winners Boxing Club owned by Mlandeli Thengimfene. Mpulampula's younger brother Monde became one of the stars of the gym. Mava Malla would become the first black CEO after the demise of the Apartheid Regime in 1994. He thus became the first boxer to achieve that feat.

Khulile Radu also became the first black chairman of the Border Boxing Commission. He currently serves as a member of the Boxing SA. The club has also produced new talent in the form of trainers. Ncedo Cecane and Luvuyo Sovasi are in the current crop as highly respected trainers in South African boxing. Mabhuti Gwavu is an academic and a long-distance runner. He says that the roadwork he did for his boxing contests as a youngster prepared him for this.

MODERN BOXING CLUB was formed by Mzukisi Skweyiya on returning to Mdantsane after being expelled from Fort Hare University due to the 1976 schools boycott. Mzukisi opened the boxing club at NU 8 and requested Boyce Zitumane to join and lead the club. Boyce Zitumane, the son of businessman and promoter Norman Zitumane, joined the club and became its manager and promoter.

Ibholomane, as Boyce was affectionately known, became a legendary boxing promoter and made the club one of the star attractions in both amateur and professional boxing codes. Zitumane was assisted by boyhood friend Dan Khetsi who as acted as a matchmaker and facilitator among, other things in all of Zitumane business activities.

The club became a legendary producer of champions like Thamsanqa Sogcwe and Mveleli Luzipho, and long after it had dismantled, the cream of the club moved to Eyethu, the club remained vibrant. This was mainly because its co-founder and promoter Boyce Zitumane was very hard working and popular – certainly one of the promoters who made the Mecca. Notable names like Mannetjie Nqezo, Vuyani Gxashe, Mongz Landu and David Gqamlana, and now Prof. Nceba Gqaleni and lawyer Ntsikelelo Manyisane have cut their teeth here and being proud products of this effort.

Later Luzipho and trainer Stephen Sam, leading a very strong contingent of amateur stars and new professional prospects that could be guessed at about ninety-five percent of the club, were very instrumental in the movement to Eyethu Boxing Club and the subsequent formation of Eyethu Boxing Club by Mzi Mnguni. The club rose to heroic standards as it produced champion after champion in the likes of Welcome Ncita, Vuyani Bungu, Hawk Makepula, Lindi Memani, Zolani Petelo and Mbulelo Botile and a large number of National champions.

AFRICAN YOUTH BOXING CLUB, also by former members of the old International Boxing club who had moved to Mdantsane, was formed at Mzoli Madyaka's house a few paces away. This club would produce among others popular stylist Tsietsi Maretloane, one of BCM's all-time greats who would later be the first South African boxer to win the newly introduced Old Buck belt. That belt remains the most prestigious belt in the history of South African boxing, and one of the most esteemed in the world.

African Youth Boxing Club is also where I won the South African Junior Middleweight championship. Highly respected Jack Jim, Fezile Maki, Wonga Lawuse, Mlulameli Caleni and Tito Dastile are also products of that gym. So is Light Heavyweight Prince Tukani, in my opinion, one of the best boxers never to win a National title. From Madyaka I was to learn the fundamentals of what would be not only my legacy but all those I came across in boxing. It would make this story.

These first four clubs in Mdantsane would form a strong competition and rivalry that would boost the love, involvement and awareness of boxing in the region to unparalleled levels for years. This exodus gave birth to new boxing clubs in Mdantsane and made the township so strong and formidable that it would challenge Big Brother Duncan Village and force a strong and fierce, but positive rivalry between the towns.

So intense was the competition that fights between both pro and amateur boxers from these two towns became special events that brought the whole of East London to a standstill. It got the attention of both males and females, young and old, as well as working and schooling alike. Boxing became the main conversation at homes, schools, busses, taxis, trains, churches and shebeens alike. This was around the time I introduced myself in the boxing circles of what was going to be the Mecca of Boxing. And introduce myself I did in the loudest of ways – with my fists. The seventies and eighties can be credited as the period when the spiraling of boxing clubs reached fever pitch in Mdantsane. The boxing craze was continuing across the length and breadth of the township in schools, car garages and beer halls. No empty building was left unused. Every unit started to have its gym. Competition became very stiff in club fights and championships. Clubs started producing prospects and star performers. Boxing fans identified with boxers living in their areas and followed them. The bragging rights had begun.

THEMBALETHU BOXING CLUB was started at NU2 by amateur LightHeavyweight Mxolisi Lubambo, and amateur boxing administrators Dan Kawa and Koko Godlo who later left to form Zimele Boxing Club.

They were joined by boxers Mzwandile Silwana and Sinda Ndlovu became the first products and reached high local amateur performers. Ncamiso Mfukuso took over the club and became the longest-serving manager until the club disbanded.

Former South African Featherweight champion Jackie Gunguza started his career here and developed to be one of the most popular boxers in the region. Under Mfukuzo, who was affectionately known as Press, the club also produced the Phike twins who started as very highly thought of prospects but soon disappeared. Memories of dynamic performers like Jomo Mpahla and Ntsikelelo Kato forever remain in people's minds. International referee and judge Andile Matika, and solid professional boxer Victor Sonaba also started their careers here while jumping between Wongalethu High School and the club. Sonaba would later meet and join forces with lifetime manager Peter Qamba.

Thembalethu Boxing Club is also where Velile Damoyi started his boxing career before moving to Zimele Boxing Club. He later joined me in Zama Boxing Club where he exhibited excellent skills that stamped him as a solid Welterweight contender before retiring and concentrating on youth development. He is now a well trained and well experienced amateur coach and a consistent member of the ECABO BOXING TEAM.

Zolile Tete also started his boxing career at Thembalethu before moving to United Boxing Club. He built a respectable record before retiring and concentrating on work. His sons Makazole and Zolani took over the baton and joined the lines of other youngsters attending the local Community Hall at NU12 under the curatorship of long-serving boxing developer Simphiwe Sinyabi.

Under Sinyabi the boys would develop into seasoned amateurs before turning professional. They are now experienced and proud owners of boxing awards, a gym and massive sponsorship. Makazole is a former South African Flyweight champion while Zolani is the current WBO World Bantamweight champion. Proud father Zolile Tete is working in the All Winners gym as a trainer.

Sinyabi would go on to produce several prospects and national champions that included his nephews, Sizwe Sinyabi is a former two time South African Junior Flyweight champion while Former South African Junior Featherweight champion and world contender Macbute Sinyabi is a firm fan favourite. Currently, Simphiwe Sinyabi is a boxing promoter. His tournaments mainly feature newcomers and upcoming prospects for development purposes.

At the club in WONGALETHU HIGH SCHOOL under the school Principal, Makhunga Mvalo were professional boxers Mzwandile Mqanto and Lindile Gangala under the management of school teacher Wilbur Sibali. They were training in a classroom.

They later left to join the International Boxing Club where Nkosana Mgxaji was working under trainer Welcome Mtyongwe. At the time Mtyongwe himself was still an active boxer. He applied both duties of training Mgxaji as well as being his chief sparring partner.

Mvalo and Sibali became Mgxaji's managers in successive periods. Mqanto took over the sparring duties and became Mgxaji's chief sparring partner. He became a solid Welterweight contender. Mzwandile Mqanto is now a successful lawyer and still retains a keen interest in boxing.

HIGHLIGHT BOXING CLUB in NU5 is well known because of the flamboyant and hardworking Pamastone Ntanga. But the founders of the club were boxers Seawater Jonas and Nkosana Ziqu. Its boxing stars were entertaining pressure fighter Mandla Booi, Lulama Mthoba, Vuyani Hanabe, Tla Mjo, Zuko Mtyongwe and crunch puncher Saxon Ngqayimbana. It is now under the capable hands of astute manager Panki Mjele and has produced among others, former SA Flyweight Champion Vuyisile Bebe, and one of the first female boxers in the Eastern Cape Bomkazi Klaas

EYETHU BOXING CLUB is, without a doubt, the most successful boxing club in the Eastern Cape. It was formed at NU 8 by businessman Mzi Mnguni after he was approached by boxers who had left Boyce Zitumane's Modern Boxing Club. They were led by trainer Stephen Sam. He opened his gym at Bulumko Primary School and started what was to be a world champion producing and globally renowned gymnasium.

At the time of their approach star boxer, Mveleli Luzipho was preparing for his rematch to reclaim the SA Junior Flyweight title he had lost to the great Baby Jake Matlala a few months earlier. Mnguni approached me to train Luzipho for the grudge match, as well as to do the initial programming and training of the club as a whole. I was already a successful and well-respected trainer, manager, matchmaker, promoter and ring announcer at the time when I had my gymnasium. I spent my time between his gym and mine. We continued together making defences of the title while simultaneously using the voluntary periods to take international flights.

Luzipho won all those fights until he lost by knockout in a WBA world title eliminator to Jose de Jesus. My agreement with Eyethu ended at that point. Luzipho was to lose the title to my boxer Odwa Mdleleni.

At the time of Luzipho's loss, the club had already been brewing many prospects that included Welcome Ncitha, Mzwandile Ncitha and a whole lot of others. Ncitha would go on and be the first world champion from the Eastern Cape, as well as the first champion produced by Golden Gloves. Vuyani Bungu, who gained experience as Ncitha's sparring partner won the IBF Jniour Featherweight title from Ncitha's conquerer and broke the defence record of a world title held by HOF world champion Brian Mitchell.

A whole lot of South African champions who later became world champions followed. They were Mbulelo Botile, Hawk Makepula, Zolani Petelo, and Lindi Memani. Former amateur star and South African Bantamweight champion Phumzile Matyila is now a successful trainer. Former South African Flyweight champion Jaji Sibali is now training boxers in Cape Town. Mzidi Dintsi is also a respected trainer of youngsters.

Bright prospects from Eyethu who showed much promise but, for some reason, never made it to the top include Ella Mfene, Mzwandile Ncitha, Mlamli Xhanga, and Malume Xhathasi. Dudu Bungu, whose brother Vuyani's success made it difficult for fans to appreciate his qualities must rate as one of the best boxers in the country never to win a National title.

His heavy burden was made so much heavier in that when the chance for him to finally challenge for the title, the title was in the hands of Zolile Mbityi, he had an awkward style and fast hands, and perhaps one of the best unsung champions this country has produced. Their twelve rounds of relentless and sometimes cruel local derby remain one of the most hectic brawls at the Orient Theatre. Young Bungu was well prepared. He put it all together but Mbityi was near unbeatable at the time.

Welsh Mnguni is one of the products, or call that producer of the gym. A nephew to legendary manager Mzi, Welsh was always the man working behind the scenes. Welsh was one of the brightest minds of boxing, with a splendid ability to perfect boxers styles and map out the strategy for fights. His mostly unsung qualities made boxing club Eyethu, the champions and his uncle Mzi what they are in boxing. Welsh made us too. Currently, Eyethu is under the management of astute academic Sihle Mnguni who has led the club in the absence of brother and founder Mzi.

Under Sihle's leadership' and top trainer Ncedo Cecane, but now without the support of Golden Gloves Promotions, the club has continued to produce new champions Phila Mpontshane, Xolisa Magusha, Aphiwe Mboyiya and Xolani Mcotheli. Perhaps as long as Eyethu Boxing Club exists the Mecca must always be assured of champions. The success of the club certainly makes it and Nick Durandt's gym the biggest producers of champions ever in South Africa.

ZAMA BOXING CLUB was the club that was to be directly and indirectly involved in creating and nurturing almost all heroes of boxing that emerged in the Border region after its formation. It made boxers, managers, trainers, promoters and ring officials. Almost all of them have a story to tell about this club, which became part of their successful careers and lives. I formed it at NU 2 with the assistance of legendary rugby player Patsa Matyeshana and my friend Welcome Mankumba. Matyeshana approached, on our behalf, the Principal of my old Mzomhle High School Mr Ben Thengimfene for a classroom to train. We later moved to the swimming pool in NU2.

In the beginning, I had my brother Nyingi, Mlulameli Caleni, Odwa Mdleleni who used to carry my kit, Vuyani Mbinda, Mxhosana Jongilanga, Clive Skhwebu, Andrew Matyila, Mthuthuzeli Thafane, Luyolo Mpofu,

Mpush Makambi, Ponto Mandela, now an advocate in the SANDF and all the youngsters who used to chase me when I did my roadwork every day. This day I stopped and told them we would run all the way to the gym. The Siko brothers Ncedile, Mayizole, Mthetho and Foreman, who were going to be a great force in boxing were also part of this group. They would later be joined by youngest brother Andile, who is now a respected imbongi and ingcibi.

It was the time we were allowed to do everything at the same time as long as we had the ability. So I became a manager, trainer, matchmaker, Ring announcer and later obtained my boxing license as the owner of Messiah Boxing Promotions named after my nickname. My club became one of the toughest competitors in the region, winning a string of regional, professional and national championships.

As a boxer, I had enjoyed and gained some of the best lessons on the skills and strategies of both training and fighting from the guys I regard as the original people of boxing. Lambert Dukashe was like a professor of boxing. He was more at home discussing the finer points, the do's and don't's and the why's and why not's of boxing. From him, I learned the basics and the finer points of the game.

Andile Tywabi was like a working machine. In his days as a fighter, he had been an energetic high voltage pressure fighter who threw punches in bunches. In the ring, there was no quiet period for him. He believed a Flyweight boxer should throw no less than two hundred and fifty blows per round. And he did just that. It was a style he wanted to instil in his boxers.

Cyril 'Old Bones' Adams was a master southpaw. As the first boxer in the region to win a South African championship in the amateur ranks, this made him the first champion ever in the region. Adams was perhaps the first southpaw of note in the region, and certainly one of the best. From him, I picked up massive information about the mind of the southpaw and fight tactics off the southpaw stance.

When I started my gym my mentors were no longer as available as before. But my different spells with them was a time well spent. I was a complete outfit as a trainer. I settled for former amateur boxer Kali Vishile to assist me to train the boys.

We also had the services of bright youngster Phumlani Mkolo who, though not an active boxer himself, had a keen interest and natural skill in setting up the game plan for fights. Mkolo would later grow up to be a seasoned and effective politician in the new government.

We would later be joined by the likes of Nkosohlanga Matshoba and Xolani Sirhunu, who were tough and bruising competitors. Also in our stable we had tricky southpaws Victor Mkhohlakali and smoothies like Nceba Dladla, Nqaba Govuza and his brothers Solly and Mlondolozi. Phila Kali, a devastating puncher became the first real drawcard of the club. Future champions like charismatic southpaws Mthobeli Mhlophe and devastating puncher Luvuyo Kakaza and his friend Mncedisi Dapo headed for Zama Boxing Club. Phumzile Dubase, a star amateur is now a respected boxing contributor and commentator. The coloured community has always been represented, though in small numbers than would be expected from such a boxing mad region. Desprough Rigney was the first Border Heavyweight champion. He won the title in stopping favourite Pietie Jacoby in the seventh round, thus becoming the first boxing champion from the coloured community of East London.

Mullen Marillier, also from the coloured community started as a boxer but later did not feel like getting into the ring to fight. He ended up being a good sparring partner for my champions as well as my advisor. The Zama club gained legendary achievements and became a nightmare to competitors. Indian boxer Lesley Naidoo started but his family business stood in the way and allowed him very little opportunity to continue boxing.

My brother Nyingi became my first champion when he won the Eastern Cape Junior Lightweight title. He was followed by Odwa Mdleleni in winning the SA Junior Flyweight title from Mveleli Luzipho. The Featherweight title followed with Mxhosana Jongilanga knocking out Gerald Isaacs in Gauteng. And the flood gates were opened. One of the most talented and attractive drawcards to come out of the region Mthobeli Mhlophe won the SA Junior Lightweight title by stopping the widely popular and highly competitive Jackie Gunguluza, Andrew Matyila won the SA Flyweight title from durable and power punching Jaji Sibali, while Mpush Makambi had to travel to Johannesburg to beat Johannes Malaza for the South African Junior Middleweight title.

Makambi was to later win the IBO world Super Middleweight title, under Mathemba Nyakathi. At around this time, the great Nkosana Mgxaji joined the club to be trained because in his words he wanted the last fight and I will not retire with a loss. So I want you to train me for this last fight.

I trained him for his last fight against tough Gauteng Rocky Mabaso. He won impressively and blew kisses to the crowd before he left the ring, after arguably the greatest and most legendary boxing campaign in the Eastern Cape Province. And true to his word that was his last fight. He did not retire with a loss. Khulile Makeba was the last of what I call my homebred champions. At this time we had Bonisile Tofi, generally known as bra Tee who, along with Nick Durandt and Willie Lock rate as the three best hand wrappers in the country. A clever and shifty southpaw, Makeba threw some of the best combination punches and the most unpredictable moves known from the southpaw stance.

He had good balance and an amazing work rate seldom seen among southpaws. He already had weight problems when he won the elimination to challenge for the SA title. Yet he was able to defend the title seven times before losing it and going straight from strawweight to challenge and win the SA Bantamweight title by knockout over Cedric Conway.

Patrick Quka, one of the best southpaws I have had the pleasure of training and watching was already a former SA Bantam and WBU world Bantamweight champion when he joined the stable. We helped him regain his SA title in a challenge against champion Sandile Sobandla whom he beat decisively in Cape Town.

He would later lose the title in his next defence in Port Elizabeth.

The club would also be joined by Welcome Ncitha for his last two fights that he drew in South Africa against Steve Robinson and lost to Lizzaraga in Miami, USA respectively.

Presently a large number of my ex-boxers are senior citizens and fathers serving in different portfolios in both the private and business sectors. My brother Nyingi now lives with his family and works in Britain. Mdleleni, Caleni, Mpofu and Makambi are senior officers in the South African National Defence Force.

Ponto is now Adv Mandela in the SANDF. Former school teacher Mxhosana Jongilanga is a government administrator. Nqaba Govuza is currently a school teacher. Nkosohlanga Matshoba serves as an administrator in the Eastern Cape Department of Sports Arts and Culture. Nceba Dladla has among his achievements that include the Ministry of Religion, is now a Service Provider for the Boxing SA office in Port Elizabeth.

YONWABA BOXING CLUB was founded by a group of boxers who

had broken away from the Zama Boxing Club. They included Mthobeli Mhlophe, Nceba Dladla, Nqaba Govuza, Nkoyi Matshoba and trainers Kali Vishile and Malizole Siko. The club did not last long as about two years later a lot of the star boxers soon left to join other clubs and promotions.

A large number of young amateur prospects soon left to join the club an active Enothole gym that was run and headed by hard-working boxing promoter Siphatho Handi. Among them were future world champions Nkosinathi Joyi and Mhikiza Myekeni. Joyi is still active as a former SA and IBF mini flyweight champion while Myekeni is one of the brightest upcoming trainers in Buffalo City.

ZAKHELE BOXING CLUB was founded at NU 1 by Cisko Mboniswa and a few other people of the neighbourhood. The club became very competitive with entertaining sluggers like Madondo Mpulampula and highly popular Fudumele Mbovane who later became a solid people's representative in his area and later a respected politician in the Buffalo City Municipality.

ZIMELE BOXING CLUB was founded in NU 2 by Koko Godlo, a former amateur boxer who would later team up with Monwabisi Guwa to form a powerful promotion under the name Real First Team Promotions.

Acting as boxing promoters Godlo and Guwa, became pioneers of boxing promotions in Buffalo City, opening doors that had historically been closed to black people. The club produced respected contenders Vuyani Mngxaso, Sixuli Madondile as well as the Nyangiwe brothers, Goodman and Goodstuff. Ntsikelelo Mona. After retirement, Mona went on to become a notable trainer in boxing.

Guwa and Godlo would later make history in the region by becoming the first promotion to organise boxing events at the East London City Hall and Orient Theater. The two venues were only events organised for white people and attended only by white people. Events held at those halls were mainly of arts and drama. Boxing was never intended to be part of the menu of events to be held there. That is until Michael Guwa approached the then East London Mayor and presented the case of boxing and the venue challenges the boxing promoters were encountering at the time. They kept their connection to the club active until it disbanded with the retirement of its popular boxers. The Orient theatre was to be arguably the most popular boxing venue in South Africa.

LUKHANYO BOXING CLUB was formed by ex-boxer Spokes Witbooi

who had just retired because of personal reasons but did not want out of the game. He came as one of the best and most vocal trainers Eastern Cape has ever produced. A strong disciplinarian and strategist, Spokes was later joined by Ndyebo Vumindaba and they worked together until Vumindaba left the gym to join Top Stars.

Under Witbooi's guidance popular drawcards as Thembile Lubisi and polished performers like SA Bantamweight champion Simphiwe Pamana were unearthed, as well as Warren Stelle. Lonwabo Makhwekhwetha Witbooi looks like he is taking up the baton. After an eventful start as an amateur, the son decided that trading the gloves was not for him and decided to serve the game differently. He is now a boxing analyst and manager. His talents have resulted in him receiving a nomination for Boxing SA Manager of the Year. Looks like there is more to come. So has ex-professional boxer Sithembele Tom who is fast developing into a respected referee and judge.

LUVO BOXING CLUB was formed by ex-national rugby player Menzi Nqodi. When he came to Mdantsane from his rural Kwelerha home he became a regular in my club in the company of then SA Featherweight champion Mxhosana Jongilanga. They grew up together. My boxers called him 'Bodyguard'. Later when he told me he had learnt enough about the game to open his gym. I was more than willing to support his dream.

Boys were approaching him in NU 15 where he was staying. They wanted to start boxing. He believed it would be his way of keeping them in line and away from the streets. We gave him a few boxing gloves and a punching bag, and he was gone. He teamed up with knowledgeable boxing fan Jack Nxitywa. And together they formed a formidable team. A few months down the line they were challenging any club, including mine.

Nqodi and Nxitywa produced awkward and popular Zolile Mbityi who won the SA and WBU world Flyweight title and several prospects that included tough Leo Dyakopu. In the process, new trainers and boxing officials were developing in the club. One of the trainers Dowie Mzini also grew to legendary status among the trainers BCM, especially after the passing of Nqodi.

Among his products were former SA and WBU Bantamweight champion Patrick Quka and polished performer Neo Seboka. Ring Official of the Year 2018 winner Phumeza Zinakile, female Ring Official, also learned her ropes from this club.

TOP STARS BOXING CLUB was formed by boxing enthusiast Bonisile Magugwana and his friend Ndyebo Vumindaba in NU 13. It produced crowd pullers like the amateur star and professional world champion Sakhumzi Mgxwalisa, former SA champion Phindile Ngingi, Mzukisi Marali and Zolani Marali - who are brothers. The club also produced the tough contenders Likhona Ciki as well as competitive amateurs like Malibongwe Shiyani and others who never turned professional. Lanky southpaw Zolani Marali won all available titles except for the world title. He is still a firm fan favourite even after his fighting days.

Magugwana also took a license as a promoter and promoted development tournaments in places as far as Indwe near Queenstown. Here he unearthed a lot of local talent including promoter Mabandla who would develop to be a formidable fight organiser in the Eastern Cape Province. Magugwana would later lose a large amount of money as a promoter when he gambled his whole pension fortune on a boxing tournament. The newly formed WBO had given the green light for Magugwana's fighter Zolani Marali to fight for its vacant Junior Flyweight title. Much against the advice of Les Muller and a lot of other experienced boxing people Magugwana took the ill-advised decision to promote the event out of his pocket and without as much a cent as sponsorship. Marali won the title, but the tournament on the other hand was a financial disaster. Magugwana lost out, disappeared, and was never seen in boxing circles again.

SISONKE BOXING CLUB was formed by Makhaya Filita at NU7 while on the other hand, he was busy working with other boxing administrators, trainers and managers, forming ECABO the new amateur boxing body of the democratic era. Among his first boxers who performed successfully at the highest level of South African boxing were Zandisile One Two Dyonashe, Mbuyiselo Xokolo, Mawethu Skweyiya, Lulama Mthoba and Thembekile Kutta. Mandla Ntlanganiso went on to serve in different portfolios of boxing in Cape Town, but perhaps his biggest achievement was when was appointed as a member of Boxing SA.

ALL STARS BOXING CLUB was formed around 1979 by pro boxer Pretty Petela and Dingaan Somtsora.

When they left Mdantsane and returned to East London amateur boxer Gqo Mahambi took over the club in 1984. He approached boxing fan and salesman Galelekile Botha to be a club manager. Together they produced boxers like Mbeko Dayile, Siseko Mabusela and Vukile Sheleni, Thembekile

Blaweni, Dumisani Bizani and Madose Ngozi.

Bra Gqo or inja yeGame, as he is affectionately known later left and trained future SA Middleweight champion Mbulelo Popla Mxokiswa. It was there that I approached him to be my assistant trainer.

Mahambi soon developed to be one of the best conditioners and strength trainers in the country. Among the success stories he has trained one can count champions Khulile Makeba, Zolani Tete, Mkazole Tete, Patrick Quka, Macbute Sinyabi and a lot of up and coming prospects in Buffalo City and Gauteng. He currently runs his fitness gym in NU 12.

PHILANI BOXING CLUB was opened at NU7 by Danile Nzimela, then president of the Border Amateur boxing body preceding MDABO and ECABO, current promoters Mlungisi Siyo and Koko Godlo, as well as the Mgijima brothers. This group of amateur leaders were succeeding the initial group of boxing developers that were led by Mr Marawu. All of them would form part of the team that founded ECABO.

Philani produced the likes of Boyboy Mgayi, Mxolisi Galada, Denqe Witbooi, Luvuyo Tyamzashe and Lulama Tyamzashe and the legendary Ali Funeka. It has lately produced record-breaking Ntlantla Tyirha, the first boxer to win the National title in only his third fight.

DOWNTOWN BOXING GYM was opened by well trained martial arts and skills expert Vuyani Madikane, as the second black manager to have his club in town after Mzi Mnguni. The gym's state of the art equipment attracted not only boxers but also all kinds of fitness seekers.

Champions like Zolani Tete and Lindile Tshemese and Siphosethu Mvula also used the gym to prepare for upcoming fights, while prospects like Siphosethu Mvula and Nkosikhona Spelimandla were groomed here. So did the amateur boxing wing ECABO who often used the gym for boxers and trainers' workshops.

The gym is now used as a part restaurant and part entertainment but still using boxing as its main theme with a ring in the centre that is mainly used for amateur boxing on Thursday evenings.

It is a thriving success and the place to visit for both young and elderly whenever one needs a treat of some boxing, music and African food in this now new student village in downtown East London.

ALL WINNERS BOXING CLUB is one of the new kids on the block,

All-Winners is determined to do just that – produce an army of winners and keep winning. Founded by Mlandeli Thengimfene and Zolani Tete after Tete returned to East London from Nick Durandt's gym, the club has grown into a formidable international competitor.

Former two-time South African champion Makazole Tete and South African Junior Flyweight champion Nhlanhla Tyirha, who though already a national champion, is still a prospect by boxing standards, also hone their skills here. So do ABU Flyweight champion Fikile Mlonyeni and veteran Eastern Cape mini Flyweight champion Loyiso Ngantweni.

Zolani Tete won his first world title here after having lost in two title eliminators under Durandt. In his new club under Thengimfene's management, Tete has won the IBF Junior Bantamweight title and vacated it due to poor representation and purse dissatisfaction after his title fight went to a purse bid.

He then moved up and won the WBO world title under new promoter Frank Warren of Queensbury Promotions and had made three successful defences of the title. His boxing prowess and Thengimfene's hard work have combined to empower the club and Last Born Promotions to break the sponsorship barriers in the boxing sphere and amass several private sponsorships.

His smooth flowing southpaw fighting style, footwork and tight defence keep opponents clutching at straws. These enormous fighting attributes have won him a large number of fans in the United Kingdom where the majority of his fights are held. A chance to win p4p status and a sure ticket to the International Hall of Fame was lost when Last Born, as he is known by his army of fans bowed out World Boxing Super Series (WBSS) before his semi-final bout against Nonito Donaire due to a severe shoulder injury. But judging by the commitment of his trainers that include his father Zolile Tete, Phumzile Matyhila, Mhikiza Myekeni, Thula Sifatyi and myself, the march to greatness continues.

According to the ages of all gyms around it in the townships and other rural villages, PHUMLANI BOXING GYM gym is practically new. That status has however not deterred it from standing up against the best in both amateur and professional categories, since it was founded by the Banjwa brothers Mthobeli and Monde in early 2000. Monde Banjwa went on to become a respectable professional before retiring due to a lack of sparring and competition for a boxer of his size in the region. He concentrated his efforts on developing youngsters. His efforts have seen him being acknowledged as one of the best producers of female boxers in the region. His boxer Nomandithini Ndyambo has already won both SA and WBF Junior Welterweight championships. Ndyambo joins international music sensation Zahara as one of the elite products to come out of this new and tiny village.

Banjwa has since joined the crew of the new up and coming boxing developers who come as trainers, managers and boxers. The new trainers' list consists of Dokes Sikhonyela, Mhikiza Myekeni, Ncedo Cecane, Luvuyo Sovasi, Phumzile Matyila, Mpumelelo Mbedle, Joe Nimrod, Thozama Gobeni, Mzamo Njekanye, Thobani Gobeni, Mzwakhe Tezu, Makwedinana Matiti and Khulile Makeba. They joined experienced mentors like Dowie Mzini, Ben Mtyaliseko, Zolile Tete, Bobbin Sityana, Mapetla Mzamo, and myself. On the manager's forum, the list includes long-serving and experienced hands like Sihle Mnguni, Elliot Mjele, Bobbin Sityana, Mongezi Smith and Mongameli Goci. The new crew of managers include Mlandeli Thengimfene, Kholisile Cengani, Lonki Witbooi, Andy Mtshotshisa and my son Mbuso Mtya.

It is because of the work of these new trainers and managers and promoters that BCM is now boasting of a rising crop of prospects and exciting performers that include Phila Mpontshane, Aphiwe Mboyiya, Thulani Mbenge, Azinga Fuzile, Ludumo Lamati, Nthlanthla Tyirha, Xolani Mcotheli, Loyiso Ngantweni, Siphosethu Mvula, Sive Nontshinga, Fikile Mlonyeni, Luzuko Siyo, Siyabonga Siyo

The commitment and determination that the current group of mentors, accompanied by the equal commitment of boxers and trainers, makes one believe in the solidity of the future of boxing in BCMM. Boxing is here for the long haul. It has survived the natural, political and social challenges imposed upon it and came out victorious. It has challenged all the odds, met them halfway. It has lived to tell the story. And more. The future of boxing in BCMM still shines and certainly looks bright.

THE BOXING ARMY, as I like to refer to these hard-working ex-boxers is the number of former Buffalo City guys who are members of the national army and other structures serving in other regions and Provinces in different parts of the country. They are acknowledged and highly respected here at home and their places of work as devoted and reliable developers of boxing.

Some are well known because they were champions, while others, though less known, are relentlessly assisting in the nurturing of the game that made them what they are today. Some of them are well known to me. Others I hear of but have never met them. These honourable soldiers of the game are, but not limited to Lindile Yam, Odwa Mdleleni, Toto Matiti, Thabo Spampool, Ben Ncapayi, Mike Nomtoto, Mzoli Tempi, Jaji Sibali, Phumzile Nxitywa, Monwabisi Tshona, Mpumelelo Ntabeni, Bond Ncamazana, Gcobani Tom, Welsh Machibela, Sanchez Dabi, Vuyani Gxashe, Mthuthuzeli Totolo, Thembisile Dayimani, Mpush Makambi, Mahlulwa Ntamo, Mickey Klaas, Mandla Ntlanganiso, Phumeza Zinakile, Namhla Tyuluba, Wilson Mofu, Makala Ntaka, Simphiwe Gceba, Sinethemba Mandyoli, Xola Moni and Musa Mgedezi.

Some of these ex-boxers and administrators are not necessarily serving in the SANDF or any armed force for that matter, but I have decided to list them all together as the Boxing Army. Those that are actually in the army have military ranks attached to their names. I hereby extend my apologies for not, as a layman, referring to them by their honours. In the words of boxing contributor and photographer Xola Moni, "Massive my former pro-boxers, keep up the good work, keep that boxing alive."

QUEENSTOWN INFLUENCE

Queenstown may be far from Buffalo City but you cannot dwell on the success of boxing in this East London and districts area without having to go through Queenstown. The main people who led the charge for the origins of boxing the now recognised Boxing Mecca have their origins in Queenstown.

They include Mzoli Madyaka and Sax Manuel. Boxing here started well before East London. It became the natural and main rival once East London and Zwelitsha started growing.

The first boxing club, Queenstown Bantu Boxing Club, is situated and practising among a collection of other sports codes. It had already been practising for some time before some members broke away and formed Lukhanji Boxing Club in Mallett Hall, which became the best-known club in the area, and the main rival of East London and Zwelitsha. Queenstown was not just a rival but a more experienced elder brother of East London and King William's Town. For some time it was much stronger, beating up the two towns in inter-club fights and championships until they started to outgrow Queenstown. And as things would work out, East London grew much faster and stronger. At the time I formally joined the Zwelistha Boxing Club, the first names I knew that were recognised as real dangers in Queenstown included juniors Tildon Magxidolo, Zama Mayola, Nceba Maseti and Maqwazima. The seniors, not necessarily in any order included Kho Tywakadi, Raymond Masimini, Mpumelelo Mkhonto, Alesta Mahashe, Desmond Skepe, Makhwenkwe Mtyalela, Mzwandile Mgidlana and Shaza Masimini.

The likes of Felix Lalaphantsi who was one of the boxers, Mzukisi Kemka who was better known as Qika, as well as a gentleman known as Mr Nobebe, Peter Bunu and others were very instrumental in the initial formation and development of boxing in Queenstown. Some of these initial boxers left Queenstown and joined boxing clubs in East London and Zwelitsha.

East London and Zwelitsha thus became big beneficiaries of this Queenstown born talent as many future stars moved and traded leather there, and as time went on even against their homeboys Queenstown. Such movements would in later years produce for East London the likes of nationally recognised contenders like Jackie Ndaliso and Themba Thole.

Xolani Kemka, a strong contender and artist became arguably the best-known fighter to move up the boxing rungs and become a national contender without leaving Queenstown. Before him, the area had already produced Heavyweight Sandi Kwaza who unsuccessfully challenged James Mathatho for the South African title, highly regarded contender Jeffrey Mankune, as well as strong contenders like Siphiwe Fuma, Nkosana Peter, Thozamile Guga, Tonotono Ralana and many others. Promoters like Fisherman Mrubatha and Mabandla as well as administrator Keith Summerton stretched their wings and played a big role in National boxing as well.

Rural districts around Queenstown also took up boxing. Indwe Boxing Club under the leadership and sponsorship of Tata Mavuso did very well while Lady Grey under Gerald Lejaka became a strong force in Border boxing. Meanwhile, while Sada was also making great strides under Wilson Mofu and local businessman Tata Rasmeni. Together they produced the likes of well known Boyboy Kondile and Mabhuti Mapeyi. Later, Mofu moved to Phumalanga where he assisted local legend Paul Tshehla in the formation and training of ABU Boxing Club. That is where local Mpumalanga's greatest pair Anthony Tshehla and Jerry Ngobeni were moulded. Presently Queenstown has lost all of its boxing glory and is struggling to raise its hand against the still vibrant Buffalo City.

MARCHING ORDERS OF ZWELITSHA

My boxing journey started in my village of Mt Coke. Like all black boys in the areas allocated to black people in the Border region of what was then Cape Province, I had only two sports codes to choose from. I could play rugby or become a boxer. My immediate choice if I could call it that, was rugby. The simple reason was that I was living in the rural village of Mt Coke. Boxing was about 10 kilometres away in Zwelitsha Township. Sticks fighting was fast becoming a thing of the past as it was regarded as dangerous and was outlawed. The stories of boxing on the radio by the duo of the legendary Given Ntlebi and Peter Bacela, as well as one Xhosa newspaper, Imvo Zabantsundu, we fast becoming news in the community.

Boxing stories written by journalists Moses Twala and Charles Nqakula made such a big impression in our minds that we somehow managed to get a copy of the newspaper every weekend. This certainly sparked the light among all the boys in my village. We started boxing among ourselves and mimicked the commentary from what we heard on the radio.

In no time we were a boxing team that was throwing fists during intervals at school. No sooner had we started this, Andile's elder brother Lukhanyo, who was friends with the Imvo Zabantsundu newspaper boxing writer Moses Twala, bought us a pair of boxing gloves.

We started to get invitations to be in programs for concerts and parties on weekends where we boxed with little or no rules. In no time I had somehow become some sort of a leader for the club. Then my mother noticed my talent and came up with a plan to have me travel to Zwelitsha on weekends.

Zwelitsha was developing by leaps and bounds in boxing in the region and was competing effectively with East London, especially the regional amateur championships and inter-club fights.

Aycliff Stengile who was a useful professional boxer at the time took interest in the village southpaw, got me to come early every time I was in town, and taught me the basics of the game. Soon I was developing a lightning jab and a jarring straight left. I was fast becoming a star of the village fights, and I started getting noticed by the real boxing people and boxers in Zwelitsha. Zwelitsha Boxing Club was formed at almost the same time as the two first clubs in East London. It was formed by amongst others, Stanley Baleni, Pres Busa, and Charles Sebe who was later to be one of the leaders of the Ciskei homeland. Among the first boxers of the club were Aycliff Stengile, Abishai Sibhene, Zacharia Pule, Amos Vangqa, and Elliot Bolani.

At the time I joined, the club had quality senior amateur boxers like Eric Mtamo, Cacile Makhenjana and Amos Vangqa, as well as junior stars like Mlamli George, Fezile Busa and Thamsanqa Mazaleni. Of all the amateur boxers that traded their boxing at the Zwelitsha Hall, Fungile Buti, Spokes Witbooi, Ruben Matewu and I, rate as the most successful boxers of the lot.

The most successful amateur boxer Zwelitsha produced was Fungile Buti. He won a string of national championships when the old Free State and Transvaal senior boxers were so tough they were flattening everything on sight. The Free State drew their strength from the mines while Transvaal was still depending on township boxing clubs. The mainly white boxers from the SADF and SA Police clubs would only come to force after the integration. Witbooi moved to Mdantsane and turned professional under legendary trainer Welcome Mtyongwe.

He had a stunning but brief career before retiring and preferring to produce his gang of boxers. He turned to train youngsters after opening up Lukhanyo Boxing Club and developed it into one of the strongest clubs in Buffalo City. He is highly regarded as a trainer and is mentioned among the best the region has produced. Mathemba Nyakathi took over the training of boxers in Zwelitsha after he moved from Ginsberg. It was here that he would produce the Maqolo twins, Wele and Babini, and their brothers Mfusi and Luthando, perhaps the best boxers he ever trained, and one of the best boxing families in the country. Ginsberg boxing prospects like Billy Mkhencele and Mathemba's brother Skhumbuzo Nyakathi followed him to Zwelitsha.

He moved the training quarters to the Zwelitsha stadium and produced such prospects as Boyboy Mazaleni, Siphato Handi, Mabhongo Diko, Xolani Diko, Boysen Diko, Charlie Soul, Siphiwe Quintana, Mike Nomtoto and several amateur prospects. Handi would develop to be a lawyer, promoter and also serve as a member of Boxing SA. As of this writing former amateur boxer, Siza Helwana is the one who is keeping Zwelitsha Boxing Club's fires burning.

CHAPTER 17

CALL IT SISA DUKASHE STADIUM

THE FORCED REMOVALS of black people to Mdantsane, in the case of East London and districts, cause the people to develop a positive side and disqualify frustration and disillusionment by creating their ways of entertainment and self-development. In a country where race determined a person's place, the removals were meant for the black people to know their place, politically and socially.

But the system could not stifle the vibrance of township life, however much the absence of facilities undermined it. As kids grew up, they identified their lines of sporting abilities by taking up any of the three sports codes available to them at that time. Boxing and rugby were for the boys, while netball was the only available pass time for girls.

Most creative activities like music and dance were taking place at small halls like Holy Cross in NU 1 and Civic Hall in NU 2. But the boat rocked at Sisa Dukashe stadium through the rise of boxing. Boxing rose to heights never imagined before and soon became the main entertainment for this 25 000 capacity multi-purpose stadium.

Built in 1970, the multi-purpose Sisa Dukashe became home for both boxing and rugby. With the rise of Nkosana Mgxaji's popularity, boxing became the most prominent sports code. Thus, the name Sisa Dukashe became synonymous with boxing. By 1972, the stadium had not yet been finished, yet there was this urgent need for a bigger boxing venue. Mgxaji had become such a massive national drawcard that the four halls in King William's Town, Duncan Village and Mdantsane were too small for the big crowds that came dancing and singing to see Mgxaji fight.

The stadium is named Sisa Dukashe after a local businessman who was a big sports supporter in Mdantsane. Dukashe was responsible for funding many activities aimed at facilitating the rise of rugby in Mdantsane and surrounding areas.

Local politician, businessman, and the entire back of arguably the most prominent rugby club of the time in the region, Mr Sipho Tanana is said to have driven to Bisho and requested Ciskei President Lennox Sebe the stadium be named after this successful businessman. Sebe agreed.

Sisa Dukashe stadium was opened for use in 1972 before the construction could be finished. There was so much demand for a big venue that the Ciskei Government was forced to agree and have the stadium used with the promise that construction would resume later and the stadium would be completed by the time the next fight was scheduled. Mgxaji fought Moses 'Blue Monday' Mthembu in front of a capacity crowd that had never seen outdoor boxing before.

The tournament became such a great success that the big crowd and the electric atmosphere was likened to the festive mood known only in the soccer derbies of Soweto. Mgxaji had arrived. There was a new sheriff in town. Boxing was never going to be the same again. Mgxaji was paid like no other black boxer had been remunerated before. His purses were likened to the paydays of Gerrie Coetzee and Kallie Knoetze in Transvaal.

When Mgxaji fought, one could feel the festive mood throughout the whole week. His fighting skills and brilliance were something never seen before in local circles. He circled the ring with the ease of a ballet dancer. He had blinding speed, throwing punches in bunches that had fans debating and disagreeing on whether it was six, seven, or ten blows that Mgxaji thew.

There was a time when the local newspaper published his punches as travelling at 250 kilometres per hour. Those were not scientifically measured conclusions but were enough to be accepted by a longing fan base prepared to agree to anything positive about their hero.

His boxing movements were like magic. His defence was impeccable. Mgxaji never blocked nor ducked punches. Instead, he relied on his legs. He moved in and out of the danger zone without getting touched by the opponent's punches while not losing his striking distance. He seldom missed. He seldom lost a fight. The name Nkosana 'Happy Boy' Mgxaji became such a craze that he became a must-see for any boxing fan anywhere in South Africa. As a result, fight week in Mdantsane became a period like no other. Business boomed in *shebeens*, shops, izirhoxo (small shops), and even homes that had rooms for hire. People came from every corner of South Africa in trains, busses, hikes and even by air.

Pick-pockets and bag snatchers were making big profits. The who's who of South African politics, entertainment and religion all assembled in Mdantsane for the big day. Boxing fans would find themselves meeting and taking photos with people they only heard of from their radios. There was no television at the time. All recognisable celebrities would be introduced from the ring. To us, it was surprising how music, sports, political and academic celebrities all assembled at ringside and did ordinary things like cheering, dancing, shouting and throwing punches in the air. Everybody would be in an ecstatic mood. People would forget themselves. Ring entry became a special event. It was Mgxaji Time. He always had to share that time with his sister Nontsizi who would not be denied her opportunity to show her skills as she would sing and dance to the awe and ululation of the crowd just as 'Happy Boy' made his entry. Everybody looked forward to his appearance.

When he finally flew out from under the stand, everybody in the crowd that consisted of no less than twenty thousand bodies crammed inside the stadium lost their minds and their whole beings and surrendered to Happyboy's control. People from all walks of life forgot their own lives and plunged into shouting, singing, dancing, shadow boxing, and doing all things that came from human and animal instincts. At one far corner of the stadium, the Shepherds Music Band would be blaring the Happy Boy entry pop song Caroline I need your love, which had nothing to do with boxing. But it became a legendary part of the period just because Happy Boy loved it. The festive mood would continue until the end of the fight. I suspect that it was only then that many people remembered who they were and would try too late to redeem some sense of dignity. But most times, it was too late. But one thing was sure. They had the time of their lives. And they would tell the story for as long as they lived. I just told mine.

Ring announcer Cecil Nolutshungu, a well-dressed man about town from Zwelitsha near King William's Town, also rose to celebrity status just by announcing Mgxaji's fights. He was the best Ring announcer of the time. The Mgxali magic also rubbed on radio commentators like Given Ntlebi and Peter Bacela. They became household names just by calling the blows and the moves of the great Happy Boy. Such was the Happy Boy magic. Outside the stadium, the lines would be so long from the bus rank to Sisa Dukashe stadium that you would step out of a taxi or bus and immediately join a long line that started at the rank itself and right up to the stadium entrance, about half a kilometre away.

Human lines would be coming from the taxi and bus rank side, from the Qumza Highway, and the NU2 side on the road from Yako's garage. The human lines consisted of people from all walks of life, men and women, young and old, and even people with disabilities.

It made no difference that the first preliminary fight would be scheduled to start at two in the afternoon. The human chains were already in place by 10 in the morning, regardless of the weather. Keeping the long lines in check became a headache. Police and volunteers would be sprinting up and down the lines with little success in controlling the crowds. The biggest headaches were the youngsters trying to jump the cues to the frustration of the elderly and those with disabilities.

One giant Heavyweight bouncer known as Boysana acquired cult status just by keeping all those lines in check. He was a killer puncher known for knocking people out with the palm. Ouh, as he was known, resembled a big bear with sledgehammer hands and a small head protruding out of a short big stomp-like neck.

He was known to be so strong that he could push or pull buses full loads of people all by himself. He seldom spoke. His voice was soft. But when he did speak to remind you to keep in line, you never failed to hear *Ouh*. He was known to be a peaceful and loving person, but no one dared to cross him. People were scared of Ouh more than they were scared of gun-carrying police officers. Yet, he never carried a weapon. Around the stadium, business was at its best, with people selling anything from roasted meat, fat cakes, pancakes and sausages. Others would be selling fruit, sweets, biscuits and chips. It was also time to bring shebeens or bottle stores closer to the action – making sure all sorts of liquor was available on demand. There were cigarettes and even Happyboy's favourite, the zol. Mgxaji's name became synonymous with Sisa Dukashe stadium. The stadium's name became known not only in South Africa but around the whole world. But little did the world know that it was still unfinished.

The only finished part was the dressing rooms and the stand that were mainly meant to be used as the boxing ringside. But it never got to be ringside because when Mgxaji started his jig to the ring, all hell broke loose. There would be vocal traditional war music, dance, praise and everything that made noise. Everybody, including police and security, would leave their posts and join the jubilant crowds.

In 1983, Sisa Dukashe stadium's fortunes changed dramatically. The Mdantsane Bus boycott dubbed Azikhwelwa was the springboard for the sudden and unexpected change of mood and attitude towards the legendary stadium. The discontentment resulted from an uprising against rising bus prices of Ciskei busses – Zezama Ciskei Amahle – mainly between Mdantsane and East London. People decided in disgust not to board the busses. Some used cars while others chose to walk from Mdantsane to work in the East London factories in Fort Jackson, Wilsonia and as far as West Bank. The Ciskei Police responded by a heavy-handed assault on everybody walking the streets.

People were forced to board the busses whether there was a need for a bus or not, whether one has the bus fare or not. All the police wanted was for the busses to have full loads of people. Things worsened to a deadly situation when it was found out that the Ciskei Police had detained people and used Sisa Dukashe stadium as a prison. There, prisoners were tortured, beaten and maimed. As a result, some lost their teeth, eyes, nails and fingers. Others were known to have lost legs and arms. Hospital staff and ambulance workers in Cecilia Makiwane Hospital, which was loosely referred to as either KwaLlona or LF Siyo Hospital, reported people being thrown on chairs depending on whom you talked to in hospitals for nurses to take care of. There was chaos everywhere.

The Mdantsane community then made a joint resolution with all sporting codes, that included the primary users of the stadium like boxing and rugby, including their fans, Sisa Dukashe stadium should not be used again under any circumstances. People believed that blood of innocent mothers, fathers, brothers, and sisters had flown in that stadium. It could therefore not be used as a venue for entertainment and recreation purposes.

The decision was taken as a matter of principle, and, as such, it had to be abided by, irrespective of losses. All of this was done in the name of looking at the bigger picture. Nevertheless, it was a terrible blow. All other venues in the region were just too small. This sorry state of affairs was magnified by the fact that Nkosana Mgxaji and Welile Nkosinkulu, a magnetic knockout specialist who had made big waves in boxing, had their careers stamped at the stadium.

Myself and Tsietsi Maretloane had carved our careers and won SA titles at Sisa Dukashe stadium. Fighting at the stadium in front of 25000 people, in an arena built to take 20 000 people, was a experience to fight and die for. That kind of crowd would bring any boxer to life. As a boxer, this would be your moment of glory for many eyes to see and many more people to tell stories about your conquering knockout punches.

Wars that took place at Sisa Dukashe stadium are still remembered by veteran Sisa boxing fans even today. People who were there to experience the atmosphere of Nkosana Mgxaji's battles against the likes of Anthony Morodi, Norman Sekgapane, Antonio Amaya, Ben Lekalake, Mzwandile Biyana, Tsietsi Maretloane and Arthur Mayisela; and it was not only Mgxaji.

Who can forget Welile Nkosinkulu vesus Peter Mathebula, Welile Nkosinkulu vs Zola Lawuse, Monde Mpulampula vs Banana Boy Sigetye, Welcome Ncitha vs Victor Sonaba, Mxhosana Jongilanga vs Zweli Ngcongolo, Mzwandile Biyana vs Bramley Whiteboy, Odwa Mdleleni vs Mveleli Luzipo, Loyiso Mtya vs Cameron Adams, Mveleli Luzipho vs Baby Jake Matlala, Zweli Ngcongolo vs Saxon Ngqayimbana, Jaji Sibali vs Johannes Miya. The list is endless.

As the People's stadium was diminishing into a white elephant status, there was already a horde of hot newcomers who were fighting and marching with their fists towards stardom and their chances to be the drawcards of the now legendary stadium. They could see it. But they could not get there. And it could not be fully developed for new drawcards.

The new blood included smoothies like Welcome Ncita, Lindi Memani and Nceba Dladla, speedsters like Odwa Mdleleni and Mveleli Luzipho. Hardened brawlers like Zandisile Thole, Ndoda Mayende and Phila Kali had the most entertaining bouts. Ring wizards like Mthobeli Mhlophe and Thembile Lubisi knew how to make the crowds come alive.

The list of boxers who made history at the Sisa Dukashe stadium is long. Knockout specialists like Zweli Ngcongolo and Mxhosana Jongilanga brought the excitement of boxing to its most incredible heights. They had tasted the feel and the magic of Sisa Dukashe. They dreamed of the day they would return to the battleground that had become their own. But it was now out of reach. For years the decision could not be changed. Sisa Dukashe stadium stood undisturbed. That is until Thathezakhe Joseph Manyathi came into the scene. Manyathi was a short, round-faced and dark-skinned fellow who always had a nice word for everyone. He spoke softly and slowly but could never miss the attention of his intended audience. If you intended to disagree with Joe, you were well-advised not to listen. Listening to him was agreeing.

He grew up in Orlando, Soweto but joined the fanfare and boxing madness of the BCM as a fan of our legendary first world champion and eternal great Welcome Ncita. Joe Manyathi came to Mdantsane around the time Welcome Ncitha was making waves as one of the best boxers in the world. Ncitha and Manyathi became close friends. With Ncita on his side, Manyathi was able to mix, spread his magic and network with boxing people inside and outside the country. He had a razor-sharp mind and a great sense of opportunity. He never failed to seize the moment. Something which singled him out even against his more affluent white competitors and until his arrival, most successful black managers and promoters. His competitors even went out of their way to lead a campaign to blacklist him. To them, he was becoming too big.

They fed some specially selected or owned members of the media with a string of false stories where Manyathi's business deals were maliciously reported. For example, they would falsely claim that he owed significant amounts of money to big companies. These were the companies from whom Manyathi and his friend Khaya Jekwa managed to secure sponsorship for all events they were involved in. Air travel locally and abroad and hired cars for teams of people were just a telephone call away. This is what angered his competitors.

We always challenged them to either come forward with proof or have them get the allegedly owed companies to lay charges. But, of course, none did anything of the sort.

Manyathi used Nçita's network to their great advantage. In no time, he was big friends and negotiating deals with boxing gurus like Don King, Emmanuel Stewart and Lennox Lewis. The new associations he made with people at the highest offices of world boxing resulted in him clinching deals and creating opportunities that changed the lives of many boxers and promoters.

He made friends here. He made enemies there. But one thing that became very clear was that people who were shut out of deserved opportunities before, because they did not belong, found themselves getting to where they were supposed to be. Without leaving the people who were there with them when the going was tough, they made sure their dreams were coming true. Then, Joe Manyathi levelled the playing fields. He was introduced to me by Ncita, with whom I was working as a trainer at the time. The three of us formed a working relationship that resulted in many trips to the UK and the USA. We later invited other boxing promoters like Koko Godlo and Zolani Moshani. From outside BCM, we had Kimberly businessman Joe Padisho and former Ginsberg rugby star Major Sihunu, who was then based in Kimberly.

Later we were joined by Zinzi Mandela. She was very influential in the negotiations that finally brought Lennox Lewis and Layla Ali to South Africa. However, the Lewis and Ali deals were dashed by financial limitations and ended up being promoted by the more polished and accomplished Golden Gloves Promotions.

Having grown up in Orlando and come to Mdantsane at a ripe old age Manyathi was quick to either find or create his Xhosa roots. In no time, he was known by the clan name Skhomo. Siphato Handi, a former boxer and promoter, gave Manyathi the nickname Master Key due to his ability to pull deals that had been tried before and were never achieved. That is how I got to know him.

Welcome Ncita introduced us, and we formed a team that was to take Ncita to the US and back to Sisa Dukashe for his last fight. At the time, I was running my Zama Boxing Club and Messiah Boxing Promotions, besides training Welcome. All of this was happening when Sisa Dukashe stadium was a pariah to the local community.

Nobody could use it for any purpose, be it training or competition. Nobody dared set foot there. Manyathi had taken it upon himself to make a plan to get Sisa Dukashe stadium to be accepted as the people's sports meeting place like before. He wanted to bring back the good old days.

It was not until we had what one could call a chance conversation with one of my up and coming boxers, young Vuyani Mbinda, that the solution to Sisa Dukashe hit us in the face. Mbinda was my boxer and, also unknown to me, was an underground political activist.

The conversation with him was about a fight I was planning to promote between him and former South African Bantamweight champion, knockout specialist Zweli Ngcongolo.

I was planning to stage the fight at the NU1 rugby stadium and tennis courts but was discouraged by the nightmarish situation, the lack of security and loose sitting arrangements would create. The two Mdantsane halls would be too small for the fight. At around the same time, Manyathi had been to every office and high ranking officer, or whoever held a position of power within the Ciskei Government echelons. Finally, he sought permission from the Ciskei authorities to call the community to a traditional mass gathering at the stadium.

He felt that such a meeting, if done right and according to the people's will, the stadium could be accepted as having been cleansed. The Ciskei authorities had no problem with that kind of arrangement. If Manyathi could achieve that feat, he would be solving their problem. But on two occasions that Manyathi tried to organise the gatherings, they had failed. Nobody turned up.

Mbinda gave us a political lecture. He informed us that Manyathi was trying to solve the stadium matter in the wrong way. Mbinda said that the reasons for the shunning of the stadium by the people were political. The solution would be political and religious. When Manyathi explained that he was talking to Ciskei politicians, Mbinda reminded him that the Ciskei politics were not only irrelevant but dangerous at that stage. People were now only listening to the '*Progressive forces*'.

He was convinced that once the progressive forces were convinced, they would take it upon themselves to call the people to the stadium. And how right this little political upstart was. The closest active political activists we knew as boxing fans were local lawyer Hintsa Siwisa and Border Sports Council secretary and Swallow's Rugby Club player Zola Dunywa. The two boxing fans, who were also widely known as political pioneers, would play a considerable role in consulting and canvassing support from the different political, civic and religious structures. Their voice and influence went so far as to reach people on the ground.

The spread of influence was far beyond what we could have imagined. Through these gentlemen's efforts, the Border Council of Churches was invited to participate in the cleansing ceremony and play a role in getting things back into order. As expected, the church certainly played a master role in cooling the tempers and changing the minds of the outraged and unforgiving communities.

Communities were invited to attend the cleansing ceremony and regain their passion so that the stadium could be used again for sports and other social activities there. What was also important was the involvement of a group of sangomas and traditional healers invited to spray and smoke away the evil spirits to create peace and good relations between the communities and the legendary stadium.

In February 1995, Joe Manyathi had his weekend. For three days, Sisa Dukashe stadium was a hive of activity. Two oxen were slaughtered, food was prepared in plenty, gallons and gallons of all kinds of drink were available. Hundreds of both male and female volunteers were on hand to help out in any way they could.

There were plenty of skilled people. Close to 10 000 thousand enthusiastic people filled the stadium for the cleaning.

People from all walks of life who had been denied the chance of enjoying themselves in all social, religious, political and sports activities for so many years came together. They prayed, praised, sang, danced, ululated, ate and drank until sunset.

Joe 'Master Key' Manyathi had done it. He was the hero. Sisa Dukashe stadium was declared The People's stadium. All the Progressive Forces and Religious groupings were represented in their big numbers.

It was back to business. Two weeks later, Messiah Promotions, I was back at the People's stadium. But this time, not as a fighter, but as a promoter. I promoted the first tournament at Sisa Dukashe stadium after many years.

Boxing was back with a bang. But was it?

The crowds no longer returned as much as they used to. What was the reason? Was Happy Boy Mgxaji with his retirement? Maybe. Was it because Welile Nkosinkulu was also gone? Perhaps! Had people lost interest because current boxers were no longer as good? Not really. Was it the economy? That people were no longer in jobs and could not afford the prices? Who knows?

The first five South African champions in the Border region were Nkosana Mgxaji, Tsietsi Maretloane, Mzukisi Skweyiya, Loyiso Mtya and Mzwandile Biyana. All of them, except for Skweyiya, won their titles at Sisa Dukashe stadium, while Skweyiya won his championship at the Great Centenary Hall in New Brighton, Port Elizabeth.

That First Five would be succeeded by several stylists and knockout specialists who resembled a pride of lions making the stadium their hunting ground. They included Welile Nkosinkulu, Mxhosana Jongilanga, Zweli Ngcongolo, Luvuyo Kakaza, Odwa Mdleleni, Mveleli Luzipho, Victor Fata, Welcome Ncita, Thamsanqa Sogcwe, Jaji Sibali and more.

Boxers who were the stadium favourites but did not win titles include Prince Tukani, Jack Jim, Volfart Rala, Griffiths Mgijima and Guy Dirty Boy Ratazayo. Others who had as much of a crowd but failed to capitalise on the stage and presence given to them were the likes of Monde Mpulampula, Nyingi Mtya, Daluxolo Tyekana, Phila Kali, Saxon Ngqayimbana, Zandisile Thole and Mandla Booi. If memory doesn't fail me, I can recall Phakamile Mpeku, Mzidi Dintsi, Victor Sonaba, Victor Mkhohlakali, Vuyani Mbinda, Elliot Zondi, Zola Lawuse, Wonga Lawuse, Jomo Mpahla, and Smallboy Tyekana also did not make the cut.

There has also been an army of outsiders who visited and became favourites among the local fans, win or lose. They include Victor Black Eagle Tshabalala, who won every fight, Thomas Homicide Sithebe, who won a lot, including the SA Featherweight title but lost only to Mxhosana Jongilanga and Nkosana Mgxaji.

Ben TNT Lekalake punished local prospects Tsietsi Maretloane and Guy Ratazayo but lost two unforgettable epic battles against Mgxaji. Peter Terror Mathebula beat Monde Mpulampula and Mandla Booi but lost to Nkosinkulu. He would revenge the loss to Nkosinkulu in Cape Town. Then there was all-time fan favourite Baby Jake Matlala.

The last big fight was perhaps one of the biggest tournaments staged in the region. It was an International encounter between South Africa's Welcome Ncita and former WBO world Featherweight champion, British fighter Steve Robinson. This mammoth of a fight was promoted by Joe Manyathi's Star Trade Promotions and sponsored by Forum Tobaccos. Legendary British promoter Barry Hearn, the founder of Matchroom Promotions, graced the event with his presents.

A few years later, Barry was going to hand over the reins of the boxing promotion to his young son Eddie Hearn who was to take boxing promotion to dizzying new heights.

Among his achievements are the engagement of DAZN, the new worldwide boxing and other sports streaming broadcast network that is putting boxing at the fingertips of boxing fans around the world like never before. Such historic media triumph all other promotional successes have landed him in the position of one of the greatest boxing promoters of all time.

But perhaps the biggest catch for this historic fighting field was the visit by undisputed World Heavyweight champion Lennox Lewis.

That rich history, unfortunately, counts for very little or nothing these days. Sisa Dukashe Stadium's days of thrills and triumphs are a thing of the past. It is still standing lonely as a church mouse. There is no boxing activity whatsoever.

Its cousin venue, The Orient Theater, now acknowledged as the home of boxing, has taken over as the meeting place of boxing. But is it enough? Why is it that after so many years of conquering the world, there is still no boxing arena with the capacity of at least 5 000 if no one can afford a 10 000 capacity venue? Meantime let's go to the Orient Theatre.

CHAPTER 18

IF YOU CAN MAKE IT AT THE ORIENT THEATRE

From time immemorial, boxing has always had its special venues where every boxer would die to fight. This wish has never been qualified into a feeling of whether the boxer just wants to fight or win there, but winning certainly has its benefits whatever the case. But the same venue is the attraction. Winning there and more so being accepted as a prime draw and favourite of such a venue lives a legacy never to be forgotten. More than anything else if the boxers are visiting. In the famous film *On the Waterfront*, Marlon Brando tells his brother Charlie, "I could've been a contender. I could've been somebody. I could've fought in the Garden."

This was when Madison Square Garden in New York was the prime venue for world boxing. Finally, it was recognised and acknowledged as The Mecca of Boxing. Boxers who fought there, especially those who scored multiple grand victories, became legends in their lifetimes. Former grand Heavyweight champion of the world Joe Louis still holds the record for world title defences at the Garden. Muhammad Ali, Joe Frazier, Larry Holmes stamped their names in the famous Garden.

Our former multiple world champion Apostle Dr Hawk Makepula, the first South African boxer to fight at the Garden, also made his mark there.

He was followed by his stablemate Zolani Petelo. It gave Mzi Mnguni and his Eyethu Boxing Club a special place in their annals of South African boxing. That honour should also go to Rodney Berman, the promoter of Golden Gloves, who was behind all of these groundbreaking achievements. It was only when television and gambling took over that boxing moved to other venues like Atlantic City. Today Las Vegas rules the roost as the premier attraction of world boxing.

Many South Africans like Mpush Makambi, Ali Funeka and Moruti Mthalane have traded gloves at the great boxing and gambling venue with great success. For any boxer, trainer, manager or promoter, an appearance in this now historic venue becomes a feat and honour to die for. But while the world gathers in Las Vegas for its fulfillment, no place in South Africa today attracts boxers and fulfils fans, as does the Orient Theater in East London. This venue has taken over the South African boxing industry as the place to be for boxing. It may not have the money nor space but makes that up by the electric atmosphere and high vibe it breathes into the fighting space and all that is inside it.

The Dramatic Society of East London was founded around 1952. About eleven years later, in 1963, the East London Playhouse was built, initially, as a Dinner or Theatre venue for whites use only. Proudly designed by architect Ben Shapiro, it became very popular. Connected to the DRAMSOC, next to the Orient Beach, East London, the Playhouse became an automatic rehearsal venue for the Society.

With the demise of Sisa Dukashe stadium after the bus boycotts and subsequent reduction in crowd numbers, there arose a need for a smaller venue for boxing. Using Sisa Dukashe as a boxing venue did not make sense anymore. The old Duncan Village Community Center had been burnt down during the riots. The Holy Cross and Civic hall, the two venues commonly used for amateur club fights and championships in Mdantsane, were still too small for the professional crowds.

It took Michael Guwa and Koko Godlo, a pair of young socialites and playboys who were successfully promoting beauty contests, to take on Plan B. Now operating as Real First Team Promotions, they had thrown their tentacles into boxing and were making a big splash in the boxing pool. They had many hot crowd favourites like National champions Odwa Mdleleni, Mxhosana Jongilanga, Jackie Gunguluza, Sidima Qina and Mbulelo Mxokiswa. But the lack of a significant and secure venue had become somewhat of a challenge. They needed to keep their charges busy for improvement and upward movement. The Promotions' last tournament had been the resounding success of the Mxhosana Jongilanga vs Zweli Ngcongolo local derby. That fight is still rated as the most prominent and toughest fight between two BCMM fighters.

Guwa, who was the leader of the promotion, did what at that time was unthinkable. He somehow set up a meeting with the white East London Mayor at the time – the last white Mayor. I was invited to the meeting. Two of my colleagues and I presented to the Mayor a case study of how we could turn boxing around in the Municipality. Our presentation was a short but amazing story of how successful boxing was in his Municipality, where it was at the time and where it was going.

We convinced the Mayor of the need to intervene and save what was growing to be the biggest success story of his town –in his own time. He informed us that the venue was designed for the arts, and he was not sure it could make sense for boxing. We were also not sure. But to our relief, he agreed to use both The Orient Theatre and City Hall for boxing.

Little did we know at the time that we were laying down the foundation for one of the greatest venues in the world of boxing – the Theatre of blood and tears or the slogan, as some fans like to call this popular venue. In entering the Orient Theatre, you get the feeling that it was meant for the arts and drama. It was never dreamed that there would ever be a need to organise a boxing event. It is a big hall with a capacity for 1300 sitting, and can easily accommodate 3000 standing and 800 sitting for our vociferous boxing choir. The seats are situated on a downward spiralling design from only one side that starts from the main entrance with one passage leading down to the stage.

The four lines of steps typically meant for up and down movement separate the seats. Boxing uses them for sitting about 500 fans in smaller tournaments. But it's about 1200 standing for big fights. It was supposed to be VIP seating and adjudicators for arts and drama, where we erect our ring.

The Orient setting means that you can watch any proceedings from one side of the house. The side entrances at the bottom on both sides lead directly to the stage – in our case, the ring and ringside if there was ever such a thing in our boxing. The location is generally used for sitting. But with televised fights, it's set up for the cameras and marketing material.

On the 4th November 1990, history was made when the first boxing tournament, a doubleheader, was held at the Orient Theatre. At stake, the two titles were the South African Junior Featherweight championship, where little-known Vuyanu Bungu defended his title against Port Elizabeth's Zolani Makhubalo and the Nationa Middleweight champion Mbulelo Mxokiswa defended against Thembelani Malahle.

But you could have fooled me. The design that was meant for the arts turned out to be the best recipe for creating intensity into the atmosphere and the great vibe that boxing is known for, especially for the kind of boxing fan Buffalo City breeds.

Buffalo City boxing fans are not your ordinary kind of fan – be it man or woman, young or old, abled bodies or with a disability. They are all the same, with vigour and enthusiasm. Buffalo City fans are ecstatic, enthusiastic, musical, talkative, active and full of drama. Sitting next to a Buffalo City fan anywhere gives the impression that you are sitting next to a very drunk person – drunk with a love for boxing.

The size and in your face presentation of the venue arouses a thrill within the combatants that they never feel anywhere else. The music and dance are spontaneous but well-orchestrated. They love their boxers to bits and make their feeling known with music and dance. They have a memorable tune to express everything happening in the ring. It could be *sisebenza ngokubulala* – loosely translated to mean 'Killing is our business' or sizakophul'amathambo, which means 'We're going to break your bones. Intimidation to the visiting opponents.'

When the action intensifies, they forget the song and start screaming, advising their favourite to stick that jab, to keep moving or their favourite advice for him to dig the body. Ayiqhashanga (He's lost it) when they feel that their man is in control. They never boo when the action is dull but will just sing niyasibambembezela (You're delaying us). But to me and perhaps to a significant number of people, the scariest and most intimidating time is when they do their thundering rendition of Uyingwe (You're the tiger).

Top boxing writer Bongani Magasela of the Sowetan newspaper tells me about his experience of having goosebumps every time he attends a tournament here. He believes there is no venue like the Orient Theatre. When it comes to excitement, that place brings up the roars. You are forced to believe that kind of assessment when it comes from a man like Magasela.

He should know. He has travelled the world and been inside the biggest and best venues in the world. He has personally experienced what they can offer.

The BCMM boxers may have played a significant role in introducing music as part of their psychological make-up. Since the days of Sisa Dukashe stadium, the music would be blasted through the loudspeakers with songs from the band, mainly overseas copied music.

The new boys have taken right back home with mainly the African Gospel music taking centre stage. But perhaps no one popularised and brought the ring entry with music to the highest extremes than Hawk Makepula. He would have the hall spellbound with Kholeka's song andindedwanga. Today my favourites are Nkosinathi Joyi's Zulu sound, ngiyashisa ngithi bhee, and perhaps the fans and everybody's favourite, traditional Xhosa song, Xolisani Ndongeni's Nank'unomeva.

The Orient Theatre's design is such that you can see and almost hear everybody when you are in the ring. Whether shouting or singing, it is all the same. It is inspirational. It is motivational. It is intimidating. It's your choice which one to embrace.

Imagine the bearing it has on the person who is just about to go to war. This in your face scenario is an upliftment for the inspired. It is a blessing for the motivated. It is opium to the confident.

You can imagine what it does to the less confident. They die a slow death before the first punch is thrown. These slogans have been known to produce the best out of the best. Confident boxers like Phillip Ndou and Hekkie Budler have risen to the occasion. Legendary Nick Durandt loved it. He trained his boxers to meet this notoriously hot fight atmosphere halfway. He believed it was the fire. So they had to fight fire with fire. So today, bright young trainer Colin Nathan primes his boxers to meet it head-on. It lifts him.

If it can bring that instinct to him, why not his well-trained athletes. That is why these great trainers want their charges to gain this Buffalo City experience before they thrust them into the international wolves.

They believe it is the best mind game and psychological warfare school in South Africa.

The local trainers thrive on it. They even join the ululating and the singing of the crowds. They believe it lifts the spirits of their boxers and extends its positive boundaries of home advantage. The fighters inhale the energy they believe is meant for them. And for them alone, not the outsiders. With every voice, they gain just that much more power over their adversary.

This is the venue where it does not matter whether you are black, white, yellow or brown. The crowds here have outgrown racial prejudices and preferences. To them, boxing comes in all colours.

As they will say in the Mafia world and language of the Italian and New York crime syndicates, the Orient Theatre is where you make your bones. If you can take the pressure of the Orient Theatre and never buckle, you can make it anywhere in the world.

So, you will be well advised never to take those fans on in their world. They are well known to cross the floor at the drop of a hat once the outsider delivers the goods and impresses them. Outside boxers have become favourites here until a local performer puts paid to that.

Those that will always have their names held in high esteem here include Philip 'Time Bomb' Ndou, Hekkie Budler and others.

Local boxers who have had some of their most significant victories at the Orient Theatre before winning international and world titles or retiring include Hawk Makepula, Vuyani Bungu, Zolani Marali, Sidima Qina and Ali Funeka. The list of fighters who made their mark at the Theatre would not be complete without the likes of Mzukisi Marali, Mpush Makambi, Mbulelo Mxokiswa, Simphiwe Pamana, Jaji Sibali, Mthobeli Mhlope, Jackie Gunguluza, Zolile Mbityi, Patrick Quka, Andrew Matyila, Toto Mokorotlo, Mabhuti Sinyabi, Makazole Tete, Lusanda Komanisi, Zolani Tete, Nkosinathi Joyi, Sikhulule Sidzumo, Thabo Sonjica, Xolisani Ndongeni and Vusumzu Bokolo.

There is a considerable number that has just made it and are now going for the stars. They include the likes of Azinga Fuzile, Xolani Mcotheli, Uyanda Bulana, Siphosethu Mvula, Phila Mpontshane, Ntlantla Tyirha, Lindile Tshemese, Fikile Mlonyeni, Luthando Ntwanambi, Sivenathi Nontshinga, Siphamadla Baleni, Loyiso Ngantweni, Ayanda Bulana, JJ Sonjica

Local boxers who have been the Oriental Theatre's fan favourites, whether they win or lose, include Jackie Pressure Cooker Gunguluza, Mthobeli Hitman Mhlope, Ndoda Happy Boy Mayende and Zolani Thambolenyoka Marali. Lunga Ntontela and Ali Funeka also made it as the Theatre's golden boys. And so did Khulile 'Real Big Deal' Makeba, Gabula Vabaza, Toto Silent Killer Mokorotlo, Nceba Whooo Dladla, Vuyisile Bebe, Dudu Bungu, Luzuko Siyo, Siyabonga Siyo, Ayanda Ramncwana, Mzolisi Yoyo, Bongani Silila, Mfusi Maxhayi, Vusumzu Bokolo, Miniyakhe Sityatha and Mfusi Maxhayi. The list is growing with the emergence of new stars.

The two boxers, who I think would have loved to fight at the Orient Theatre, are legends Dingaan Thobela and Brian Mitchell. I am sure they would have loved to show off the skills that made them so great in front of that enthusiastic welcome and electric atmosphere. They are constant visitors now as commentators and contributors.

Brian Mitchell made a career of fighting in the townships that were his black opponents back yards. That was when it was not yet fashionable for whites to be in black townships or residential areas. Let alone fighting there.

Mitchell was not intimidated. He did what he had to do to the best of his abilities. And his best was always better than his opponents best – wherever it was happening. Our crowds missed out on landing a hand in making perhaps the greatest boxing career to date by a South African – a Hall of Fame career.

Dingaan Thobela had the kind of style that would have mesmerised the Orient crowd. The locals love skilled showmanship. They love fighters who can mix power, lightning speed, high-class punch combinations and overall boxing finesse all at the same. What a treat that would have been.

The Orient Theatre has its own stories that can sometimes be unbelievable. Xolani Sirhunu and Norman Zwilibi were two deadly punchers contesting for the Border Junior Welterweight title. Everybody knew there was going to be a knockout as soon as the fight was announced. But no one ever expected the way it happened. In the fifth round, both boxers spotted the target and threw their known killer punches – at the same time. Who can forget that day of the double knockdown?

Both caught each other flush on the forehead, exactly where both were aiming. And down they went on their backs. Referee Tsuka bent down between them to be as close to their ears as possible. With each hand going up and down right in front of their faces to make it easy for them to pick up the count if they could hear or see him. It was hard to tell. But no one could blame the crowd because there was dead silence in the hall.

People were paralysed. Their voices were lost.

They had never seen such a spectacle in their lifetimes of boxing. The referee started the count as both boxers struggled to get their limbs under control. They fumbled with their hands. They somehow found the ropes and began to pull themselves up. They discovered none of them could maintain his equilibrium. They held the ropes and soon fell back on the ground, only to try and get up again. It seemed like forever. At around count number five, the crowd recovered. They had regained their voices, and the noise started stronger than it had been before. The count was going on, and it seemed like forever.

I was Sirhunu's trainer, and I was manning his corner, and together with my two assistants, we were shouting our voices hoarse. So was Zwilibi's corner on the opposite side of the ring. We all knew that whoever beat the count would win the fight. At the count of seven, both boxers were back up, hanging on the ropes, their knees buckling and unable to hold on for long.

According to the rules, as long as they were still hanging as supported by the ropes, they were still down, the count would continue. So it came to which boxer would step away from the ropes. Unbelievably at the count of eight, Xolani Sirhunu stepped away from the ropes and started staggering away towards the centre of the ring. The referee continued counting Zwilibi out as his back still lay on the ropes. It was a knockout win for Sirhunu.

Small as it is, the Orient Theatre is the venue that boxers and their trainers from the length and breadth of South Africa regarded as the place to stamp their names and gain genuine boxing acknowledgement as true greats of the game.

Until Buffalo City gets the kind of venue its boxing deserves – Mdantsane Indoor Center, Gompo Hall and Orient it is. *Makuliiiiiiiiiiiiiiiwe.*

YOU CAN BOX AT HOME

While boxing was growing in the townships around East London, King William's Town was doing its share towards the growth and development of the rural villages. But, like in all rural villages and townships that were keen on boxing, there were no rings.

Nor there was material to build or erect rings. So people had to make do with what they had. We were lucky to have my elder brother Lukhanyo Mtya who was a solid rugby player. He took an interest in what the youngsters were doing and bought us our first set of gloves. He later used his truck, free of charge, to deliver the boxers wherever they had to compete. But, from the beginning, younger brother Stoto was never drawn into boxing.

The local team consisted of my cousins Andile Mtya and Phetelo Mtya and several other boys like Mluleki Dlova, Thamsanqa Mnyanda, Thembile Tyatyaza and Mvuyo Mpanza. Later on, we were joined by the likes of Mbuyiseli Tyatyaza, Mnumzana Gxaleka, Bobo Xaso, Monwabisi Mdoda, Siphiwo Paliso, Monwabisi Mdoda and Nkosinathi Ngceba. The boxing bug had bitten. Once the boxing bug bites, you stay bitten. There was no way of stopping. So rings were made from lines drawn on the sand to desks in places like Mdantsane, where they could box in school premises.

In Mt. Coke, we started our rings first by erecting a human wall and later by stacking wood on the ground. My home village was to develop and produce myself firstly as South African Junior Middleweight champion, my brother Nyingi. He would win the Cape Province Junior Lightweight title when he beat Ngcambaza Mbaduli in Zwelitsha. He went on to unsuccessfully challenge Hall Of Fame world champion Brian Mitchell.

Nyingi was undoubtedly the toughest and bravest of the family. But he had one glaring weakness that forced his early retirement from the ring – he was very prone to cuts. He used to joke that, personally, with his opponents, all he had to do was faint, and he would bleed.

The third professional was Siphiwe Quntana, who became a solid performer under trainer Mathemba Nyakathi in Zwelitsha. He stayed long enough at home to make the local club a formidable and well-respected competitor. He was a good leader and teacher for the youngsters. It was sad to see him leave the village because of work commitments. And when he left, boxing died in our village.

Highly thought of prospects Anele Gxaleka and Luvuyo Somhaya turned professional in Mdantsane but retired after a few fights without realising the promise they showed as amateurs. Meanwhile, my youngest brother Lulama was developing as an excellent referee and judge. He is now widely recognised as one of the best referees in the world, with many world title fights under his belt, especially as a referee.

Zolani Bongco also started as an amateur boxer but soon veered to officiating. He found his voice as a boxing Ring announcer. He is now an award-winning Radio Announcer with Umhlobo Wenene Radio. Our cousin Vukani also became a solid amateur boxer but chose to abandon boxing once he reached tertiary. Perhaps the best move. He is now a very reliable analyst of the game.

I can brag and claim to be the brightest boxing product of my village. My younger brother Lulama comes second. And brother Nyingi comes third. We always tell anyone who will listen that we never joined boxing. We were born into it. Our father was a boxing fundi in East London. Essentially he was somewhat of an expert in the sport. Our brother Lukhanyo planted the seed with the first set of boxing gloves. And our cousin Lundi Majangaza, though younger than me, was the first boxer we looked up to in the family. Uncle Khayakhulu, a boxing manager and trainer who was one of the founding members of boxing in Port Elizabeth and districts, was always an inspiration to us even when we were fighting opponents from Port Elizabeth, where he was based. We owe him a lot.

Boxing is widely perceived to be easier on entry than other sports codes. There is said to be very little one has to do or have in terms of resources to make it successfully to the top. That is partly true if one considers the kind of armoury and finances other sports codes demand at the door.

We sometimes take for granted the actual requirement of being professional boxers, and most people go into boxing without even trying to have the necessary equipment. But, unfortunately, this poses a great deal of danger for the youngsters because the equipment that many youngsters need for protection is essential but not easy to get.

This naivety and seemingly careless state of affairs is brought about by the conditions of poverty and squalor that the young kids and their trainers come from. The interest and determination to continue with boxing is never deterred by the lack of facilities. We also found ourselves in a similar situation when we started boxing. It was the same in other rural villages and even in the townships like Mdantsane and Zwelitsha, where boxing was already thriving.

Milk cartons were used as boxing gloves. There was no knowledge of protecting the knuckles, thumbs and wrists. Imagine the damage these utensils were causing on the unprotected eyes, lips and noses. Cloth, cotton wool, or folded plastic were used as gum shields to protect the gums and teeth.

We had no boxing rings. That was taken care of by human circles or lines drawn on the ground. Those who were lucky to have the nod of a sympathetic school principal to use one of his classrooms had it better because they could use the desks and put them in a circle as the boxing ring. That was mainly the case in the townships. Things have since evolved with time. Although things are not as perfect as they should be, beginners can now join a reasonably equipped gymnasium with the necessary equipment for beginners. An adequately equipped gymnasium can prepare a youngster with the following material for his protection;

Headgear is essential for the protection of the head, especially the forehead and the eyes. In addition, it assures a certain measure of lessening the pain so that a kid can focus while learning. Amateurs use it in both sparrings in the gym and actual fighting. Professionals use it in sparring in the gym to protect against injuries in training.

The mouth-guard protects the mouth-parts, especially the gums and the teeth. Protection of the teeth is essential as they tend to loosen up, grind against one another, and cause other damages to other mouthparts on getting hit with specific punches.

Boxing Gloves are used for both sparring and fighting. They protect both the boxer and the opponent from serious injury to the head and body. They also protect the fists and knuckles of the fighters.

Hand-wraps must be used at all costs, both in training and fighting. They are used to protect the knucklebones and wrists to keep the hands of the boxer. The hands are the most delicate part of the boxer's body and must be kept safe at all times. The boxing ring is still a dream for some boxing clubs for both professional and amateur boxers. They still train in makeshift rings and only get the real thing in the actual fight. But at the list, it's not all gloom and doom.

THE RICH TALENTS OF GINSBERG

Ginsberg is a small township on the banks of the Buffalo River next to King William's Town in the Buffalo City Metropolitan, Eastern Cape. It was named after a member of parliament of the Cape Colony, Senator Franz Ginsberg. As was the case with other townships where inhabitants were drawn from farms and rural villages to be closer to the towns for purposes of cheap labour, so did the people from predominantly rural backgrounds who flocked to this new residence to seek work nearer to King William's Town.

No one could know that this small space would in future be a breeding ground for political, academic and administrative giants that would change the face and make their mark forever in the annals of South Africa.

Among icons who call Ginsberg home are globally known and revered anti-apartheid activist and founder of the Black Consciousness Movement, Steve Bantu Biko, Executive Chairman of The Platform for Public Deliberation, among his many caps, Professor Xolela Mangcu, as well as respected administrative guru Mthobi Tyamzashe. The rich presence of different talents meant that Ginsberg was always going to be a force to be reckoned with in any social activity, including boxing in the Eastern Cape and the rest of the country.

Boxing started here almost the same time as Zwelitsha. The first known founders of boxing here include Mr Mtolo and Mthunzi Mpondo. The most successful amateurs were Mthuthuzeli Mooi, Thozamile Mpondo, current Siphetho Mlonyeni, Spintshintshi Kamteni, Thobekile Sobopho, Billy Mkhencele, Nkosomzi Moss and Ruben Matewu. Except for Moss, Matewu, Mkhencele, Mpondo, Socutshana, Nyakathi and Mooi, Ginsberg produced more successful amateurs than professional boxers.

Nkosomzi Moss became the most successful boxer from Ginsberg. He won the South African Junior Featherweight championship when it was still the prestigious Old Buck Belt—earning him acknowledgement as the first boxer from King Willam's Town to win the Old Buck Belt. Mthuthuzeli Mooi, my former opponent, whom I beat, of course, was later to be a boxing promoter. This is also the home club of Mthobi Tyamzashe, the first black chairman of Boxing SA in the new democratic South Africa – after the Apartheid Regime. Mthobi was the first chairman under the South African Boxing Act 11 0f 2001, as introduced by then Minister of Sport Ngconde Balfour. However, there is no more boxing in this once busy sports-mad township that was home to the legendary Star of Hope Rugby Club, one of the most vibrant and most productive rugby clubs in the region.

Stanley Christodoulou, South Africa's internationally acclaimed boxing official who has been involved in boxing since 1963 with over 200 world champions in his career.

Team Dida Boxing Promoter, Meme Dipheko (left), a nominee for the Most Promising Promoter of the Year category in the Boxing South Africa Awards 2018, with her husband and boxing trainer, Dida Dipheko (middle) and boxer, Thato Bonokaone (right). Photo: Siso Naile.

From left to right: Marvelous Marvin Hagler, American professional boxer and film actor who competed in boxing from 1973 to 1987 with Berman and Roberto Duran. Photo by Jeff Ellis

Baby Jake Matlala who held the South African junior flyweight title and four world titles: WBO flyweight and WBO, IBA and WBU junior flyweight titles with Theo Mthembu who must be considered as one of the greatest trainers and managers in South African boxing history. Pictire: African Ring collection

The late Leighandre 'Baby Lee' Jegels in action against Liliana Gonzales from Argentina at the Orient Theatre in East London. File Photo Image: ALAN EASON

Phillip Ndou celebrates after he defeated Welcome Ntshingila during their fight at The Redemption 2 Double Header IBF Championship at Carnival City. Photo ENCA

South African Zolani Tete scored a spectacular and dominant eighth-round knockout over Paul Butler to retain his IBF junior bantamweight title in Liverpool, England.

Boxing returns to the Orient Theatre in East London after months of inactivity due to the Corona Virus pandemic.

The late Mzi Mnguni is flanked by champion boxers Nkosinathi Joyi, left, and Simphiwe Konkco. Image: ALAN EASON

Boxer Muhammad Ali steps away from a punch thrown by boxer Joe Frazier during their heavyweight title fight at Madison Square Garden in 1971.

Welcome Ncita, Simpiwe Vetyeka and referee Roberto Ramirez during the vacant IBO International Boxing Organisation bantamweight title bout between Simpiwe Vetyeka and Eric Barcelona at Emperor's Palace on the 11 July 2009 in Kempton Park, Gauteng, South Africa.
Image: Lefty Shivambu / Gallo Images

Ayanda Matiti during the 2018 Boxing SA Awards at Boardwalk Casino and Hotel on February 02, 2018 in Port Elizabeth, South Africa. Picture: Michael Sheehan / Gallo Images

Bukiwe "Anaconda" Nonina is the first local woman champion to claim the ownership of BSA's championship belt. Photo: Facebook

Multiple award winning boxing promoter Mbali Zantsi is on a mission to make women's boxing fashionable with the same opportunities as men.

SWEAT AND TEARS

CHAPTER 19

THE FUTURE OF BOXING IN THE EASTERN CAPE?

It is maybe a surprise why East London and surrounding areas were the last regions to take up boxing in the country. It is may also be an even bigger surprise that no sooner had boxing started there; it was producing the more polished boxers in the region, the great fan numbers, the jealously involved crowds at the venues, the incredible enthusiasm and the undoubtedly clear understanding of the game as to challenge anyone and anywhere.

It took less than ten years for East London and surrounding districts to take over all the facets of boxing in South Africa. How did that happen? Maybe one can trace this involvement, enthusiasm and talent back to the pre-Colonial days of the people in what is mainly *Xhosaland*. Stick fighting, music, poetry, and dance have always been part of the culture in this region. Therefore, it is fitting that the tactics and rhythm of boxing jelled easily with the kind of fighting they were born into.

The art and science of the two is the same. This area has a particular brand of boxing that is different from other parts of the boxing world. It is exciting. It is rhythmic. It is unique. And as South African history will tell, boxing between black and white boxers in front of racially mixed crowds was forbidden and could not be sanctioned. All positions were appointed and controlled by the Government.

The amateur level had to be run by an army brigadier who had proved his position and belief in Apartheid Rule and was against racial integration of any kind. He would make sure that there were separate white, coloured and black tournaments and championships. Such tournaments were run by governing bodies according to their colour or race. The white group was the main body.

The blow that finally broke the back of the racial hold on boxing came in the form of international sanctions. The Barcelona Olympics were coming, and South Africa was forced to send non-racial teams. Not to be outdone by this new pressure that went as a stronger challenge, the SA Apartheid officials simply selected non-racial groups but still made sure that most officials came from the white body. There had to be two white judges and one black judge for each contest. The black judge was always overruled.

The above scenario was not practised in the Border region of the Eastern Cape, which is now known as Buffalo City. There was already unofficial or secret mixed boxing in the area as black, coloured and white boxers were already visiting the different racial gymnasiums, sharing training facilities and sparring together. The white boxers included promising talents like Louis Olivier, Keith Kyle and Pietie Jacoby. He was to win the white South African amateur championship when he beat Grant Forbes in the finals in 1971.

The coloured boxers were led by Peter Shelton, known as one of the best-coloured boxers in this area. He never had the chance to turn professional because of the strict Apartheid conditions. He was soon to be followed by such talents as Solly Renkins and Cyril Groupe.

Around about the same time as Shelton being one of the top boxers, journalist Benito Philips was making waves as one of the leading boxing writers in the region. All of these illegal meetings were happening under the secret guidance and leadership of Les Muller, who had made the giant step of meeting up with the black-boxing leadership. As a white man, he used his racial advantages to advance boxing in the Border region.

Things turned around on January 13th 1979, when all segregated boxing was finally banned. In his book entitled "No Punches Pulled," renowned fight analyst Terry Pettifer writes, "On that historic date, Justice H. W. O. Klopper delivered what may rightly be termed the most significant and far-reaching speech in the annals of South African sport."

Justice Klopper took advantage of one of boxing's most significant events – the King Korn Boxing Awards. At a packed Carlton Hotel, he made the announcement that would formally eliminate all racial segregation and dismantle all racial titles in South African boxing. Our boxing finally received the International stamp of approval and was accepted around the boxing world as normal.

Almost immediately, big businesses recognised the opportunities and mileage that boxing and television could create for their brands. Gigantic companies like Southern Sun, Ronnie Bass Sigma, King Korn, Nashua, Old Buck Gin and Ellerines plunged in with massive sponsorship. This period unquestionably enabled boxing to develop and emerge as one of the three leading sports codes in South Africa. The other codes being rugby and soccer.

This financial windfall, especially from King Korn, Ellerines and Old Buck Gin in the townships, started blowing up. These companies set up a meaningful trend of township boxing that would introduce itself in a boxing style accompanied by a wave of music, song, dance and vocal crowds never seen before in the financially secure but less enthusiastic white South Africa.

East London and Mdantsane townships led the new charge. These townships had mainly black and a few white and coloured boxers. Local promoters heaved a sigh of relief at the new injection as this would go a long way towards ensuring that they did not only depend on the gate takings to recoup their losses or gain some much-needed profit. Since the beginning of boxing in the region, local promoters like Eric Gabelana, Boyce Zitumane, Mfana Jekwa, Salinga Mzamo, Daliwonga Mkhosi, Wridge Qeqe, and later Michael Guwa, Koko Godlo, Mzi Mnguni, Tsele Thembeni, Zolani Moshani, Mlungisi Siyo, and a whole lot of others and myself as Director of my own Messiah Promotions, had to dig into their pockets for purse monies and logistics.

In King William's Town and surrounding districts, the promoting charge was led by Wridge Qeqe, who was later joined by Cyprian Mheshe. There were no sponsorships to back up the promotions.

Ntshoto kept King William's Town rural villages like *Ezilaleni*, *Ngxwalane*, *Kalkop*, *Zondani* and others alive by having those villages busy. He promoted numerous non-profit development tournaments and billed local boxers. A young Mathemba Nyakathi, Chris Pondo and promoter Ntshoto would take up the promotional duties later. Currently, boxing is still going on, though at a much slower pace. Andile Champ Bakubaku and Xolani Jamani have now joined Chris Pondo. Together they are keeping the fires burning. They are luckier than their counterparts in other areas in that local boxing fan and businessman Maduna Magongo who lives in Ndevana near King William's Town, continues to fund boxing as he was doing with Mathemba Nyakathi and Monwabisi Guwa of the legendary Real First Team Promotions.

Magongo expects nothing in return. To him, it is just for the love and development of the game. Other than that, there were no sponsors. Currently, Magongo assists new kid Mfundo Botha who is busy with grassroots level boxing in the King William's Town rural areas.

The large crowds that always filled the venues ensured that the promoters gained much more than they lost. Sisa Dukashe stadium in Mdantsane naturally became the most popular venue. Long lines could be seen from as early as ten in the morning for tournaments that would only start at 13h00 in the afternoon. Business boomed as taverns and shops had to deal with the influx of people from all walks of life.

Police would be challenged to the limit while trying to control the lines. As a result, vital and feared people like Boysana emerged as the guys to control long lines of impatient fans who wanted to jump the lines to the gates as soon as possible. Boysana used to knockout such intruders with an open palm. He became an instant hero.

It was, however, not all good news for local promoters, managers and trainers as the competition with their white counterparts started to put on the heat. The white folks had more influence on the boxers because they had more lucrative sponsorships and naturally more paying power than the black promoters. They were also more seasoned and more imaginative businessmen. It was not long before the better black boxers and prospects drifted towards the white promoters, managers and trainers.

While the bigger part of the country was losing boxers to their white counterparts, the Eastern Cape, especially Buffalo City, faced a different version of the situation. In these parts, it was not the boxers living for white counterparts. Mzi Mnguni, a businessman and a newcomer to boxing, forged ties with big promoter Rodney Berman of Golden Gloves. Their relationship made sure that all prospects under Mnguni were guided to the top of the IBF world rating and finally to world title fights.

Boxers such as Welcome Ncita, the IBF Junior Featherweight champion, Vuyani 'The Beast' Bungu, who was to become the IBF Junior Featherweight champion, Mbulelo Botile, IBF Bantamweight champion and Zolani Petelo, the IBF MiniFlyweight champion; benefitted heavily from their association with Mnguni.

Other boxers who won world titles because of this relationship were Lindi Memani – WBU Mini Flyweight champion and Hawk Makepula, the first multi-world champion from the Eastern Cape. It was no surprise that all good prospects left their stables to join Mnguni. He became a legend in his lifetime. His boxers became heroes.

It was the emergence of a young red-headed motor-mouth called Nick Durandt and a white promoter of Serbian origin Branco Milenkovic that dramatically loosened the grip on Mnguni's hand on the local scene. Durandt was a sound and well-grounded trainer-manager who also enjoyed a good relationship with Golden Gloves. BCM boxers started crossing the gym floor, disregarding long-living relationships and the benefits of being with Mnguni. They flocked in big numbers to Durandt's stable. Other boxers stayed in their gyms with their local mentors who had started them on the road to boxing success.

Under Branco, they still received attention and gained International and world title fights. This was something unheard of since the emergence of the Mnguni/Berman relationship. Branco had successfully broken Golden Gloves' hold on the world boxing scene. The changes were there for everyone to see and every deserving boxer to enjoy.

Unlike Berman, new promoter Branco did not have an impregnable select line of managers and trainers from whom to get the boxers to promote to world status. He was prepared to work with any trainer or manager who had good boxers and was prepared to work with him. This promotional strategy saw him take control of the best boxers across the country, especially the Eastern Cape Province, Gauteng and Limpopo. Boxers did not have to leave their people. He became very powerful and influential, gaining much respect both inside and outside South Africa.

He secured international connections, and his tentacles covered all big three sanctioning bodies, namely, WBA, WBC and IBF. He also had a firm grip and influence on the Government corridors, subsequently promoting big tournaments in the boxers' home venues with the help of Government funds. But when Branco's champions that included Mzonke Fana, Noni Tenge and Zolani Tete, lost their IBF World titles without defending them in the ring, he seemed to lose a lot of his clout among South African fans. He was accused of having pulled the plug on the boxers by using his influence within the IBF to have them stripped of the tiles. Their sin, they complained, was to ask the promoter for better purses.

Boxing was booming on one side, with TV and sponsors creating stars and heroes like no other time in the past. But on the other side, tensions began to loom between the TV channels SABC and its competitor Supersport.

This rivalry also impacted the black promoters as they were finding it more and more challenging to compete with their white counterparts in what was now becoming more of a business than a sport or, as was expected, a social obligation.

While it can be effectively argued that television played and still plays a significant role in marketing and popularising boxing, it is also a big contributor to the demise of crowd attendance in the venues. The years between 1980 and 2000 can safely be described as the period when television showed both sides of its influence. Positively it brought to the sport of boxing the prosperity that is the goal of every sports code.

Negatively the empty seats it created in fight venues were fast becoming more numerous than the occupied ones. Its homely effect kept people watching boxing from their comfortable lounges at home with their families.

It consequently created many armchair commentators and analysts, who developed to be avid and knowledgeable contributors and boxing fans without ever attending a fight venue to watch a live boxing match.

Different views on whether TV killed or strengthened boxing have been expressed, but mine is that the personal opinion depends on where one is standing. TV brought boxing action to millions of viewers at home and other gathering places. It became an enormous marketing phenomenon which was to take boxing to higher levels and introduce its star performers to future generations. But the slump in live attendances has always been condemned by hardcore boxing fans and promoters.

There has, however, been some consolation to promoters from TV payments for live coverage. The influence of TV also created another form of rivalry among promoters and fans across the racial divide. From its initial days as MNET, DSTV's Supersport had signed a long term contract with

Golden Gloves, who only used the gambling Casinos as their promotional venues in mainly the Northwest Province and Gauteng.

The geographical locations and the business of the Casinos naturally make for a white man's venue. And so it followed that Golden Gloves' paying customers became mainly white fans, and their main drawcards were white boxers.

The Eastern Cape, especially BCM, gained enormously during this period. New opportunities were created by internationally connected boxing writer and analyst Leonard Neill, who became an international boxing agent. He took a liking to the local fighting style. He used his influence with international promoters for local boxers to gain world ranking, resulting in them earning opportunities to fight for world titles.

Eastern Cape boxers who took advantage of Neill's connections and won world titles recognised by the new mushrooming world sanctioning bodies were Sakhumzi Magxwalisa – WBU Super Bantam, Mzukisi Sikali – WBU Junior Flyweight and WBU Junior Bantamweight, Patrick Quka – WBU Bantamweight, Mpush Makambi – IBO Middleweight, Wele Maqolo – WBF Mini Flyweight and Zolile Mbityi – IBO Flyweight.

The above period up to perhaps the year 2000 is strongly regarded and celebrated as the best and most industrious period for boxing in the Eastern Cape, especially Buffalo City. It produced the best boxers, trainers and promoters.

The year 1999 even promised to be the biggest year when negotiations were at advanced stages to promote a Mandela Belt tournament that would feature Lennox Lewis against Evander Holyfield for the world's Heavyweight championship.

Local Daily Dispatch journalist Mxolisi Ntshuca was deeply involved in the negotiations for the Fight of The Decade, and also what would be the biggest fight ever staged in South Africa, to happen in Buffalo City. He was acting as a consultant for businessman Motto Mabanga who intended to organise the event in conjunction with Don King Productions.

Such ambitious intentions would have buoyed our region and fixed its position firmly on the same level of international visibility as did the Rumble in The Jungle for the Democratic Republic of Congo, another African country. But in this case, the intentions floundered because of the non-existence of a suitable venue for such a fight in Buffalo City.

Gauteng had already lifted its hand to take the stage as the next venue before the negotiations fizzled out. In the last twenty years, the situation has changed so dramatically, and standards dropped so low in the field of local boxing promotions that no sane person would even dare contemplate presenting such a proposal. The political atmosphere is cosy and friendly enough to allow all world sanctioning bodies to operate in the country without questions. The economic situation is, however, totally disagreeable.

With the exception of the WBU, the sanctioning bodies are still visible and in full practice. The newcomers are the WBF and the IBO. They are also the busiest. The WBA and WBC, the oldest sanctioning bodies globally, are only active as far as their regional titles are concerned.

These regional titles are ten a penny. But the promise of a respectable ranking and eventual chance at the world title remains just that – a promise. All that these titles do is provide a safer route and opportunities for promoters and their prospects who dodge the tougher SA title route and vie for the easier opponents and more winnable fights rather than take on their tougher SA contenders and the National title. The busier sanctioning bodies who deliver on their promises of world rankings on winning their regional and international titles are the WBO, WBF, IBF and IBO. South Africa boasts of several world champions on all these four sanctioning bodies.

The WBO and the IBF are the more internationally recognised and supposedly credible, and respected sanctioning bodies of the four. The future of Eastern Cape boxing can only be predicted by the numbers and capacities of its boxers and promoters. There have, however, emerged new players and new ideas on the local horizon that promise an unpredictable but also very interesting view for Eastern Cape boxing. Past promotional ventures were able to produce heroes and heroines from all facets of the game – against all odds. But the question that curiously arises is whether the current situation is conducive for a revival of the happy successes of the past. At this writing, the Eastern Cape cannot even afford to stage world title defences involving its single WBO world Bantamweight champion Zolani Tete.

The situation further raises the question of the uncertainty of whether the current crop of promoters, on whose shoulders our pockets rest the future of our boxing, can overcome the historic challenges of economic demands and compete effectively in the international arena. Can they withstand the monetary demands, logistics and all other requirements that make for big international events?

Local hopes have been positively aroused among the boxers, fans, managers, trainers, and other promoters. The IBF has recently announced that local promoter Terris Ntuthu of Rumble Africa Promotions won the purse bid to stage a world title elimination contest for boxer Azinga Fuzile. It is a boxing first and a historic victory for South African boxing that could mean that perhaps there is a light at the end of the tunnel.

Of the more than forty licensed promoters that are supposed to be operating in the Eastern Cape Province, only three are actively promoting. Except for that, they only promote at the international and world level. That leaves development fights and still to be developed boxers out in the cold. A future without development or nursery tournaments is no future at all.

In just the past two years, much to the dismay of the local boxing fraternity, three promotions that had landed a big hand and showed a lot of promise for the future in successfully delivering mammoth events are no longer operating.

That has undoubtedly led to the demise of local boxing. Seemingly the main reason, among others, for such hasty retreats by the promoters have been the breakdown of working relations with Boxing SA, the regulatory body of boxing in the country.

Without going into the intricacies of such disagreements, it is just hopeful that the different parties will, in time, smoke a peace pipe for the good of boxing. Without promoters, there is no boxing.

For some time, the Imonti Consortium that was formed by a group of boxing enthusiasts who included Andile Sidinile, kept the boxing fires burning. Sidinile, a former amateur boxer who would later serve as a Boxing SA board member, formed his own Sijuta Promotions. This ambitious promotional career started like a house on fire. In a few years of promoting boxing, his promotional outfit soared in stature and rose to become one of the brightest boxing houses in the country.

Armed with a long boxing experience and networking skills, Sidinile made great strides nationally and internationally, consulting and making deals for his own and other promotions and stables.

Working relations with world-class promoters like Bob Arum and Oscar De La Hoya resulted in world-class local fighters landing long deserved and profitable opportunities. From such links, Simphiwe Vetyeka became the first South African boxer to unify two world titles, the IBO and WBA

Featherweight titles when he beat 58 fight unbeaten WBA champion Chris John in Australia. Also in the offing were upcoming quality fights for the Siyo brothers Siyabonga and Luzuko. Sidinile even lured female boxing sensation Leahandre Jegels from Karate to conventional boxing and promoted her to a national and Pan African champion in only nine fights.

He also enjoyed excellent working relations with The Money Team of P4P great Floyd Mayweather Jr.

His boxing tentacles went as far as Germany and Saudi Arabia, countries with no history of sporting or boxing relations with South Africa. With his Sijuta Promotions as one of the licensees, the future of South African boxing looked very bright until serious disputes with the regulatory body, BSA, emerged. Such fallout would lead to him discontinuing his active involvement and working mainly as an agent. Sidinile is still well connected and operating extensively at the international level, using his networks to clinch deals for boxers, ring officials and promoters as a consultant or agent. One hopes that his problems with the governing body will soon be sorted and be a thing of the past. Boxing needs as much talent from as many angles as is possible.

Mamali Promotions was formed by former unbeaten professional boxer and current lawyer Siphaho Handi. He was appointed as a Boxing SA Board member in 2002 before retiring to take up a promoter's license. Unlike his fellow promoters in King William's Town like Mathemba Nyakathi, Chris Pondo and Champion Bakubaku, who concentrated on small tournaments and relied on their East London counterparts for bigger fights, Handi shot for the stars from the beginning with considerable success. The promotion had the best boxers of that period and staged their big fights at the Orient Theatre. Among the leaders in the pack were crowd pullers who would be legends of what is generally known as The Boxing Mecca. Nkosinathi Joyi is perhaps the greatest fighter that Mamali Promotions guided from the beginning to a world championship.

In winning the South African mini flyweight title and later conquering the world as IBF champion, Joyi became a local drawcard and an all-time great. He was to be succeeded by female sensation Noni Tenge, who won the WBF and IBF Welterweight titles, assuring her undisputed position as the best female boxer and a pioneer for South African female boxing. In addition, Female world champion Unathi Myekeni (WBF) and Lubabalo Msuthu (WBF) are also products of this success.

The saddest moment was when the promotion and the boxing fraternity had to come together to mourn the death by car accident of Ludumo Galada. Many people were convinced he was headed towards being the best boxer in the region.

Unfortunately, his hand also bowed out of boxing, taking all those skills with him and leaving boxing all the weaker for it. Fortunately, they always come back. As the saying goes, "Once the boxing bug stings, they usually stay stung."

Besides national champions and upcoming prospects, there are about ten genuine quality contenders for world title challenges tightly controlled by contractual obligations among the three local giant promoters.

One would be accused of being pessimistic in observing that the blistering pace at which the boxers change allegiances is such that it could result in a state of inconsistency. It has always been the reason for the demise of many stars and prospects who promised so much but failed to reach the desired destination. When they shift promotional allegiances, the new promotional outfit usually has its own trusted managers and trainers.

Last Born Promotions, founded in 2015, is the newest of the three big promotions in the Eastern Cape Province. Named after its champion Zolani Tete, the promotion under Director Xolani Mapunye, who is assisted by co-founder and manager Mlandeli Tengimfene, has seen the promotions rise to international status in a short space of time.

In less than three years, it has already formed strong working relations with UK based Queensbury Promotions, one of the leading boxing houses in the world. Thanks to WBO world champion Zolani Tete who impressed the British crowds and was promptly secured under contract after winning against the then-unbeaten prospect, British boxer Paul Butler.

That association with such a successful promotion has boosted the Last Born's efforts and seen it sour to the skies and fly and compete effectively with already established promotions in the country.

In this period, it has managed to successfully promote nine national and international fights that include two fully-fledged world title fights. That is a small number, and chicken feed, compared to the big international giants against which the promotion will be competing. Still, it's a massive achievement in local standards by which success is measured.

That clout has powered the promotion to sign a good number of upcoming prospects that include national champion Nhlanhla Tyirha and international champions Fikile Mlonyeni and Loyiso Ngantweni.

Among the attributes that qualify it to be a promotion for the future has been its ability to succeed where most of its older competitors have failed. Last Born Promotions has succeeded in securing private sponsorship for its tournaments as well as its All Winners Boxing Club. This is in contrast to the majority of its competitors, many of whom rely on Government funding to promote tournaments and boxers under contracted to their promotions.

It will be interesting to see if Last Born Promotions, with its connections firmly attached to the international successes of Queensbury Promotions in England, will continue to grow bigger and stronger.

To maintain that status, it will need to adopt the kind of high professionalism that is the key to succeed at that level of competition. Its challenges, however, do not reside overseas. The bulk of them is residents right back home within themselves as individuals, in some cases their partners and their competitors.

Negative habits and practices are the well-known local setbacks that have ruined many a bright future for local groups, especially the boxers. But perhaps the most significant burden for the success of Lasborn Promotion, in this case, lies on the shoulders of its world champion Zolani Tete himself, the partner who has also landed his ring name to the promotion.

A big part of the outfit's success at the top will also depend on whether Zolani Tete keeps his head on his shoulders and does not fall into the same trap of ill-discipline and ill-preparedness that has always been the Eastern Cape boxers' downfall when they approach the top. The promotion's international relevance depends on him keeping on winning.

Xaba Promotions's Director Ayanda Matiti has promoted arguably the biggest tournaments in the Eastern Cape over the last ten years.

The Xaba executive that consists of matchmaker Abbey Mnisi, Adv Tandokazi Loqo, and Project & Marketing Manager Mrs Dibakazi Matiti, has organised high profile events that have attracted some of the biggest crowds since its launch in 2008. The event's themes have gone beyond the normal boxing confines and attracted people from all walks of life. Even those that have not been historically connected to boxing. It has been the promotion of choice for managers, trainers and upcoming prospects.

Matiti's massive negotiating and networking skills have resulted in him forming important and groundbreaking partnerships. Such far-reaching deals have succeeded in producing co-promotions with partners outside of his Province, thus earning him strategic opportunities to take charge of organising boxing tournaments to celebrate almost all strategic political commemorations and events in the South African calendar and boxing tradition.

Big promotions like Sijuta and Mamali that rivalled Xaba for some considerable periods in the last five to ten years are no longer in the running, for one reason or another. Xaba Promotions' events and the number of boxers contracted to the promotion through managers with close working relations make it nearly impossible for other promoters to effectively organise preferred matches without approaching and seeking permission from his promotion fit. At this point, only Rumble Africa Promotions and Last Born Promotions seem to be competing effectively, due in part to the large number of champions, contenders and prospects contracted to them, as well as their non-dependence on government funding to do their tournaments.

Xaba's master strategy that strangled many other promotions and saw them either not promoting or leaving the game was in using its negotiating powers and financial muscle to sign contractual agreements and promote large numbers of boxers holding influential positions in the rankings many champions per division as possible.

Such signed boxers include but are not limited to South African champions Makazole Tete, Miniyakhe Sityatha, Lwandile Sityatha, Mzolisi Yoyo, and the massively popular duo of Macbute Sinyabi and Xolisani Ndongeni. Others have been famous international players like Gideon Buthelezi and Ludumo Lamati. The effect was that he had a stronghold on each and every division and deciding who fights who at a certain point in time.

This power is at its most glaring when the champion and the mandatory contender, as well as the first five or six contenders in a division, are all contracted to Xaba Promotions. This does not sit well with other promoters as they find themselves forced to go through or negotiate with him at every point. It has led to the courts of law being worked overtime, like never before in South African boxing.

Xaba Promotions does not only promote in Buffalo City as is the case with other promotions, but its tentacles are spread all over the country to as far as Gauteng, Limpopo, and Northwest Provinces. That makes it a formidable national player. Its Headquarters are, of course, in East London where it's all happening, as usual.

The big events, which are usually stacked with Pan African, International, Inter-Continental and South African title fights, are held at the Orient Theatre and The ICC at the beachfront in East London. The partnership with Premier Hotels and Resorts has added more punch to an already powerful fighter. Rumble Africa Promotions is a highly professional outfit that has already transcended its own and boxing fans imaginations.

Formed by Director Terris Ntuthu, its biggest ambition is to compete at the highest level of world boxing. If one has to judge by the giant steps, it has taken in less than five years of boxing life, and it is maybe safe to say that this promotion is already there. Among its achievements are the cream of South Africa's top-class performers. You can count Azinga Fuzile, who was rated the brightest South African prospect for world honours in its kitty. As of this writing, Fuzile may have lost that rating after Russian Asavat Rhakimov knocked him out in an IBF world title eliminator.

Former boxing amateurs stand out now. Seasoned and unbeaten professionals Ludumo Lamati and Sivenathi Nontshinga, and dynamic performers like Siphosethu Mvula and Lerato Dlamini, and a lot more, form part of the RAP team.

RAP has as its CEO female trailblazer Nomfesane Nyathela and COO Camagu Luvo, who were instrumental in RAP winning an international purse bid for Azinga Fuzile's elimination contest against the cream of international promoters vying for the same competition. This was the first achievement not only for a South African promotion, but also a first for female boxing. Maybe there's more on the way.

Gauteng based and Internationally connected training wizard Collin Nathan forms a significant and influential part of RAP as an advisor. His influence was not more visible than when the promotion successfully clinched a working professional relationship with MTK. This UK based international management group has made great strides in professional boxing worldwide.

This move has already paid great dividends and gained massive strides in empowering the promotional giant that is RAP. With a self-sufficient company like Rumble Africa that can draw from its resources to organise its boxing activities, boxing is certain to keep on rumbling.

The new MEC for Sports Arts & Culture, Fezeka Bayeni, not only showed her concerns on the uncertain future of local boxing but threw her punch by sponsoring and facilitating an urgent three-day workshop that succeeded in committing the divided promotional groups of local promoters to a harmonious working relationship.

The workshop, headed by HOD Mzolisi Matutu and his officials, long time boxing fans, Bafundi Makubalo, Gugu Adams, and Andiswa Skiti, came out with a turnaround strategy that ensured the spreading of skills and empowerment of all participants. This will create a more favourable atmosphere conducive to closer working relationships and more opportunities for boxers and other participants in all facets of the game.

Maybe the direct involvement of Government is what is needed in a turnaround strategy that aims to forge public/private partnerships with a view to shape and influence managerial, operational, financial, as well as all other spheres that will make the game of boxing a sport of choice for all.

Maybe with a new team led by Tando Zonke, the future will be instrumental in facilitating changes that may even end up reinstating the Eastern Cape Provincial Boxing Governing Body.

Such a governing body would make it much easier for the Province to produce that kind of activity to live up to its widespread recognition as the MECCA OF BOXING.

It would also create a solid platform to uphold and preserve its rich boxing and other sports legacy for generations and generations to come. Such boxing achievements would even succeed to influence the re-awakening of the sleeping giants like rugby and cricket, who have a rich history of developing and producing all-time greats at the most difficult of times. This would go a long way towards making this Province great again.

The new team of the Promoters Association consisted of:

- » Chairman; Tando Zonke
- » Deputy; Khaya Majeke
- » Secretary; Bongani Zulu
- » Deputy; Monica Goci
- » Treasurer; Sibongile Nkebe

Additional members are;

- » Mlungisi Siyo
- » Tando Nqanqali
- » Khwezi Booi
- » Xolani Mampunye PRO
- » Thobela Ngodwana.

CHAPTER 20

THE BIGGEST FIGHT THAT NEVER HAPPENED

From the time that boxing started in the 1950s, here in Buffalo City, especially in the East London – Mdantsane area, we have seen great boxing talent develop into extraordinary fighters. Buffalo City has always been the birthplace and breeding ground of immense boxing talent.

No sooner had youngsters in this impoverished region taken up the sport of boxing as a career of choice did we start to see an emergence of boxers who were prepared to stake their lives in the ring. For some, boxing was nothing more than a source of income, and many *pugilistic genii* emerged here and blossomed to national and international standards.

Buffalo City has especially been active and dominant in the lighter divisions, from mini-Flyweight (47, 63kgs) to Lightweight (61, 24kgs). Every title in those divisions, Flyweight, Bantamweight, Featherweight and Lightweight, plus all their junior classes, has always been regarded as lost when in a boxer's hands from another Province when matched against a fighter from Buffalo City. That is not surprising as it has to do with the general size of the people there. Even fighters who were big enough to campaign in the heavier divisions have been unsuccessful, especially when matched against opponents from the Gauteng province.

There have, however, been a few exceptions – myself as the former SA champions, Mpush Makambi and Mbulelo Mxokiswa can be counted as those exceptions. As the first boxer from this area to win the SA junior Middleweight title, Mpush Makambi won the SA Middleweight title and became the first IBO world champion in winning the Super Middleweight title. Mbulelo Mxokiswa also won the SA Middleweight championship. Maybe the unluckiest boxer not to win the SA Light Heavyweight title was Prince Tukani, who lost to future WBA Light Heavyweight Piet Crous.

Their fight remains one of the best fights seen yet in South African Boxing rings. The question has always been asked as to which division has produced the best performers in Buffalo City? I believe that the Bantamweight division has, without a doubt, been our most talented division up to now.

It started with the emergence of the wonder boy Mzukisi Skweyiya, followed by the dynamic Welile 'Ali' Nkosinkulu. Local boxing fans always have and will always lament the fact that politics of the time robbed them of seeing the greatest local fight that could ever be imagined. Why! Because it never happened.

This fight would have matched the best local boxing talent, at a time, when they were both at their best. If people had contracting skills, attitudes and personal lives, it was the two. Where Nkosinkulu was loud and dynamic, confronting opponents and predicting rounds in which he would knock them out, Skweyiya was quiet and unassuming. Where Skweyiya was tactical and defensive, Nkosinkulu was speedy and reckless. Nkosinkulu was a one-punch knockout artist, Skweyiya was the consummate technician who took an opponent down piece by piece.

Skweyiya was a master defensive mode, ducking, rolling, riding, blocking, parring punches, whereas Nkosinkulu was a stand-up, guards up, brutal and killer puncher. Where Nkosinkulu was ignorant and politically naïve, Skweyiya was a brilliant and intelligent scholar. The only two things that were common to them is that both boxers could fight. Both boxers were pretty boys. Crowds love handsome boxers. I know because I was a pretty boy myself. Historically BCM has produced great Bantamweights, perhaps the best division in the region if one considers the achievements of boxers in the division. Think of Skweyiya and Nkosinkulu, as the trendesetters. Then consider and measure all the greats that followed them. They read like a who's who of the Boxing Hall of Fame. The list consists of Mbulelo Botile, Gabula Vabaza, Simphiwe Vetyeka, Mhikiza Myekeni, Khulile Makeba, and

Phumzile Matyila; all of them having held the South African Bantamweight title. Add Zolani Tete, former IBF junior Bantamweight and current WBO World Bantamweight champion.

Both Nkosinkulu and Skweyiya would have had their hands full against any of the champions mentioned. But there is such awe and aura in their names and performances that is so stunning and long-lasting – it is incredible. Of all the local derbies that have happened and those that have not happened, none rates close to this imagined fight among local boxing fans. I have been to bus and taxi ranks, rugby and soccer tournaments, school events and everywhere else, fans still cry about how they missed out. And they are in disagreement as to who would have come out victorious in that encounter.

Both boxers had been star amateurs. They were already better known and bigger drawcards in the amateur divisions than many professional champions of the time. Nkosinkulu had moved through the amateur ranks like a whirlwind, mowing down all known opposition. He was even known to move up the divisions to challenge respected and feared performers much heavier than the Featherweight division. But once he turned professional, he was happy to settle in the Flyweight division until he outgrew the division and moved up to Bantamweight, where he was more comfortable. That's where he built his legacy. Mzukisi Skweyiya had a cult following in Duncan village, where he grew, even as an amateur. Surprisingly I already knew about Mzukisi while I was still in my rural village, well before I got the opportunity to box. Skweyiya won the SA amateur title when he beat well known, and until that time, unbeatable amateur champion Paul Sikabopha Tsehla.

When South Africa was beginning to waver from its strong policies of racial separation, boxing was always upfront in leading the country in tackling such issues organised a multi-racial National championship in the then Transvaal. As could only be the case, there were two white judges to one black judge for each contest that put a black boxer against a white boxer. You can imagine the split decisions for white boxers as winners in all competitive fights. The referee would also be white and would be docking the black boxers for even the silliest of fouls. In fact, in most cases, there were no fouls at all. Skweyiya, as was expected among the black folks, knocked out everybody put in front of him. That is until the finals, where he could not stop Gregory Wagner from winning the title. The contest was so clear with Skweyiya overwhelming Wager, hitting him with everything except the kitchen sink. When Wager won, as had always been the case, all other fights before, the media that included black journalists like Theo Mthembu and Harold Pongolo described it as the robbery of the event.

I have had numerous conversations with my old friend, former boxer and trainer Spokes Witbooi. We discussed and disagreed on this matter when we were still boxers, and we continued to disagree. We both happened to be club-mates and sparring partners of both boxers. He was with Nkosinkulu. I was with Skweyiya. We were both firm in our beliefs that it would have been a tough and entertaining encounter. We disagreed on the outcome. So did everybody we talked to. Ironically amid all the hullabaloo about them, the two boxers seldom if ever talked about each other. There was this distant and quiet respect between them. Spokes Witbooi believed and still does that Nkosinkulu was the best local product ever. "He had blurring hand speed and accuracy unseen in a very long time. He was confident and completely believed that no one could beat him," says Witbooi.

As a young upcoming prospect, I am reminded of how Nkosinkulu walked over to the great Peter Mathebula and told him to win and keep winning because Welile was looking for him. "I will knock you out," boasted Nkosinkulu to the amazement of all boxing fans who had attended the weigh-in, Mathebula included. Even after Mathebula had swept the ring with Monde Mpulampula on that day, Nkosinkulu still reminded him that, "I'm coming for you."

While Nkosana Mgxaji is rightfully credited with popularising boxing in the Eastern Cape and especially putting Mdantsane or East London on the world map, Nkosinkulu undoubtedly popularised the weigh-in. Both these areas are now part of Buffalo City Municipal Metro. And both have become the pride and joy of the City's boxing heritage. Nkosana possessed rare natural qualities that made him stand out in a room full of other boxers. He was charming. He was brash. And he was confident. Added to that, he could fight. His potential opponents were always called out and told how far they could go. He would do this show of bravado in a weigh-in event where he was not part of the bill. He would take it to extremes on the weigh-in of his fight. In the ring, he was a relentless fighting machine. He liked the eyeball to eyeball stare, stood in front of his opponents, and dared them to fight. Many of his opponents avoided that stare and refused to make eye contact as it was believed that Nkosinkulu used magic, and his gaze cast a spell on his opponents. He threw punches while at the same time talking to his opponent and making faces. He remains the only boxer to be able to challenge Mgxaji in terms of crowd-pulling. He, unfortunately, did not finally get to eclipse Mgxaji on the crowd attention because his career was very short. It folded just as fast as it had risen.

Both boxers' careers were short. Nkosinkulu's ignorance and naivety were to be his downfall. As soon as he tasted fame and adoration of the boxing fans, he surrounded himself with new people, some of whose agendas were not boxing aligned. At a time when political attitudes were at boiling point, Nkosinkulu allowed himself to be absorbed by people who were feared members of the then sinister security police.

He left his long time trainer and manager *Ntaba Mtyongwe* and was managed and trained by Willie Ncoko and Charles Sebe. People started to see him driving beautiful cars when the old Nkosinkulu they knew would hit the road or be in the gym. His performance took a dive, and he started losing fights he should have easily won. He was not working for the police, nor did he commit any deeds that would have him accused of being an out and about sell-out. But some pockets of people regarded his actions as selling out. He was young, illiterate, naïve and ignorant of all the political rumblings and changes around him. He was just a boxer. The old teachings of sticking to boxing and leaving politics to politicians firmly found room in his mind. But those days were fast becoming a thing of the past.

Such teachings were becoming irrelevant and intolerable. But Nkosinkulu could not comprehend such revolutions around him. He came from an impoverished family where his grandmother was the provider and breadwinner. It was rumoured that his biological parents were somewhere in Cape Town. They may have been some truth in this rumour as Cape Town is where he fought his last fights. It is where he finally settled. He still lives in Cape Town.

These new people in his life were giving him the kind of life he was not used to. All his toys had changed. Fast and flashy cars were a far cry from the carts he and his friends used to push when he was already a star amateur boxer. Loud, blurring car music and fast food had replaced the small home radio and staple home food. Beautiful girls were a new experience for him. And he loved every minute of it. But credit to him, he was not big on alcohol, smoking or anything of that sort. To him, it was just about having a nice time – letting the good times roll. But boxing was taking a back seat and a hard knock. His abilities were diminishing very fast. The little dynamo of energy that was Welile Nkosinkulu was getting soft and vulnerable. Things came to a head when his mentor Mtyongwe was transferred to Peddie, far away from everything that had to do with boxing. This new move put paid to any hope of Nkosinkulu every regaining the form that made him the terror of the Bantamweight division – the darling of the fans. Skweyiya, on the other hand, was the epitome of respect and dignity. A handsome, quiet and intelligent political activist. He was a student at Fort Hare University. The first boxer to win a South African boxing title while a student. He was never fully fit for his fights because of academic commitments and political activities. But he was still good enough to make the best and most accomplished boxers look ordinary.

While there were students like Khaya Ngqula and myself to help him prepare for fights, study duties would always call, and as such, we could never stick to a strict program for training. Besides sparring with me, him a Bantamweight, and me being Welterweight at the time, there were other ex-boxer students, especially from East London and the old Transvaal, who were always ready to help with sparring when academic duties allowed. They included guys who are now leaders in the South African academic and social fields. I have forgotten some of them, but I remember Peter Ngatane, Luyanda Ngoma, Mandla de Beers, Cosmo Maho, Boyce Mbha, Mazembe Ndzondo and several other youngsters from the neighbouring village, kwaNtselamanzi in Alice. Khaya Ngqula and Mthobi Tyamzashe were always on hand to help. Ngqula also worked as our cornerman. Skweyiya had to make do with what he had. In June of 1976, we came back to an empty Fort Hare University. Other than big numbers that marked a massive police presence, the campus was empty. Skweyiya, Ngqula and I had attended a boxing tournament in Port Elizabeth. We had known before leaving that something was bubbling. But we never anticipated a rapture of such magnitude.

One that would turn around the very face of the country and the lives of the people – forever. We were allowed to collect our belongings and get the hell out of there. Such was the life and boxing of Mzukisi Skweyiya. He was one of the most complete fighters I have ever seen. A boxer-fighter who could box skilfully or go toe to toe, depending on what the opponent was bringing or not bringing. His technique and ring generalship allowed him space to execute risky but effective moves within dangerous zones of his opponents best qualities – within the pocket and come out untouched. He also had knockout power in both hands. One can only imagine how far he could have gone if he had just a little bit more time to train. Witbooi is adamant that Nkosinkulu's blistering pace would be too much, and Skweyiya would be out-gunned. He rightfully makes an example of a common opponent Daniel Hlahane. Both contested against him. Skweyiya fought a draw with Hlahane. Nkosinkulu knocked Hlahane out in three rounds. I think the reason there is a matter of style. Come forward fighters were easy meat for Nkosinkulu. He met them halfway. Against Skweyiya, he would miss and pay as long as the fight lasted.

Witbooi argues that the penchant for ducking punches is precisely what would play into Nkosinkulu's hand and give him victory. "Skweyiya's wide stance plus that love for ducking punches and spending almost all of the time making an opponent to miss would have been his downfall against Nkosinkulu who had an exceptional work rate," argues Witbooi.

Nkosinkulu 's fighting style made him a boxing fan's darling, aside from his brash nature and prediction of the rounds in which he would knock out his opponents. He was right most of the time. His 'seek and destroy' style accompanied with hands that went out like thunder and lightning made him a minute thrill performer. His knockout abilities with any punch made it difficult for one to look away lest one missed something – his opponents could not afford to lose focus even for a split second. He was known to have fists that created thunder and lightning on his opponent's heads every time he landed. But this, I think, is the same style that would make him easy meat for a formidable technician like Skweyiya. For Nkosinkulu's swarming style left him wide open, especially for impeccable counter punchers. Skweyiya would set him up with angles and make him punch thin air.

That lack of defence resulted in Nkosinkulu being stopped by opponents like Nkosana Tolbert in his first fight and Joseph Ngubane. He was set up with a jab and damaged with a straight right hand. So did Zweli Ngcongolo, who knocked him out. Mathebula also knocked him out in a rematch.

Witbooi argues that Nkosinkulu was no longer the same killing machine in those fights. I argue that it should not be an excuse as Nkosinkulu was still south of 30 years of age, still a youngster by boxing measures, and still supposed to be in his prime when such fights happened. Nkosinkulu, fast and powerful as he was, in contrast to Skweyiya, was also easy to read and anticipate his moves, especially when the fights were longer. Unlike

Skweyiya, Nkosinkulu had no excuse to come to the ring in less than prime condition. He had all the time. Skweyiya, on the other hand, was always on the run from the security police. There were times when he could not finish his training sessions. I doubt if there was any fight that he prepared thoroughly for and came in hundred percent condition – except for when he prepared for his South African challenge against Christopher Dlamini. For that fight, Skweyiya went and stayed for three weeks in Alexandria. Only two people knew about that, his training assistants Khaya Ngqula and myself.

The fight never happened because soon after the 1976 schools boycott, the police pressure became so consistent and dangerous that in 1978 Skweyiya, with stablemate *Lindile Yam*, now a General in the SANDF, quietly and secretly skipped the country and went into exile. Not even his closest friends like me had a hint of his preparation to elope, nor his actual departure until he had been gone for weeks. And he has so diminished a boxing career that undoubtedly would have been one of the best by a South African boxer at any time.

Mzukisi 'Wonder Boy' Skweyiya died in Botswana in a car accident. He retired unbeaten. Ironically, amid all of this hullabaloo of debates, discussions, disagreements and even fights about who would win in their wishfully upcoming fight, the two boxers seldom if ever talked about each other. There was this quiet and distant respect between them. Can you imagine how far the two talented pugilists would have gone if they had not met but continued with their careers side by side? Imagine if Welile Nkosinkulu had maintained the demanding training program and strong self-belief and discipline he had under *Ntaba Mtyongwe*?

What if Mzukisi Skweyiya did not have to run away from home to fight and die for his people's freedom and Constitutional rights? What if he was born into all the rights he deserved as a human being and citizen of his country? What if he was free to do, say, move, and associate with whomsoever he chose? What if he had all the time to engage and practise the sport that he loved so much and had the talent to challenge the best in the world? What if they had all the wishes mentioned above and eventually fought? We can only imagine.

CHAPTER 21

SCHOOLS BOOST MECCA BOXING

School sports have always been known as the breeding ground for all sports. Kids learn their sporting skills at an early stage at school, making it much easier for their minds and bodies to grasp.

It is also where teachers and coaches can identify those children that show exceptional talent. It also makes it easier to implant the religious practice of the sport even if the kids gravitate towards other interests in future.

From the beginning of boxing in the BCM, schools played a significant role in the awareness and development of boxing. It was because of such a relationship that boxing created such a massive vibe and activity. As Duncan Village was the leading township of boxing, one of the local founders of boxing was a school teacher named Thamie Nomvete. He would soon be joined by other teachers like Barnie Lebethlwane and Andrew Nkone in the administrative supervision of boxing tournaments. That group preceded a young and hardworking Mlandeli Vazi, who would take Duncan Village boxing to much greater heights by encouraging the majority of local primary schools to engage in weekly school tournaments. Mdantsane would soon follow suit. Though it took longer than other regions to take up professional boxing and had to rely on KZN for help, it was not long that this region took over all of the South African boxing once it started. It became the home of boxing. Many champions here, myself included, are products of such school development. This was partly due to the scarcity of halls that could be used as gymnasiums.

School principals were requested to allow boxers to use classrooms as gyms. Consequently, it was natural in a place like Mdantsane and neighbouring villages to have almost all the boys joining the boxing within the school premises.

There was such a resounding boom of boxing that schoolboys would represent their schools in inter-school tournaments and be back in the ring on Saturday representing their club.

There was plenty of action and learning. Almost every school had a boxing club and a couple of recognisable prospects. All these activities went a long way towards making boxing the number one sport in the region.

Ironically, school boxing is now completely dead. Maybe it goes with the perception that boxing itself is no longer the beloved sport it used to be, not only in this region but the rest of the country. I do not for a second believe that boxing is dead, but I am first to admit that it is by far no longer what it used to be. The slump in boxing numbers and competition can be put squarely on the fact that for the last two decades, school boxing has been completely shunned.

Perhaps my greatest disappointment borders on the fact that numerous attempts have been made to both past and current political appointees from the Provincial Government to the National Government to allow for the return of school boxing. We are confident of the role that boxing can play to decrease the strong reality of drug abuse and violence that is in high abundance and on the rise in schools.

Boxing has been historically known to implement verbal and practical measures among its practices to keep boxers on the straight and narrow. However, the time taken to commit mind and body to boxing practice and other extramural activities has been known to occupy the redundant space and brought such tendencies to the lowest levels. But all such attempts have been to no avail. Instead, there has just been a string of promises made in meetings as well as public addresses. Having been the first boxer in South Africa to turn professional as a university student and as a subsequent product of school boxing myself, I have personal and first-hand knowledge of what such association has and can still achieve. I am what I am today because of it. So are a lot of other people I know. And so is Buffalo City. That is why we never lose hope.

My taste of school boxing coincided with my introduction to the game. Right from the very beginning. The Principal at my school, Imiqhayi Secondary in Mount Coke, Mr SK Ngqangweni, allowed the local boys to use the hall as a gym. That started a boom for boxing that even attracted boys from the neighbouring villages. School Principals in other villages began to see boxing as a deterrent to alcohol and drugs for the youngsters. And so they opened up their schools to boxing and started interschool boxing in the evening after rugby and netball matches.

Nowhere was this phenomenon of boxing stronger than in Mdantsane, especially at Mzomhle High School under Principal Aubrey Bomela and later ex-Robben Islander, Ben Thengimfene. I was to benefit, and by extension, boxing was to benefit from the two sports developers, respectively. They were, just like every other parent in the region, as mad and committed to boxing as could be expected.

Founded around 1966 in NU1, Mdantsane Mzomhle was a highly respected school in the region. It boasted of high-quality education, professionalism among its staff, cleanliness, respect and dedication among its students. So it came naturally that it became a leader among other schools in all sports codes. Rugby matches between Mzomhle and neighbouring Hlokoma High School became legendary meetings.

Hundreds of people would overload the small NU1 rugby field as people would skip work and come to watch because these rugby matches were held on Wednesdays. These matches produced great spectator-friendly rugby stars like Patsa Matyeshana from Hlokoma as well as bright performers like Khayakhulu Qabaka, Mpumelelo Thantamiso and Zamikhaya Gxabe.

Mzomhle athletics and netball teams were also winning everything from scores in the field and performance awards. Girls like Nokuzola Mashologu and Nolose were always fan favourites wherever they performed. Sprinters Edward Sinani, affectionately known as Segge and Bantu Gqirhana's running escapades, were for the movies.

At this time, almost every Lower Primary, Higher Primary and High School had a boxing gym and school boxers. Such was the interest of boxing among the Mdantsane community and the schools around Mdantsane that Bomela came shot of introducing boxing as part of his school syllabus. Maybe he was denied by academic rules and regulations. But he still officially set aside a classroom and declared it a boxing gym. A school teacher, Mthuthuzeli Baduza, was appointed to look after the boxers.

Bomela went a step further by appointing ex-boxer Lungisa Dukashe as the special trainer to the young boxers. The Mzomhle Boxing Club's tournaments were held at Holy Cross Hall across the street. Its star performers included but not limited to Boy-Boy Mpulampula, Mzwandile Mqanto, Nduwa Qunta, Lulama Njikelana, Lwazi Njikelana, Monwabisi Goje, Fufu Mehana and Monde Mpulampula.

The club became perhaps the best boxing club Mdantsane club in 1972 when it swept the majority of titles in the Border championships. Boy-Boy Mpulampula, Mzwandile Mqanto, Nduwa Qunta and myself won the Border championships. In the same year, BoyBoy and myself were awarded the Mzomhle High School Sports Awards.

At Mzomhle Boxing Club, we had tough competition from Lovedale and Healdtown Institutions. Healdtown boasted of tough boxers like Smuts Ngonyama, Zama Mayola, Lucas Ncetezo, Tshiwula, Vuyo Nomvete, and National amateur champion Phakamisa Soka. The students and the local communities loved boxing and would pack the halls to watch interclub fights. On the other side, in Alice, Lovedale College already had professionals like the famous Tshume brothers Ngqika and Phalo. They were excellent and entertaining prospects who were known to give the legendary Nkosana Mgxaji a good run for his money. The college also boasted of respected competitors like Mzwandile Mqanto, who went there after Mzomhle and Lungile Gangala, Bafo Qabaka and a good number of others.

In 1979 I returned to Mzomhle with my manager Patsa Matyeshana. The same challenge of scarcity of boxing gyms that is still prevalent today forced us to approach the Principal and ask for the same old classroom for a boxing gym. Thengimfene has spent six years in Robben Island from 1967 as a political prisoner. On his return, he had taught in various schools that included Woodlands St Thomas, School of the Deaf and Khulani High School in Mdantsane before taking up the post of Principal at Mzomhle. He was now Life President for Wallabies Rugby Team. He was also an ardent fan of Nkosana Mgxaji. He gave us the classroom. And Zama Boxing Club was born. The rest, as they say, is history.

Against all odds, boxing in the BCM has made it to the international headline. If BCM is going to retain its position as the BOXING MECCA, one of its immediate actions will be to find out what made it to be so successful in the first place. And they may find that the answer is staring them straight in the face. Boxing should be returned to schools where local schools should be persuaded to afford a boxing activity that will entail two hours of boxing lessons per week firstly to introduce the kids to boxing. The aim may not be to make them contest or to practise as boxers but to teach them the basics of boxing for self-defence and the basics of the game.

This program would also create jobs for ex-boxers, giving them something to fall back on after their boxing days. In addition, at least two local boxers could be allocated to the closest school for such classes so that they could walk to and from work.

The government could allocate funds for such activities if there is political will. If this will existed and such programs could be sustained during the Ciskei and Transkei rules, I believe it can be done now. And it was done better. And much easier.

The school program succeeded in raising boxing in the region to international levels. It created and ensured boxers, boxing fans and activists for life. Our boxers became some of the best in the world. Boxing awareness among the communities makes for even young girls to have the confidence to defend themselves. It made Buffalo City the home of boxing – the Boxing Mecca

CHAPTER 22

WHEN DEATH MAKES NO SENSE

I was on my way from Frere Hospital where I had visited my boxer, Clive. If I can recall correctly, it was maybe my 15th visit in the seven days he had spent in the hospital. He had been rushed and admitted there from his fight at the Orient Theater; knocked out in his fight. I had spent most of the time there with boxing secretary Les Muller as he had also been a constant visitor.

Clive had been lying on the bed comatose and lost to the world for seven days. He was not responding to treatment. The doctors had tried everything they could with little success. All sorts of attempts had been made in our presence every day. But to no avail. Finally, on this day, the nurse who had always been in attendance most of the time came out completely different.

She had changed. The free-spirited and hopeful mom who kept assuring us not to worry because things were going to be alright, was gone.

On this day, instead of looking at the patient, she looked straight into my eyes and addressed me. She told me that though Clive was sleeping, still and looking dead to the world, he was still with us and could hear us talking. He understood all that we were saying. She told me that as one who had been with him for so long, I was the one who could release him. She said to tell him, if his condition was painful and he was suffering, he should let go.

We would all understand. I knelt next to the bed and whispered in his ear. I told him that this was the seventh day that he had been away from us. If he felt pain, any kind of pain, he must give himself to God. I told him that one day, I did not know how long it would take, but I would do something for him. To keep his memory. This book is dedicated to him.

I remember as I parked my car in front of the house in my Mdantsane home, the phone was ringing. I rushed into the house and picked up the phone. "Is that you Mr, Mtya?" asked the lady on the side. I recognised the voice immediately and said yes. "He is gone," she said. I was strong enough now. And I understood. I thanked her and hung up the phone. On the way from Frere Hospital, the sad feeling of helplessness and imminent loss has risen so much that I could not control myself anymore. It had been simmering underneath every day from when it had become evident that there was nothing more we could do when the ringside doctor requested that he be taken to hospital. The feeling in my chest had now reached boiling point. I parked the car on the side of the road, and I cried loud and long. I was strong enough when the call came from the hospital to inform me of his death.

Clive Sikhwebu had passed on. My son had gone too. I had known Clive as a young boy growing up and playing with other boys around my house. He was staying close by across the street opposite mine. His grandmother looked after him and his brother.

These boys and some of their friends in the neighbourhood had grown up watching television with me in my home as I was the only one who had a TV set at the time. They would run after me when I did my roadwork. It was inevitable that they would end up being boxers.

When they finally made the decision and started boxing for competition, my club was the natural place for them to formally learn the trade some of them would choose as a career. I was their natural manager and trainer. I was their mentor.

Clive, who depended on his grandmother for his livelihood, was able to convince her to let him stay with me. She agreed. I, therefore, took over his entire life. I looked after him from his clothing, his school fees, and every bit of his life. He became my son. Now he was gone. And I had to go and break the news to his grandmother and other members of the family. Up to that time, the most challenging job I had to do. We had then started our journey together to make Clive Sikhwebu a star performer with the kind of all action and power punching style that made him the darling of the Orient Theater fans. He was one of the star attractions and best-loved boxers in the then Border region. His untimely death added his name to a list of other fatalities that resulted from boxing activity. Such casualties include boxers who have suffered short-term and long-term injuries.

When not about performances, victories, and defeats, debates and discussions on boxing are mainly centred on its casualties and fatalities. The arguments always start on the *whys* and end up on the hows. To many people, even to those who work and practice it every day, it does not make sense. Since it started in this region between the late fifties and early sixties, boxing has changed many lives. For better or for worse. But which side has the bigger numbers between the two is debatable.

Why then are all efforts, studies, and debates centred on death? I think it is because death in any form shakes people down to the very roots of their being. It is the very end of it all. Its existence has had people coming to grips with its unavoidable existence. They have had to understand it. But do they find it hard to accept it? They traverse into the farthest spaces and most profound corners of their natural, academic, and spiritual experiences to understand death and its realities. But death never makes sense.

This experience inevitably dug deep into my own emotions, and I have always tried as much as I can to take steps of my own to minimise injuries and death. I know there are a lot like me in all boxing gyms and arenas around the world. Like everybody who is in boxing and millions of those who love and embrace the noble art, I have never joined the chorus of those who have had reason enough to call for the banning of the game.

Like every boxing practitioner, I try to study and learn what causes death in the ring to reduce fatalities to the lowest numbers. In this case, I joined many people who were, and are, still trying to make sense of it all. It is the understanding of everybody involved that this game is a dangerous game in its very nature. You always read and hear the stories of deaths and near-deaths. But you seldom think that it will happen to you or anyone close to you. I also think that I am biased because I love this game so much. I am one of those people who have been gripped by this animalistic phenomenon and declared blood sport that is also ironically acknowledged as a sport of art and beauty. From my earliest days, I have always been fascinated by what boxing writer Terry Pettifer describes as the thrill of seeing two superbly conditioned athletes matching against each other in a confined, roped, punishment pit. I am not alone.

What has always made sense to us as people who are involved in the sport is how to make boxing safer. Brian Wysonke is an avid boxing fan who has dedicated most of his time and donated much material assistance to the game. Like many of us, he loves boxing and decries the loss of life that occurs from time to time. He says, "There are several sports like motor racing and motorcycling where the chances of getting injured and even dying are higher than other sports like golf, swimming, triathlon, and tennis. Many sports carry a risk."

The first and significant shift boxing made was to stop that ancient practice of going underground and into corners to practice its art. When it finally came out into the open, boxing attracted and gained various professionals who landed their skills and expertise to reduce death and injuries in the game. The experts came from a variety of academic disciplines that included, fortunately for boxing, medical practitioners. Aligning itself with professionalism was a masterstroke for the fortunes of boxing. It had proved that it had come in from the cold. It was ready to be counted. To make its point, South African boxing became the first sports code to ban boxers who tested HIV positive. This came around the early eighties when thirty-three South African fighters tested positive for the virus in one year. The exclusion of HIV Positive fighters was to go a long way in ensuring that measures were being taken from time to time to make the game safer and more acceptable. Considerable numbers of these professionals are now holding strategic and influential positions in boxing administrations.

Boxing commissions, organisations, medical groups, and individuals have thus landed significant support in advising and enhancing the push in the quest to make boxing safer. In recent times many changes have been made. Initially, there were no boxing rounds. Pugilists fought until one could not go on anymore. The introduction of rounds improved that.

The introduction of rounds meant that boxers could rest after the prescribed round. Such arrangement was still not satisfactory as the schedules themselves were too long for human consumption. The number of rounds was then reduced to what for a long time was fifteen rounds for world title fights. The organisations agreed to shorten the fifteen rounds to twelve rounds for title bouts. And as a rule, a boxer being knocked down three times in one round would automatically be considered a knockout loss.

Medical practitioners and scientists have also done immeasurable research and advised on ways and means of, where possible, curbing and reducing boxing fatalities. Such medical research and experience among boxing practitioners have revealed that many boxers carry conditions and injuries from their training sessions in the gyms to the ring. This is mainly a consequence and a combination of ignorance and inexperience among the handlers and the boxers themselves.

Thanks to the contributions by our doctors like Peter Ngatane and *Mzwakhe Qobose* of Gauteng, as well as East London's Siyabulela Bungane, the punishment index was introduced. Current fight supervisors have to register the punishment the boxer receives in each fight. Such statics are used for measure and reference in deciding whether the boxer should take the next fight, take a prescribed rest, or be ever allowed to box again. This information is important and kept for consideration even where the boxer wins what is considered an easy fight. But the one clear rule which is also visible to the spectators is the BSA adopted requirement that all tournaments must have two doctors in attendance. The purpose is to ensure that if one doctor has to leave with the injured boxer to a hospital, there is still a doctor left behind to ensure that the tournament continues under strict medical supervision. The hospital must have been booked before the fight and must be no farther than fourteen kilometres. A tournament cannot begin without the presence of such doctors, an ambulance, and paramedics. Another strict measure aimed at securing the life of the boxers was the rule introduced in South Africa to ensure that a closer look is taken at any boxer contesting in more than five fights within one year.

One of the main reasons behind boxers' ultimate undoings is the punches they take in the gym even before they take the journey to the ring. Boxers have to spar almost every day in preparation for upcoming fights. Sparring sessions have to be monitored. Sometimes when they are struggling with weight. And, even worse, sparring with opponents far bigger in size and weight. The day-to-day effect of punches they take, especially to the head, takes its toll if it goes unchecked tall.

Hundreds of boxers who die or are permanently disabled suffer from brain damage, eye impairments, kidney failure, or even breathing complications. Such injuries are at their most damaging, or boxers become more prone to them when their food intake and liquid consumption are drastically reduced. This dangerous practice is exercised to slim down to the lightest weight limit possible. Sometimes the effort itself is the killer. Boxers like to fight at the lowest weight as they believe it gives them a size advantage in being bigger than their opponents in the same division. It subsequently results in them under drinking, under-eating, and over-training. In the end, over-training brings about the same results as under-training. However, because of the practices I have mentioned, some boxers do not get in the ring in their best shape possible. Some boxers come in the best form, where injury or death results from fatal blows that could not be foreseen.

Boxers who carry too much weight between fights are also not doing themselves any favours. Dropping 10 to 15 kilograms in two weeks before a fight is the surest way to a fatality. Trainers have a massive job to do in the way of advising the boxer on the above matters, as well as being actively involved in the training. For sure, a trainer can assist as long and as much as humanly possible but cannot follow the boxer around every minute, all around the day. He cannot stay with the boxer all day to see what they put into their mouths. He also cannot kick the boxer out of bed to do roadwork. And so it boils down to the discipline and professionalism of the boxer himself.

As if that was not enough, I was to experience a somewhat similar feeling, but in reverse years later, when two boxers suffered untimely deaths at the hands of my boxers. I thought I knew exactly how the parents of the lost sons must have felt. I felt like reaching out and assuring them that it was God's will and that everything would be alright.

I wished I could tell them that their loved sons had died in the game that they loved so much. Maybe they would understand if I told them in the way amaXhosa have historically accepted the despair of loss and expressed their determination to keep life going on nonetheless. I wished I could say "*Akulahlwa mbeleko ngakufelwa,*" which in English translates to "do not despair or never give up."

It sometimes becomes a massive task to be involved and defend boxing. Even worse, practice and compete, or train people to compete. Boxing is a sport people choose for one reason or another. It has helped some boxers and their families beyond expectations - taking them from a place of destitute to a space of wealth and opportunity. It has produced a better life for those who have benefitted from boxing, especially those who have had a higher level of success than most.

The same, however, cannot be said about the gloom and doom some families have had to endure at the loss of their sons and, lately, their daughters. Sometimes boxing shoots itself in the foot to the point of losing its defenders. It forces many people to decide that there can be better ways to develop their lives. But some people choose to stick to it for better or for worse. Clive Sikhwebu was one of them.

There have been some unreported deaths due to ring injuries, especially in the amateur ranks. Some reports show that the first known ring death in the Border region happened in the late fifties or early sixties in Grahamstown.

Reports on the matter are that the said boxer, whose last name was Mbovane, died after a contest against East London's Kotikoti Sophila. Permanently injured boxers from ring activities include Simphiwe Mfaniso and Luvuyo Tyamzashe. And so are these heroes from Buffalo City alone who lost their lives in the game that they loved so dearly, Nceba Gobhozi, Vuyolwethu Booi, Samora Msophi.

At the writing of this account, I was saddened beyond belief as I receive the news that one of the boxers I was training, South African Bantamweight and WBA Pan African Flyweight champion Leahandre Jegels, had just been shot in the street and died. I take a few minutes to shed some tears and recover from this shot below the boxing belt at large.

Though her death is not ring related, it is still boxing-related and is a shuttering loss for her family, friends, and the boxing fraternity. She was shot after a high-speed car chase on her way to the gym as she was preparing for her next fight on the 5th of October 2019. She was shot and killed by a man known to her.

This unfortunate incident happened in August when South Africa celebrates Women's month. This is a month set aside for celebrating women for, among other things, their power, contributions, and achievements in the development of all human nature. We should have been celebrating her rise to the top in such a short period, Baby Lee, as she was affectionately known by her army of fans, was already a former multiple amateur Karate champion when she joined boxing. A lightning-fast and heavy-hitting pretty girl who had won all nine of her professional fights, seven of them by knockout, Jegels was undoubtedly destined for greatness and assured of her place among the greatest of South African boxing. And this had to happen. May her soul rest in peace.

To all of those who died in their pursuit of ring achievements and greatness, here in South Africa and across the world, my heart goes out to you, your families, and your fans. You will forever remain treasured in the hearts and minds of boxing fans and all people who wish for a good life for all.

CHAPTER 23

MDANTSANE GIRLS ROLL WITH THE PUNCHES

Wherever they are, Buffalo City women always have a way of showing off where they come from.

Whether by choice or by mistake, the boxing language and skills that they display in conversations or just their rough and tumble playing habits have a way of separating them from your normal girls.

Like the boxing boys they play within the streets back home, their language and style are all boxing orientated. Buffalo City women are still the only women who can accurately analyse a fighting style or fight contest.

One would be amazed at how women took up boxing in the Buffalo City area. It would make one believe that female boxing was legalised much earlier. This results from the region's love for boxing that has seen it jumping first and taking all boxing opportunities available.

Women in Buffalo City took up boxing lessons long before it was legalised. In fact, there was so much frustration among many women that white East London female boxer Sandra Almeida ended up taking advantage of her New Zealand citizenship and took up a professional boxing license and made her debut there before she could be allowed to box legally in South Africa.

Amanda Ngutha was one of the first-star quality female amateur boxers in BCM. She and other young girls like Noni Tenge, Bomkazi Klaas, Namhla Tyuluba and Unathi Myekeni had already made their mark in the South African amateur boxing scene. Ngutha was undoubtedly destined for great achievements like her fellow competitors but unfortunately passed away before realising her dream of fighting as a professional.

When Sports Minister Ngconde Balfour, a former rugby player and a big fan of boxing, announced the legalisation of female boxing in South Africa in 2001, there was no question as to which region in which Province would lead the charge. Women like Nonkongozelo Ndiki of Duncan Village and Nontsikelelo Mqengqeni of Mdantsane had already made their presence felt among men in the political sports field of the NSC. Mqengqeni would later join Siya Vabaza as the first two female boxing ring officials.

The Boxing Mecca had already promoted a string of amateur fights featuring girls as young as ten years of age. When this announcement finally came, Buffalo City already had seasoned female boxers who were not only ready to fight as professionals but were also well equipped and experienced enough to challenge the best in the world.

BSA was given the mandate to get female professional boxing on the way. It fell directly on my desk to deliver female boxing for the country. But there was only one small thing – the government did not put forward the budget to carry the mandate. To make matters worse, it was the period between 2006 and 2008 when BSA was going through its most challenging financial challenge yet. National Treasury and the Sports Department were not releasing the BSA grant due to financial mismanagement.

Fortunately, though, BSA was at the time running a boxing development program called the Baby Champs. Funds for the project came from SABC, Gauteng businessman Gibson Thula, and material assistance from all Provinces where the tournaments were held. It became advisable to piggyback female boxing on the Baby Champs program.

Boxing SA chairman Adv Dali Mpofu and the board had agreed to let this new, untested program operate for a year as a Pilot Project, after which a decision would be made about its future. It had been a big success and was running for the second year.

The female program once included and running was so successful that sixteen girls that came through as winners at the finals were turned professional. Female boxing flourished within the Baby Champs and produced National, International, and world champions among boxers, ring officials, corner women, and promoters. The Baby Champs Program was hailed as the most effective development program in South African sport.

The majority of such winners were from Mecca. Among them were Noni Tenge, Unathi Myekeni, Amanda Nguta, Bomkazi Klaas and Namhla Tyuluba. Myekeni went on to win the National title and a series of international wins against world-class opponents.

This prompted BSA to allow Mbali Zantsi and her Showtime Promotions to promote the first Women Only tournament in Durban in 2006. Women ran that tournament in all its facets. Male officials were spectators. It was the first tournament of its kind in the world.

Noni Tenge won the SA title and went on to become the first South African woman to win a world title when she won the IBF World Welterweight title. She remains the only boxer in South Africa, of any gender, to win four world titles in two weight divisions. Bomkazi Klaas lost two attempts at the South African Middleweight title when she was beaten both times by Gauteng's Queen Shabalala. Lanky performer Namhla Tyuluba decided to pursue a career as a ring official. She has developed to be one of the best judges and referees in the country. Ngata, unfortunately, passed away after a short illness before she could realise her dream of fighting as a professional.

Many newcomers took on the baton and were running with it. They included National champions like Nomandithini Ndyambo, Sharadeen Fortuin, Asandiswa Nxokwana, the late Leahandre Jeggels, Noxolo Makhanavu, Nwabisa Mbopha. Currently, the crop of prospects is led by Siphosethu Nxazonke, Babalwa Nonqonqotho, Nozwelethu Mathonsi, Nosipho Ngqondelana, Xolelwa Soka and a lot more who are coming out of the amateur ranks.

The coloured community has been represented by one boxer whose talents and achievements, though produced by one person, represented more in numbers. Leandre 'Baby Lee' Jegels came into the boxing field like wildfire. Pretty, charming, and a bundle of energy, she showed flashes of talent seldom seen among the female folk. In a short spell that numbered only nine fights, she had already won the South African Bantamweight and Pan African Junior Bantamweight titles. Her unbeaten record and seven knockouts had won her a legion of fans and assured her a future as the face of female boxing. She was on her way to the gym when she was fatally shot by a jealous boyfriend, thus ending a brief but exciting career. Her place is assured in the annals of South African boxing history.

The local women folk have also covered other facets of boxing. Siya Vabaza and Nontsikelo Mqengqeni were the first women to take the ring as judges and referees. They were instrumental in mentoring the likes of Namhla Tyuluba, Phumeza Zinakile and Thandi Nqodwana, who joined later and have already made great strides as referees and judges, winning a lot of regional and national awards.

Groundbreaking Female promoters Mbali Zantsi from Showtime Promotions and Sibongile Matiti, who was with Zbassy Promotions, have made sure female boxers are kept busy. Furthermore, they canvased the support of female political and social legacies to be celebrated in boxing by female boxers in the best female fashion possible. Meantime Nomfesane Nyatela is breaking new ground as CEO of Rumble Africa Promotions which is perhaps one of the five leading promotions in the country.

Notably, at the time of this writing, Golden Gloves Promotions, Eyethu Promotions and Xaba Promotions have become the three biggest promoters in South African boxing. In this time, they have been firmly entrenched as the leading players since female boxing was legalised about ten years ago. Unfortunately, my view is that they have not used their experience, massive international network and financial capacity to develop and enhance female boxing in the country. That credit could mainly go to Mbali Zantsi's Showtime Promotions, Koko Godlo's Vukani Promotions and Branco Milenkovich's Branco Productions, in that order.

BOXING AGAINST CRIME

BCMM has also taken full advantage of the relationship made by BSA and Correctional Services. Many agreements that are made in this fashion are usually for PR purposes. They never get off the ground. But this one was different. Specially organised by SABC host Dumile Mateza and shown live one Friday night on SABC 2. Mateza put then Correctional Services Minister Ngconde Balfour and myself, and asked why the two entities could not agree to a co-working relationship.

Balfour was in full promising mood and committed on air for us to formalise a mutually beneficial exercise whereby the two entities would share some skills in which BSA would especially lend to the rehabilitation program. Veteran boxers would be allocated to prisons within proximity to where they reside. As the agreement was laid out, they would train the inmates in boxing basics and discipline. Mateza promised that he would hold both of us to it.

True to Balfour's commitment, I received the call the following Monday from the DG for Correctional Services Fezile Siphamla. We set up a meeting and drafted the agreement. The Correctional Services agreed to fund some parts of the projects if any of the inmates challenged or defended Provincial or National titles. The program took off very well in the Eastern Cape, Gauteng and KZN. But the biggest and best results emerged from the BCMM.

Training sessions were held in separate camps by different boxers around the country. In Gauteng former boxers Johannes Miya, Jan Bergman, Lehlohonolo Ledwaba and Keith Rass led the development. In BCMM, Luyanda Kana, Welcome Ncita, Vuyani Bungu, Khulile Makeba, and many others made their way to the local prisons. Luyanda Kana, who is now an award-winning match-maker, was already working actively in the Boxing Against Crime project as an inmate. Several tournaments, including the Baby Champs, were held inside the Correctional Services premises, wherein many prospects emerged. Two National Championships were held in Eastern Cape and Gauteng. Some inmates were allowed out of various prisons in the Eastern Cape to go and compete outside. This opportunity resulted in two inmates for the BCMM prisons, Mzukisi Roberts and Sabelo Jubatha reaching the finals of the Baby Champs development program. Roberts became the outright winner. On being released from prison after finishing his sentence, Jubatha used the skills and experience he has gained through the window of opportunity created by this relationship and won the South African Featherweight championship. That was a first for South African boxing.

SAKHISIZWE BOXING CLUB AGAINST CRIME

Political inmates formed this club as a continuation of a project they had started inside. They were serving death sentences when fellow inmate Rev Makhenkesi Stofile who was also in jail serving a sentence imposed on him by the then Ciskei Government, advised them that they should form a boxing club and fight crime from inside.

He convinced them that they would soon be out of jail even though they had been sentenced to death. The death sentence was later outlawed in South African courts. But they were still serving and now pinned their hopes on parole.

True to Stofile's prediction, the five were granted parole by then-President Thabo Mbeki on 11 May 2002, after serving fourteen years at Mdantsane Prison - the Middledrift Maximum, St Albans Maximum Prison, Parensi Prison and finally East London Prison. The parole had been preceded by a visit to them in prison by ANC Heavyweights Terror Lekota, Smuts Ngonyama, Baleka Mbethe and Steve Tshwete. By now, Rev Stofile was the Premier of the Eastern Cape and he was using his power and influence to assist the project as much as he could. The group, which included Luyanda Kana, Monwabisi Kana, Mandlenkosi Jakavula, Mziwabantu Katsikatsi and Mabhongo Jamela, had done a lot of work inside prison, advising newcomers on what to expect and how to behave in jail. On their release, they were invited to parliament, where Stofile introduced them as people who had done a lot of work as inmates and would continue to make sure that people who were out of jail would stay out and those who were out would not go in.

Premier Nosimo Balindlela, who took over as Premier after Stofile, also encouraged the group to carry on. She provided them with boxing equipment and assisted in finding training premises for them. Sakhisizwe Boxing Club Against Crime was officially opened at NU1 Mdantsane in 2002. As was expected, youngsters from NU1, where the club was based, flocked the gym from the first day. Almost all of them would develop to be the champions and crowd favourites that are the toast of boxing fans today. They were Lusanda Komani, the Yokose twins, Lwandile Sityatha, Mawande Matross and Thobani Mbangeni. Mbuyiselo Klaas and Monwabisi Kana were already professional boxers from Yakuza and United Boxing Clubs, respectively. Their involvement enhanced public interest among the fans.

Monwabisi Kana took up a promoter's license so that the club could be self-sufficient and not depend on other promoters who serve the interests of their own boxers and use other boxers as cannon fodder.

The club served its purpose as many former inmates started joining, and the club grew in recognition and awareness. Tournaments involving current and former inmates were held in open spaces in Malls and taxi ranks. All tournaments were used to spread the message for youngsters to stay away from crime and drug abuse. The ex-inmates would address the crowds and even tell them what happens to people in jail. Strong support was coming from the government and individuals. The Department of Police under MEC Dennis Neer offered them transport to travel around the Eastern Cape Province. The owner of a neighbourhood gym Nkululeko Vellem and former professional boxer Ntsikelelo Goniwe offered monetary donations and material assistance. Goniwe even offered his minibus to assist the club.

One inmate Mzukisi Roberts was even released for a day to successfully engage in a tournament in Mdantsane. South African Featherweight champion Sabelo Jubatha and South African Bantamweight champion Lindile Tshemese are products of this project. They started boxing from the inside as inmates and came out to excel and win the national titles after their release. Luyanda Kana laments the fact that the Sakhisizwe Boxing Club is no longer operating. It still has the equipment, but there is no gym anymore due to the refusal of the school to give them space. Kana has gone on to be an award-winning matchmaker.

In 2008 BSA started talks with SANDF to strengthen amateur boxing by opening boxing clubs in the military bases like it used to happen during the Apartheid Era when soldiers and the police used to win the majority of National titles in the South African amateur tournaments. In a generous gesture to facilitate this process and develop boxing from the grassroots level, SASCOC President Gideon Sam joined the process and committed to assisting in sourcing funding and facilitating this new and unprecedented search for talent. The team that included BSA, SANDF and SASCOC toured the country from town to town in all Provinces.

We invited active ex boxers, current boxers, and interested people who had never boxed before to come and get tested. In a total of 107 young male and female boxers that were discovered, thirty-seven of them had never boxed before. They just had a natural talent, and we selected them because we felt that they could be developed. The majority of boxers chosen came from the Eastern Cape and KZN. They were registered for careers in the army as soldiers, as well as boxers and officials. The last report I had was that only three of them had left the SANDF. Many of them have advanced to higher levels in all facets of boxing.

CHAPTER 24

FOR THE LOVE OF BOXING

South African boxing has attracted so many different people. They have come for very various and diverse reasons. Such reasons have varied from their pasts and experiences to their dreams and aspirations. They have thus seen boxing as fulfilment or as a pursuit of their dreams.

Boxing is, by its nature, an addictive sport. People who realise their dreams keep plucking in even when they have nothing more to reap or prove. Those who lose keep on trying and hoping that one day, they will find their life-changing win. It is like the Lotto.

I am not talking in this case about boxers, but the people who assist and advance the boxers one way or the other. These are the fans, promoters, managers, trainers, sponsors and donors. There are a lot of them. They come in big numbers from various places. Some are in full public view and are known in boxing circles. Others work quietly outside the public view, but their results and products are as clear as crystal. I can now think of the few that come to mind.

MADUNA MAGONGO leaves in Ndevana, a semi-rural village just outside of King William's Town. This little village, which Ex-Ciskei President Lennox Sebe built, firstly as a residence for members of the Ciskei

Defence Force, but later developed into a fully-fledged residential village, is now a sprawling residential area with everything that one would expect to get, gain or develop in a rural or urban area. Ndevana is a mix of life.

Maduna, his clan name, and as he is affectionately known, is a successful businessman who has achieved much and survived through all the political and economic changes that have taken turns changing people's lives. For better or for worse. He hangs in there, adjusting and evolving strategy like a skilled boxer. He should because boxing is the love of his life.

Maduna has spent all his business life funding or donating massive amounts of money for tournaments to happen. He has never asked for anything in return. While big professional sponsorships release their funds after ensuring their visibility for marketing purposes and keeping financial records for tax rebates, Maduna either does not know that or does not care. He does it for the love of the game. The only thing he asks for is a verbal report of whether the tournament was a success or not.

Promoters from his area have made it big on, especially development tournaments in the townships and rural villages where the big-time promoters never think of whether boxing exists there or not. Such promoters include but are not limited to Mathemba Nyakathi, Chris Pondo, Xolani Jamani and amateur boxing development organisers like Mfundo Mchenge.

Maduna has also sponsored big-time promotions whose fights received large TV promotions and were of national or international level. Such promoters were Michael Guwa and Koko Godlo of Real First Team Promotions, Mathemba Nyakathi of Star Promotions, as well as my Messiah Promotions. The Messiah Promotions event that featured SA champion Mthobeli Mhlope and Thembile Lubisi were funded by Maduna, as were all Tournaments that Real First Team promoted. His most favourite boxer was South African Junior Flyweight champion Odwa Mdleleni. Maduna still carries on. But he is now concentrating on funding amateur boxing. He deserves a lifetime award.

LESLEY FLAVELL lives in Johannesburg, Gauteng. She is a businesswoman and a fervent horse breeder. Boxing is the love of her life. She owns a number of successful boxing-exercise health and fitness gymnasiums around Gauteng. She thus has taken advantage of the new awareness, and boom in boxing orientated training among fitness fanatics to her Warriors Gym's advantage. Her gym is manned by boxers who also regard her intervention in their lives as a lifesaver and a blessing. It is here that they maintain their boxing life while preparing for life after boxing.

The majority of her beneficiaries, especially those from Buffalo City, have their skills honed in developing other people's skills and fitness levels. Our boxers have found a home in her gymnasium as personal trainers making a living. They call it a home away from home.

The money they earn from training clients and teaching them the basic skills of the noble art, and especially their fitness, is enough to pay for the boxers' rent, food and other basic necessities of daily life. It makes living home looking for greener pastures in Gauteng all the easier and affordable.

Buffalo City boxers, whose skills are known and in demand in such gyms, have been known to take full advantage of the opportunities she has created. It is well known among training fundis that high altitude training is the best preparation for any high endurance sports code. The thin, dry air is the best exercise and training for any conditioning and durability challenges. Boxers from outside Gauteng who want to leave their low altitude areas in preparation for big fights in high altitude areas are allowed to use the gym for free.

Buffalo City boxers who have been known to use her gym include WBO world champion Zolani Tete, Xolisani Ndongeni, Nhlanthla Ngamntwini, Makazole Tete and a lot of others. For example, the car that was bought as an Urban Warriors' brand for Zolani Tete was later used by Xolisani Ndongeni. The car is now owned by IBO world mini flyweight champion Simphiwe Khonco. Buffalo City can use more people like Lesley Flavell.

MANDISI NTSOTHO is not well known among your average boxing fans or boxers. But his contributions, especially where he stays and what he did, can not go unnoticed. Many people do not know him as well as they do many others who have made far lesser contributions and commitments than him because all his promotions were strictly in the rural villages, away from everything.

He paid for everything and all logistics but never made a cent in return. His tournaments were mainly in rural villages like Elalini, Kalkop and Ngxwalane. His boxers were the likes of Junior Middleweight Mbeki, who carved a good name for himself before he disappeared, good prospect Mahlubi Mfikili and Gwayana. His tournaments were for free, proving that his intention was to create awareness of boxing in the rural villages. And in this, he succeeded. He made such a significant impact out of his pocket. Without gaining anything in return, many prospects he produced left for greener pastures after gaining some exposure and experience from his non-profitable shows.

TSELE THEMBENI's tough-talking township style and lingo would never get you to realise you were talking to a lifelong businessman. That is until he told you so. Born and bred in the rough Duncan Village streets, Matsele grew up in the gyms. He was one of the first juniors when Cornet Dunjwa opened Nompumelelo Boxing Club in 1970. But instead of pursuing ring success, he found success in business and preferred to be a boxing promoter and donor.

With his own Development Boxing Promotions, his biggest stars included popular SA mini Flyweight, SA Bantamweight and WBC International champion Khulile Makeba. But a lot of his donations went to tournaments and fighters he did not himself promote. A lot of promoters came to him for assistance to fund their tournaments. So did a lot of boxers.

My Messiah Promotions tournaments that featured Mpush Makambi's defence of the SA Middleweight championship were funded by Thembeni, as did boxers like former WBA world champion Simphiwe Vetyeka. It is promoters and donors like him that made the sport so prominent in this region.

ZOLANI MOSHANI. If there was ever a person with a perpetual smile and a loud laugh like Zolani Moshani, I still have not met that person. Moshani was a taxi owner and boxing promoter who organised his events while also funding other promoters' tournaments, gyms and boxers. His passion was for boxing to rise. And this he did by putting lots of money on many people who had no way of paying him back.

When Moshani died, so did a big part of boxing. While he made money from boxing, his main source of living came from the taxi industry. His friends were boxers, trainers, managers and promoters. We never thought he had enemies. It was hard to imagine there could be anybody who would wish any harm to such an easy-going and generous fellow. That is until he was gunned down near his house in Mdantsane.

VUSUMZI NGWENYA is the son of former Cape Town boxer David Ngwenya. He is a businessman licensed as promoter Real Deal Promotions but never used his organisation to organise fights for profit. He, instead, used it to generate funds and sponsor the career progress of boxers and their stables. The first boxer to gain from Ngwenya's donations were former South African Junior Flyweight, Bantamweight and WBC International Flyweight champion Khulile Makeba. The next boxer to benefit was former South African Flyweight and WBU Flyweight champion Zolile Mbityi.

Both stables benefitted from financial donations for gym equipment, transport and other boxing necessities with no conditions attached. Vusi even paid for himself and his friends to tournaments where his sponsored fighters were competing. Both boxers did not disappoint as they won national and international titles in different divisions.

DAN MAPHALALA is one of a kind. Boxing people alike regard him as a friend and someone to rely on. I did not know much about his life outside of boxing. But I know that boxing people, especially boxers and developing promoters, have relied on him for ages. He is the reason some boxers made it in life. And as would be the case when it came to boxing, the biggest beneficiaries were boxers from Buffalo City.

This Johannesburg businessman owned a hotel in Berea and turned it into student accommodation. But he offered free accommodation and meals from outside Gauteng, especially the ever big and talented numbers of boxers from the Eastern Cape and his Province of Limpopo. This made life so much easier for those who were also doubling up as students. All boxers had to do was turn up, and they had a home.

Boxers from other African countries outside of South Africa were there. They came by air, train, taxis or hitched their way to Johannesburg from Zimbabwe, Botswana, DRC and Nigeria. A lot of them did not know the hotel nor the address. They would ask for directions once they landed at or Tambo Airport, Park Station or Noord. Once there, locating Maphalala's place was never a problem. Everybody knew Danny Mapeee.

Boxers who stayed at his place were contracted to big-time managers like Nick Durandt, as well as promoters like Branco Milenkovic and Rodney Berman. But Maphalala, though a promoter himself, never made his generosity to them a condition for signing fight contracts with his promotion. They were free to come and go as they pleased. Even small promoters would travel from the Eastern Cape, Limpopo and even Gauteng to ask for loans or donations from Maphalala to meet the deadlines for purse monies. A lot of those funds were never paid back. I stayed at Maphalala's place for two years with four boxers and my assistant trainer - free of charge.

KHAYA JEKWA was born into boxing. When he was born, his father, a former fierce rugby wing for Swallows Rugby club, was already a successful boxing promoter. Much to his father's displeasure, and a businessman, Khaya did not follow his father's footsteps into rugby nor boxing but preferred to play soccer. He was good enough to be spotted by Orlando Pirates' talent scouts and was on his way to Johannesburg for trials that his father got wind of the unblessed journey and fetched him just in time at the airport as he was about to board for Johannesburg. That was the end of his soccer dreams.

Long after his father's death, Khaya, now a businessman, decided to get involved in boxing. But again, not as a boxer, promoter, nor anything else but as a donor. Khaya became big friends with Joe Manyathi and, as a lifetime fan of Welcome Ncita, it became a good mutual relationship. Businessman Khaya Jekwa thus became a big donor towards Manyathi's majority of boxing projects. Manyathi did not have the money.

Khaya could afford it. So he made things happen. He paid for a lot of the car hirings, hotel bookings and overseas trips. He was expecting nothing in return. He was known as Don King's son in the US due to his looks and resemblance to the greatest boxing promoter that ever lived.

JOE PADISHO AND MAJOR SIHUNU are business partners from Kimberly. Sihunu was originally from Zwelitsha, where he was a star rugby player. He made the connection between Joe Manyathi and his friend and Kimberly business partner Joe Padisho. Together they joined Khaya Jekwa in funding Joe Manyathi's projects.

Joe and Sihunu made it clear from the beginning that theirs was only a donation. All they needed was to be part of all trips and be present in all meetings. This, to them, was a new enjoyment and experience in a game that they loved so much. Their inclusion made the job easier for everybody, including other partners like Koko Godlo and myself. It meant that there was enough budget to include and cater for everybody. The whole team was there in Don King's offices in Miami when King granted Daily Dispatch journalist Mxolisi Ntshuca the interview that Ntshuca had been craving for all his life. And as we all waited in Don King's office, expecting the big man to walk in as per appointment, Ntshuca was shaking in anticipation. He could hardly believe that this moment would ever come. When Don King finally walked in and declared in his loud voice, "my brothers from Africa," Ntshuca strode forward to shake his hand and shouted to no one in particular, "the mother of all interviews."

PATRICE MOTSEPE is a South African mining businessman. He is the founder and executive chairman of African Rainbow Minerals. His business interests cover gold, ferrous metals, base metals and platinum, among others. He has worked his way so successfully up the business ladder that he has earned recognition as South Africa's first black billionaire. In 2012 named South Africa's richest man.

Motsepe is better known, especially among the poor black communities, as a developer and philanthropist who has used his wealth to uplift the standards of the less privileged, especially in sports, arts and culture. He also reached out to assist and alleviate the plight of this boxing mad community in BCMM. His gesture would reach out to developing every boxing facet in the region. And that was the best strategy. He requested a list that would include every official and operating boxing club in Buffalo City and donated training equipment for every one of them. He then made his donation in correspondence with the Eastern Cape Boxing office and ECABO, the amateur wing. This strategy indeed served the purpose. As was initially planned, the equipment was distributed equally. It reached every club, new or old, irrespective of how many boxers or champions trained there. Fifty-seven boxing clubs turned up. Each club received equipment to the tune of R 15 000. That was enough to furnish each gym with every bit of boxing gear except the ring. And we all said Huntshu Motsepe

ANDILE ALDRIN NCOBO is a former High School Principal, a lecturer, General Manager of Premier Soccer League, and also formerly known as a FIFA soccer referee.

His love for boxing has seen him supporting the game in a quiet and unobstructed way that very few are aware of. Ncobo's house in Sandton, Gauteng, has been used as a camping house for boxers from Eastern Cape like world Bantamweight champion Zolani Tete, Nkosinathi Joyi and others. Whenever these boxers have wished for a stay and train in Gauteng to take advantage of the high altitude, Ncobo has offered his house for free, sometimes taking up to ten boxers and trainers at the same time. This arrangement was made possible courtesy of the hardworking and helpful former Eastern Cape Minister of Sports Recreation Arts and Culture, Pemmy Majodina.

PHILIP SILVER is a South African attorney who migrated and now lives and practices in Australia. Before relocating to Australia, my boxing promotion was one of the beneficiaries Silver assisted financially to fund boxing tournaments. He made the donations while expecting nothing in return. His selfless gestures also assisted in the development of boxers like Philip Ndou. It was just for the love of the game.

BORDER EASTERN PROVINCE RIVALRY

Port Elizabeth/ Uitenhage and neighbouring districts have historically enjoyed a friendly rivalry with the Border. This rivalry has produced many wars in both boxing and rugby. Perhaps it is safe to say that without this area that is now mainly Nelson Mandela Municipality, our Border region could not have reached the position it enjoys in world boxing today.

As a late starter in boxing, it needed all the assistance it could get. The closest opponent was the Port Elizabeth/Uitenhage. Between these two regions, an opponent or a ring official was always a telephone call away. At the helm was boxing fan turned administrator Welcome Duru who could turn around and be ring announcer at the drop of a hat. Ring announcing meantime was made a class act by the powerful voice of Stan Mosia, and sometimes by the enthusiastic historian young Mike Phantsi.

It was always a treat to leave our area and, as a local team, spend amazing weekends of boxing in Port Elizabeth and Uitenhage. Among the promoters we could always count on for our excellent and close working relations were the likes of Sipho Mthoba, Speedo Nondumo, Ambrose Dlula, Monde Ndlaleni and Zolisa Mlahleki. These promoters made sure that every weekend was a boxing weekend. They kept the competition and interest in the game running high. What kept the interest so high was that boxing people could simultaneously work as promoters, managers, and trainers. And there was work aplenty for everyone involved. Managers and trainers included, among others, Badman Vellem, Chief Masemola, Kola Fulela, Mncedisi Kortman Thobile Mali, Frans Mini, Davis Goliath, and my uncle Knight Mtya.

The people were among those you always had to deal with for fights in their region or the Border region. They were constant visitors as teams ushering their boxers in our rings for action. A lot of them became our heroes and role models. My uncle became my mentor. The list of boxers is very long. It includes fighters who made the Border region their own. They frequently came and won fights at Sisa Dukashe stadium, Zwelitsha Hall, East London Community Center, and lately, the Orient Theatre. Boxers who readily come to mind include crowd favourites like Christopher Dlamini, Zim Makitakita, Fikile Qubantu, Thomas Vumazonke, Vuyo Tulwana, Aubrey Peta, Brown Bomber Mqina, Terence Makaluza, Leslie Pikoli, Xhanti Singaphi, Ngqika Tshume, Phalo Tshume, Phumzile Madikane and many more. These were the main crowd-pullers that always filled the Great Centenary Hall, now known as Nangoza Jebe in Port Elizabeth, Zwelitsha Community Hall in King Williamstown and Duncan Village Community Center in East London.

The Sisa Dukashe fan generation will undoubtedly treasure for a long time, memories of how Vuyani Nene became a giant killer beating such popular and multi-talented local winners as Odwa Mdleleni, Nqaba Govuza and Mveleli Luzipho.

Close on Nene's heels as local crowd favourites would be Phindile Gaika, Phumzile Madikane, Mthobeli Ndzandze as well as the Mbaduli brothers Ngcambaza, Mpisekhaya and Dlebusuku. Some of these boxing greats did not turn their backs on the game after their boxing days. Instead, they decided to plough back their hard-earned knowledge to teach and develop the youth in the game.

Such greats as Ace Makaluza and Leslie Pikoli would join long-serving officials like Thembisile Kiti and Mbambaza as ring officials. In contrast, Mthunzi Mapitiza, a former ring official, moved in and out of the region to assist Eastern Cape service provider Phakamile Jacobs in fight supervision. The Border region, especially Buffalo City Municipality, owes many thanks to Nelson Mandela Bay Municipality.

RING ANNOUNCERS

Ring announcing is not just about standing in the middle of the ring and calling the names of the boxers and officials. It is a skill all by itself. It is about looks. It is about style. It is about making an impression. The Ring announcer is about as important in making the fight as the boxers themselves. A ring announcer makes or breaks fights. He wakes the boxers up. He motivates the fighters. The way his voice vibrates all through the roof of the venue, as he calls the boxers' names, snaps them to a realisation that it's fight time. The response from the crowd seals it all.

Ring announcing has its challenges, none of which is more important than correctly pronouncing the names of the boxers. It also has its benefits, none of which is more important than giving the announcer more engagements. And more so making him a celebrity. Announcers prepare for the moment, for the thousands of people watching and listening to them. Of the ones who have graced our ring and called the shots at the Duncan Village Community Center, Zwelitsha Hall and Sisa Dukashe stadium, those who readily come to mind are Cecil Nolutshungu, Lambert Dukashe, Loyiso Mtya, Mzileni and Zolani Bongco. But once the tide turned and all contests plus new promoters turned up at the Orient Theatre and Mdantsane Indoor Centre, so did the emergence of new Ring announcers.

The current announcers who are taking boxing into the future include former rugby wing Lucky Makeleni, who has been at it for the last fifteen years. He is still young and fresh enough to hang in there for much longer. It does not end there. From time to time, we have had prolific and nationally acclaimed announcers like Putco Mafani and Carrol Manana taking on our rings and feeling the space with well-trained voices.

Even our iron lady of the game, Siya Vabaza Booi, has sometimes found herself being hurled into the ring to do it. Siya and one of my personal favourites, KZN's Phumlani Msibi are always called upon to save the situation when the currently used announcers are unavailable. Their understanding of the game and the fans always comes in handy. Vabaza Booi made her first appearance in professional boxing as a Ring announcer.

Msibi is a commentator for Supersport. He is one of the most informative commentators I know. Also in the mix is Devon Curer, better known among boxing fans and social media as Dev DC, a new white kid from CapeTown. His boxing tentacles have resulted in close relationships between us and the rest of the world. He is undoubtedly global. Buffalo City promoters have no qualms in flying him from Cape Town to call our fighters to war. He is worth every cent.

Siya Taho is a radio DJ. He is new on the scene. But his formidable presents and tenor voice have already created a movie opportunity for him. He was selected to call the fight as ring announcer and fight commentator in the new boxing movie Knuckle City shot at Mdantsane Township. Another first for Buffalo City. I also got a lifetime opportunity myself as a trainer of the boxer who plays the leading actor. And as ring announcer Siya Taho will roar, "Ladiiiieeees and Gentlemen, waiting time is overrrrrrrrrr." He is certainly the future.

BUFFALO CITY RING OFFICIALS

The first generation of Ring Officials in what is now known as the Eastern Cape office of Boxing SA started with the first professional tournament in October 1965. It began as Border Boxing and Eastern Province. Then it was the Border Boxing Board of Control before its present state. They were all white officials recruited by Les Muller from different sports codes and other social activities. They were Arno Oberholster, Piet Kruger, Pietie Jacoby Snr, Swanie Swanepoel and the Van Zyl brothers. The chairman was Marcus Temple from Cape Town. Muller became secretary.

The white officials were later joined by the first group of black officials who included Ndidi Gcilishe, Abishai Sibene, Alfred Sizani, Mava Malla, Mgwebi, Mzwandile Tshabalala, Tokota, Sheshe Dunjwa, Lulama Mtya, Phakamile Jacobs, Allen Matakane, Nangoku Thethani, Andile Matika, Siya Vabaza Booi and Siphiwe Mbini; among the longest-serving officials are Sheshe Dunjwa, whose career is as old as boxing in this region. He was one of the first junior boxers in Duncan Village before a brief professional career. He was one of the first officials to serve in the Transkei Boxing Control Board before returning to East London to join the Border Boxing Board. He has gained a lot of experience as a referee and judge at both National and International levels. Lulama Mtya has developed in stature to be one of the most experienced referees and judges in South Africa after joining the board as an official among the group that can be described as the second generation. He is the first official in the Eastern Cape to officiate in a world title fight. He was a fight judge in Phillip Holliday's knockout of legendary Jeff Fenech in Melbourne, Australia, for the IBF Junior Lightweight title.

The second generation is mainly the black group of officials that joined from around 1980. After a short stint as an amateur boxer, Mtya joined the professional ranks as a referee and judge. He has built up an exceptional career, officiating at all levels and winning multiple BSA awards. He has a strong following as a fan favourite referee wherever he goes.

Hall of Fame and former world boxing champion Brian Mitchell regards Mtya as the best referee in South African after world champion status Hall of Famer Stan Christodoulou. Simphiwe Mbini also belongs on this list. A former amateur boxer at the famous International Boxing Club, he joined the board in 1985 and was trained by Arno Oberholster as a judge. He has officiated in all sanctioning bodies as referee and judge, except for the IBO.

He has attended the Ring Officials' Conference in Paris and has won the Boxing SA Ring Official of the Year award. Andile Matika, who also rates as one of the best ring officials in South Africa, started as an amateur boxer at Thembalethu Boxing Club. He soon dropped the glove and built a career as a referee and judge. As a referee, Matika has developed a keen eye that seldom misses a ring misdemeanour and quick legs that carry him and put him at the right places all the time. He is well recognised for his excellence and has won several national awards. He has added to his achievement by gaining selection as the IBO's African Fight Supervisor.

Siya Vabaza Booi's entry was not as easy as her male counterparts. She was the first woman to participate as a ring official after growing up in a boxing family. She came across fierce objections from boxing officialdom that included the secretaries of both Provincial and National offices, Les Muller and Stan Christodoulou, respectively. South Africa was introducing new and sometimes historically taboo democratic changes. There was still this uneasiness against women in boxing.

I thought the prejudicial attitude against her was unfair as South Africa was changing at the time. I just joined her struggle fought on her side, and soon some attitudes, including those of Les Muller and Stan Christodoulou, began to change. I forced her in as ring announcer in one of my tournaments as Messiah Promotions at Dukes, Mdantsane Hotel. That changed Muller's attitude for good. He agreed to use her sparingly in the more minor bouts of development tournaments. And what a success she developed to be. The rest, as they say, is history. But the man who has been there since the beginning of local boxing is none other than the longest-serving official in South Africa, Louis Smith. Born on 1st April 1927, Smith did some little boxing with all other youngsters when boxing started but was already at a ripe age to compete on a serious note.

He soon looked for something else to do. He has been working as a Glove Steward from day one of boxing in the Border region. As I write, he is still fresh and spritely, doing his exercise daily at the age of ninety. The current group consists of Thandi Ngodwana, Allen Matakane, Simthembile Tom, Mandisi Mkile and Zola Naki. Award winners Phumeza Zinakile and Namhla Tyuluba are registered and operating excellently in the Gauteng Province.

CHAPTER 25

THE FOUNDING FATHERS OF THE BOXING MECCA

Perhaps no one person or group of people deserve the title of Founding Fathers of the Boxing Mecca than the gentlemen listed below. Upon remembering how they grew up, realizing the challenges they faced that could have made them worse people had they succumbed, they felt that something had to be done. The ungainly life they had endured as they were growing up had to be restructured so that future generations would be better prepared and armed to strive for a better life. To their limited skills, sports activities for the youth was the best way out of that quagmire.

While other people chose rugby, cricket and netball according to their skills and experience, this group settled for boxing. They started it and carried on doing it against all odds. Against all odds. Look where we are today. Well recognized across the globe.

MZOLI MADYAKA can rightfully be called the Father of boxing in BCMM. Originally from Queenstown, his parents moved to the old West Bank, East London where his businessman father brought his kids up with a keen interest to follow his business interests. Like his father, he developed a keen business mind. Such qualities were to assist later in the quick decision-making abilities and a rare sense of opportunity that made boxing what it is in BCMM today. The growing aroma and interest in the qualities and skills of boxing among his friends and community lured Madyaka into the journey that would make his region the home of boxing. He joined a group of young men who decided that the time had come to make boxing a reality among their community.

They started recruiting youngsters who were idle and interested in boxing. Once the first gymnasium, generally accepted as the International Boxing club was formed, there was a need for competition. Soon there were active and learning gymnasiums. Inter-club fights became a weekly activity. A string of prospects was developing among young and learning trainers. Boxing was growing every day. The need for growth in space for learning and training, opportunities for more fights, as well as general development, were growing. It was at this point that Madyaka used his leadership skills and business acumen to lead the charge of local boxing to higher places. In agreement with the only white member of the team at the time by the name of Les Muller and other members that included schoolteacher Thamie Nomvete, four prospects were identified as ready to turn professional.

The four amateur stars were Lawrence Ndzondo, Alesta Mahashe, Stanley Toni and Cornet Dunjwa. There was no official boxing board at the time, so the four boxers had to be taken to Natal, now KwaZulu-Natal to turn professional. It was left to Du Toit, as he was known, to drive the boxers in his car, and at his own expense. The rest, as they say, is history.

LES MULLER was a white youngster of German origin who played Provincial rugby and cricket. He was also keen on other sports, especially those that were not mainly practised among his white communities. There was already some keen boxing interest growing among his white folks, but Muller had a keen interest in what was happening on the other side of the world.

The other side was just across the street, in the townships. The stories he was hearing from the black employees who came to his home and the neighbourhood to work in the gardens and kitchens aroused his interests beyond fear. A chance meeting and a conversation with Edgar Miya, a social worker who worked at the Duncan Village Community Center, would change his life forever. Muller was introduced to Madyaka, Nomvete, Gidana and other boxing people. Legend has it that after the meeting with the boxing tribe, Les Muller turned black. His whole life changed and was devoted to helping and developing local boxing to international heights.

Muller's involvement, as the only white person at the time, would lead local boxing to the professional status, create the Border Boxing Board of control, introduce other white officials to referee and judge in tournaments and generally lead local boxing into the future. So committed was Muller in sticking to his home roots that he even turned down an offer of the job to lead South African boxing.

ERIC GABELANA was the first promoter of the region. Born in Queenstown, he came to East London as a youngster. He had done some boxing and was one of the people who opened Duncan Village Boxing Club, the second boxing club in East London. He trained with the boxers but did not pursue competitive fighting. He instead concentrated on his business interests.

When professional boxing started he promoted the first fight. The main fight was staged as an exhibition between Gabriel Fighting Gash Dlamini and Rhodesian, (now Zimbabwe) George King Marshall Jetu. The rest of the preliminary bouts were official professional fights that featured the new East London Professional boxers in their debuts. The main fighting exhibition had a controversial ending when Jetu jumped out of the ring and declared "Me no fight no more, house full smoke." But history had been made. Professional boxing had been born in Buffalo City. Was it a boy or a girl? Whatever it was, things were never going to be the same again.

Gabelana went on to share the promotional stage with another leading promoter and businessman Nimrod Zitumane. Between them, they promoted the likes of crowd-pullers Simon Sali, Monde Mbhangxa and Lawrence Ndzondo. Other top performers of the time included Lambert Dukashe and Cornet Dunjwa until the mass movement to Mdantsane. Soon after this first group of what one would call the First Generation of boxers in the region, would emerge a young, charismatic whirlwind who would change the face of boxing. His name was Nkosana Mgxaji. He was nicknamed Happy Boy after his ex-boxer brother died. The brother's name was Happy, and he was known as Happy's boy.

After the mass Apartheid movement, almost all the good boxers, including Mgxaji were staying at Mdantsane. The great careers of the First Generation, the likes of Sali, Mbhangxa, Ndzondo, Dukashe and Dunjwa started and ended in Duncan Village, East London. The Mdantsane group that included me, and was led by Mgxaji on the turnstiles, was the Second Generation. The attitudes of the boxers, as did the attitudes of the fans were changing. The language of boxing was also changing. Mdantsane was a mixed bag. As against the first generation of Duncan Village commonly referred to as *bantwana baseKasie* or in rugby terms *abantwana beVetkoek*, we were, as boxers there, a mixture of *Amagungqayi, amanali, imirhangqolo, imincotsho, amagubu, iminyolwa, omasitshaye.*

These were new derogatory names used to identify all sorts of personalities, styles and habits that came with the people, especially boxers from the rural villages, like myself. This new township dictionary entry described anything from rural origins to easily and carefully selected opponents with little or no chance of winning. The names or terms were supposed to be derogatory to the people for whom they were meant. But people fell in love with them.

At the opening of Sisa Dukashe stadium, Eric Gabelana promoted the first fight there between Nkosana Mgxaji and Moses Mthembu. He also followed that up by bringing Bingo Crooks from the UK, the first overseas opponent for Mgxaji. At this time boxing was like a drug in Mdantsane. People were *boxaholics*, always either high or needing a fix. Every Unit and every school had a boxing gym. Mgxaji himself became one of the best in the world training in a classroom and using desks as rings for sparring under candlelight.

BOYCE ZITUMANE took after his father Nimrod as a promoter, but founded his promotion and named it Modern Boxing Promotions. Commonly known as *ibholomane*, a phrase used to refer to his almost white look, Boyce was a short rotund, lovable fellow who always seemed like he was rushing somewhere. It was difficult to share a conversation with him as he was always on the way and had to talk to you at the top of his voice because the distance was lengthening. But there was only one person who made him sit down to negotiate – Nkosana Mgxaji. To talk to Nkosana was to talk money. He was the drawcard, the money maker. Every promoter wanted to talk to him. And he knew it only too well.

Boyce Zitumane became the most popular promoter of the time. He was known to get so excited he would let all entrances open and get everybody to go and watch once Mgxaji once the Mgxaji Parade hit the road to the ring. Other promoters were forced to follow the same practice. Even the Police, as there was no private security to ensure order in events at the time, would leave their posts and go watch Mgxaji strut his stuff. It was free for all to see.

MFANA JEKWA was once a fast and furious rugby wing for Swallows Rugby Club, perhaps the most popular rugby club in East London. But once the boxing bug bit he was in boxing like there had never been anything else in his life. Jekwa always maintained that while Mgxaji was the main drawcard, promoters should not forget that he was not fighting alone. They should thus pay the preliminary bouts just as well.

He took care of the upcoming boys like myself. He was upfront in producing the next drawcard Welile Nkosinkulu and perhaps the most complete fighter of them all Mzukisi Skweyiya. To Jekwa, no one could beat Skweyiya. Not even Mgxaji if they could fight in the same division. He nearly gave up promoting when he heard that Skweyiya had skipped. He was close, as he said, to clinching the biggest Eastern Cape fight of them all – Skweyiya vs Nkosinkulu.

WRIDGE QEQE, a businessman from Zwelitsha near King William's Town was the only promoter from outside the East London-Mdantsane area to compete effectively with Mdantsane Big Five namely Eric Gabelana, Boyce Zitumane, Salinga Mzamo, Mfana Jekwa and Daliwonga Mkhosi.

It was his confidence accompanied by a big rough voice and deep pockets that gave him the power to stage big fights right in the heart of East London. He was aware that there were moves to keep him out of EL/MDA as he had KWT all by himself. But Wridge would not budge. He felt that the fights in King could only be for developing boxers. The money was at Sisa Dukashe. He was right. His big promotions landed him the right to be recognised as one of the people who made the Mecca.

THAMIE NOMVETE was a teacher who resigned when the Apartheid Government introduced Bantu Education. He had a keen sense of care for youth development. Such qualities assisted and made him stand out when it came to programs and projects of social upliftment. When the call for boxing came he realized that his academic qualifications would be best suited for helping the youth. The boxing team used to, among other things teach and warn the boxing youngsters against street tendencies like abuse of liquor, smoking and stealing. He became the first manager of International Boxing Club and led the Father Club to a long and lasting history of our boxing and produced many other clubs.

SAX MANUEL is one of the leading proofs that BCMM was the last part of South Africa to take up boxing. In less than five years of practising professional boxing this region was ruling boxing. He was a musician who came to East London from Queenstown and joined the weekend shows in the Duncan Village halls. The music shows, *KwaNomtatsi*, it's where the local people let loose and enjoyed themselves on weekends.

Boxing in Queenstown where Manuel came from had already been going on for more than thirty years. When Manuel realized the keen interest the local youth had in the game, as well as the unrelenting efforts of the elders to get their youth in boxing, he donated a set of boxing gloves to the founders. His music and showbiz experienced enabled him to be used as a ring announcer from time to time in amateur boxing shows.

DUMILE GIDANA was one of the youngsters of the time who joined but never boxed. He did secretarial jobs like writing letters for challenges, organizing interclub tournaments, trials and championships. When professional boxing started he became the first matchmaker and timekeeper until he retired from active boxing.

SHELLOCK NGCOBO was a big man with a grumpy voice who used to visit different gyms and show the boxers the ropes. We did not know at the time, only to learn later that he was the first recognised trainer in the region. He had been one of the first amateur boxers but did not turn professional. He thus became the first trainer of the International Boxing Club.

He was checking the clubs and teaching the basics. I think that was the right thing to do because a lot of our boxers were still fighting on natural talent, without the basics. They have been known to fold under the relentless pressure of top-class pressure cookers because natural talent can only go thus far. It needs a lot of development and support. Advanced steps are being taken by some of the current trainers to put more emphasis on the boxing basics as well as durability training. The aim is to tackle this challenge from the initial stages of the kids' training.

DAVID TSHAKA can safely be acknowledged and recognised as the second trainer in the region. He is said to have started the practice of taking up the lead training of boxers at the early stages of Duncan Village Boxing Club, the second club to be opened in East London. His reign was somehow longer than his *co-old* timers because he was still there training the youngsters - Zandisile Thole and Ndoda Mayende, when the next generation of trainers like Spokes Witbooi, Mathemba Nyakathi, Stephen Sam, and myself introduced ourselves.

EDGAR MIYA has his place in history. Nothing much is known about him. Edgar Miya makes this list because he saw the need to introduce a white man to our boxing. That was the thing to do at the time. Without Les Muller where would be our boxing today? Thank God for Edgar Miya.

DUGGAN is also another unknown hand that helped our boxing. Only known by his Irish name or surname of Duggan, nobody knows whether this was his first or last name. Even veterans like Cornet Dunjwa and Lawrence Ndzondo who were there at that time as youngsters cannot give a clue into the clearer identity of this white man. What is well known is that he was not South African. That he came from England. But one thing he did was visit the first clubs and teach the guys how to train for boxing, as well as how to box. So the first basics of boxing in BCM could be named after him as the Duggan Boxing Basics. Glory be to him.

After Gilbert Gidana retired from active boxing, I took over his activities of matching and fight organising for the Big Three Promoters. I had learnt a lot from him. It thus became natural that the promoters would ask me to do these things. What angered my father, however, was that I was still an active boxer. And unbeaten at that. He felt that this was interfering with my training. He was right. "This boxing first interfered with your studies. Maybe you will write a book about all this you are learning," he let out the prophetic words in anger one day. "I am writing the book now dad, you planted the seed, thank you very much. Please bless this effort. And may you rest in peace."

THE PEOPLE WHO POPULARISED BOXING

NKOSANA HAPPY BOY MGXAJI was ahead of his time. How he popularised boxing in not only the Buffalo City but the Eastern Cape at large is in almost every chapter of this book. He remains, without winning a world title, the greatest and best product of boxing in this region. But I am sure of one thing. If Mgxaji had come fifteen to twenty years after he did, he would have been one of the GOATS (the greatest fighters of all time.)in the world.

SIMON '*SORE FINGER*' SALI was the first drawcard of the region. He used to draw people as an amateur wherever he went. As a professional the Duncan Village Community Center, the Zwelitsha Communal Hall and the stadium in East London were his places. He had everything that makes a drawcard in any kind of life you choose. A drawcard makes people stop everything they are doing to see him do his. In Sali's case, it was boxing. He had the prerequisites that make for magnetism. He had charm. He had confidence. He was pretty. And he could box. Please do not confuse this because it has been proved that being ugly can be a charm on its own. What is more – Simon Sali could box. Legend has it that when he was knocked out by Mackeed Mofokeng at the Rubusana Grounds in East London, some women cried until they reached home.

Husbands had their hands full calming them down. And the husbands understood. Simon Sali's face had been damaged – maybe forever. But he did come bigger and better than ever before. But some women never came back, lest they see him being knocked out again.

MONDE MBANGXA was small for boxing in his time. He would have done so much better these days where people of his size have been catered for by creating lighter weights. Mbangxa was fighting as a Flyweight those days, which was a division for the smallest men. But the opponents were still much bigger than him. But he had such a good set of skills, defence and crowd-pleasing style that the crowds in East London and King William's Town loved to watch him. And only the best could beat him.

LAWRENCE 'SLOW POISON' NDZONDO was open-faced and friendly. One of the few boxers with whom you could still open up a reasonably friendly conversation on the week of the fight. He was a living example that boxing can also be a gentleman's game.

That is why people loved him win or lose. He had a crowd-pleasing crafty style that kept him from receiving unnecessary punishment. One of the best boxers never to win a South African title.

PREMIER BOXING LEAGUE (PBL)

Dicksy Ngqula is one of the most recognisable faces in South African boxing. Unquestionably one of the finest commentators of boxing, he has rubbed shoulders and exchanged microphones and ideas with his co-commentators, the likes of Bert Blewett, Dumile Mateza and myself.

He is certainly one of the brightest young men I know, with an astute knowledge of the game. It was natural that when he called me one day when I was still running operations in BSA, and requested a chance for him and his company PBL, to present a boxing development idea, what he described as a world-class Boxing League that is proudly South African. I was excited. But within a few minutes of his presentation, I was astounded, confused and desperate for him to stop. The idea to me was unworkable in boxing. Maybe he should take it to soccer or rugby, but this was certainly the wrong office for boxing. However, the ever persuasive Dicksy persisted to present his case. Listening to the presentation of this project, named The Beginning I had never in my life ever envisaged a scenario of boxers competing across all divisions for one prize. To me I think, and I know a lot of boxing people think as well that a Flyweight must fight a Flyweight, a Lightweight must fight a Lightweight.

How could a Bantamweight contest with a Middleweight and a Heavyweight? But Ngqula had it all worked out. They do not have to fight physically, but they can do on a points system, he said. When he had done going through it all his presentation and his sums, I was sold. It was the first idea of its kind in boxing. Anywhere in the world. His immediate wish was that the first season would cover the divisions from Mini Fly to Lightweight. His reasoning there, rightfully of course was that for purposes of the League the more feasible divisions for matching would make for a smoother and less turbulent start.

Due to limited numbers and potential for attractive fights some matches would be made on special weight limits to allow matching across divisions on agreed weight limits without endangering boxers. This would be the case, especially where there was less talent in a division. In boxing, it's called Catch-weight.

The second wish was that the PBL tournaments be held in Hemmingways, Buffalo City in the Eastern Cape and Gold Reef City in Gauteng. He believed that those were the venues that could form a solid base for marketability and fan likeability for the PBL. They would put the spotlight back into the backing. Boxing's image would be elevated. And as he would keep on saying advertisers follow audiences.

For purposes of entertainment, we had to make sure of the impact each bout would leave in the minds of the fans. Generally, championships are scheduled for twelve rounds, however, for that purpose, we agreed that the fights should be scheduled for six rounds. The rules and regulations covering tournaments and actual fights would not be tampered with. Everything had to go according to the BSA book. Only the supremely talented top 24 boxers from the most talented divisions would be invited to participate.

Perhaps the biggest gain for the boxers and boxing as a national game was the big marketing strategy that the PBL brought. The enhanced image of boxing would further benefit other promotions in terms of crowd attendance, as well as the attraction of sponsorship. This would also pay big dividends for the managers, trainers and Ring Officials. And when it started it all came together. Boxing was the talk and the view throughout all print and electronic media. With social media having recently entered the fray and introducing itself in a big way, Ngqula and his company made sure that the PBL was the first and last thing people talked about.

The boxers were well marketed with appearances ranging from public appearances as individuals and groups, radio, TV and newspaper interviews as well as public sparring sessions. Perhaps the biggest bait for the fans, once they got to the venue, was the entertainment. That kind of treatment was unknown in boxing circles. The fans walked the red carpet. So was the ring entry. There was a hospitality lounge for celebrities. There was music and dance, music and dance all the way. This worked down well with especially the Buffalo City fans. There was also a Betting platform, something new to South African boxing fans. The setting was different.

The prize for the fighters, especially the overall winning fighter was the kind of purse local boxers were not used to. The boxers were guaranteed R80 000 per six-round fight. At that time, the amount was only paid to boxers defending their national titles. Six rounders had to be happy with R6000. But it was the handsome R1, 5million prize money for the winner that killed this lovely project. The winner would be the boxer amassing the highest score in terms of the points and bonuses allocated per winner.

As Director of operations in Boxing SA at the time, this proposal was put forward, I had been part of the initial negotiations. Unfortunately by the time more extensive discussions were engaging and all agreements were made between BSA and PBL Pound 4Pound I was no longer there. I was not privy to the final agreements. I was an interested spectator when the games began. I attended all the events merely as a boxing fan. It was when Ndongeni could not be paid his prize money that I got wind of what had brought about the collapse of this ambitious project.

All the boxers were fully paid the contractual purse monies in all fights whose agreements rested in the BSA office. But the event company, PBL Pound 4 Pound could not pay the final award of over a million rand to the overall winner, crowd favourite Xolisani Ndongeni. This was due, I was informed, to the withdrawal of the sponsors. Boxing SA could not pursue the matter as they had no legal agreement papers or contracts lodged with them as the regulating body of boxing in South Africa. PBL's agreement with BSA was only for the purse monies of the boxers lodged with the regulatory body before the tournament. Such agreed-upon money was duly paid to the boxers through the office of BSA.

The prize money which was the one quoted at more than a million rand was the agreement made between the boxers and PBL. There was no binding agreement for BSA to enforce the agreement to pursue a legal route that would result in the payment of Xolisani Ndongeni. And so ended a project that had captured the minds and won the admiration of boxing fans across the country. A commercial strategy that would have changed the fortunes of South African boxing.

UBUNTU BOXING FOUNDATION (UBF)

This organisation was founded in 2018 by a group of ex-boxers who initially identified to start a project that would look after the welfare of other ex-boxers who are in need. This concept was fuelled by the lonely death of ex-boxing star Sexon Ngqayimbana who was found in his home about three days after he had died. The group seized the moment and collected donations from local businessmen and individuals to organise a memorial service and then make sure that the local hero received the dignified funeral and send off that he deserved.

To date, UBF has successfully organised more than thirteen funerals and memorial services of former champions, both former world, South African champions and those who did not become champions.

Also as part of the campaign for a better life for needy boxers, UBF has visited and delivered groceries to the homes of more than sixteen needy ex-boxers, especially those who are destitute and bedridden. Skills development is also in the pipeline to make sure that the boxers of the future are better equipped to deal successfully with the economic and social challenges faced by the past boxers.

Since its foundation UBF has taken broader and more creative steps making means to preserve the legacy of past boxers, contributors and administrators. Print and electronic information is in the process of being sought and collected in a bold bid to the bank as much local boxing history as possible. The group aims to ensure that such vast deposits of print and electronic information will finally be available to everybody at the press of a button.

As of January 2019, as part of the Museum and Heritage initiative, the group has been organising memorial lectures of all the legends who contributed immensely to boxing. This is a continuous process that has already seen Nkosana Mgxaji, Les Muller and Mathemba Nyakathi being honoured.

The UBF office consists of;

- Executive Chairman, Lindi Memani
- Vice-Chairman, Xolani Sirhunu
- Executive Secretary, Vuyani Mbinda
- Ass Secretary, Lungiswa Ntontela
- Treasurer, Dudu Bungu
- Co-ordinator, Vuyolomzi Mtekwana
- Media Liasing Officers, Luyanda Kana and Dokes Sekhonyela
- Additional members, Pheleka Ntontela, Siyasanga Myokwana, Linda Madyaka.

LAST BORN PROMOTIONS

Perhaps one of the boldest moves that can help change lives and advance youth development in South Africa, especially in the Eastern Cape Province, is the historic partnership that has been forged by the Last Born Promotions or All Winners Boxing Club with Monkstown Boxing Gym in Belfast, Northern Ireland. This bold and wide-ranging agreement takes advantage of the love and commitment to boxing by both camps and uses the noble art as a platform and launching pad.

Such far and wide-ranging agreements were made during Zolani Tete's visit to Belfast for the defence of his WBO world Bantamweight championship.

Team Tete used the Monkstown Boxing Club not only as its training quarters for the fight but also as a negotiating table for a much-needed development project for the youth of the Eastern Cape. "This is a dream come true," says Mlandeli Thengimfene, the manager for Team Tete, who was forefront in creating and forging this relationship.

All-Winners Boxing Club is a relatively new boxing club in Mdantsane. It is hardly four years old but already has a world champion and several proven competitors like Nhlanhla Tyirha SA Junior Flyweight champion) Fikile Mlonyeni (ABU Flyweight champion), Loyiso Ngantweni (Eastern Cape mini Flyweight champion), and prospects Xolisa Nonkonyane, Athenkosi Nxayiphi, Uyanda Nogogo, Lithemba Goje, Sinethemba Nolawo, Okuhle Ngake, Yamkela Phaliso, Mhlanganisi Sogcwali, Malachi Sobolo, Sakhele Thuso and WBF female Junior Featherweight champion Unathi Myekeni.

The above prospects are members of the All-Winners Boxing Club and are set to be among the first beneficiaries of the groundbreaking deal. The club's promotional arm, Last Born Promotions, named after its first champion Zolani Tete's nickname is already enjoying a strong international relationship with UK based Queensbury Promotions that promotes Zolani Tete's fights. Monkstown could not have come at a better time for a new bright idea to develop and enhance boxing in this region.

Monkstown is a pioneering education and sports project which works with over 1 000 young people each year across Monkstown, Rathcoole and North Belfast Communities. Their mission is to change people's lives through sport, education and personal development so that they can fulfil their personal life goals.

The club has received several awards for its work including, The Best Education Project in the UK in 2015, as well as their success inside the ring. Their philosophy is to develop champions outside the ring also. As part of their programme of work, they provide young people with life-changing opportunities that include volunteering, obtaining new qualifications and more recently international travel. "As I am sure you will agree the opportunity to travel at a young age can be life-affirming and these experiences can help shape the young person's future and outlook on life," says Lead Youth Worker Amy Stewart.

In 2017 Monkstown Boxing Club took a group of young people from the club along with a group from the Colin Glen Trust to Poland, which was their first international youth exchange. From this, young people have been passionate about the benefits of such projects and, through a relationship developed between world boxing champions, Carl Frampton of Belfast, Northern Ireland and South African Zolani Tete are now in the process of planning an international exchange to the Eastern Cape in South Africa.

This project will provide an opportunity of a lifetime for a group of young leaders from the local community to travel to a different continent and work with some of the most disadvantaged children on the planet. Eight young people alongside two Youth Workers will travel to East London in the Eastern Cape. In preparation for this visit, these young people will participate in a range of sessions with a focus on team building, diversity and South African culture in preparation for the voluntary work they will be undertaking.

Additionally, the young people will complete various qualifications including Level 1 in Youth Work Practise, Sports Aid and Sports Leadership. These qualifications will provide the young people with confidence, knowledge and skills that they can transfer to their work in South Africa.

When in South Africa the young people will be volunteering across various charities including Orphanages, Schools and Townships in Mthatha and East London, supporting children with school work, meal preparations and experiencing the African culture. As a project of this scale comes with costs, young people will endeavour to raise the bulk of their costs through various events and activities such as ballots, car wash, bag packs, a boxing show and many more. The collected amount will not just pay for transport and accommodation while in South Africa, but more importantly much-needed supplies and clothing for the children that will be visited.

At the writing of this chapter, Monkstown Boxing Club is contacting its local business to help reach their fundraising target and be part of this life-changing opportunity for young people.

"We can only achieve these goals and carry out this life-changing work with the support from generous individuals and the local community. These generous donations will help us make a difference to those less fortunate," says Monkstown 2 Mthatha South Africa Project leader Amy Stewart. Need more be said?

CHAPTER 26

THE MEDIA

From the time boxing began in South Africa, the media has always been a friend and stuck with boxing through all its ups and downs. The Eastern Cape as always, and like in all other spheres of life, has the shortest end of the stick. It has not had the fortune of access to the big numbers of readily available media for creating awareness and love for this big homegrown product.

Unlike its sister Provinces like Gauteng, KZN and Western Cape, the Eastern Cape has had to do with three or four media houses. But this small number, especially print and radio media, made the loudest noise and made sure that boxing receives the biggest attention they can master.

Three of these media giants like Mhlobo Wenene, Daily Dispatch and Imvo Zabantsundu were already announcing the news when boxing began in South Africa. As the Eastern Cape and more specifically Buffalo City happens to be the last region to take up boxing in the country, it is safe to say that the media was already much experienced in dealing with this new phenomenon when it landed on its lap. They certainly did a great job.

RADIO BANTU now UMHLOBO WENENE is a national Xhosa language radio station that has been a friend of the boxing world since it started in South Africa and especially the Eastern Cape. It started as Radio Bantu. It was later changed to Radio Xhosa before settling on Mhlobo Wenene.

The station has assisted with all news dealing with announcements of upcoming fights, weigh-ins, and all other matters relating to marketing the fight and boxing in general. The ringside commentators in fights broadcast live from the venue have been nothing short of spectacular.

Radio commentator Given Ntlebi's booming voice and spectacular presentation of fights from ringside made him a legend in his lifetime. He popularised boxing to thousands of listeners across the country. Peter Bacela added humour in explaining boxing moves and reactions. He was never lost for comparisons.

Lately, the new generation of commentators has taken boxing marketing to new levels. Levels not seen before, especially when it comes to profiling individual boxing participants like boxers, managers, trainers and promoters. Such new blood include dedicated and knowledgeable personalities like Zolani Bongco, Sterra Ngqezana, Loyiso Sitsheke, Monwabisi Jimlongo, Mluleki Ntsabo and a whole lot of up and coming youngsters in the community radio stations that are mushrooming across the country. It is also worth noting that they go beyond just making announcements and breaking news, they are also always involved in creating and introducing ideas to improve boxing. Zanoxolo Bongco, unfortunately, passed on so early. He was one of us.

DAILY DISPATCH: When it comes to the origins and history of boxing in the Eastern Cape, the Daily Dispatch newspaper is far and wide ahead of the many other media sources that have popularised boxing in the region. It has introduced the game to individuals, groups and households beyond our wildest imaginations.

It being older than boxing in the region and country means that when boxing was born in the Eastern Cape the DD, as it is affectionately known, was one of the midwives. Courtesy of the Daily Dispatch, the story of boxing reaches more than twenty-five thousand readers a week. Such distribution has been the case since 1965, the year of the birth of professional boxing in Buffalo City. According to reliable reports, the first edition appeared as The Daily Dispatch and Shipping and Mercantile Gazette on the 10th of September 1872 under its first editor Massey Hicks.

This historic success was achieved after a string of major difficulties that nearly aborted the birth of the newspaper. Such challenges included but were not limited to, the lack of premises to house the press and newspaper, as well as having to deliver printing material from King William's Town via my home village Mount Coke, the only road to East London at the time, by wagon. Hicks had promised the first publication by 10 September. And true to his promise he and his hardworking team met the deadline.

Perhaps the origins of the newspaper's legendary liberal stance, by which it stands to this day and which was to come in as a major boost for our boxing for generations to come, is the historic document that was found in 1960 when changes were being made to the old newspaper. The groundbreaking document reportedly originated from Cecil Rhodes in which he said he would be happy to lend the Daily Dispatch 500 pounds to help buy equipment, as long as it adhered to its policy of fair treatment to all races.

This discovery served as a reminder that the newspaper's founding fathers had no intention of treating people according to race or colour.

As boxing is a predominantly black sport that draws its participants from the poorer classes of society, it was always going to be a big challenge for it to gain visibility. Unless it could be able to forge good relations with a wide-ranging media. These few words sealed a relationship and a love affair with a local race group, mainly AmaXhosa tribe that, unbeknown at the time was to develop and embrace a game that would develop it into the giant world-class competitor it is today.

This courageous stance was emphasized as a reminder when the incoming editor at the time took the reigns. The new editor Donald Woods who took over in 1955 at around the time that boxing started in East London was destined to have brutal wars with the Apartheid regime, which enforced racial discrimination, for years to come. Born in Elliotdale, Transkei, Woods remains the most famous editor of the newspaper.

He stood firm on the newspaper's tradition of fair racial treatment which came from Rhodes and made it a condition for the fund. Woods and the Daily Dispatch stood against racial discrimination through thick and thin. Like local boxing to the rest of the country, the Daily Dispatch went head-on and matched the most profitable newspapers in the country like the well funded Sunday Times and The Star. Local boxing benefitted largely from this relationship and grew by leaps and bounds.

The year 1963 proved to be a great year for local sport in general, and boxing in particular when the Daily Dispatch appointed former East London rugby player and the national selector on the African Rugby Board of

SA, Gordon Qumza to its editorial staff. Furthermore, over the years, the Daily Dispatch newspaper has fielded such wise and knowledgeable sports journalists as Leslie Xinwa, Charles Nqakula, Glyn Williams and Wellington Sangotsha to name nut a few. Among them, they introduced and launched the widely successful and popular Indaba edition that would make boxing's popularity to dizzying levels. Xinwa edited Indaba for a while.

Charles Nqakula who had previously worked as a political journalist for Imvo Zabantsundu would later serve as Minister of Defence and later Minister of Safety and Security in the new South Africa.

He would also have Xinwa appointed as his spokesperson in the Department of Safety and Security. The later generation of contributors after the previously mentioned pioneers included hard-working and penetrative journalists like Mxolisi Ntshuca who also served as a member of the National Rating's Committee under the South African National Boxing Control Commission.

Currently, a youngster by the name of Mesuli Zifo has gone beyond being a journalist or boxing writer to be one of the activists for credibility and transformation in the game. He has been part and parcel of all major projects and moves aimed at making boxing a better and more presentable game. Zifo has also served in the Boxing SA awards committee before resigning.

IMVO ZABANTSUNDU was the first black newspaper founded in South Africa. It was published in King William's Town by writer and teacher Tengo Jabavu in 1884. Before the establishment of Imvo Zabantsundu, there were a few African language newspapers that were printed as missionary journals only to advance literacy and Christian awareness. They did not provide any space to cater for political or cultural news. It was this lack of space for African politics and opinion that aroused Tengo to create a forum for the African thinkers to air their views on policies made by the government – in their isiXhosa language.

IsiXhosa would make sure that news was understood in all corners of the country especially by Xhosa speaking people working in faraway places from home like the mines. Miners especially those coming from the Eastern Cape have always been well known for their love of boxing and sports in general.

It was through this newspaper that when boxing finally began in the soon to be boxing mad Border region, the birth news of this game spread far and wide, producing interest in the game that would set a blazing trail across the country. It created a craze and awareness that would not be matched anywhere in South Africa and gave birth to boxers and followers alike in both male and female genders.

Imvo Zabantsundu's list of boxing journalists included fight specialists like Moses Twala, Charles Nqakula, Elliot Mtshozeni and Preston Mareka who made sure that their excellent writing skills matched the newspaper's far-reaching tentacles and thus providing a wide pool of knowledge for sports lovers and making sure that sport was widely spread and popularised.

Boxing benefitted widely from this project.

Among other media houses that have been in the forefront of updating and keeping boxing news in their pages, keeping the public informed on upcoming fights, results as well as profiles on boxers and administrators, are Gauteng based national newspaper The Sowetan, Sowetan Sunday World, Daily Sun and the Sunday Times.

Their journalists include, among others, the late Harold Pongolo, Percy Qoboza, and the doyen of South African boxing Theo Mthembu. The new crop includes Bongani Magasela, Pule Mokhine and Sandile Xaka. Lately, Isolezwe Newspaper has followed the tradition set by their predecessors Xhosa Newspaper Imvo Zabantsundu from the twentieth century. Imvo Zabantsundu walked the extra mile to popularise our boxing.

Contributions by journalists like Benito Phillips who worked for other media houses cannot be forgotten. Such contributors certainly took our boxing to the levels it is enjoying today.

CHAPTER 27

WITH A LITTLE HELP FROM FRIENDS

From its beginnings and its rise to the top of the boxing ladder, the Eastern Cape region has benefitted a lot from some people from outside this Province who assisted in every way they could. Their contribution to the sport has nothing short of great. They have come from all categories of boxing, like administrators, managers, trainers as well as the media. Those who readily come to mind are, in no particular order;

STANLEY CHRISTODOULOU

At the time that boxing started growing in South Africa the man at the helm of boxing in the country was none other than Stanley Christodoulou. He was Secretary of the South African Boxing Board of Control. He called the shorts for everything to do with boxing in the country. A highly intellectual, dominant and likeable figure, Christodoulou had a deep passion for boxing that went far beyond the call of duty. He used the power vested in him, so to speak, to express and fulfil that passion, thus carrying South African boxing to the highest levels of international participation and influence. He took advantage of the close working relationship he had successfully forged with the WBA, as well as his learnings from this leading international sanctioning body, to formulate the way forward for South African boxing, especially its Rules and Regulations. The WBA was the only leading international sanctioning body at that time that was happy to work with the South African boxing fraternity when the country was the pariah of the world due to its Apartheid Rule.

Christodoulou enjoyed unwavering support from Justice HWO Klopper, Chairman of the South African Boxing Board of Control during a great length of his reign in office. His close relationship with Les Muller, the Secretary of the Border Boxing Board of Control in the Eastern Cape region ensured that everything and any assistance that was meant to develop and advance the interests of the game in the new boxing region was facilitated from the top – and without much hassle. From time to time Christodoulou would visit the region to oversee the running of tournaments, as well as all other aspects of boxing like judging, refereeing and other general aspects in the improvement in boxing in the region. He was certainly impressed with the talent and enthusiasm of boxing and acknowledged this region as the home of boxing.

RODNEY BERMAN

One can safely say that Rodney Berman delivered The Mecca to the space of world champions. In the almost 130 years of South African boxing, and almost 60 years of professional boxing in Buffalo City, nobody has done more in ushering this region onto the world stage than Berman. In the process of making his promotional boxing outfit the best and most professional outfit in Africa, and certainly one of the best in the world, he made South Africa and particularly the Buffalo City region the best boxing community in Africa.

Having made Welcome Ncitha the first world champion for his Golden Gloves Promotion, he also made him the first product of the Eastern Cape to win a world title. More were to follow. Soon after Ncitha lost the title in his eighth defence to Kennedy Mckinney, an aggressive but smooth and defensive and pressure fighter Vuyani Bungu was to win the same title from Mckinney and make record 13 defences of the world title. Bungu's rise had been masterminded under Ncitha as a sparring partner and co-feature in the preliminary bouts. Berman achieved these feats by firstly recognising boxing as show business, secondly identifying the business acumen and boxing prowess of Buffalo City's Mzi Mnguni whom he brought under his wing, and thirdly embracing the IBF as a sanctioning body to work with while it was still struggling to convince the boxing fraternity, promoters and managers that it was an organisation with much value to offer in the boxing world. Berman and his American partner Cedric Kushner can lay claim to having made the IBF.

The networks and tentacle reach of Golden Gloves spread so far and became so influential that all South African champions and world-class contenders under Mnguni's control gained IBF world rankings and were subsequently offered world title fights. Which they almost all won. He then proceeded to create world title opportunities for Mbulelo Botile, Lindi Memani, Hawk Makepula and Zolani Petelo. The turnaround and opportunities that Berman brought for the Buffalo City region, known as the Boxing Macca, will go a long way and will influence mindsets and working strategies for generations to come.

THEO MTHEMBU

One man that Less Muller credited with teaching him the finer points and details of the game was Theo Mthembu. This highly intelligent journalist and boxing manager-trainer was already experienced as manager and trainer of well known Dube Boxing Club in Soweto. The club was born and bred by such legendary champions as Levy Madi, Hebert Hlubi, Alfred Buqwana, David Mankga, as well as Sisa Dukashe's crowd favourites Baby Jake Matlala and Anthony Blue Jaguar Morodi.

Dube Boxing Club was the first club of professional boxers from outside the Province to engage with our first professional boxers. Less Muller used all those opportunities to engage and learn from this wise old man known amaXhosa as *Isisele senyath*i (a well of knowledge). It was ironic that Nkosana Mgxaji, Buffalo City region's first champion won the SA title from the very Dube Boxing Club, which as history will show, was a teacher of boxing to many greats. Mgxaji beat Anthony Morodi in Orlando stadium for the South African Junior Lightweight title. Mthembu was in Morodi's corner. Mgxaji's corner was manned by Thamie Nomvete.

DAVID MASIKE

This friendly and eloquent boxing man is unknown to BCM fans. The simple reason is that he works within the amateur boxing code. The last I checked, he lived in Soweto, Gauteng and is well known to the SANABO and ECABO boxers and administrators. His importance in boxing history and legacy is his connection with Buffalo City's first champion, Nkosana Mgxaji. He is the only man from outside the region who can boast that he made Mgxaji a champion, further raising the profile of boxing in this boxing mad region.

When Happy Boy lost his first attempt at the SA Junior Lightweight Title by a points loss to Anthony Morodi, his first defeat as a professional after an unbeaten record of 35 fights; the main reason that boxing analysts blamed for Mgxaji's loss in a fight that the majority of fans thought he had won was that Mgxaji was slapping. Mgxaji engaged in three more fights before he challenged Morodi again for the title. This time Team Mgxaji decided to take no chances. They approached trainer Masike to fine-tune Mgxaji for the big contest.

Masike had to make emphasis on Mgxaji's punching abilities. He was taken to Masike's Soweto home and stayed there for a month and a half while Masike worked him every day. On fight day the results were there for all to see.

Mgxaji had lost none of the qualities that made boxing writer Terry Pettifer rate him the speediest boxer in South Africa. But he had done away with much of his slapping and was punching with more knuckle and more authority and newfound power.

Mgxaji came home as the new South African Junior Lightweight champion. It was his 36th fight. And he was to fight 71 more fights and retire a hero. But we must never forget to remember the name David Masike. He is one of the friends from outside who gave BCM boxing that little extra push towards the destiny of being known as The Boxing Mecca.

STANLEY VOKWANA

Very few people know that it took a Cape Town businessman to risk all his finances and invest in a world title fight for Nkosana Mgxaji.

That man was Stanley Vokwana. At a time when there was no sponsorship for fights, especially those promoted by black promoters and featured black boxers, promoters relied on the gate takings to make their profit. And if you saw what usually happened in East London, they got their money back, and much more.

This is why there was a feeling from the East London fans that Vokwana should have promoted the world title fight between Mgxaji and WBA world champion Sam Serrano in Mdantsane. It is generally believed that he would have made his money back. But the promoter naturally had more confidence in his own town and people.

Suffice to say that the tournament was a heavy financial loss, more so because Mgxaji also lost by knockout and failed in his bid to be the first Eastern Cape boxer to win a world title. The Boxing Mecca had thus failed in its first attempt at a world title. But Vokwana had tried.

BERT BLEWETT

For a long time, Bert Blewett was recognised as the mouthpiece of boxing – very vocal about his love for boxing. A strong boxing fan with a keen analytical mind, Blewett never seemed to fail to make his point under the most difficult of situations. If it was about boxing, Bert had his ways. He served boxing in many ways and in many institutions that included print and electronic media, as well as an administrator. I met Bert in the early 2000s when we were partnered by SABC to do boxing commentary and analysis on TV. We went off like a house on fire and hit the world of boxing with an African style, eloquence and deep knowledge of the game they had never heard from this side of the border.

Walter Mokoena and Brian Mulder, a popular anchorman and well-informed boxing analysts and commentators at the time for SABC SPORTS affectionately referred to our combination as the gruesome twosome, and it stuck. In 2006 we won an International award for excellence in boxing commentary and analysis. Bert will always have a place in the minds of the boxing people in Buffalo City. When they saw him, they saw boxing. And he loved the boxing atmosphere they provided. He always said that it produced the best out of him. And truly it produced the best out of everybody. And the best of Bert Blewett was certainly the greatest.

DUMILE MATEZA

The most loved and mimicked voice of any commentator I know, that is the voice of Dumile Mateza. Anyone and everybody who heard him do commentary on any sport, especially his favourites, boxing and soccer, they want to hear him again. And they want to do it like him.

I remember going to a Lower Primary School in Potsdam. I was still fresh from my boxing ring days and the kids knew me as a boxer. So when I was introduced they started doing what all Eastern Cape kids do when they see a boxer. They started shadow boxing. One of them, incidentally we shared a name. He was also Loyiso Mtya. And soon enough some were doing a live commentary on the number of fights on view. Different comments started flowing in the air. It went on like *"uthande ukungxabalaza unkabi phesheya phaya,"* *"nanko ebanjwa ngelikhohlakeleyo lasekhohlo, iyoooo ngumntwana kabanina lo ubethwa kangaka,"* were some of the comments flying in around.

It was Dumile Mateza's voice all the way. Dumile is very objective and vocal. But perhaps his biggest asset is his independence. Fluent in IsiXhosa, English and Afrikaans, he says things exactly the way he sees them and has never been known to be in anybody's pocket. And he does not wait for tomorrow to air his views.

Dumile Mateza was never angrier than the night he was part of the commentary team that covered the now notorious Technical draw that decided the fight between Harold Volbrecht and black hero Arthur Mayisela. He screamed his voice hoarse asking what was happening, especially when referee Alfred Buqwana indicated that he was stopping the fight but was overruled by Board secretary Stan Christodoulou. To this day he has not changed his mind to the fact that South Africa's first technical decision was a plain robbery.

Why Dumile is on the list of friends who helped build the Mecca from outside is because he is from Port Elizabeth. He has never stayed in the Boxing Mecca. But boxing to him has always been about the Mecca because it is, after all where all things boxing have been happening. His voice on radio and television, as well as his in-depth knowledge and love of the game, helped the Buffalo City region a lot. You just have to say *Unkabi phesheya phaya*, and everybody knows who you're talking about.

KHALIFI CALEB MABELANA

KC Mabelane is one of the people from outside the BCM region who played a big and progressive role in the development and governance of South African boxing, especially in the then Border region of the Eastern Cape now known as Buffalo City. Mabelane was already a seasoned administrator when he joined Fort Hare University as a lecturer in the middle

80's. He was already acting as an advisor to Fort Hare University's All-Sports Committee when the Eastern Cape Government took advantage of his expertise and experience to set up its boxing structures.

As a lecturer at that time, and more so during the Apartheid Era, it was not fashionable for lecturers to interact freely and be friendly with students as KC was doing. It is this unofficial role that introduced him to the chairman of Fort Hare boxing Siphatho Handi and fellow boxing activist and developer Khulile Radu. That role introduced him to the local government officials. Mabelane was roped in as part of the team to research and recommend the layout for the running of the Border Boxing Commission which would be run by Less Muller and later Khulile Radu as chairman.

Working closely with the South African Tertiary Institutions Congress (SATISCO) under the presidency of Sindisile Maclean, as well as the National Sports Council under President Mluleki George, he became a pillar of strength and a reservoir of experience.

These connections made sure that his input into the BCM region would be along the lines of progressive politics. Local boxing could not have chosen a better man to pave the way towards the Mecca status it enjoys today. After leaving Fort Hare with an unwavering love for boxing, KC was voted into the Board of the South African Boxing Control Commission under Chairman Dr Peter Ngatane.

LEONARD NEIL

Leonard Neil was in many ways like Joe Manyathi. He, like Manyathi always unlocked doors that were historically slammed shut and keys were thrown away for black boxers, especially in the Eastern Cape.

As a journalist, he worked for the Rand Daily Mail, Sun International and Golden Gloves Promotions. It is this experience and knowledge of the game that made him fall in love with East London boxing.

He believed that East London boxers were the most talented boxers in the country, and their trainers were the best. He was however not happy with the way such talent was usurped. He used to come and book himself into a hotel at the beachfront where he would hold meetings with us to discuss the strategy of how to gain more opportunities for our fighters. He was immensely popular among the licensees here.

He then used the working relationship he had with Promoter Mike Segal, with whom he was now working, to secure fights, world rankings and finally, world title fights for Patrick Quka, Sakhumzi Magswalisa and others. Other people he was closely working with within BCMM included promoter Zolani Moshani and Daily Dispatch journalist Mxolisi Ntshuca.

JEFF ELLIS

Jeff Ellis has served the game as a fighter, a matchmaker, a board member and lately a collector of memorabilia of boxing as a whole. He always makes moves and takes on new ventures that will market boxing locally and across the globe. As a personal friend, he has helped my boxing activities under some of the most difficult situations in this game. In this way, his assistance has in many ways also spilt over to assisting the Buffalo City boxing vehicle.

Ellis has almost every picture of everybody ever involved in boxing. It is also surprising that he has the largest collection of boxing pictures of the Eastern Cape, especially Buffalo City boxers and administrators. When the question, "Where did all the white boxers go?" came from parliament in 2005, Jeff was the man I turned to for assistance to get the white boxers back into boxing. Together we went door to door convincing a lot of white kids who had turned their backs on boxing because of the game's own version of Swart Gevaar. Big numbers of white boxers had been scared away. Roping him in was a masterstroke. Together we brought them back into the fold.

RON JACKSON

Ron Jackson's collection of boxing is unmatched in South Africa. Probably one of the biggest collectors of boxing memorabilia. Jackson has been quick to assist with any information that has to do with upliftment and improvement of the sport of boxing. He has a deep knowledge of the history of boxing and has helped me personally and everybody else, including Less Muller. His contributions, in writing, on television as well as on a personal basis have assisted immensely to make the country's boxing what it is today.

RUBEN RASODI

It is one thing to spot talent. It is quite another to correctly identify one who will go all the way to the top. Ruben Rasodi did just that. He proved not to be one of the best spotters, but a friend who helped the Boxing Mecca from the outside of the Mecca boxing circles. Ruben Rasodi is the lifetime matchmaker of Golden Gloves Promotions. He has won a string of awards that include perhaps the biggest award for Long and Meritorious Service to Boxing, that we both received together in 1985.

He is credited as the man who spotted Welcome Ncita when Golden Gloves was looking for a good black kid who would go all the way to the top. Rasodi was spot on with that talent. It is history now, Welcome 'Hawk' Ncita went on to become the first world champion to come out of the Eastern Cape, a Golden Gloves world champion, and the last Apartheid Era champion. What a feat. And we can only thank Ruben Rasodi for that.

PETER NGATANE

Peter Ngatane is a man I have known from our days in college, through the boxing streets, halls and rings right up to the time I served under him as an administrator in Boxing SA. A servant of boxing who has been in the game for so long because he loves it. Ngatane makes more friends than enemies, and those that remain enemies are there because they choose to be enemies. Not him.

Peter Ngatane is a former amateur boxer, one of the guys we used to rope in as sparring partners for Mzukisi Skweyiya at Fort Hare. After his college days, he was recruited into the South African National Boxing Coordinating Council (SANBCC) to provide guidance and leadership in the sport. He was to move up the boxing ladder until he took over as chairman of the National Boxing Commission after the death of Mike Mortimer, while Stan Christodoulou served under him as Executive chairman.

It was at the insistence of local licensees and final demand from Sports Minister Steve Tshwete that the National Commission resigned in 1998. However, when elections were held in 1999 Ngatane was democratically elected as Chairman of the Gauteng Commission. This Commission under Ngatane was hailed as the most professionally run Provincial Commission in the country for a long time.

Perhaps his toughest and most testing time was after he was appointed as acting chairman of the South African Control Commission after Mortimer. A movement called the Boxing Reconstruction and Development Association (BRDA) had appealed to Minister of Sport, Steve Tshwete not to appoint Ngatane to succeed Mortimer as chairman. The BRDA, which has formal structures in the then Provinces of that time known as Border and Gauteng regions, and other areas like the Free State, Natal, Eastern Province and Western Province were adamant in their stance.

Even as Mortimer struggled for his life in hospital, intense lobbying was in progress and local boxing pioneer Les Muller was also in the running for the position. The movement alleged that if Ngatane was appointed to the position no development of boxing would take place. Even big boxing giants like matchmaker Jeff Ellis, former vice president of the Africa Confederation Khaya Ngqula and promoter and trainer Carlos Jacamo supported the move. Their hopes were raised when Tshwete announced in a national awards banquet that he aimed to introduce changes in the running of the national body. But then to the amazement of everybody Tshwete appointed Peter Ngatane. Since then Ngatane has served on and off and on until now as the Chairman of Boxing SA. Whenever there is chaos in South African boxing Ngatane has always been the man any Sports Minister calls to quell the flames.

The latest call came from Sports Minister Thulas Nxesi when he recalled Ngatane to the board and returned him to the chair. At the time of writing, he was still serving as BSA chairperson. His biggest quality as chairman of BSA has been that he has never let himself be run by promoters.

There is a tendency in South Africa where Board Members assume the positions in the highest office to serve certain promoters. Promoters are by nature businessmen. So it is in their nature to seek the weakest links and have influence in the office. A lot of members soon find themselves being proxies of promoters and doing anything to put such promoters ahead of others. Ngatane has always been his own man, not bending even when some of his fellow members pressure him to make specific decisions. To Ngatane, if it does not serve the more positive interests of boxing, he keeps his peace. Through all these ups and downs Ngatane has always had a special place in his heart for boxing in Buffalo City. This originates from his days as a student at Fort Hare University.

He and his friends would travel to Mdantsane to watch boxing at Sisa Dukashe stadium. They used to arrive on Friday and stay at their favourite tavern Emthini and leave on Sunday. He has also made numerous trips to the region as a member of SABCCC, Fight Supervisor for the WBC and also as BSA chairman.

He has always been the man to call to douse flames when they have flared up in this boxing mad region, even during the days of Less Muller, Mzi Mnguni, Khulile Radu and myself. Mzi's power in the game always made him difficult to control, athethe kuthethwa. Buffalo City licensees are the best of friends. But not all the time. Peter Ngatane was always the man to tame them. He would often say, "Mzi I am not going to allow you to hijack my meeting." But in the end, they would shake hands in agreement. Ngatane does not make permanent enemies. That is why he has been good for BCM boxing. That is why he is good for boxing overall.

ADV. KRISH NAIDOO

Krish was unquestionably one of the most outspoken critics of racial sport in South Africa. A soft-spoken but eloquent character with an unyielding tenacity, he was the man to look out for when Boxing SA needed an administrator after the resignation of CEO Thabo Mseki in 2004.

Boxing at the time was at its lowest ebb, struggling to come to terms with the new Boxing Act that was racially inclusive. It was inclusive by propaganda but not in actual actions.

The BSA's new business outlook, which included having to account to auditors for its finances, did not make things easy. South African boxing was not used to that.

With impeccable credentials in politics, law and sports administration, Naidoo had to amass all his skills and experience gained especially from his days with the National Sports Council (NSC). His understanding of development in sports as well as the vision of inclusivity that at the time was new in the South African social scene put him in good stead in leading boxing through these trying times.

He understood only too well the history and dynamics of boxing in the Eastern Cape, especially East London or Mdantsane and surrounding villages. He could not have come at a better time.

BOXING FANS FOR LIFE

The Boxing Mecca is proud of its standing among the best in the boxing world. It has produced the best of boxers, trainers, managers, promoters, ring officials. And guess what? It has also produced the best of fans.

The following three gentlemen are those who come to mind first as boxing fans for life for only one reason – they were there from the beginning when amateur boxing started in the mid-50s, they were already full fans when professional boxing was advancing in 1965, and they are still here now. They never miss a fight. Big or small.

They made the Mecca. The three fans are Reggie Klaas, Ken Ntenteni and Ngenisile Ngcani. Mlandeli Sabotage Dabeni is very young but makes the list because of his enthusiasm and energy in boxing tournaments. He is generally known as the ambassador of boxing.

CHAPTER 28

HISTORY-MAKERS IN THE MECCA

Boxing is made great by the men and women who bravely walk into the ring to face their opponent. Their heroism is not just about taking or throwing punching, it goes much deeper than that. It is about discipline, being prepared both mentally and physically. For many, it's about facing their demons, their bad habits and rising to be a fighter of world renown. In my books, the following names have done just that.

CYRIL ADAMS: A youngster still fighting as a junior boxer. Cyril Adams introduced the Border region to championship levels when he won the South African amateur title in 1960. He thus became the first of many champions that would follow and take local boxing to international levels.

WELCOME NCITA: The first Eastern Cape boxer to win a world title.

Welcome Ncita grew up in Mdantsane. And like all other kids his age, he started sparring in the streets with other boys. There were no boxing gloves, so sparring gloves were milk cartons. He also played a little bit of kicking the ball in the streets of the already boxing mad township. It was a no brainer then that boxing would be the winner. And so he joined the throng of youngsters that started at Boyce Zitumane's Modern Boxing Club and later to Mzi Mnguni who opened the Eyethu Boxing Club for them.

This association was going to lead to the world stage. Welcome became a brilliant amateur. He had at that stage of his development what I usually refer to as a riotous style that comprises pressure fighting, throwing volumes of quick punches with little or no head movement nor blocking of any sort. But he was still difficult to hit because of very fast legs and unpredictable footwork that put him in and out of the line of fire. That made Ncita a very difficult target to nail.

He did not have much in terms of power, perhaps his footwork could be blamed for that, but he made up for that with a high work rate. And he always won against the best. He hit the professional ranks with a blaze and a trail of victories that left the Buffalo City fans baying for more. But the most satisfying victory that sealed his local accomplishments and catapulted him into the international scene was also the one that made some fans take his rise to the top with a pinch of salt.

Ncita beat local favourite Victor Sonaba fair and square in one of the legendary local derbies that have set this region apart from others. The contest was so enthralling and relentless that a rematch was imminent by public demand. Ncita never gave Sonaba a rematch. You can credit that to his shrewd manager Mzi Mnguni.

On the Northern side of the country in Gauteng, International promoter Rodney Berman and his Golden Gloves outfit were spreading their wings into the black market. They wanted a bright young black kid who could go all the way to the top. Their reasons were both for business and political purposes. Their matchmaker Ruben Rasodi recommended Welcome Ncita in Mzi Mnguni's Eyethu stable in Mdantsane. Ncita's boxing career, Mnguni's managerial skills, and Buffalo City's boxing legacy would never be the same.

In no time Ncita, undoubtedly, through the connections of Berman and partner, South African born American Cedric Kushner, gained an IBF ranking that saw him surprisingly move from Flyweight to an IBF world Junior Featherweight title challenge without ever fighting in the division. The title was in the hands of Frenchman Fabrice Benichou. It was held in Tel Aviv.

This fight had two historic challenges that would impact greatly on Ncita's performance, victory or defeat. Firstly and positively South Africa was still in political ecstasy and buoyancy in the recent release of Nelson Mandela after twenty-seven years in jail. Secondly and negatively manager Mzi Mnguni had to leave all fight preparations and the fight itself. Mdantsane was ablaze. Mnguni had to fly back home to protect his businesses from being burned down.

The opportunistic riots that sprang up after the overthrow of Ciskei President Lennox Sebe as leader of the Ciskei Homeland by General Oupa Gqozo, had taken the region by surprise. Business properties were being burnt down and there was a spree of looting on a scale never seen before.

Mnguni's sudden departure to protect his businesses meant that for the first time in his professional career Ncita would take the ring without his mentor in his corner. Mnguni need not have worried. His businesses back home were protected by boxing fans turned comrades who had formed a protective human wall around the properties of known comrades to save them from destruction. Such is the power of boxing in this area.

Meantime in Israel, Welcome Ncita danced circles around IBF Junior Featherweight champion Fabrice Benichou in front of a mesmerised crowd of French fans and took the title by way of a unanimous decision to become the first Eastern Cape boxer to win a world championship. He also became Golden Gloves Promotions' first world boxing champion.

VUYANI BUNGU: The first BCM champion to hold a record number of world title defences for a South African.

At this stage of BCM boxing, Bungu still stands tall among the greats of this talent-laden region. Following in the footsteps of legends like Nkosana Mgxaji and his stablemate Welcome Ncita, it was always going to be difficult to gain the honour of being recognised as greater than these giants, unless he did something special.

He had to earn it. And this he did with the kind of aplomb no one expected. After campaigning successfully as South African Junior Featherweight champion, a title he won in his second attempt from Fransie Badenhorst, Bungu, management and promotion were satisfied he was ripe for anything the world could offer.

Kennedy Mckinney was holding the title he had won from Bungu's stablemate Welcome Ncita. It was time to get the title back to manager Mzi Mnguni's stable. Winning the IBF world Junior Feather-weight title was one thing. After all, he was not the first boxing champion the region ever produced. But defending it a record 13 times and surpassing Brian Mitchell's twelve defences was a mammoth achievement.

He lined up his defences at the Carousel Casino his favourite venue. His nickname may have been The Beast, but the casino and his fans there called him The Carousel Kid. He vehemently turned down the challenges of Felix Camacho, Mohammad Al Haji Nurhuda, Victor Llerena (twice), Laureano Ramirez, John Lewis, Pablo Osuna, Jesus Salud, Kennedy Mckinney, from whom he won the title, Enrique Jupiter, Danny Romero, Angel Barotillo and Ernesto Grey. With that, he broke the record and stamped his legacy.

A defensive magician in a style that is always regarded as reckless, Bungu walked after his opponents with one of the most underrated jabs in boxing. His jab was not your usual jab. Normally that punch is thrown on the back foot or standing still, as it is meant to either keep opponents away or keep them checked.

Bungu used the jab to its fullest use. He pressed forward with consistent bobbing and weaving while using the jab to open up the opponent's defence and keep him on the backfoot. And to cap it all, Bungu fought with a high guard and never dropped it. This kind of attack forced his fights to be on the inside. He was well prepared for that. He threw some of the best combination punches you will ever see in a boxing ring.

That is also what confused his opponents. His jab allowed him to adjust and fight as effectively at long range as he did on the inside. This made it difficult even for the best strategists in the world to predict and compromise his line of attack. Bungu's record puts him among South Africa's all-time greats.

LES MULLER: Les Muller's story is as long as the boxing story in the Eastern Cape Province. A lot of his achievements and pioneering work are in every category of this book. This is because he started professional boxing in the Border region of the Eastern Cape.

As the only white man at the time who was prepared to come to the townships and rub shoulders with black people, it became automatic for him to take the leading role as all facets of life, boxing not excluded, needed a white man for things to work out.

Les Muller formed the first group of ring officials in the Border under the chairmanship of Marcus Temple who headed the Cape Province Boxing Board of Control. Locally it became the Border Boxing and Eastern Cape that later became Border Boxing Control Board. Now under Boxing SA, it is the Eastern Cape office under service provider Phakamile Jacobs.

Muller had to form this group by convincing other white sportsmen who were interested in working in the townships. He was able to bring people like Piet Jacoby Snr, Swannie Swanepoel, Arno Oberlholster, Piet Kruger, and the Van Zyl brothers. Muller then went on to formulate the rules, train officials and licensees, assist in matchmaking, assist in the logistics of organising tournaments and piloted local boxing into the world stage. Muller became everything, and without pay. And when local boxing started to find its feet, Muller also realized that the political tide was changing. He started preparing for the future. He recruited DV Mapisa into the board and also started mentoring Mava Malla and Phakamile Jacobs to get them ready to govern boxing after him.

DV MAPISA: Douglas Vakele Mapisa came to Mdantsane in 1968 to open a school as principal. In 1975 he was appointed Sports organiser by the Ciskei Department of Education. He went through a variety of sports activities as an administrator before he retired. His keen interest, knowledge and experience in sport forced the Eastern Cape Board to have him elected as its first black chairman. He retired due to ill health.

MTHOBI TYAMZASHE: When Sports and Recreation Minister Ngconde Balfour needed to implement his idea of a new Boxing Act and a new National boxing body, he appointed Mthobi Tyamzashe from Ginsberg in the Eastern Cape, as the man who would steer the new board and South African boxing. The new national boxing regulatory body to be called Boxing SA would be run under the new South African Boxing Act 11 of 2001.

Mthobi Tyamzashe was born in Uitenhage where he started his boxing activities fighting as a Bantamweight and later played rugby as a scrumhalf at St John's College. After graduating from Fort Hare he joined Spring Rose Rugby Club and became its secretary in Ginsberg where he continued his love for boxing at the local Ginsberg Boxing Club. He was secretary of the Border Rugby Union when he was recruited by founding member and then president of the National Sports Congress (NSC) Mluleki George to be the organisation's national secretary in 1989.

In 1994 Tyamzashe captured one of the top posts in South African sport when he was appointed Executive Director of the National Sports Congress, the country's major sports body. By the time Balfour appointed him to lead South African boxing and turn around its fortunes, especially after years of isolation, Tyamzashe had already served in the administration of SARB as well as DG for the Department of Sports and Recreation. He was now working for media giant Vodacom as CEO. Thus local product Mthobi Tyamzashe became the first black chairman of Boxing SA.

MAVA MALLA: Adv. Mava Malla started his amateur boxing career in 1976. He retired early as a professional boxer and decided to resume his studies at Fort Hare University where he pursued a Law degree. He was later recruited by his former trainer Boyboy Mpulampula and served in the East London and Border Boxing, being selected as the secretary in 1978.

Les Muller recruited him to serve as referee and judge in the professional ranks where he became one of the young black officials in the predominantly white group. Muller started to get more involved in Mava's career and insisted that he formally join the Border Boxing Control Board wherein he mentored him for better things.

Once he was officially inside the Board Malla began to push for changes that were meant to make professional boxing a better home for black officials. First among those was getting black ring officials to be allowed to officiate in National title fights, something that was meant only for white officials. Black officials who participated in International fights were not paid. Only the executive director was paid at the time.

Malla challenged that until it was changed. Black officials started being paid. He was also involved in discussions that led to Welcome Ncita being allowed to jump from Flyweight and directly to the IBF world Junior Featherweight title. Les Muller mentored Malla on fight supervision and other boxing logistics until he was appointed to the National Commission in 1987. Malla's academic status, his knowledge of fight organisation and his experience as a ring official in the Border region proved to be enough acquisitions to see him appointed as the first black CEO of South African boxing post Apartheid in 1998. He also holds the accomplishment of being the first ex-boxer to ascend to such a position in South Africa.

HAWK MAKEPULA: Apostle Dr Hawk Makepula holds several firsts through his life as a boxer, as well as in life after the ring. He made his first by being the first black athlete to lift the South African flag for TEAM SOUTH AFRICA in the 1996 Olympic Games in Atlanta.

That was followed by being the first South African boxer to fight at the legendary Madison Square Garden in New York, USA. And in winning three world boxing titles, Makepula became the first South African boxer to be a Triple world champion. Together with Jake Matlala, they became the first South African boxers to engage in a unification contest for two world titles. Makepula thus unified the IBO and WBO LightFlyweight titles.

MZIMASI 'MZI' MNGUNI: Firstly all the boxers in this list of people who made history by gaining achievements never seen or heard of before were managed by Mzi Mnguni. He became the first manager from the Eastern Cape to produce a world champion when Welcome Ncita did the honours. Vuyani Bungu who succeeded Ncita in winning back the IBF world Junior Featherweight title and defended it a record thirteen times was also a product of the Mnguni managed Eyethu Boxing club. The next world champions Mbulelo Botile, Lindi Memani, Zolani Petelo and Hawk Makepula were all managed by Mnguni. He became the first manager to achieve such a feat.

PHAKAMILE JACOBS: Although he never became a boxer in any way, Phakamile Jacobs grew up with boxers and was always around the boxing clubs and rings. He always had a passion for the game and learned as much as he could. This gave him enough knowledge and boxing awareness to start as a referee and judge when black ring officials were introduced in the Eastern Province and Border area of the Cape Province. He soon became one of the best referees in the country. Les Muller's mentoring also saw Jacobs being understudy to him in 1996.

In 1999 Jacobs was then appointed as secretary of the Border Board after Les Muller suffered a stroke. He thus became the first black secretary. Boxing SA was later to change the status of the Provincial offices, curtailing some of the powers, and having service providers reporting directly to head office. Jacobs became service provider and later Eastern Cape Provincial Manager when BSA again reviewed the positions of the provinces. He currently serves in that position. The huge size of the Eastern Cape Province and the number of tournaments have forced that there be an understudy to help out. Mthunzi Mapitiza of Port Elizabeth has been filling the gap effectively. Former boxer Nceba Dladla has taken over since the passing on of Mthunzi Mapitiza.

LULAMA MTYA: Lulama Mtya rose from his days as an amateur boxer to a leading referee and judge. He was nominated as one of the top ten officials in South African boxing before the IBF nominated him to officiate the IBF Junior Lightweight Title fight between South African Phillip Holiday and Jeff Fenech in Melbourne, Australia. He became the first official from the Eastern Cape to officiate in a world title fight.

SIYA VABAZA: Siya Vabaza holds a number of firsts in South African boxing. She was already a pioneer of female boxing refereeing and judging professional boxing during the Apartheid Era. That was long before female boxing was legalised by The South African Boxing Act 11 of 2001.

She is currently a well-travelled and experienced Ring official, having shared the boxing stage with some of the best boxers in the world, at home and abroad. A double award winner of both the Boxing SA Female Ring Official of the Year as well as Boxing SA Ring Official of the year, she is a proud winner of seven boxing awards in total.

NOFOTI TSENENE: Nofoti Tsenene was a businesswoman from Port Elizabeth when she decided to help in the development of boxing. As there were no sponsors nor television she put on money to promote development as well as national tournaments. She became the first female boxing promoter in South Africa.

MBALI ZANTSI: Mbali Zantsi and her Showtime Promotions was the first boxing promotion to organise an all Female boxing tournament in South Africa and the whole world.

The bumper tournament that was held in Durban, KZN featured upcoming South African female prospects, as well as South African champions against overseas opponents. The whole tournament was promoted, supervised, refereed and judged by female officials.

NONI TENGE: Noni Tenge has been the face of female boxing in South Africa since female boxing was legalised in 2006.

After an illustrious amateur boxing career, Tenge was one of the first female professional boxers to turn professional. She fought her way up the national and international rankings, beating a long list of tried and proven professionals from around the world before she was given the green light to challenge for the WBF and later the more prestigious IBF World Welterweight championship. Tenge won and thus and became the first South African female boxer to win a world championship.

SIMPHIWE VETYEKA: Simphiwe Vetyeka has won four world titles including the South African Bantamweight title. He won the IBO Bantamweight and Featherweight tiles in 2009 and 2013 respectively, then won the WBA Featherweight title in December 2013. Winning three world titles confirmed his status among the best fighters South Africa ever produced. But winning the WBA title against legendary Chris John in Australia while holding the IBO Featherweight crown meant that for the second time South Africa had a unified champion. This achievement ensured Vetyeka's place among the best in the world.

TSIETSI MARETLOANE: If the nickname of Pretty Boy that I always hear bandied about every day could be given a chance to choose for itself who deserved it most, it would certainly choose Tsietsi Maretloane. One of the most exciting fighters I have ever seen, Maretloane was not only handsome and charming, but he was also very brave. Although he was slick and quick and could have easily won fights while moving away, Maretloane never stepped back from a tough challenge and was always ready to engage. His style made for exciting slug fests.

He would have been a fan favourite had his career coincided with the introduction of television in South African boxing. Unfortunately, his time was ahead of TV. He was the black South African Featherweight champion when he met his white counterpart Freddie Rust for the Supreme Championship in Cape Town. In beating Rust, East London's Maretloane became the first South African boxing champion to win the prestigious Old Buck belt

AMATEUR BOXING FIRSTS

The amateur wing of boxing also achieved a lot of firsts in its endeavour to develop and enhance the state of boxing in the country, specifically in the Eastern Cape. ECABO, the Eastern Cape Amateur Boxing Organization was founded in 1995 by former boxers and amateur boxing administrators that included Mabhuti Gwavu, Khulile Radu, Sakhiwe Sodo, Andile Mofu, Wilson Mofu, Mzolisi Kota, Makaya Filita, Boyboy Mpulampula, David Qotile and Thembisile Gacula, among others. They decided to take this step after the last championships of the old Cape Province were held in Kimberly. The CP consisted of Border, Nothern Cape and Western Province.

After the unification of South African amateur boxing, the local group ECABO, now under the national SANABO, produced a lot of firsts as follows. Thembisile Gacula became the first ECABO president. He would also be elected as the first PRO for SANABO as well as the first internationally qualified official. Boyboy Mpulampula was selected to become the first black coach of the national team in 1991. He was the national team coach for the 2000 Sydney Olympics.

Andile Mofu became the first SANABO president, as well as being the first AIBA 3 Star coach and international instructor. He also led the national team as coach for both the 2004 Athens and 2012 London Olympics. Vuyolwethu Mtekwana is the current ECABO president.

From those beginnings, the group of international trainers has risen considerably. Former boxers professional boxers Velile Damoyi and Happy Mngqibisa have since qualified as two star international trainers after Mpulampula and Mofu. They qualified with Pumeza Xawuka, making her the first local female trainer to qualify at that level.

BOXING HEROES LOST TO THE POLITICAL STRUGGLE

Today is the 11th of August 2019. As I write this story I am reminded of the heroes that our boxing lost to the struggle. Today marks exactly 34 years ago, on 11th August 1985 to be exact, when 19 lives were lost, brutally taken away by the South African Defence Force (SADF) and other security forces in Duncan Village, East London which is part of the Buffalo City Municipality Metro today.

Among those killed in the massacre was a six-month-old baby, two Buffalo City boxing prospects namely Zandisile Thole and Oupa Mapai. This goes a long way to prove that our boxing people have never been just boxing people or boxers, but have been involved in all human endeavour, as citizens of the country.

Other boxers and club administrators who were detained without trial and brutally tortured during that period include Bandile Sizani, Batyana Dunjana, Mongezi Goci, Ryan Mapisa, Thethinene Jordan, Mahlulwa Ntamo, Small Menziwa, Ganda Hashe and Lulamile Filizwe. This brings to mind other boxing heroes who were forced by the unbearable circumstances of the time to flee the country and go to exile overseas and in other parts of the African continent.

Some of them came back after the demise of Apartheid and playing different roles in society. Others sadly lost their lives and came back either as corpses or were seen again. Not known if they are still alive or lost their lives.

Gideon Vakala was one of the star boxers of the first generation and is probably the first local boxer to flee to exile. Had he stayed he would have been in the first group debutant. He is back home in East London and is living a quiet life with his family.

Charles Nqakula was a journalist for Imvo Zabantsundu and later the Daily Dispatch. He and other journalists of his time like Moses Twala, Gordon Qumza, Lesley Xinwa and Benito Philips are credited with writing with a kind of style that firstly popularised boxing in the Border region, and then broadened it nationally. They are said to have coined the term Boxing Mecca. When Charles Nqakula fled the country and went into exile, our boxing suffered a terrible loss. He was back however after the demise of Apartheid and has played a major role in the new democratic South Africa.

Mzukisi Skweyiya was an unbeaten South African Bantamweight champion when he left the country due to unbearable pressure that made it practically impossible for him to concentrate on training for his fights. He had beaten every worthy opponent in both the Flyweight and Bantamweight divisions and was left with only two opponents, Welile Nkosinkulu and Peter Mathebula. Skweyiya died in a car accident in Botswana and did not come back with the rest of the returnees.

Boy Mnyaka's story is a surprise. One would not be out of turn in naming little Boy as one of the first people in the gym when Duncan Village Boxing Club, the second oldest boxing club was opened in East London. But somebody else would ask how such a young boy could be at such a place at that time. Which is where the answer lies.

Boy Mnyaka was so young. He grew up in the Duncan Village Boxing Club. However, because of his age, he did not start training immediately, but just came in and sat there every day, doing all the little things a youngster of his age could do in the gym. And he was on every trip that the club undertook across the Province. So it was that he attended every tournament when the new professionals started contesting. He was in King William's Town, Queenstown and Port Elizabeth.

When he finally started training effectively, now at Nompumelo Boxing Club, it did not take him long to be such a bright amateur that a decision was taken to immediately turn him professional. He was now at the Golden Gloves Boxing Club in Mdantsane. But that was as far as it got. Because after a few fights, Boy White Lightning Mnyaka skipped the country and went into exile. He is now back and staying in Queenstown. All that boxing talent has aged. Jomo Mpahla was a star amateur and had just turned professional when he left the country. That certainly put paid to a promising professional career. He died in exile. I did not get the circumstances surrounding his untimely death.

Lulama Mthoba left as an amateur but was already too old to continue his boxing career when he came back. He was preparing to get back as a trainer when lost his life in an accidental death by fire.

Luvuyo Vabaza of the famous Vabaza boxing family was the first fighter in the family. He was already a professional boxer and had built a respectable record when he left. He died in a stabbing accident after his return.

Lindile Yam is now a General Lindile Yam in the SANDF. He is still very active in boxing development matters within the army. A very good amateur who was a favourite of the legendary Mzukisi Skweyiya, unconfirmed reports are that they skipped the country together. Yam turned professional at the Modern Boxing Club as one of the prospects for the future. A few fights later he was gone.

Mpush Makambi is the only boxer and struggles soldier to go into exile and still come back to South African in time to recontinue his professional boxing career and finish as a world boxing champion. Why he is on this list is because of how far he could have gone if his career had not been disturbed. He resumed his career after his return to South Africa with a bullet on his leg, courtesy of a shot from the SADF during one of the skirmishes.

Lion King, as I nicknamed early in his amateur days because of his killer instinct, disappeared after a rosy amateur career and a good start in the professional ranks. He was still in his teens, and his future in boxing looked very bright. He however disappeared, and I was to hear from him about ten years later. He phoned me from Las Vegas and told me he wanted to resume his boxing career.

After leaving South Africa he had settled in Zimbabwe for some years as a soldier of APLA, the military wing of the PAC. He had moved to the US with two bullet wounds on his leg after a skirmish with the SADF.

The bullet wounds, as he said, were still a big challenge but were not serious to a point of him being unable to exercise, run and box. But they would hinder his ring mobility and leverage for the rest of his boxing career. But his immense talent and punching power always helped him to overcome his challenges.

He felt he was now ready to box again and wanted to know if his South African boxing licensed could be transferred into an American licence or anything of that sort. I advised him that the best for him would be to present himself to a gym and tell them he was a boxer. I knew he was good enough to pass any test they gave him. Which they did. After a few months of sparring, they felt he was ready to turn professional in the American way. He went through the American turning system and was granted a fighter's license.

Five fights later, and all wins, South Africa was changing. The banned political organisations like the ANC, his PAC and all others were unbanned. They could all come back home. Makambi also packed his bags and flew back home. He won five fights at home before challenging for the South African Junior Middleweight title. He lost in the first attempt on a points decision against champion Gregory Clark. He won in his second attempt when he outpointed Johannes Malaza in Johannesburg.

Makambi went on to show his true mettle as a boxer when he flew to London on seven days notice and knocked out their home-favourite Adrien Dodson in the eighth round to win the IBO world Super Middleweight championship.

He thus joined a few elite South African champions like Gerrie Coetzee (WBA Heavyweight champion), Thulani Malinga (WBC Middleweight champion) Dingaan Thobela (WBC Super Middleweight Champion) in winning a world title in the heavier divisions.

CHAPTER 29

WHO SPOILED THE BUFFALO PARTY

Buffalo City has sometimes had its dreams come crashing down at the most unexpected moments. Just when the fans regarded their boxers as demigods who could never be conquered, someone would come and spoil the party. It has never been easy for any fans, especially the Buffalo City boxing choir, to see their hero being outplayed, worse in a fighting game like boxing where he is subdued and helpless, being out-boxed, out-foxed, out-punched and sometimes even being beaten to submission, to the disbelief of the local followers. This disaster that grows to awful proportions, especially to the overconfident followers, has been caused by visiting fighters who never succumbed to the skills of the local boxers, nor were subdued by the paralysing psychological effect of the local fans. It once caused a riot.

In 1982, with his record closing in on a hundred fights, one of the very few boxers to have achieved such a feat in South African boxing, the other being Anthony Blue Jaguar Morodi and Enoch Schoolboy Nhlapo, Nkosana Mgxaji was already at the end of his career. His boxing prowess had left him. He was no longer as fast and elastic as he used to be. His skills were now just good enough to keep him winning some carefully selected opponents. He was still a hero to his fans and a big drawcard. To them, nothing was wrong as long as their man was still winning. To the promoters, he was still the money cow. It came as a surprise to the more knowledgeable fans when it was announced that he had challenged, and was granted a fight against the very dangerous South African Junior Welterweight champion Arthur Mayisela. The Gauteng based champion was brave and confident enough to come to East London in the Eastern Cape, the challenger's own Sisa Dukashe stadium. Mgxaji did what he was now adept at doing, keep his loyal fans happy with his slipping and sliding moves.

He survived as usual and was crowned the new champion. But Mayisela and a section of the crowd thought the champion had done enough to retain his title. Mayisela was a very angry man when he flew back to Johannesburg. He promised to come back and regain his title with vengeance. And he did.

Arthur Mayisela grew up in Meadowlands, Soweto. People who know him describe him as having grown up as a streetwise, rough and tough kid who was able to look after himself and always ready to sort out his street affairs with his fists. This made him one of the most feared youngsters in his area. And he gained the nickname Pantsula. So it was no surprise to those who knew Mayisela when he started attending the local gym.

Perhaps boxing also turned him around and away from what could have been worse. His meteoric rise in boxing was what put him in a position to match his skills against the man regarded as the god of boxing in the Eastern Cape. The rematch was held at the BRU Grounds in East London. And the man who returned to East London for the rematch was the street fighter. Perhaps Mayisela's ring entry told the story before the fight even started. It was the most fearsome ring entry I have ever seen, perhaps equal only to the one Mayisela orchestrated on his way to meet. This time Mayisela wanted to do it all by himself. He had no intention of leaving it to the judges. Clear signs were there from the first round that Mayisela was a very angry man.

There was no feeling around. Mayisela went straight after his man, and did not allow Happyboy room to manoeuvre his usual survival tactics of slipping and sliding or turning around his opponent and clinching. He attacked relentlessly and when Mgxaji tried to come in close to call on his respected speed of hand, Mayisela roughed him up with his elbows and shoulders. He even used his head. He was well known for such tactics.

After seven rounds of relentless pressure and sustained punishment, Mgxaji could not take it anymore. He indicated to the referee that his mouthpiece was stuck in his throat. He could not continue with the fight.

I was close enough to the action and well experienced to know that there was no mouthpiece problem. The champ had taken enough roughing up and punishment from an angry young challenger. There was a new camp. Nkosana Mgxaji was bowing out gracefully.

I was a ring announcer for the fight. And when the referee waved the fight off, I rushed up the ring steps. As I was bowing under the ropes to enter the ring, I felt the first bottle thrown hit my shoulder. Then more bottles and missiles came flying. I turned around to face Mayisela's corner and saw my friend and NSC leader Khaya Ngqula rushing from the other corner towards Mayisela. From the corner of my eye, I caught a glimpse of ring official Phakamile Jacobs and Cape Province Boxing Chairman Marcus Temple diving under the ring. Temple had a gun in his hand. At that moment, I said a little prayer for him not to shoot. He did not shoot.

The East London Police who were always present in boxing tournaments quickly formed a protective body around Mayisela, his team, Dicksy Ngqula and myself. We all pushed forward through the crowd and safely into the dressing room. But the mini-riot was over as soon as it had started, and there were no injuries to anyone. Just that Mayisela had spoiled their party. It was the first time that local crowds had reacted like that when their boxers lost.

It has never happened again. Not even when the next idol lost in what at the time was the biggest fight held at Sisa Dukashe stadium. Welile Nkosinkulu was in an elimination fight, the winner of which was guaranteed a challenge for the WBA bantamweight championship.

It was the first official elimination bout for a world title for any boxer here. It was the closest thing to a world title fight. To the local fans, this was a world title fight. At this time the horde of fans that filled the stadium that day believed that no one could beat Nkosinkulu. He would win the elimination and go on to win the world title. Both by knockout.

But the fans went into an unusual quiet mode as the co-eliminator, Puerto Rican Julian Solis ducked under and around Nkosinkulu's crisp and lightning-fast combinations. He stuck close to Nkosinkulu in what in today's terms is described as fighting in the pocket. Solis countered Nkosinkulu's charges with body and head movements, making him miss with his best-aimed punches that had caused damage to many opponents before. But not this one. Nkosinkulu was his confident self, attacking with intensity every quarter of the way. He wanted to catch Solis coming in but could not get a perfect punch or combination to satisfy his mission. The fight became intense and competitive to a point where people began to enjoy the boxing clinic from two diverse styles fought at close contact. And they roared ALIIIIII each time Nkosinkulu scored with one of his specials. But those roars were few and far between. Solis did not give much space to be hit. And when he was announced as the winner, the crowd readily accepted the judges' decision.

They stood up and clapped their hands, satisfied that the better man had won. They respected Solis for putting up such a splendid exhibition of boxing and wished him well. They still loved Welile Nkosinkulu and would still come back for him. But Solis had spoiled the party.

He has stopped Nkosinkulu's march to a world title. It would take a few more years before Welcome Ncita would fulfil the dreams and aspirations of his people and take Eastern Cape boxing to the next levels it had never known before by winning the IBF world Junior Flyweight title.

CHAPTER 30

CAN MIKE TYSON FLOAT LIKE A BUTTERFLY?

Trainers are always faced with the challenge of making a success of every boxer they train. Needless to say, that is impossible. Boxers are always looking around for the trainer who will make them the perfect fighting machine. Also near impossible. It has become a day to day exercise for boxers to move from one trainer to the other for whatever reasons they can think up at that moment. It is much easier for a trainer when a young and still learning prospect walks through the door. It is however not so easy when a veteran contender or champion who is already long in the tooth walks in. The main objective for the new trainer is always to improve the newcomer. But what is always the tricky part is whether to make adjustments here and there to improve the style. This usually needs doubling up on that jab, taking one more step forward after that punch, feinting before throwing that killer hook or cross.

The other option is whether to completely change the fighter as one does to a car engine. There is no easy answer to this. What then is the most important thing to do or to change? For this new relationship to be a success is it the boxer who has to change? Is it the trainer? I think this needs a considerable amount of shifting from both of them. Remember that two success stories are coming together. It's the boxer who has been successful while doing things one way. He now comes to a trainer who has produced champions and other successful boxers by making them do things in a certain way. The state of mind of the boxer gets tested against the skills of the new trainer to introduce new thought processes and tactics. There are cases where the two just readily merge. There are, however, also situations where it is not so easy, especially where a lot more adjustments that were initially thought of, come to the fore.

Imposing the will and the style of one on the other is always a no-no. This can produce the worst results, to a point where questions could be asked as to why the boxer changed trainers In the first place. It becomes important that the trainer comes up with a strategy of only polishing what is already there than saying he will be teaching new tricks. As a trainer, you also have to be diplomatic. Boxers, especially already successful ones hate being made like they are being taught how to box. The mindset, body dynamics, habits and abilities become the most important aspects for the trainer to deal with.

It is always important how the fighter views the new coach, and what or how much he expects from him. Remember that the boxers have had two or three trainers before. And they made a success of him. Now he comes because he experts the new one to take him to the next level. Comparisons are always inevitable. Being successful depends on the relationship and adaptability between the boxer and the trainer.

Every trainer will be the trainer, implementing his style according to his views, abilities and experience. He will come with new tricks to improve on the defence, offence and delivery. Sometimes the biggest challenge here comes with the training program. Trainers do their work differently. The new trainer never wants to do the same way as the previous one. That is why it becomes dangerous for a boxer to change trainers too much. He should try and do the change to a small limit. The reason here is that the strategies are usually different and easy to overlap and sometimes confuse. That is the last thing the boxer needs.

WHAT THEN MAKES A GOOD TRAINER?

There is a mountain of factors that come together for a boxer or any other athlete to be considered great. They include talent, dedication and discipline. But central and very important among them is the person behind the boxer, who guides, pushes, motivates, coaches, and even forces the boxer to do all the necessary undertakings and adjustments necessary to achieve the intended goals.

Talent alone is not enough to make a boxer reach their potential and goals. Dedication alone does not motivate nor push one to the highest limits of concentration and preparation. The discipline itself may be inborn in the genes, but it still needs guidance to gain relevance. It has been proved in all ways scientifically and practically possible that being naturally endowed with all above and have them locked somewhere in your body or mind is one thing, but you still need someone to unlock and direct the true potential and lead it to actual and meaningful achievement.

A good boxing trainer will achieve this and more. There are living and good stories from rings around the world where fights have been won by the trainers or the men in the corners, rather than the fighters themselves. One needs to look, listen and learn from them. South Africa has its legends in this category.

All the greatest boxers and achievers in the world have a trainer or a coach that is central to the preparations and whose plans and actions go a long way towards achieving the intended results. Such people range from teachers, strategists, conditioners, strength and fitness instructors, analysts, cheerleaders, motivators to friends. Having a good trainer is among the most important factors to push all of the above in improving the boxer's ability and chances of winning against the very best that competition can offer.

Even to the trainer or coach, there is more than just enthusiasm, passion, knowledge and experience to succeed in the chosen role- that of making the boxer a winner.

The role of the trainer in boxing has been so well maintained and preserved since the beginning of this most original of all sport itself that it has become a career for a lot of people. It has proved to be so important that many professional fighters have teams of trainers, each one specialising in different expertise relating to boxing.

As I try to go through and analyse all the different types of trainers in all the gyms and rings, I will start with the first and most original, but yet most overlooked of all. This is The Guy up the street. This is the person in the line who spots the talent and passion of the youngster and goes out of his way to assist. Even using money out of his pocket to make the youngster realize his dream. He gets so involved he goes out of his way to learn the finer points of the game to lend value to his advice. Some of these people are fortunate to climb the ladder with the boxer, and also bask in the limelight when their charge achieves fame and fortune. Others are not so lucky. They are dropped on the way and are never even mentioned in passing.

Why I call him The Guy Up The Street is because of the way it usually happens. This person is usually one who lives in the same street and gets interested in the youngster's efforts, the friend who the youngster grows up with and learn a lot of things together, the father, older brother or the guy he started going to the gym with or met and trained with. That person usually becomes the boxer's first coach. He knows the boxer better than anybody else.

He knows his likes and all things that make him uncomfortable. He knows exactly how he feels in all kinds of situations. He has the answers to all the boxer's needs. He is the one that believes in the boxer even at a time when nobody else does. With him around, the boxer gains confidence that the whole energy to conquer is within reach.

Every boxer, big or small, brilliant or average, experienced or not, need someone they can trust, in training and in going to war. A boxer needs that familiar face, understandable utterances and recognisable body language, in the corner, especially when the going gets tough. It is a combination of people he has grown to know that has been with him through thick and thin.

One he has learnt to trust. That trust is built over time. Through thick and thin. It goes beyond friendship. Pain, sweat and tears form the rocks of its foundations. From mutual feelings of pain. From an understanding of attitudes, habits and tendencies. Celebrating victories together as well sharing disappointment. This bond is earned. It is trust that has been built over time. That's why I love this game.

CHAPTER 31

SO NEAR AND YET SO FAR

Few other sports reward their heroes and achievers as much and as generously as boxing. The practice of awarding can be traced back to 800 AD. In some cases, boxers were rewarded with food for life. Legend has it that the Emperor Galicula of Rome rewarded his victorious boxers with young virgins. With modern times the awards have changed. Besides medals, trophies and belts, boxers today even carry cash and vouchers back home.

Such recognition is not only restricted to boxers but also to a variety of other people who work within or are connected to boxing. In the USA for instance there are awards for Excellence in Boxing Journalism and Broadcasting.

The British Boxing Board has an award for Sportsmanship. Back to boxers, the Ring Magazine started the annual custom of naming Boxer Of The Year in 1928. In South Africa, the custom was started by the monthly publication, Boxing World. The practice has now become so widespread that no Board, Commission or Sanctioning body can proudly regard itself as a regulator of boxing but still miss the opportunity of naming and rewarding its winners. It was such a relief but no surprise when we received the news that South Africa's own Gerrie Coetzee will be honoured in the USA.

Coetzee, widely regarded as the most talented Heavyweight this country has ever produced, realized his ultimate dream by winning the WBA Heavyweight title in his third attempt. He achieved this feat by knocking out Michael Dokes in the 10th round in Richfield, Ohio. He thus became the first non-American to win the heavyweight crown since Ingemar Johanssen pulled the trigger on Floyd Patterson way back in 1959.

While there is no doubt in my mind that all boxing loving South Africans will wholeheartedly welcome Gerrie's honouring, I must submit my wondering of whether by this award bestowed on him, we as South Africans must sit back and rest comfortable and satisfied, believing that this is enough. May I ask if the accolade is the apt recognition that we deserve or are we being thrown a bone or dropped a crumb or two as an afterthought? This opinion is not much on the award headed Coetzee's way, but on the one where I believe he and other South Africans deserve more recognition – The Boxing International Hall Of Fame.

For decades the African continent, in general, has produced gladiators that not only conquered the world by sheer boxing skills and achievements in the square jungle but were also highly recognized and respected by boxing fans and historians at home and away. It came as no surprise when they were justly selected and inducted into the International Hall of Fame. These all-conquering heroes who received the historic and gigantic call that would have them leave the prints of their fists on the wall of heroes and forever entrench their names in the annals of boxing are Nigeria's Dick Tiger, Ghana's Azumah Nelson and South Africa's Brian Mitchell. The fourth man and the only one outside of boxers to come out of this continent and receive this honour is the referee and Judge Stan Christodoulou. But considering the whole continent of Africa's impact in the international boxing arena, and all the great African pugilists that have graced boxing rings around the world against the best fighters other continents could offer, is it fair that we deserve to boast of only three boxers and one ring official? Coming closer home could South Africa that has achieved so much for boxing inside and outside the ring, only field one boxer and one ring official? Seriously?

South Africa's efforts in the boxing landscape have even revived crumbling international sanctioning bodies and struggling promoters. This makes Brian Mitchell the only boxer from South Africa to be considered good enough to make the grade. I personally refuse to believe that this honour is enough. I think South African boxing has produced a fair share of boxers, writers and promoters, and thus deserves more recognition than we are receiving, why so few from so many? The Boxing International Hall Of Fame offices is based in Canastota, New York, USA. It honours boxers, trainers, writers and other contributors to the sport worldwide. Ceremonies are held each year to conduct the induction of nominees. Inductions are handled by the American Boxing Writers Association and an International panel of boxing historians. This event is one of the biggest annual sports honours in the world, certainly the most colossal and final recognition one can receive and enjoy in the world of boxing. It equals the biggest awards that other sports codes and the movies bestow on their legends. It attracts the who's who of personalities from across the globe including present and former champions of boxing and other sports, as well as Hollywood celebrities.

Boxers must have been in full retirement for five uninterrupted years before they can be available for nomination. Being recognized and available does not however guarantee a place and first print on the wall, as the nominees still have to be voted for the final induction. A lot of gladiators still lose the final vote and have to wait for the following year, maybe finally making the grade after three, four or five years from the first time they got the call. Some boxers, the real and undoubtedly greats, get the vote and are successfully inducted in their first year of availability. The appointment of these history-makers comes as a result of not only the influence and impact their ring records commanded as they gloved and punched their way in the square jungle across the boxing venues of the world, but by the social, religious, political and/or any other humane legacies they left behind.

In the South African context, all boxing participants and fans who have followed Brian Mitchell know that he remains the only white boxer in the country to carve his career by venturing out of the comforts of the suburbs, and conquered all opposition right in the township venues that were his opponents' backyards. Thanks in part to his courageous and progressive manager-trainer Maurice Toweel who steered his early career. He made his bones fighting in the townships, especially in Mphathlalatsane Hall in Sebokeng, and Uncle Tom in Soweto, where he fought and beat the best boxers of his time who were predominantly black amid their crowds, in their backyards.

The nurturing Mitchell received at this early stage of his boxing life honed him mentally for his destiny. This was when it was not yet fashionable for white athletes to ply their trade in the townships and locations. It was the turbulent times in the history of a then divided South Africa. These brave outings by Brian Mitchell would go a long way towards proving sport as a great unifier. History will attest that the episode was his best school, yet unknown at the time as he would develop into a formidable world champion who would be forced by the sanctions imposed against his country for its Apartheid Policies to defend his title on foreign soil. His perfect conditioning and mind of steel enabled him to withstand the hostilities hurled at him in far away from home countries as England, Panama, Italy, France, Puerto Rico, Spain and the United States. He certainly deserved the call to the Hall of Fame. Stan Christodoulou reigned firstly as secretary and later as Executive Director of the South African Boxing Control Commission. He became incredibly popular overseas as a referee, particularly with the WBA, the first and original world sanctioning body. Working hand in hand with the WBA, he is widely credited for formulating the aspects of our statutory body, and firmly putting South African boxing on the world map.

He now operates as a freelance agent and is still active as a referee and judge in Africa and Europe. He has served as referee and judge in more than 200 hundred world title fights across the globe, He certainly deserved the call. But why has there have been such rarities of African, particularly South African boxers who reached the pinnacle of world boxing and stayed there, but failed to receive that all-important call? A strong case could be made of Welcome Ncita who not only became the first boxer in his Province to win a world title but also like Mitchell went on to conquer the world away from home. Twenty of the fights in his impressive record were amassed on foreign land in countries like France, Italy, Panama and the USA. Six of those fights were successful title defences of the IBF world title. Vuyani Bungu's record of defending the IBF world title a record thirteen times has been celebrated and ululated for as long as possible. His achievements place him among the best boxers of his era. Held the IBF junior Featherweight crown before vacating it unbeaten to campaign as a Featherweight. Among his victories stands his impressive annihilation of former Olympic Gold medalist and IBF champion; American Kennedy McKinney and add to that, one of America's hottest prospects who was hailed as the next big thing, Danny Romero.

Thulani 'Sugar Boy' Malinga became the first South African to win what is widely regarded as the most prestigious of all world belts – the WBC green belt when he soundly beat Nigel Benn to win the Super Middleweight championship. After losing it to Italy's Vincenzo Nardiello in a hotly disputed decision, Malinga came back to regain the title by thrashing British

Robin Reid. Incredibly Malinga still went on to win the Super Middleweight version of the WBF. By this time he was in his seventeenth year as a professional. The WBA is widely recognized as the first or original world sanctioning body. It only had to compete for space and recognition after some of its members broke away to form the WBC on or around 1960. More members broke away later to form the IBF and the WBO. The WBA and WBC remain the two most prestigious and respected sanctioning bodies. Dingaan Thobela, who is regarded by many boxing fans and fundis as the most talented boxer ever produced in this country, is the only South African ever to win both titles. One other name that deserves a place under the sun is Bert Blewett. One of the most recognizable faces not only in South African boxing but also in International boxing. Unquestionably the finest boxing editor and analyst I have had the pleasure of working with. His work on radio and TV was enormous, he and I won an International award for excellent boxing commentary.

We were referred to as the Gruesome twosome. During the dark days of apartheid, Bert campaigned fearlessly to abolish segregated fights, rating and sitting in fight venues. He accepted a job as a writer in the Sunday Tribune only on the condition that he wrote about black boxing as well as white boxing. His book The A-Z Of World Boxing is a masterpiece.

This brings me to Rodney Berman who has powered the Golden Gloves Promotion into the most formidable and successful enterprise in the 125 or so year history of South African boxing He has guided and masterminded all the biggest successes of South African boxing. With a vision and the eye of an eagle, he spotted the IBF in its conception and forged ties that would create opportunities to produce the likes of Welcome Ncita and Vuyani Bungu. He took South African boxing by the scruff of the neck right out of its straight jacket and taught everyone who would look and learn that boxing is show business and should be marketed accordingly.

Why then does it seem that all of these escapades by our fighters and contributions by other personalities outside the ring have not been recognised by the powers that be? Maybe the reason lies in the power of numbers and the subsequent bias of the vote. The majority of the boxing writers who vote come from America, followed by Europe. Naturally, their main focus rests on the home heroes before they cast their eyes somewhere else. Coming back to the boxers, the list I have mentioned above, with perhaps the exception of Thobela, were fighting and winning right in front of the voters, where it counts most – the very heartland of boxing recognition – the United States. They surely could not have missed them. Could it be that the reasons for our contributors and boxers to be overlooked lie within their track records? Could their contributions and accomplishments not measure up to the required and acceptable international standards? Could it be that they come from the wrong Continent and do not have the complexion to make the connection? Could the boxers have missed the fights that mattered? Did they perhaps fail to heed the call when history beckoned with fights that were poised to catapult them to *superstardom*, fame and fortune? Did they lose when it counted most?

Did they fail to deliver on the fights that could have made a difference – fights that could have made the whole world sit up and take notice? Did they miss their flights and could not land on the most important days and fights of their lives – the fights that would have defined them and made them live forever. Were our boxers not good enough?

Were they not necessarily prepared for the contests whose calls go beyond physical talent and capabilities to challenge their mental strengths, their opponents' and those of their minders? Or is there another reason?

Perhaps if we could come up with answers to some of the questions above, we would be halfway towards achieving what to us and our boxers has always been a dream to strive for. As of the time writing this piece we have world-conquering champions who have been competing at the highest level and winning- at home and abroad. One can but wonder how far they will have to go or what they have to do to get recognition and receive that call. They are Hekkie Budler, Moruti Mthalane, Zolani Tete and promoter Rodney Berman. To us, these boxing heroes have done and delivered all that boxing requires to be honoured as the deserving heroes of the sport. We South Africans from our side believe that they deserve every recognition that the world of boxing can offer. Or do they? You be the judge.

CHAPTER 32

NEW IDEAS TO IMPROVE BOXING

Since the beginnings of boxing, all sorts of programs and projects have been implemented for the improvement of the status of boxing across all its facets. Foremost in the vision of boxing's designers and activists has been the final presentation of boxing as a smooth and seamless professional outfit, that one can choose as a sport of choice, and even recommend without a doubt. It is hoped that such noble objectives if applied with proper foresight and preparation, will make the game more marketable and acceptable.

Since 1994 the year that brought the dawn of democracy, Sports Ministers Steve Tshwete, Rev Makhenkesi Stofile, Ngconde Balfour and later Fikile Mbalula have tried and tested many ideas aimed at achieving this goal. Projects have been implemented. There have been some successes. Also just as many failures. Some projects are currently on. Below are some of the initiatives that have been implemented. Enter The South African Boxing Act 11 of 2001.

Sports and Recreation Minister Ngconde Balfour began his term when boxing was still run by The South African National Boxing Control Commission as mandated by the South African Boxing And Wrestling Act 39 of 1954. Under that Act and its rules and regulations, the Minister is the sole custodian for sport and Recreation in the country. Balfour discovered that his quest for an enabling environment for all South Africans to participate equally in boxing were heavily disabled by the Act that he had inherited.

Balfour dreamed of a boxing entity that was run as a business or on business lines. In his view, the only way for boxing to operate effectively and similarly, if not exactly in line with the world's best practices, would be to set up a Boxing Act that would be conducive to the introduction of such relevant practices. What this meant to him, is that the old Act Boxing Act that mandated the office of the South African Boxing Board of Control as the regulator of boxing in the country had to be reviewed. A new Act that would allow for new policies and legislation had to be introduced.

On 5 September 2000, an interim structure known as the South African National Boxing Control Commission under the chairmanship of Adv Rod Solomons and CEO Dumile Mateza, that had been set up to review the South African Boxing Bill made a presentation to the Sport And Recreation Portfolio Committee to report on the processes and route to be followed in not only specifically reviewing the Boxing Bill but to go the extra mile of cleaning up boxing in the country. The month of September 2000 was set aside for public hearings, deliberations and voting. The Bill would then be debated in National Assembly on 5 October 2000.

The National Boxing Convention that was convened by Ngconde Balfour at Sea Point, Cape Town in 2001 dwelled specifically on the South African Boxing Act which at that time had no rules and regulations, as well as look at the envisaged dispensation of the unitary structure that would be the new National Commission in the country.

While this historic move was both well received and exciting to the boxing fans, there was something that at the time might have been missed due to the excitement. This was the question of the powers of the Provinces.

Granted, the Unitary Structure was formed, but it was without any legal framework dealing with the powers and authority of the erstwhile Provincial Powers. This went in the face of the recommendations from stakeholders around the country who were adamant that the Provincial structures continue operating as they had been doing during the old Boxing Act under the Apartheid Regime. It then becomes clear as things are working out now that though neither the Convention of 2001 nor the new National Boxing Act abolished the Provincial Boxing Commissions, they have lost their power.

The view of keeping the powers of the Provinces intact stems from a variety of factors that include but are not limited to; that sport is a national heritage that has provincial competence and provincial origins, and that the stronger the Provincial structure, the bigger and stronger the Provincial activity, for example, the Border Boxing Control Commission, the Eastern Province Boxing Control Commission and the Transvaal Boxing Control Commission. The issues of operations to be left to the Provinces to drive that the National Structure must only deal with Policy matters and determine the strategic direction that must be followed in consultation with provincial structures.

Boxing promoter Siphato Handi who was in the forefront of discussing the way forward as we prepared for the new dispensation is adamant that at no stage during the deliberations was the total abolition of provincial structures ever envisaged and resolved. While the big step was taken in taking South African boxing forward, it may have been the removal of Minister Ngconde Balfour that the provinces have lost their powers, to the demise of boxing. South African boxing still has to revisit the oversight, and it was as a result of such giant steps and then subsequent passing of the Bill that South African boxing began to pave the way forward towards the dream and to make boxing more inclusive and progressive. It led to the reviewal and restructuring of the old South African Boxing And Wresting Act 39 of 1954. Upon completion, the new South African Boxing Act 11 of 2001 was launched at a lush gathering in Vodaworld in May 2002. The new national federation in charge of South African boxing was officially named Boxing South Africa [BSA]. The choice of venue was strategic in that South African boxing had just introduced Vodacom as the new major sponsor of boxing.

New sponsor Vodacom's CEO Mthobi Tyamzashe, a former general secretary of the National Sports Council and later South Africa's director-general, was named as the new chairman of the equally new Boxing South Africa, the country's new federation in charge of both amateur and professional boxing. He replaced businessman Gibson Thula who was chairman of the South African Boxing Control Commission after the resignation of Adv Rod Solomon.

SIBONGISENI SIDZATHANE

This is a dyed in the wool boxing fan who knows and loves the game so much that he took the brave decision to dig into his pocket and started a monthly boxing magazine. The idea was pushed by the desire to announce upcoming fights, report on fight results, do profiles on boxers, managers, trainers and promoters, as well as generally spread the boxing news. This was a move that would market boxing. And for as long as it continued it certainly did.

He was forced to discontinue the venture after carrying on for more than two years without getting funding to assist him. Down went another grand idea in a poor Province.

THE MATEZA/ZIFO REPORT

In 2009, the then Minister of Sports and Recreation, Makhenkesi Stofile came into office with a huge experience in politics and sports. As a founding member of the National Sports Council, generally operating as the sports arm of the ANC, he and his comrades had aimed to uproot all sorts of racial prejudice in sport. When he assumed office and checked its sport code's symptoms, he realized the difference and worked on each sport accordingly to its ills. He appointed a Committee of two that were, sports commentator, historian and analyst Dumile Mateza, and partnered him with experienced Daily Dispatch journalist Mesuli Zifo.

Their mission was to conduct a nationwide tour that would interview groups and individuals. This was aimed at collecting the inputs of the interviews about the status of boxing and how, in their opinion, it could be improved. In their investigation, the Committee targeted a diversity of boxing experience ranging from journalists to boxers, promoters, managers, fans and other stakeholders with close attention to the boxing.

Based on their terms of reference, the Committee prepared and centred their questions on, but not limited to, the world's best practices with special emphasis on administration in developing countries, how sponsors and donations could turn around South African boxing and make it self sufficient, how should the Provinces be governed, and should Boxing as a sport continue to be governed by an Act of Parliament?

The Examination into Boxing South Africa titled The Report 2009, was presented to a hall full of licensees from all Provinces in the presence of Minister of Sports and Recreation Rev Dr Makhankesi Stofile. Its recommendations, which were largely based on the medical safety of the boxers, were discussed by the licensees and Boxing SA members present.

MBUYEKEZO BOXING CHANNEL

This channel was co-founded by Siyabonga Mbulelo Chophiso and Apostle Dr Hawk Makepula in 2004. Mbuyekezo is a Nguni word that translates to 'reward'. MBC was formed to reward and look after the good of everyone involved in the sport of boxing. Hawk Makepula is a household name, a boxing legend, a three-time world champion and a flag bearer for the 1986 South African Olympic Team in Atlanta. Chopiso, his partner is a businessman in Mdantsane.

A leader in space and satellite technology application, Chopiso balances his pioneering in coordinating the development of satellites that orbit space with memories of how his former boxing career got him sharing the boxing ring with Patrick Quka, Mzidi Dintsi and the late Clive Sikhwebu. Mbuyekezo's presence is meant to facilitate the BCMM's charge towards its boxing's commercial appeal, which has been lagging behind for some time now. This has left a lot of boxers in a poor state, physically and sometimes mentally. Makepula used the experience he gained from the game and the technical skills of his partners to turn around this unacceptable state of boxing affairs. This they felt, was the result of the poor arrangement of the media and broadcasting rights. "MBC aims to use the power of technology to transform the role of the media in boxing and contribute towards the sport's long term sustainability and the welfare of stakeholders – boxers and managers. The Data costs and access to the internet now remain a huge challenge to achieve this goal," says Chopiso.

Mbuyekezo enjoys strong support from professional and amateur wings of South African boxing. At the time of this writing, it has covered more than 200 hundred tournaments in all Provinces, across the length and breadth of the country, and has as a result, lots of volts of boxing archives from between 2008 and to date.

MBC also has strong support and working relationships with amateur wing SANABO and its Provincial (ECABO) and Regional (MDABO). It has thus become such a strong brand in SA boxing that it has started its pay-TV platform. MBC currently broadcast its content online through its platform *www.mbuyekezoboxing.co.za* and on YouTube. MBC continues with its vision of covering boxing events, news and interviews. It would like to see itself as a leading media platform for local boxing that streams live content and can contribute to the preservation of the history and heritage of this sport, recognise and reward the legends and everyone else who has contributed to the success of boxing in the mecca. The MBC TEAM Siyabonga Chopiso (Chairman and CEO), Apostle Dr Hawk Makepula (MD), Thembal Chopiso (Production), Petronela Gubevu (Manager), Xolani Moni (Photography), Phumzile Dubase (Commentator), Ncedo Jeku (Commentator), Ndoda Somhlahlo (Operations), Dumisani Sondlo (Broadcasting Strategy And Advisor)

THE BABY CHAMPS.

This project was conceptualised and implemented. It was a Boxing mass participation program, managed and conducted by BSA admin staff. The program responded to a call from parliament for BSA to bring back all race groups, especially the minority groups back to boxing. BSA was put in a position to respond with a program that would be relevant to such a call.

At about that time BSA administrator Adv. Krish Naidoo had presented an OUTREACH PROJECT to Mthobi Tyamzashe and the BSA BOARD. Part of the project is the introduction of minority groups as participants in mass participation projects organised by BSA. The project would not only help in developing boxing but build and improve its image as a sport of choice. This project coincided with my roping into BSA as a PRO.

As soon as Naidoo put me in the picture about the new BSA project, as well as his desire for me to assist in any way I could, I took this as the opportunity to introduce to him a boxing program I had always thought would benefit the development of all boxing facets.

It would create opportunities for contests and better competence for all boxers, promoters, and ring officials irrespective of their clubs, provinces or contractual obligations, thus affording them better chances of competing more effectively against firstly themselves, and then against the rest of the world. It would implement ways that could help these boxing facets to practise, learn and pit their skills in projects relevant to their respective competencies.

They would train and contest in mass participation challenges aimed at laying down a solid foundation equally, and across the provinces. It would result in a national final. Krish Naidoo was well experienced in sports activities, its dynamics as well as its politics, having cut his teeth in the NSC.

When I presented the project Naidoo was ecstatic. The sound of it talked to the country's vision of equal opportunity for all. But as he was not clued up to the boxing specifics and applications he needed me to take him through it step by step. His reasoning here was that he would have to personally and practically believe in it to assist in putting a clear presentation to the board. And we both knew that BSA chairperson Mthobi Tyamzashe was a man of perfection.

The BSA board accepted the proposal in principle but could not adopt it officially because they were already at the end of their term and could not bind the next board to a project they did not know.

Tyamzashe did not return as a board member. This meant that we had to present the proposal to the new board under chairman and ex-amateur boxer Adv Dali Mpofu.

The new board readily accepted the project on the condition the first one would be a pilot with only seven divisions competing. What made the idea especially acceptable was the opportunity it provided for boxers who had famously would turn professional, year after year, only to encounter the stress brought about by never get to fight because they were either in the wrong stable, wrong manager or wrong town.

This was especially the case in the Eastern Cape. The new program would cater for all boxers with less than five fights as professionals. We were on. Only two main challenges were facing the introduction of the Baby Champs. The first challenge was the absence of funds. The second was the absence of white boxers. It was the first time since the advent of boxing in South Africa that there was such a low number of white competitors in boxing.

This meant that without the special and urgent attention to these challenges, this important development project would never see the light of day. This is where SABC's Programs Director Joe Visagie showed his passion for sport, especially the sport of boxing. Visagie pledged on behalf of SABC, an annual amount of R720 000 towards the project.

The BSA board voted R150 000 for its side of the deal For the fruition of the rest of each tournament per province I travelled to all the Provinces with a request for them to lend material support for the Baby Champs project every time and anytime the project would be held at such province. Every province agreed to assist with the venue, accommodation, catering, hospital, ambulance and ring.

As would always be the case the Eastern Cape Province was the first one to take up the opportunity with DG for Department of Sports Arts and Culture DSRAC in the Province Bubele Mfenyana. Hot on the EC's heels was Ms Mnumzana, Free State MEC for Sport who guaranteed her province's assistance in the program including the Final and awards. Joe Maswanganyi, Limpopo's MEC was next. Now was time to tackle the political and racial challenge. It was time to get back all young white boxers who had turned their backs from the game. This is where I called upon experienced ex-boxers, former BSA board member and current promoter Jeff Ellis and requested him to help me in bringing back the white fighters. Jeff Ellis organised the meetings. We talked to individual boxers, families and clubs. The stories were interesting. A lot of them had been told that they would be forced to fight in the townships. All of them loved their boxing and wanted to come back. But they could not risk their lives.

The most interesting extraordinary I had held was one at the SABC offices with the Oosthuizen family. Charles Oosthuizen was a former tough and relentless South African Middleweight champion. His sons Charles Jnr and Tommy had followed in his footsteps and had gained national colours as amateurs. He was now in retirement but could not allow them to fight under the circumstances. His wife cried when she relayed the story of how they had denied their sons to carry on with boxing because of the stories they had been told. Her sons wanted to box. I was at pains to explain this untruth and even went as far as showing her a program listing where the tournaments for the year would be.

The Oosthuizen's found out that yes, the program contained townships and rural areas where all the boxers would be fighting as boxers irrespective of race. There were a lot of mainly white venues as well. Ms Oosthuizen must have cried again when Charles Jr was crowned The Winner and new Baby Champ 2005. And maybe, even more, when Tommy Oosthuizen won the South African Lightheavyweight championship. Two of my most satisfying moments in boxing. I cried too when I was awarded the Chairman's award for leading the way in the development of boxing in the country. The following year we had our tournament in a mainly Indian area where businessman Imran Khan paid for the venue, the ring and catering. Like in many other areas where the Baby Champs had landed, it was the first time that boxing had been held there. For the first time, boxing was taken to both rural and suburban places like KwaXuma in KZN, KuGatyana in Transkei, Tzaneen in Limpopo. Malls in Germiston, Carlton Center and

Pretoria were used and produced crowds of up to five thousand. Prisons in Gauteng were also used. Development Promoters Xaba, Gilmore and White Velvet won the BSA awards for Most Promising Promoter of the Year for 2005, 2006, and 2007 respectively. Ring Officials Ms Sylvia Maphangula and Sylvia Mokaila won the BSA awards for Most Promising Ring Officials of the Year. Ms Siya Vabaza Booi won the Award for Best Ring Official of the Year.

In 2008 The Baby Champs program had to be discontinued due to SABC's inability to guarantee the R720 000 sponsor. That was the time the National broadcaster was beginning to face financial challenges. But in the four years that it had been on its winner and star contenders who had gained more skills, experience and marketability from the project had won;

- » 12 South African champions, including two females
- » 6 International champions including two females
- » 6 world champions including two females.

The winners included all South African racial groups. The kind of development brought about by this project did not only cover the people working in the ring, like boxers and Ring Officials, but it also stretched to the offices and brought the best out of the staff and as well as the provincial service providers. Its success depended on the understanding of the rules, especially the new special rules meant for the project. Special congratulations go to the BSA board as well as BSA manager Krish Naidoo and staff members in the BSA office like Abram Khambule, Nomsa Mdluli, Josh Steyn, Gugu Rhadebe, Vecqueline Jacobs, Daphney Hobyane, Vuvu Mali, Sikhumbuzo Motha, Talifhani Khubhana, Tumelo Kekana, Lillian Dewee and volunteer Zandile Sokhela.

Boxing SA Provincial service providers, Phakamile Jacobs, Les Andreasson, Mickey Klaas, Archie Nyingwa and Solly Matsimela were on standby on a 24-hour basis for any emergency cases that could need their services in the middle of the night. Boxers were always travelling long distances overnight across the Provinces. The Service Providers played a big role in working awkward hours to make the project the success it got to be. Sometimes weigh-ins had to be conducted during the awkward hour to satisfy the twenty-four-hour health rule between the weigh-in and the actual fight.

The first Baby Champs Belts for the winners were donated by American company CAPE ALOE FEROX WORLDWIDE INC. The company was introduced to Boxing SA by KZN promoter Lionel Khubeka. Luyanda Kana and Boyboy Mpulampula donated money to feed the EC boxers on all trips across the country. The gestures by these gentlemen made things much easier for the project as well as the boxers. The Baby Champs program received acclaim and recognition as the best development project in SA sports. But no endorsement could come bigger than the one from former South African and WBA world Heavyweight champion Gerrie Coetzee.

In an interview that was held with him about his boxing life, he could not stop himself from heaping praise on the development opportunities the Baby Champs program that was going on at the time was creating in all facets of the game. Coming from a legend like Gerrie Coetzee it was worth a million words. But perhaps the biggest initial boost for the Baby Champs came from people who were, and are still seldom mentioned when it comes to the success of the project. They were there when the project was pitched and voiced their commitment to assist from the beginning, when a lot of people, especially experienced boxers still doubted whether the project could get off the ground.

They are businessman Gibson Thula who used his funds to assist some of the tournaments, especially those in his home Province of KZN. Close on his hills was Sandy Hattingh. Sandy was a big boxing fan who also used her funds to develop boxing in Ekurhuleni Municipality. She secured accommodation for the Baby Champs teams wherever tournaments were held in town with hotels and casinos. The Baby Champs was the ultimate exercise in boxing development, and real teamwork, the likes of which have still to be seen in South African boxing.

MANAGING THE BOXER'S PURSE

One of the biggest challenges facing the sport of boxing has been the inability of boxers to hold on to their hard-earned finances. Some big earnings over long and short periods depending on the career of the boxer or boxer in question, extravagant spending and the final disappearance of such hard-earned wealth have been widely reported. One businessman approached the boxing fraternity with an idea that was meant to tackle this anomaly and put it to bed once and for all. He was prepared to use his finances on the first few boxers signed under him, to make sure that the new idea has a profound and lasting beginning. Butityi Konki is a Uitenhage born businessman and boxing fan.

Having grown up in the boxing township of KwaNobuhle, Konki grew up admiring the tales of Uitenhage's previous boxers like Aubrey Peta and Brown Bomber Mqina, while in his adulthood he closely followed the career of perhaps the best product of that region in any sports code, Vuyani Nene. While he spent a lot of his business earnings donating to many sports codes like soccer and rugby in his hometown, Konki's main soft spot and interest was always boxing. And so he began to think and to plan how he could assist boxing and its boxers in a manner that talked to his expertise and experience in financial skills he gained as Director of his own company BK Investment Holdings and other business interests. He believed that a strategy that empowered and enabled boxers to effectively and profitably invest their earnings for the short and long terms would go a long way towards enhancing their capacity for successfully packaging themselves and their activities. This achievement would set them up as brands. Konki started his project with Philip Ndou, Ali Funeka and Simphiwe Vetyeka, three of the leading boxers in the country at the time. In no time he had stable of fighters that included Mfundo Gwayana, Thabo Sonjica, Thembelani Maphuma, Zolani Tete and Leli Mbilase.

BK Investments Pty Ltd became the first company to ensure that Boxers' purse money is used to secure monthly salaries for them. This was contrary to what had always been going on, and still is the case, where boxers are allowed their direct purses and use them irresponsibly, and mainly to their demise. Konki made sure each boxer had a bank account with Investec Bank, one of the leading banks in South Africa. This happened even though the ordinary boxers did not qualify for such banking facilities due to their income standing. These purse monies were held in each boxer's account and paid on a monthly basis to meet their commitments and personal needs. No monies left the account except when payments were made to BK Investments for purposes of reimbursement.

In addition, BK Investments Holdings as per the management and sponsorship agreements would further pay each boxer an additional amount to assist the boxers in their needs. Mzonke Fana was paid a bonus of R50 000 over and above his fight purse for winning a world title. BK Investment Holdings bought attire for its boxers to be worn at special events and social gatherings. The boxers attended special trips and workshops. All travel and accommodation expenses were paid for by the company. When Mfundo

Gwayana, one of its contracted boxers faced being stripped of the title for failing to defend within the stipulated time, BK Investments requested Port Elizabeth promoter Ms Nofoti Tsenene to organise the fight. All fight arrangements including boxers' purses, travel, accommodation and other logistics were paid for by BK Investments. Ms Tsenene's promotion to all fight profits for its effort. This was in addition to the humane gesture made to Samora Msophi's extended family when they lost their son after a fight.

The company raised R120 000 which was used to renovate a four-roomed house for the family. Boxers, Luvuyo Tyamzashe and Simphiwe Mfaniso who suffered permanent injuries after boxing bouts were given big amounts of groceries for Christmas. There however rose some challenges that were never anticipated. They led to misunderstandings and accusations. Mainly among them was that boxers expected BK Investments to make payments to them as and when they wanted. This practice, according to BK did not make business sense.

It was taking the boxers exactly to the practice of wily-nilly spending. Furthermore, BK Investment Holdings Pty Ltd made sure that to enforce this discipline, its boxers signed Powers of Attorney over to BK Investment Holdings Pty Ltd to make sure that firstly monies paid into the boxers' personal accounts were used for the correct purposes and secondly, The Receiver of Revenue was paid what was due to them from the purse monies. This, in the long run, did not go down well with the boxers. Some outside advisors were suddenly highly influential in the boxers' lives.

It was decided among all of them that the agreements be discontinued before further accusations could be made. One of South Africa's boxing greats, former triple word champion Simphiwe Vetyeka had this to say about Konki, "I liked the way BK negotiated with a promoter for the boxer's purse in the presence of the boxer. It was different from the situation we were used to of just getting informed of your purse and you had to take it or leave it." In my opinion that I voiced as I was part of BSA at the time, Konki's idea was the best when it came to saving money for especially life after boxing. It was an idea that came either to the wrong crowd or it was the right idea at the wrong time – an idea that was ahead of its time.

CHAPTER 33

THE HEADACHE OF SETTING THE RANKINGS.

When I was appointed as Boxing SA's Director of Operations in 2008, I was given the task of drawing up the SA Ranking's system and be in charge of rating South African boxers monthly. I had to draw a new system to replace the existing one that after thorough perusal, BSA had decided that had too many glaring weaknesses that some licensees were using to their advantage, to the exclusion of better deserving boxers. Given my experience in the game as an ex-boxing champion, manager, promoter, trainer, Ring announcer, analyst, writer, matchmaker and PRO of Boxing SA, it was supposed to be smooth sailing. I plunged into it. It was not easy. And I dare say it is not easy for anyone. It has never been easy. Never will be.

Historically, the rating of boxers is a king-size headache suffered by whoever is unfortunate enough to be tasked with this cumbersome and thankless exercise. It happens to the best, be it an individual, a select committee or an entire organization. The very nature of ratings, being the lifeblood of boxing, decides the careers of boxers and influences the plans of promoters, managers and trainers.

Friends have been known to disagree. Foes have been forced to kiss and make up. Rankings have forced them to do business. Love them or hate, rankings or ratings if you like, are here to stay. You may as well get to know how they work. One would define ratings as a system of evaluation or assessment of the boxer as against the others in terms of skills, experience and accomplishments. What makes it so unique is that it can neither be measured mathematically nor can it be proved scientifically. It is all in the eye of the beholder and needs colossal knowledge of the boxers, understanding of the dynamics of the game and fairness of the person or persons who are given the daunting task.

The challenge always lies with the criteria used to rate boxers. Boxers are rated in terms of their ACTIVITY, RECORDS, QUALITY of opposition and their POTENTIAL. How one defines the above mentioned criteria and whether those qualities weigh the same when it comes to the final placing of the boxer in the list of the best, determines the final decision. Point is; there is no particular order.

ACTIVITY, in any terms, is the state of doing or pursuing your practice. It is movement and liveliness in your chosen career. The education and experience acquired in the process are immeasurable and it shows amongst boxers. A more active boxer stands a better chance of being seen, analyzed and rated as he or she is more visible. What the eye does not see, the brain will not dissect and rate. That is why boxers are persuaded to take that walk to the ring as much as they possibly can. Activity has always been known to be the best teacher.

The record of the boxer contains the list of all opponents he has met in his career. QUALITY opponents with different styles give him the added advantage, exposing him to different skills and attitudes. That exposure bodes well for investing in the improvement of his skills, stamina and experience. Sometimes the boxer with fewer fights may have more improvement and experience than the one with more fights simply because of the quality of the opposition he has met on the way.

This brings us to the quality of opposition. QUALITY means an inherent or distinguishing character in a boxer. That quality may be the one that places him above the rest in terms of excellence or superiority. In boxing, it may be a certain kind of style, a punch, experience, stamina, resilience, strength and extraordinary skills. A boxer who fights against some or all of those attributes in his record stands a better chance of learning and thus getting a better rating than one who has a longer record or is unbeaten against inferior or nor so good quality opposition.

POTENTIAL means capability or the possibility of doing or possessing. What one will have may not be in existence at the time, but performances may show an inherent ability to grow, develop or come into something. That trait can only be spotted in an active boxer who has been exposed to different quality opponents. The old system of rating boxers and approving them for title fights simply because they have won Provincial titles or have beaten somebody in the ratings is a thing of the past.

The system of sanctioning according to Provincial championship status was relevant when South Africa was geographically demarcated into four provinces namely, Transvaal, Cape Province, Natal and Orange Free State. The new political dispensation changed that and as a result, there was no more competition in new provinces like Mpumalanga, Northwest, and the Northern Cape. All boxers must go through a qualification system before they can challenge for the South African title, irrespective of whether they are rated in the top ten or not. This will empower the ratings and make sure that all boxers go through an experiencing and toughening process that will improve the quality of fights.

The rating system needs to be reviewed and compounded from time to make sure that it stays relevant to the dynamics, attitudes and expectations of each decade or century. Boxing South Africa introduced this new provision after having to endure a lot of mismatches in fights that were approved according to the status quo. This is why we are taking this next step to create an opportunity for the public and the boxers or trainers themselves to do the ratings.

The whole problem emanates from Regulation 17(3) (a) of Boxing Act 11 of 2001 that allows any boxer in the top ten the right to fight for the title.

The rating system as was drafted further rules that after losing in a championship bout or any fight while he is in the ratings, the boxer drops down no less than three notches depending on whether the loss was by knockout or points decision.

If a boxer loses badly he drops five notches or even out of the ratings. That is where I found myself disagreeing with the system. What the system does not address is firstly the quality of the fight itself, secondly, the quality of the opponent the boxer lost to, and thirdly the records, activity and abilities of the boxers underneath him/her who were fortunate to lose first and are now moving up at his expense. A good boxer of high quality usually finds himself dropping to below mediocre performers, some of whom last fought when they were beaten by the champion.

Experienced managers and promoters exploited this anomaly when choosing opponents for their champions during the voluntary defence period by going for the weakest opponents. This gave rise to a lot of mismatches that were bringing the noble art of fisticuffs into disrepute.

After noticing the compromising effect this practice was causing on the value, the impact and importance of our titles, Boxing South Africa introduced a new provision that has already forced elimination contests to decide new champions.

As I said from the beginning the system of ranking boxers is a mammoth headache. I may not have come with the best system of ranking boxers, but my point of departure was that, while not overlooking the fact that a beaten boxer must lose some of the statuses he enjoyed before his defeat, it should not be an automatic decision that everybody ranked under him/her is better quality. When the International Boxing Organisation (IBO) introduced its computerised ranking system everybody thought that all the ills of all ranking systems would be solved.

Its rating system would elevate the IBO and lift its status to gain recognition as the most credible sanctioning body in the world, Maybe it was time that all national and international sanctioning bodies should turn to this new system and employ its new rankings system. But it was not to be. The search for the fairest, most effective and globally accepted system of ranking boxers continues.

CHAPTER 34

UNIFYING AMATEUR BOXING

Amateur boxing, now known as Open boxing or Olympic style boxing, emerged in the mid-nineties as a result of the feeling among some participants and spectators that professional boxing was rather too dangerous and, to some degree immoral. They felt, as a result, bound as a matter of principle to absolve themselves by steering clear of the constant controversies that always followed and bedevilled what was referred to as prizefighting. They opted to follow and practice what they regarded as a more scientific and safer style of boxing. This project proved to be highly popular and successful, immediately finding favour with schools, universities and armed forces. In the South African context, amateur boxing has been practised successfully and competed effectively with the rest of the world. It has however been South Africa's Apartheid Policy of segregating people along racial lines and dictating where, when and whom they should contest, that has resulted in the country bearing the brunt of the rest of the world and being excluded from all sports, arts and cultural activities.

Few people are aware and can thus realize the effects of the polarising dynamics that divided South Africans along racial lines before 1990. The history of traditional and cultural divisions among the different races was further deepened and solidified by regulated and legally enforced racial laws that made it impossible for the people of different races in this country to know, understand, trust and accept one another across the colour lines. It was not surprising that once the political landscape necessitated a change to non-racialism and unification, these diverse racial attitudes became the stumbling blocks in the quest for desired satisfactory settlements. Such changes were unavoidable if people were to live equally and acknowledge the rights of others to enjoy equal opportunities in their sport of choice, which in this case was boxing.

Amateur boxing, the cornerstone of boxing development anywhere in the world found itself in the middle of such biases, opinions and agendas as it endeavoured to wriggle itself toward unification within itself. The equal opportunities for all racial groups that such unity would secure was a prerequisite for South Africa boxing to regain unqualified acceptance for participation in all activities by the rest of the world. African countries were preparing their teams for the upcoming All Africa Games which are the passageway to the Olympic Games that had been set for 1992. The keyword which was fast becoming the new normal in South Africa was non- racialism.

Up to 1991, the South African boxing amateur code was made up of mainly four organizations namely, the South African Amateur Boxing Association (SAABA), South African Amateur Boxing Union (SAABU), South African Amateur Boxing Council (SAABCO) and South African Amateur Boxing Federation (SAABF). All the above organisations were running boxing separately based on racial lines. They could not engage in any form of mixed participation with one another, be it inside or outside the ring. Needless to say that the whites-only SAABA, with its immense finances brought about by political affiliation to the Apartheid Government, had been historically the most powerful of all the amateur organisations.

SAABA was also resisting the changes and fighting with all its might to stick to the status quo which was its power base. However its opponents, the historically underprivileged and less powerful organisations, especially mainly black only SAABCO, were comfortable and confident in that they had the leverage brought about by support from the anti-apartheid pressure group, the Mass Democratic Movement that had impetus across all political affiliation. Influenced by the unbanning of all political parties in then-President de Klerk's speech on 2/11/1990, pressure for non-racial unity was unstoppable and growing by leaps and bounds from inside and outside the powerful and rigid Republic of South Africa.

The South African Non-Racial Olympic Committee (SANROC), the National Sports Council (NSC) and the National Olympic Committee Of South Africa (NOCSA) were at the forefront of such political awareness and pressure. Their international connections provided much of the needed funds. Their guidance ushered in a new political landscape. New views and understanding of the daily social and political developments surrounding the people and structures were the order of the day. With sports by nature being part of the national culture and heritage, transformation formed an integral part of the new political agenda as was the case with all other political, social, cultural and other activities. Unlike professional boxing, Amateur Boxing is a national concern. It represents the country.

The overarching political change was audible and visible. The negotiations for a non-racial unitary amateur boxing structure were mandatory as they formed the entire transformation. This was what the whole world put as a price for South Africa's re-introduction into the international sports fold. It was something new and unimaginable in the history of the country. Expectations from all pillars of society namely the workers in and out of employment, the students of tertiary and higher education, as students young and old were part of the youth movement, the masses on the ground in the form of resident associations, as well as from participants both at home and abroad, were revived.

Thrown out of the windows and gone were the old fashioned but well-respected responses where sportsmen were taught, and would gladly echo sentiments for unity and equal opportunity for all, but on the same breath still exclaim that they were sportsmen, not politicians and would live politics to politicians. The renewed questions that needed a speedy address with equally urgent answers were whether one could divorce sports from politics. Or whether there could be normal sports in an abnormal society.

As would be expected once the talks began after much shoving and screaming, the negotiations that finally took place from the 20th January 1991 were never smooth sailing. It took six marathon meetings of intense negotiation that were firstly mediated by veteran strategist Does du Plessis, before he was replaced, to agree.

The SAABA leadership under Commandant Welgemoed, Commandant Green, Brigadier Pretorious, Lieutenant Attie Botha, Mr Robertse, was said to superimpose themselves over others and using what SAABCO delegate Khulile Radu referred to as the master-servant approach.

It was clear that they came prepared with facts and advice from their own backers. The SAABA team believed that there was no need for unity – that SAABA should be the home for all. They believed and were adamant that they could send their team to compete internationally without the unity of non-racialism as guided by SANROC/NOCSA. Attie Botha was quoted as saying, "We do not have to start a new structure SAABA is the authentic body." They even went further and tried to push SAP, SADF and Railways to join the talks as separate entities. This move, if accepted would tip the scales in their favour and guarantee them their dominance and votes when it came to consensus or majority decisions. It was this kind of behaviour and resistance to change that, according to analysts, deprived the SAABA members of understanding the broader state of affairs, and resulted in them staging a much-publicised walkout in one of the meetings.

All weekend newspapers of that time carried the story of the SAABA representatives who were singling out and blaming Mabuti Gwavu, a member of the opposing SAABCO in particular, who was always regarded as too militant, as the person who caused all the trouble. The SAABCO team comprised of Koko Godlo, Khulile Radu, Mabuti Gwavu and other members who were receiving weekly tutoring and advice from NSC members like Mluleki George, Mthobi Thyamzashe, Zola Dunywa, Khaya Ngqula, as well as soccer administrator Sticks Morewa.

These briefings gave them added advantage to better understand and explain what was expected of the prospective new order. Their undoubted preparedness and confidence resulted in them dominating the meetings much to the clear frustration of the opposing teams. The negotiations were fraught with entitlements, expectations and secret agendas arising from the diverse backgrounds of the representatives.

The SAABCO team would subsequently come out of the meetings very satisfied with the outcomes of what had now become a war between them and the top brass of SAABA that included experienced administrative heavyweights as already mentioned above. They would later be the team to draw the constitution and even its preamble for the unified non-racial new amateur boxing body in South Africa.

Interestingly the walkout attracted the indulgence of the all-powerful NOCSA, resulting in an urgent invitation to the warring factions with a stern command to present a clear report about preparations for the All Africa Games. The conditions required all united federations that met the nonracialism criteria to prepare teams, and those that were in the process of unifying to speed up their processes. This had the final effect of making the anti-change groups realize that the wagon was moving on with or without them. They would be left behind and would lose out.

Finally, in the sixth meeting that would change the history of boxing in South Africa, a twelve-member Transitional Committee was nominated. The Committee was made up of 3 members from each of the four amateur bodies ie SAABA, SAABU, SAABCO and SAABF. Among the requirements

The Committee was mandated to deliver, perhaps the most important was to draft a constitution, Identify potential threats to unity, raise funding, ensure winding up and closure to all erstwhile bodies and, organise a date for the inauguration. Amazingly the Transitional Committee worked excellently together. The two influential leaders from the previously opposing groups were Brigadier Soon Pretorious (SAABA) and Mabuti Gwavu (SAABCO). They had been engaging like two bulls in one kraal when the preparatory gatherings started, had now found and understood each other. They now shared one desired destination of working together like one, for a game that they both loved.

They continued meeting and discussing certain prickly matters on and off the official meetings to make sure that the transition was easier and to stick to the principles of unity and nonracialism as required by the conditions. This combination worked wonders and started yielding the desired results

The Constitution was adopted and the inauguration of SANABO was set for Johannesburg on 23 February 1991. Before the elections for the new South African National Boxing Organisation (SANABO) executive all groups were allowed to break to canvass support. Interestingly the SAABCO group were very keen to have one of their candidates land the strategic and influential Secretary-General position. But they had two names in the offing and had to decide between Khulile Radu and Mabuti Gwavu. The wise and vastly experienced Khaya Ngqula whose council had always been sought by the group was in favour of Khulile Radu. There was the general feeling among them that Mabuti Gwavu was too militant. His radical stand would stick out like a sore thumb and would not allow for smooth sailing once the democratic boat started moving.

It was felt that he might not be supported by the rest of the groups come voting time. Khulile Radu was regarded as an unassuming master of negotiation with good foresight. But tough-talking businessman Koko Godlo won the day by convincing his group that Gwavu's attitude had already won him a lot of support among the other groups. He felt that he would have no problem winning the majority vote. In the end, Godlo was proved right as Gwavu scored a landslide victory to become the first Secretary-General of SANABO in a racially mixed history-making executive that included;

- » Brigadier Soon Pretorious – President
- » Mr Vernon Phakathi – Vice President
- » Mr Mabuti Gwavu – Secretary-General
- » Commandant Eric Green – Deputy Secretary-General
- » Mr Chris Robertse – Treasurer.

Boxing has always played a special and leading role in the breaking down of racial barriers in South African sport. It came as no big surprise that, for the 1996 Atlanta Olympic Games, a far-reaching and groundbreaking decision was made to have boxing hold the South African flag and leading TEAM SOUTH AFRICA by Mdantsane Flyweight Hawk Makepula when the country was accepted into the international fold for the first time in more than 30 years. This category of South African noble art, originally known as amateur boxing has since undergone a lot of reforms in terms of its rules and regulations, statutes and by-laws. This evolution began with the changing of its name from Amateur Boxing to what is known today as Open Boxing.

This name changing decision was taken to make the game more marketable as well as to attract sponsorship. It was felt that a more professional name had to be adopted. The amateur reference brought about the feeling or understanding of people not knowing what they were doing. The new Open boxing was more accommodating and inspiring. Nonracial boxing, which was historically taboo, is the new normal, was on the move and growing more popular among all communities. Today boxers, trainers, managers and promoters work together under non-racial rules and circumstances. Ring officials, both male and female work all tournaments around the country without racial nor gender-based restrictions.

Lots of changes in both competition and training gear have been improved. New rules have been introduced to make the game safer, more accessible and easier to understand. Where boxers were only categorised as junior and senior, today they are fight divisions like Schoolboys, ranging from 13 to 14 years, Juniors ranging from 14 to 15 years, the Youth from 16 to 17, as well as the Elite from 18 to 40 years of age. These measures are meant to curb mismatching against much older and more experienced competitors, a practice that has cut short a lot of youngsters' careers.

Once the boxers reach the level of Elite boxers, they are regarded as experienced enough to be able to use their boxing, especially their defensive skills to protect themselves. Protective gear like headguards, that they have been using in competitions as younger boxers in the growing stages are taken off. This is meant to prepare them for the professional ranks where no headgear is allowed. Where professional boxers use 8-ounce gloves for certain divisions, open boxing uses 10-ounce gloves. 12-ounce gloves are then used for all the heavier boxers who weigh 69 kilograms and more.

As Open Boxing or Olympic Style Boxing, as it is now known, grows and keeps growing, it has begun to face its challenges. Splinter groups and factions have arisen from within their own ranks. New rules and regulations from the international mother body AIBA have posed serious challenges to its working relations with the country's professional body Boxing SA. This current state of affairs has given rise to uncertainties and questions of whether Boxing SA which, according to the mandate by South African Boxing Act 11 of 2001, is the regulatory body in charge of all boxing activities in the country, will be able to perform its obligations to the amateur body. This same question of recognition or none thereof also stretches to the South African Sports Council, as well as the international amateur body AIBA. Time will tell if the mother bodies will recognize the new splinter groups or seek to unify them.

CHAPTER 35

THE COVID-19 KNOCKOUT

Below are my layman's unofficial understanding and summary of the virus and its devastating impact on the sport of boxing at large. One certain thing is that boxing as it was known before this paralysing onslaught will never be the same again. As of this writing, the world's original human contact human sport has taken a knee and is down for the proverbial count. Whether boxing beats the count before it reaches ten and can resume and come back fighting resiliently like before, is a story for another day. This is courtesy of an attack from an unseen opponent whose deadly blows result in an infectious disease. It leaves many people dead and others disabled for life.

I am not yet in a position to know whether those who are fortunate to regain full recovery can still be healthy enough to be able to box or participate in any other physically challenging sport code, can do so as effectively as before they contracted the virus. Medical experts describe the invisible challenger known as Corona or Covid-19 as being caused by a yet unidentifiable virus. Here below is a layman's unofficial understanding and summary of the virus and its devastating impact on boxing and its participants.

The new virus and subsequent disease were unknown until symptoms reportedly emerged in Wuhan, China in December 2019. According to South African Government medical reports, it was in March 2020 that the first patient in South Africa consulted a private doctor showing symptoms that were diagnosed as those common with the disease. On 5 March 2020 Minister of Health, Zweli Mkhize confirmed the spread of the virus to South Africa. On 15 March, the President of South Africa Cyril Ramaphosa declared a national state of emergency that would bring all movements in the country to a standstill. It effectively meant that people should stay at home. Only essential services would be exempted. The President also announced the formation of the National Coronavirus Command Council to take charge of all government initiatives meant to monitor and arrest the spread of the virus. On 23 March a national lockdown was announced. The lockdown started on 27 March 2020. It meant that boxing activities of all sorts would be among all other social activities included in the lockdown. Boxing activities were halted with immediate effect.

Medical research has identified the most common symptoms of Covid 19 as fever, tiredness, and dry cough. Further research has discovered that some patients may have aches and pains, nasal congestion, runny nose, sore throat or diarrhoea. These symptoms are a direct and serious challenge to all training and fight practises for boxers, coaches, trainers and boxing fans.

Even though health advice has been loud and clear about how people should protect themselves by wearing face masks, constantly washing their hands and keeping safe distances from one another, such precautions would not be enough and effective to curb the spread of the disease in any boxing sphere. Firstly boxing by nature is a contact sport. This close contact starts from basic learning, fitness training, and right up to the competition. Competition time brings together all participants, administrators, health officials and fans crammed together under one roof. Training in general causes people to breathe much faster and harder, thus causing a faster spread of disease. There is also a lot of coughing, sneezing as well as spitting.

This has raised the important question of whether boxers or other athletes should wear face masks during running and exercise. Even before medical advice from health specialists came out advising against people exercising while wearing masks, boxers and trainers had already experienced the difficulty in breathing posed by the mask.

The ability to breathe comfortably and inhale the large quantities of air that are needed by the body during such strain is reduced. This makes it impossible to sustain high volume running or skipping. Sparring and pad work became a no go zone as close contact with the sparring partner, as well as close contact with the coach during pad work are an unavoidable necessity. Boxing could in no way be able to arrest the chain of transmission among its people. There could be no training. No training meant that there could be no contest. The coronavirus had dealt boxing a paralysing blow.

As President Cyril Ramaphosa declared a three-week national lockdown on March 27 of 2020 and later extending it to five weeks, Boxing SA was quick to heed the official announcement and follow suit. BSA Director Of Operations, and later Acting CEO after the resignation of CEO Tsholofelo Lejaka, Ms Cindy Nkomo wrote to BSA licensees, "No professional boxing gym or Boxing South Africa (BSA) licensee should arbitrarily resume training in gyms before compliance inspection of each gym is completed by BSA and written approval is received from the Minister of SPORT."

She advised the boxing fraternity to be patient and wait for the government to decide when boxing activities would be resumed. She further promised that BSA would continue to assist in making sure that all impediments to the resumption of boxing would be tackled to make sure that boxing complied with all protocols, once resumed. And BSA lived up to this promise. This decision once communicated resulted in all gyms being closed. Some boxers continued to exercise and keeping in shape by doing programs within their homes hoping that the lockdown period would be short and they would be free to resume the game. The majority of boxers depend on boxing for their earnings and very livelihood. The strength of this blow was somehow lessened to some extent when National Minister of Sports Arts and Culture Nathi Mthethwa announced a National Relief Fund that was meant to ease off the economic challenge on the sportsmen and women in the country.

Boxing SA took advantage of this manna and put forward the lists of all its categories whose earnings had suffered a knockout blow from postponed or cancelled competitions due to the virus onslaught. Extra steps were taken to make sure to find out and assist all eligible licensees so that they could lodge their applications in time and not miss out on the deadlines. It was sad, however, to realize that the pandemic also meant the end of the road for the older boxers. Old age may have caught up and been much against them by the time boxing activities resume. On June 11 2020 the Minister of Sport Arts and Cultural Activities made an official request to all codes under his department for them to detail how best their codes could resume their different activities under strict Covid-19 conditions meant to protect their participants.

BSA had until 26 June 2020 to submit the prepared report and have it delivered on time. On 9 July 2020 BSA received the much-anticipated approval from the Minister. But it was only for non-contact training, not full contact boxing

On July 11 2020 Boxing South Africa held its quarterly meeting, part of which was to discuss and make resolutions that were meant to prepare themselves and the boxing fraternity on the anticipated approval for the resumption of boxing and other contact sporting codes.

While happily accepting and appreciating the Minister's approval, BSA realized that, based on their experience about the conditions of local gyms, they still needed time to ensure that gyms met the expected health and hygiene standards required for the safe resumption of training, before allowing the boxers to resume training activities.

BSA set such a review period of the gyms to finish before allowing boxers back into the gyms. Later communication announced the official resumption training by 1 August 2020. Such arrangement was on condition that the gyms complied with conditions as set out after the inspections were conducted and results analysed.

Among the resolutions passed by the BSA appointed Medical Medical Committee placed in front of its participants before being allowed to resume training were, but not limited to,

a] training only, no sparring and fighting,

b] trainer/manager to accept BSA appointment as Compliance Officer,

c] COVID-19 results for boxers and trainers to be submitted to BSA,

d] Gyms to submit their training programs after inspection,

e] Gyms to be disinfected and cleaned every day

f] Only licensed boxers must attend

g] No spectators allowed and

h] Personnel over sixty years of age had to undergo special tests to be presented to BSA before being allowed back into the gyms.

Key to these plans was the safety of all personnel in the training spaces, the safety of their equipment, the safety of procedures as well general safety of all concerned and practising within the boxing space in any way in boxing at large. At the time of this writing, Boxing SA has announced the resumption of tournaments and full contact fighting. This announcement has come out with specials rules and measures to ensure health and safety for all concerned. Boxing is back until further notice.

Perhaps the biggest drawback brought about by the pandemic is the inactivity of boxers. This is a result of the ban on boxing tournaments and other sporting events. This left South African boxing in limbo, boasting only two South African bred world champions, Moruti Mthalane [IBF] and Kevin Lerena [IBO]. There is also Junior Makabu, a Congolese-South African professional boxer plying his trade in South Africa, if one could include him in the list.

With a lot of tournaments having been cancelled or supposedly postponed, BSA finds itself in a position where they have little or no good reason to organise the much-revered boxing awards. The most important step to take at this stage would be to pull together with the promoters and all other stakeholders to arrange tournaments and make boxing happen again. But the art of pugilism as we have grown to know and practise it has changed. Things will never be the same.

Despite poor gym conditions with old training gear, fighters still flood the gyms during training times. Picture: Leon Sadiki

Former International Boxing Organization (IBO) Welterweighter champion Thulani 'Tulz Evolutions' Mbenge. Photo by Gallo Images

Mbulelo Botile a retired South African professional boxer who was a world champion in two classes, bantamweight and featherweight.

Loyiso Mtya and Brian Mitchell in 2010 at an awards ceremony Emperors Palace.

Loyiso Mtya and Mthobeli Mhlope after a training session when Mhlope was the reigning SA Featherweight champion. Mtya managed and trained Mhlope.

Simphiwe Khonkco and Hekkie Budler after their 2015 hectic title fight for the WBA Minimum weight title at Emperors Palace that Budler won on points. Khonkco is a Transkei boxer.

Chief Mangosuthu Buthelezi and Tap Tap Makhathini. Makhathini had won Supreme SA Middleweight championship that made him the champion of both black and white boxers.

Patrice Motsepe with Former World champion Zolani Tete. Motsepe had visited Mdantsane to donate a wheelchair to Tete's mother.

after a tournament in NASREC in 2010 Loyiso Mtya was analysing the Ring Officials' performances.

Moruti 'Baby Face' Mthalane ; Image by ANTONIO MUCHAVE

Irrepressible Dingaan Thobela ranks among SA's greatest fighters. Pic: Jon Hrusa

Brian Mitchell defending his WBA junior lightweight title against Alfredo Layne at Sun City. Mitchell knocked him out in the 10th round. Photo: Gallo Images/Sunday Times

Doing the Mdantsane shuffle, boxers dream big in the gym of champions - Eyethu Boxing Gym in Mdantsane, East London - where Ncedo Cecane, boxing trainer and former South African flyweight champion, produces champions. Photo by Masi Losi

Knuckle City is a 2019 South African crime sports film written and directed by Jahmil X.T. Qubeka. It was screened in the Contemporary World Cinema section at the 2019 Toronto International Film Festival.

Young pugilists in action during a previous boxing tournament held at Mdantsane City Shopping Centre in the Eastern Cape's boxing mecca of Mdantsane. (Photo: Supplied)

ABOUT THE AUTHOR

Loyiso Mtya is a former professional boxer, trainer, manager, promoter, commentator and acting chief executive of Boxing SA.

When Loyiso "The Black Messiah" Mtya was a young boy, he did not have to cross the street to know about boxing, his home was the home of the fighters. During the mid-60's his father, Wilson Bill Banguxolo Mtya was responsible for transporting the very first Eastern Cape (Mdantsane) professional fighters in his vehicle as a driver.

Often referred to as the fighter, the trainer and the leader, Loyiso Mtya was born into boxing. Mount Coke, the small village in the Eastern Cape is where it all started when Loyiso's Cousin Lukhanyo Mtya bought two sets of boxing gloves and gave them to Loyiso to start the amateur boxing club. Since that day he has never looked back, his life has been dedicated to the sports of boxing from playing different roles as:

- » Amateur Boxer,
- » South African Champion,
- » Boxing Trainer,
- » Boxing Manager,
- » Boxing TV commentator,
- » Boxing Administrator,
- » CEO of Boxing South Africa

Loyiso is the former South African junior middleweight champion, winning the vacant junior middleweight non-white title when he stopped Morgan Moledi in Mdantsane in 1977. He was one of the incredibly dangerous southpaws from Mdantsane, arguably the biggest junior middleweight ever in South African boxing, standing at 1.89m tall. In the ring, he has faced the likes of Gert Steyn, Terrence Ace Makaluza, Joseph Hali, Cameron Adams, Bruce McIntyre, and Coenie Bekker. His success as a fighter was around his powerful boxing brains, he was excellent in figuring out his opponents.

After he hung up his gloves in 1982 having turned professional eight years earlier, Mtya ventured into training boxers and promoting the sport. Qualified as a teacher by profession - Loyiso Mtya used his academic skills to communicate effectively as a trainer, to get the best out of his students (fighters). His success as a boxing trainer has been mysterious, to say the least, he trained great fighters such as Mxhosana "Tshawe" Jongilanga, Odwa "Old Bones" Mdleleni, Khulile Makeba, Mthobeli "The Hitman" Mhlophe and Zolani "Last Born" Tete – to name just a few.

When he is not thinking or talking boxing, Loyiso Mtya is writing boxing articles for the Daily Dispatch Newspaper – most of which culminated in the publishing of this book. Most recently he played a key role acting as a trainer of the lead actor on the boxing movie Knuckle City. With his passion for the boxing fraternity, he has been instrumental in the development and running of the following projects when he was with the BSA:

- » Produced two female international champions since the inception of the Baby Champs project.
- » Four young boxers from the Baby Champs program became world champions
- » Two female boxers from the Baby Champs program won international championships
- » Three female ring officials officiated in world title fights.

During his time at BSA, Mtya engaged in stringent cost-cutting measures and discontinued formerly outsourced programmes. The approach resulted in BSA paying off all its debts inherited from previous administrations and boxing was able to report a profit of more than R2 million after being in the red for a long time. All of which proved his sports administration prowess.

In many ways, Loyiso Mtya has played a key role in the development of boxing in South Africa, taking it from where it was back then to where it is today. His contribution to the sport is invaluable.

BIBLIOGRAPHY & NOTES

ARTICLE: The Guardian - Apartheid in the ring | LINK: https://www.theguardian.com/books/2002/feb/09/sportandleisure.highereducation

BOOK: Dancing Shoes is Dead - A Tale of Fighting Men in South Africa | Author - Gavin Evans | Publisher - Doubleday, 2002 | ISBN: 038-560-2375, 978-03856-023-7-2

BOOK: Mama's Boy - Lennox Lewis and the Heavyweight Crown | Author - Gavin Evans | Edition Illustrated | Publisher - Highdown, 2004 | ISBN: 190-431-7766, 978-19043-177-6-0

ARTICLE: Sowetan Live - Baby steps may save SA boxing, Loyiso Mtya says | LINK: https://www.sowetanlive.co.za/sport/boxing/2020-05-22-baby-steps-may-save-sa-boxing-loyiso-mtya-says

ARTICLE: Sunday Times Heritage Project – From The Street Shuffle to Glory | LINK: https://sthp.saha.org.za/memorial/articles/from_the_street_shuffle_to_glory.htm

BOOK: The Boxing Album: An Illustrated History | Author - Peter Brooke-Ball | Publisher - Southwater; Updated new edition (31 Jan. 2012) | ISBN: 978-17801-905-8-7

ARTICLE: Sunday News Zimbabwe - Bulawayo Bomber undeterred | LINK: https://www.sundaynews.co.zw/bulawayo-bomber-undeterred

ARTICLE: Sunday Mail Zimbabwe - Moyo keeps boxing title | LINK: https://www.sundaymail.co.zw/moyo-keeps-boxing-title

ARTICLE: Screen Africa - Inside the making of Jahmil X.T. Qubeka's Knuckle City | LINK: https://www.screenafrica.com/2020/01/08/film/film-content/inside-the-making-of-oscar-nominated-knuckle-city

BOOK: Under Our Skin: A White Family's Journey through South Africa's Darkest | Author - Donald McRae | Publisher - Simon & Schuster Ltd (28 Feb. 2013) | ISBN: 978-18498-313-7-6

ARTICLE: Show Me Online Magazine - SA Boxing Champions honoured | LINK: https://showme.co.za/durban/news/sa-boxing-champions-honoured

ARTICLE: Sunday Times Live – Doing the Mdantsane shuffle: boxers dream big in the gym of champions | LINK: https://www.timeslive.co.za/sunday-times/news/2020-03-08-doing-the-mdantsane-shuffle-boxers-dream-big-in-the-gym-of-champions

BOOK: Greatest Boxing Stories Ever Told: Thirty-Six Incredible Tales From The Ring | Author - Jeff Silverman | Publisher - Lyons Press; New e. edition (1 Nov. 2004) | ISBN: 978-15922-847-9-5

BOOK: Boxing Nostalgia: The Good, the Bad and the Weird | Author - Alex Daley | Publisher - Pitch Publishing Ltd; First edition (30 Nov. 2018) | ISBN: 978-17853-145-5-1

ARTICLE: Mali Boxing - Loyiso "The Black Messiah" Mtya | LINK: https://maliboxing.com/2018/04/30/loyiso-the-black-messiah-mtya

VIDEO INTERVIEW: Mbuyekezo Boxing Channel - Mla Thengimfene and Loyiso Mtya Interview | LINK: https://mbuyekezoboxing.co.za/mla-thengimfene-and-loyiso-mtya-interview

BOOK: The Greatest: My Own Story | Author - Muhammad Ali | Publisher - Graymalkin Media; Illustrated edition (17 Nov. 2015) | ISBN: 978-16316-804-9-6

ARTICLE: News24 - Last Born firm on new trainer | LINK: https://www.news24.com/sport/othersport/south-africa/last-born-firm-on-new-trainer-20170715

ARTICLE: Sowetan Live - Plan to take boxing to a new level ready | LINK: https://www.sowetanlive.co.za/sport/2013-05-08-plan-to-take-boxing-to-a-new-level-ready

RADIO INTERVIEW: Player FM - Loyiso Mtya on Boxing SA | LINK: https://player.fm/series/vision-view-sports-radio-on-air-interviews/loyiso-mtya-on-boxing-sa

BOOK: Unforgivable Blackness: The Rise and Fall of Jack Johnson | Author - Geoffrey Ward | Publisher - Yellow Jersey (8 Jan. 2015) | ISBN: 978-02240-923-4-0

ARTICLE: Sowetan Live - 'Last Born' Tete paid for zigging when he should have zagged against Casimero | LINK: https://www.sowetanlive.co.za/sport/boxing/2019-12-06-last-born-tete-paid-for-zigging-when-he-should-have-zagged-against-casimero

BOOK: The A-Z of World Boxing | Author - Bert Blewett | Publisher - Robson Book Ltd (April 1, 1997) | ISBN: 978-18610-500-4-5

ARTICLE: Sowetan Live - Mtya takes issue with knockdown rule | LINK: https://www.sowetanlive.co.za/sport/2014-06-06-mtya-takes-issue-with-knockdown-rule

ARTICLE: Sowetan Live - 'Baby champs must return' | LINK: https://www.sowetanlive.co.za/sport/2014-01-30-baby-champs-must-return

ARTICLE: ENCA - Boxing elite gather to remember Baby Jake | LINK: https://www.enca.com/south-africa/boxing-elite-gather-remember-baby-jake

BOOK: No Baloney: A Journey From Peckham To Las Vegas | Author - Frank Maloney | Publisher - Mainstream Publishing; New Ed edition (2 Sept. 2004) | ISBN: 978-18401-889-8-1

ARTICLE: News24 - Boxing is a path from poverty | LINK: https://www.news24.com/News24/Boxing-is-a-path-from-poverty-20010420

BOOK: No Punches Pulled | Author - Terry Pettifer | Publisher - Full House Productions (January 1, 2000) | ISBN: 978-06202-547-0-0

ARTICLE: NEWYORK Times - A Hollow Sporting Footnote in Apartheid-Era South Africa | LINK: https://www.nytimes.com/2012/10/21/sports/gerrie-coetzee-vs-john-tate-in-apartheid-era-south-africa.html

ARTICLE: Evolve Daily - The History And Origins Of Boxing | LINK: https://evolve-mma.com/blog/the-history-and-origins-of-boxing

ARTICLE: The Citizen - The Orient Theatre – Mecca of SA boxing | LINK: https://citizen.co.za/sport/sport-columnists/120096/the-orient-theatre-mecca-of-sa-boxing

BOOK: My Life and Battles: By Jack Johnson | Author - Jack Johnson | Publisher - Praeger Publishers Inc., U.S.; Translation edition (30 Sept. 2007) | ISBN: 978-02759-996-4-3

ARTICLE: Sunday Times - Eastern Cape's Orient Theatre no longer fit for big boxing events | LINK: https://www.timeslive.co.za/news/south-africa/2015-09-07-eastern-capes-orient-theatre-no-longer-fit-for-big-boxing-events

VIDEO: BlogTalk Radio - Boxing History - South African Apartheid and Sun City | LINK: https://www.blogtalkradio.com/knucklesandgloves/2020/10/10/boxing-history--south-african-apartheid-and-sun-city

ARTICLE: The Citizen - SA black boxers continue to thrive in post-apartheid era

| LINK: https://citizen.co.za/sport/south-african-sport/boxing/2024173/sa-black-boxers-continue-to-thrive-in-post-apartheid-era

BOOK: Pound for Pound: A Biography of Sugar Ray Robinson | Author - Herb Boyd | Publisher - Amistad; Illustrated edition (2 Mar. 2006) | ISBN: 978-00609-343-8-5

WEBSITE: Brand South Africa - Boxing: SA's world beaters | LINK: https://www.brandsouthafrica.com/people-culture/sport/features/boxing10

ARTICLE: Brand South Africa - From Mdantsane to the world: The Eastern Cape's champion boxers | LINK: https://www.brandsouthafrica.com/people-culture/sport/sport-health/east-london-boxing-capital-of-south-africa

ARTICLE: Sowetan Live - Boxing South Africa responds to ring chaos | LINK: https://www.sowetanlive.co.za/sport/2011-08-02-boxing-south-africa-responds-to-ring-chaos

BOOK: Dark Trade: Lost in Boxing | Author - Donald McRae | Publisher - Simon & Schuster UK; UK ed. edition (5 Jun. 2014) | ISBN: 978-14711-353-7-8

ARTICLE: Sowetan Live - Champs get their belts at long last | LINK: https://www.sowetanlive.co.za/news/2010-05-28-champs-get-their-belts-at-long-last

WEBSITE: Rangers - Famous Boxers from South Africa | LINK: https://www.ranker.com/list/famous-boxers-from-south-africa/reference

ARTICLE: SABC News - Professional boxing loses its punch in Mandela Bay | LINK: https://www.sabcnews.com/sabcnews/professional-boxing-loses-punch-mandela-bay

BOOK: FLOAT LIKE A BUTTERFLY: Muhammad Ali: The Greatest Boxer In History | Author - Tony Fitzsimmons | Publisher - Independently published (24 May 2017) | ISBN: 978-15213-676-1-2

ARTICLE: Dispatch Live - Strike the right balance always | LINK: https://www.dispatchlive.co.za/sport/2015-08-14-strike-the-right-balance-always--

BOOK: Boxing | Author - Bob Mee | Publisher - Apple Press (1997-10-31) | ISBN: 978-18507-678-6-2

ARTICLE: Sowetan Live - Moyo boxing ban shocks EFC supremo | LINK: https://www.sowetanlive.co.za/sport/2014-07-17-moyo-boxing-ban-shocks-efc-supremo

BOOK: On Boxing | Author - Joyce Carol Oates | Publisher - Bloomsbury Publishing PLC (Published in 1997-09-04) | ISBN: 978-07475-376-6-3

ARTICLE: Sports24 - Title fight criteria reviewed | LINK: https://www.news24.

com/Sport/Title-fight-criteria-reviewed-20080904

ARTICLE: News24 - Women's boxing blues | LINK: https://www.news24.com/news24/Archives/City-Press/Womens-boxing-blues-20150429

ARTICLE: Sowetan Live - dream come true | LINK: https://www.sowetanlive.co.za/news/2010-04-21-dream-come-true

BOOK: Making Of A Champion: A World-Class Boxer Hardback | Author - Don Wood | Publisher -Capstone Global Library Ltd (Published in 2004-10-29) | ISBN: 978-04311-893-7-6

WEBSITE: Boxing SA - Hall of Fame | LINK: https://www.boxingsa.co.za/hall-of-fame

ARTICLE: Daily Maverick - Lords of the Ring: The past, present and future of SA boxing | LINK: https://www.dailymaverick.co.za/article/2019-06-17-lords-of-the-ring-the-past-present-and-future-of-sa-boxing

ARTICLE: Supersport.com (Online) - Colourful history of SA boxing | LINK: https://supersport.com/boxing/history/news/170829/colourful_history_of_sa_boxing

ARTICLE: Zoutnet - New boxing promotion launched | LINK: https://www.zoutnet.co.za/articles/sport/8023/2010-02-05/new-boxing-promotion-launched

ARTICLE: Supersport.com (Online) – The story of boxing's transformation in South Africa | LINK: https://supersport.com/general/news/200423_The_story_of_boxings_transformation_in_South_Africa

BOOK: 12 Greatest Rounds Of Boxing | Author - Ferdie Pacheco | Publisher - Pavilion Books (Published 2004-10-06) | ISBN: 978-18610-580-5-8

ARTICLE: BBC News - Nelson Mandela: Six things you didn't know | LINK: https://www.bbc.com/news/world-africa-22006386

ARTICLE: News24 - 'Fire and Ice' what SA need | LINK: https://www.news24.com/news24/fire-and-ice-what-sa-need-20011008

ARTICLE: Mail & Guardian - SA women's boxing is on the ropes | LINK: https://mg.co.za/article/2010-06-18-sa-womens-boxing-is-on-the-ropes

ARTICLE: Sunday Times Live - Optimism, but SA boxing faces huge challenges | LINK: https://www.timeslive.co.za/sunday-times/sport/2015-03-01-optimism-but-sa-boxing-faces-huge-challenges

BOOK: Little Book of Greatest Moments in Boxing | Author - Graham Betts | Publisher - G2 Entertainment Ltd (Published 2014-08-28) | ISBN: 978-17828-125-5-5

ARTICLE: News24 (City Press) - Boxing league's fight night floored | LINK: https://www.news24.com/news24/Archives/City-Press/Boxing-leagues-fight-night-floored-20150429

ARTICLE: News24 (City Press) - Boxing SA perturbed by lack of interest in women's boxing | LINK: https://www.news24.com/news24/Archives/City-Press/Boxing-SA-perturbed-by-lack-of-interest-in-womens-boxing-20150430

ARTICLE: News24 (City Press) - Great fighters who just couldn't take it | LINK: https://www.news24.com/news24/Archives/City-Press/Great-fighters-who-just-couldnt-take-it-20150429

ARTICLE: Sowetan Live - Mateza Stung by Criticism | LINK: https://www.sowetanlive.co.za/news/2009-11-11-mateza-stung-by-criticism

BOOK: The Fighters; a Pictorial History of SA Boxing | Author – Chris Greyvenstein | Publisher: Don Nelson; 1st edition (January 1, 1981) | ASIN: B00186R2AG (Amazon.com)

ARTICLE: Sowetan Live - Fight goes to purse bids | LINK: https://www.sowetanlive.co.za/news/2007-08-30-fight-goes-to-purse-bids

BOOK: The Life And Times Of Stanley Christodoulou - The Remarkable Story Of World Boxing's Championship Referee And Judge | Authors - Stanley Christodoulou, Graham Clark, David Isaacson | Publisher - Staging Post | ISBN: 978-1-9284-401-6-1

ARTICLE: Sowetan Live - Media have influence on halls of fame | LINK: https://www.sowetanlive.co.za/news/2010-04-20-media-have-influence-on-halls-of-fame/

ARTICLE: Sowetan Live - BSA plans to take new champs to big rings | LINK: https://www.sowetanlive.co.za/news/2007-01-23-bsa-plans-to-take-new-champs-to-big-rings

ARTICLE: News24 (City Vision) - Boxing allowance a pittance | LINK: https://www.news24.com/news24/SouthAfrica/Local/City-Vision/Boxing-allowance-a-pittance-20151028

ARTICLE: Fight News - The greatest night in South African boxing history | LINK: https://fightnews.com/the-greatest-night-in-south-african-boxing-history/75174

BOOK: The Holyfield Way: What I Learned about Courage, Perseverance, and the Bizarre World of Boxing | Author - James J Thomas, Evander Holyfield (Commentary) | Publisher - Sports Publishing LLC (July 1, 2005) | ISBN: 978-15967-001-9-2

GLOSSARY & ACRONYMS

PRO – Public Relations Officer

SADF - South African Defence Force (the South African Army during the Apartheid era), changed to SANDF - South African National Defence Force (the South African Army post the democracy in 1994)

CEO – Chief Executive Officer, the CEO presides over the organization's day-to-day operations. The CEO is the person who is ultimately accountable for a company's business

COO - Chief Operating Officer (COO) is a senior executive tasked with overseeing the day-to-day administrative and operational functions of a business. The COO typically reports directly to the chief executive officer (CEO) and is considered to be second in the chain of command.

CFO - Chief Financial Officer (CFO) is the senior executive responsible for managing the financial actions of a company. The CFO is the third-highest position in a company and reports to the CEO.

WBA – The World Boxing Association, formerly known as the National Boxing Association, is the oldest and one of four major organizations which sanction professional boxing bouts, alongside the World Boxing Council, International Boxing Federation and World Boxing Organization.

WBC – The World Boxing Council (WBC) is one of four major organizations which sanctions professional boxing bouts, alongside the World Boxing Association (WBA), International Boxing Federation (IBF) and World Boxing Organization (WBO).

BBC - British Broadcasting Corporation.

BCM - Buffalo City Municipality also often referred to simply as Buffalo City.

BRU - Border Rugby Union Grounds in East London.

USBA or INTERNATIONAL - United States Boxing Association International.

DAZN - Pronounced Da Zone, DAZN is a global over-the-top sports subscription video streaming service. The service carries live and on-demand streaming of events from various properties as well as original programming.

ECABO - Eastern Cape Amateur Boxing Organization

Transkei Boxing Act - Under the Transkei Act during Apartheid Rule, boxing in the homeland was run under its own rules and regulations.

Tsotsi - in South Africa this refers to a young urban criminal, especially one from a township area.

Kombi – in South African it refers to a minibus, especially one used to transport passengers commercially.

Homeland Act - The Bantu Homelands Citizenship Act, 1970 was a Self Determination or denaturalization law passed during the apartheid era of South Africa that allocated various tribes or nations of black South Africans as citizens of their traditional black tribal "homelands," or Bantustans

Homeland – The Bantustans or homelands, established by the Apartheid Government, were areas to which the majority of the Blacks population was moved to prevent them from living in the urban areas of South Africa

Bantustans - a Bantustan (also known as Bantu homeland, black homeland, black state or simply homeland; Afrikaans: Bantoestan) was a territory that the National Party administration of South Africa set aside for black inhabitants of South Africa and South-West Africa (now Namibia), as part of its policy of apartheid. In a generic sense, Bantustans are regions that lack any real legitimacy, consisting of several unconnected enclaves, or which have emerged from national or international gerrymandering.

Township - In South Africa, the terms township and location usually refer to the often underdeveloped racially segregated urban areas that, from the late 19th century until the end of apartheid, were reserved for non-whites, namely Indians, Africans and Coloureds.

National Party - The National Party, also known as the Nationalist Party, was a political party in South Africa founded in 1914 and disbanded in 1997. The party was an Afrikaner ethnic nationalist party that promoted Afrikaner interests in South Africa.

IBF – The International Boxing Federation was officially formed in April 1977. At first, it was treated as a regional sanctioning body aligned with the United States

Boxing Association. Then in 1983, the IBF was recognized as a major sanctioning body.

SANBCC - South African National Boxing Coordinating Council

NSC - National Sports Council

ANC – The African National Congress (ANC) is the Republic of South Africa's governing political party. It has been the ruling party of post-apartheid South Africa since the election of Nelson Mandela in the 1994 election

PAC – The Pan Africanist Congress of Azania (formerly known as the Pan Africanist Congress, abbreviated as the PAC) is a South African Pan-Africanist movement that is now a political party.

BBM - Border Boxing Movement

NBA - The National Boxing Association is a global sanctioning organization for male and female boxing matches.

FIFA - FIFA stands for "Fédération Internationale de Football Association" and is the international federation governing association football (to distinguish it from "union football", i.e. rugby).

NPO – Non-Profit Organization (NPO) is not driven by profit but by dedication to a given cause that is the target of all income beyond what it takes to run the organization.

FBI – FBI stands for Federal Bureau of Investigation. "Federal" refers to the national government of the United States. "Bureau" is another word for department or division of government. "Investigation" is what we do—gathering facts and evidence to solve and prevent crimes.

SABC - The South African Broadcasting Corporation (SABC) is the public broadcaster in South Africa. and SABC TV - Refers to South African Broadcasting Corporation Television Channels.

PBC - Premier Boxing Champions

BCMM - Buffalo City Metropolitan Municipality is situated on the east coast of Eastern Cape Province, South Africa. It includes the towns of East London, Bhisho and King William's Town, as well as the large townships of Mdantsane and Zwelitsha. *See also BCM or Buffalo City.*

PED - Performance Enhancing Drugs are substances that are used to improve any form of activity performance in humans.

KO – A knockout (abbreviated to KO or K.O.) is a fight-ending, winning criterion in several full-contact combat sports, such as boxing or kick-boxing and other mixed martial arts or sports involving striking.

EL – East London is a city on the southeast coast of South Africa in the Buffalo City Metropolitan Municipality of the Eastern Cape province.

EC - Eastern Cape is one of the provinces of South Africa. Its capital is Bhisho, but its two largest cities are East London and Gqeberha.

KZN – an abbreviation for Kwa-Zulu Natal (previously known only as Natal)

ECBPA - Eastern Cape Promoters Association

SAP - The South African Police (SAP) was the national police force and law enforcement agency in South Africa from 1913 to 1994; it was the de facto police force in the territory of South-West Africa (Namibia) from 1939 to 1981.

SAPS - South African Police Service (SAPS) is the national police force of the Republic of South Africa post the Apartheid era coming into effect in 1995.

UBF - Ubuntu Boxing Foundation

SATISCO - South African Tertiary Institutions Congress

BRDA - Boxing Reconstruction and Development Association BCMM

ECBPA - Eastern Cape Promoters Association

G.O.A.T - Greatest (Fighter) Of All Time

SANROC - The South African Non-Racial Olympic Committee

NOCSA - National Olympic Committee Of South Africa

SAABA - South African Amateur Boxing Association

SAABU - South African Amateur Boxing Union

SAABCO - South African Amateur Boxing Council

SAABF - South African Amateur Boxing Federation

SANABO - South African National Boxing Organisation

SANBCC - South African National Boxing Coordinating Council

Border Council of Churches - The South African Council of Churches (SACC) is an interdenominational forum in South Africa. It was a prominent anti-apartheid organisation during the years of apartheid in South Africa. Its leaders have included Desmond Tutu, Beyers Naudé and Frank Chikane. It is a member of the Fellowship of Christian Councils in Southern Africa.

Apartheid - In South Africa, it refers to a policy or system of segregation or discrimination on grounds of race. Apartheid is an Afrikaans word meaning "separateness", or "the state of being apart", literally "apart-hood" (from Afrikaans "-heid").

Shack or shacks – a shack (or, less often, shanty) is a type of small, often primitive shelter or dwelling. In South Africa, this often refers to temporary accommodation put together by squatters.

Black Homelands Citizenship Act (1970) - Bantu Homelands Citizenship Act, 1970 was a Self Determination or denaturalization law passed during the apartheid era of South Africa that allocated various tribes or nations of black South Africans as citizens of their traditional black tribal "homelands," or Bantustans

The Group Areas Act (1950) - Under the Group Areas Act (1950) the cities and towns of South Africa were divided into segregated residential and business areas. Thousands of Coloureds, Blacks, and Indians were removed from areas classified for white occupation. The Group Areas Act and the Land Acts maintained residential segregation.

Boxing Act 11 0f 2001 – a law promulgated to create synergy between professional and amateur boxing; to establish a Boxing Commission known as Boxing SA; to promote interaction between associations of boxers, managers, promoters, trainers and officials and Boxing SA; and. to provide for matters connected therewith.

Bantu Education - in South Africa under apartheid was the official system of education for black South Africans enacted by The Bantu Education Act of 1953.

The Bantu Education Act of 1953 - was a South African segregation law that legalized several aspects of the apartheid system. Its major provision was enforcing racially separated educational facilities.

Baddest - in Urban slang, means the coolest, the toughest, the best.

Indaba - indaba (pronounced in-dah-bah) is an important conference held by the izinDuna (principal men) of the Zulu and Xhosa peoples of South Africa. The term "Indaba" comes from the Zulu and Xhosa languages. It means "business" or "matter"

Bantu - relating to or denoting a group of Niger-Congo languages spoken in central and southern Africa, including Swahili, Xhosa, and Zulu.

Ubuntu - ubuntu means "I am, because you are." The word ubuntu is just part of the Zulu phrase "Umuntu ngumuntu ngabantu", which literally means that a person is a person through other people.

isiXhosa - the Bantu language of the Xhosa people, one of the official languages of South Africa.

AmaXhosa – means or refers to Xhosa speaking people (amaXhosa, amaMpondo, abaThembu and amaMpondomise). The Xhosa are a South African cultural group who emphasise traditional practices and customs inherited from their forefathers.

Bra (brah) or bru - an informal term for "my friend" or "mate", deriving from "brother." In Township speak, it is often a sign of respect to some older with no relations to the person being spoken about.

Muti or uMuthi - Pronounced moo-ti refers to Medicine in general however in the South Africa context it refers to traditional medicine, from the isiZulu or isiXhosa muthi.

Sizakophul'amathambo - 'We're gonna break your bones. Intimidation to the visiting boxing fight opponents.'

Unkabi phesheya phaya - loosely means the strong guy over there.

Andindedwanga - I never walk alone

Ukugqwakaza - cattle on locked horns like they are fighting when they're actually playing.

Ukucweya - done by men or boys when they hit and block in fighting an action when they are not hitting the target. Same as ukugqwakaza in cattle.

Ukucweya - in boxing is also the same as ukugqawakaza. However, in boxing, it is more intense, very close to the actual fighting. Sometimes even more. It is called sparring.

Nank'unomeva - Nomeva is a wasp. This is a Xhosa traditional song.

Inkunzi - literally means a bull. In Xhosa tradition, it refers to the champion among boys in stick fighting.

Ingwenya – a Nguni (e.g. Zulu, Xhosa and siSwati) word for a crocodile. However, among Xhosa people, this also refers to anyone with a considerable measure of success.

Umrhabulo - political education or enlightenment

Oxholovane – a Xhosa manner of speaking which refers to the main man or the man of the moment

Gawul' eshiya - One who never looks back or has no follow up.

Shebeen - in South Africa, is an informal licensed drinking place in a township.

Inja yeGame - tough guy

Isirhoxo - spaza shop or small shop usually located in the township

Uyingwe - You're the man

Ululating - a reverberating screaming sound made by women as a sign of appreciation or encouragement.

Kombi – in South African it refers to a minibus, especially one used to transport passengers commercially.

Makuliiiiiiiiwe – this is a call for a fight to start or continue, literally meaning "let's get on" or "let the fight begin."

Akulahlwa mbeleko ngakufelwa - keep on trying until you succeed.

BOXING WEIGHT DIVISIONS

There were traditionally eight weight divisions in men's boxing. More divisions were added, and professional governing bodies now recognize a total of 17 weight classes, which had their current names established by the major boxing organizations in 2015. The upper limits of these classes are delimited as follows:

- » Minimum Weight, 105 pounds (48 kg)
- » Junior Flyweight, 108 pounds (49 kg)
- » Flyweight, 112 pounds (51 kg)
- » Super flyweight, 115 pounds (52 kg)
- » Bantamweight, 118 pounds (53.5 kg)
- » Super bantamweight, 122 pounds (55 kg)
- » Featherweight, 125 pounds (57 kg)
- » Super featherweight, 130 pounds (59 kg)
- » Lightweight, 135 pounds (61 kg)
- » Super lightweight, 140 pounds (63.5 kg)
- » Welterweight, 147 pounds (67 kg)

- » Super welterweight, 154 pounds (70 kg)
- » Middleweight, 160 pounds (72.5 kg)
- » Super middleweight, 168 pounds (76 kg)
- » Light heavyweight, 175 pounds (79 kg)
- » Cruiserweight, 200 pounds (91 kg)
- » Heavyweight, unlimited

In all world and national title fights, weight limits must be strictly observed, although fighters are often allowed by contract to weigh-in the day before a fight. If a boxer is over the limit, he is normally given a short time in which to make the stipulated weight. If he still fails, the bout usually proceeds, but if the overweight fighter wins the bout, the title for which he was fighting is declared vacant.

In Olympic-style amateur boxing the weight divisions for men are:

- » Light flyweight, not more than 108 pounds (49 kg)
- » Flyweight, 115 pounds (52 kg)
- » Bantamweight, 123 pounds (56 kg)
- » Lightweight, 132 pounds (60 kg)
- » Light welterweight, 141 pounds (64 kg)
- » Welterweight, 152 pounds (69 kg)
- » Middleweight, 165 pounds (75 kg)
- » Light heavyweight, 178 pounds (81 kg)
- » Heavyweight, 201 pounds (91 kg)
- » Super heavyweight, any weight over 201 pounds (91 kg)

There is no universal agreement on weight divisions within women's professional boxing, but amateur weight divisions are:

- » Flyweight, not more than 106 pounds (48 kg)
- » Bantamweight, 112 pounds (51 kg)
- » Featherweight, 119 pounds (54 kg)
- » Lightweight, 126 pounds (57 kg)

- » Light welterweight, 132 pounds (60 kg)
- » Welterweight, 141 pounds (64 kg)
- » Middleweight, 152 pounds (69 kg)
- » Light heavyweight, 165 pounds (75 kg)
- » Heavyweight, 179 pounds (81 kg)
- » Super heavyweight, any weight over 179 pounds (81 kg)

Women's Olympic boxing is restricted to just three weight classes:

- » Flyweight, 106 to 112 pounds (48 to 51 kg)
- » Lightweight, 123 to 132 pounds (56 to 60 kg)
- » Middleweight, 152 to 165 pounds (69 to 75 kg)

ACKNOWLEDGEMENTS

To my wife, Nosambeso Lulama Constance, who has been there and worked through all the trials and tribulations, making sure that this book project and all other successes are achieved. Thank you Mnkabane, Mboyi, Majeke nomthi wembotyi.

To my children and grandchildren, whose presence and influence pushes me to reach out and gain beyond my normal personal limits. Ukwanda kwaliwa ngumthakathi.

To my brothers and sisters, as well as all members of my extended family and clan, amaQadi amahle, oNgcwina, oNgcinase, oMbushe, oWungushe, oMdlana, oMbinyashe, oDeku oMcilongo, omabiyangodaka, omaphilakuzenzela, omalaleqhingeni. Thank you for your genes that have made me the man I am. It is because of you that I can face this world and trade punches for punches without fear and expecting no favour. I am firm and I am fair. To my friends who have volunteered a lot of ideas to make this book rich and brimming with information, thank you!

Many thanks to Lonwabo Rani, Duma Buntu Maqubela, Zuko Blauw and Balungile Jamela. That's my formidable team that has continued to contribute towards the development and refinement of this project through all challenges. Thank you guys for believing in me and standing by me through thick and thin. Your contribution and effort have been invaluable.

This book would not be complete without acknowledging all those people who played a quiet but significant role behind the scenes to make Eastern Cape region the Mecca of boxing. They were big in their personal roles as businessmen and women, legal gurus, political activists, religious leaders, law enforcement officers and many the many other roles they played. They are, in no particular and not limited to the following individuals; Fikile Siyo, Papa Nomtshongwana, Sipho Tanana, Lennox Sebe, Charles Sebe, Pharmacist Mthimkhulu, Mpumelelo Nkonkobe, Charlie Nkonkobe, Phumelele Mrhwashu, Hintsa Siwisa, Matayiti Jwayi, Steve Tshwethe, Makhenkesi Stofile, Stanley Baleni, Wilson Mtya, Lukhanyo Mtya,, Tebro Nobongoza, Mncedisi Jekwa, Xola Pemba, Aubrey Bomela, Ben Thengimfene, Mlandeli Vazi, Mxolisi Makhongolo, Mazembe Khamanga, Tshawe Gordon Nginza, Dubs Msauli, Friday Kom, Ben Ntonga, Wandile Tutani, Vernon Mamo Ngani, Mzukisi Mcanyangwa, Mkhuseli Mcanyangwa, Willie Ncoko, Nceba Matoti, Braam Magqabi, Mr Ciliza, Simo Mjo, Mr Botha, Mzwandile Caga, Mbuti Adonis, Gilbert Wartle, Albert Tshetu. KT Wotshela, Foreman Skunana, Frank Magcoba, Mqondeni Bottoman, Eddie Makeba, Mr Sonjani, Mr Nontloko, TV Manyela, Brown Mngxaso, Lunga Mbi and Oom Xol Ncwayiba.

There were also women like Sis Tammie Woji who was the owner of Emthini Tavern. This used to be the watering hole for boxing fans from around the country. There were also Thandiwe Maliwa, Nomalungelo Gabelana, Nozuko Tyatyaza, Nontsikelelo Jamela, Winnie Maretloane, Noyoli Woji, Tutu Siko, Maggie Mjo, and my mother Winnie Mtya. May their souls' dwell in our boxing rings and make our boxing and all its participants safer.

My gratitude would not be complete if I do not say *Huntshu* to DAIMLER, the local Mercedes-Benz Group plant that has been boxing's biggest fan base from the beginning till now.

Last but not least, to you, dear reader, thank you for believing in the works of my hands. This book would only be in vain if not for you to read it. God bless you as you read this book.

INDEX & REFERENCES

A

Acting
  CEO 190, 377
Adv. Dali Mpofu 91
African
  culture 48, 52, 65, 67, 90, 114, 130, 135, 138, 145, 146, 149, 289, 290, 363, 365, 367, 368, 369, 371, 395
  traditional religions 48, 52, 65, 67, 90, 91, 92, 94, 95, 114, 130, 135, 138, 145, 167, 169, 277, 293, 297, 298, 299, 303, 365, 375, 379, 392
Ali Funeka 46
Amanda Ngutha 272
Amateur boxing 84, 152, 179, 180, 192, 193, 272, 330, 331, 367, 369, 372
amaXhosa 149, 268, 313
AmaXhosa 307
AmaXhosa tribe. *See also* Xhosa speaking people
Amphitheatre 143
ANC, 335, 354
Ancient Greece 141
Andrew Matyila 130, 186, 188, 218
Apartheid 52, 91, 135, 152, 162, 169, 178, 181, 224, 277, 293, 295, 307, 348, 352, 367, 368, 389, 391
  Government 52, 91, 135, 152, 162, 169, 178, 181, 224, 234, 277, 293
  rule 52, 91, 135, 152, 162, 169, 178, 181, 224, 234, 277, 293, 295, 307, 312, 317, 319, 348, 352, 367, 368, 389, 391
Apartheid Era 277, 317, 319, 330
Apartheid Rule 162, 178, 234, 312, 412.
  See Apartheid
Atlantic City 214

B

Baleka Mbethe 276
Bantu Education 167, 295
Bantu Holomisa 158
Bare-knuckle
  boxing 149
BBM. *See* Border Boxing Movement
BCM 62, 66, 83, 179
Benito Philips 234, 333
Bert Blewett 298, 315, 349, 391
Bible of Boxing 137
BK Investment Holdings 361, 362
black

promoter 49, 50, 51, 52, 53, 63, 64, 66, 88, 91, 135, 136, 138, 149, 153, 165, 193, 198, 201, 324, 331, 347, 349, 368, 390, 392

Black
  Boxing Heavyweight 49, 50, 51, 52, 53, 63, 64, 66, 88, 91, 135, 136, 138, 149, 153, 170, 317, 319, 324, 327, 328, 329, 331, 368, 390, 392
  people in South Africa 49

Black managed 64
black promoter. *See also* Black Promoters
Black trainers 64
Bloemfontein 169
Border Boxing Board 172, 289, 293, 312
Border Boxing Commission 181, 317
Boxing 145
  analyst 116, 136
  clubs 174
  Control Act in South Africa in 1923 146
  event management companies 50
  fans 47, 61, 63, 83, 91, 96, 111, 130, 131, 372, 377, 378, 379,
  gloves 47, 63, 86, 87, 88, 89, 117, 118, 362, 368, 369, 370, 389, 390,
  license 187
  licensees 90
  manager 222
  promoters 136
  trainers 112
  venue 48
Boxing Act. *See also* South African Boxing Act of 2001
Boxing development 272, 280, 298, 334, 360, 368
Boxing gyms. *See also* Boxing gym
Boxing International Hall Of Fame 346, 347
Boxing Journalism 345
Boxing managers 63, 66, 415
Boxing Mecca 153, 162, 177, 196, 242, 261, 272, 291, 314, 315, 321, 333
Boxing SA 91. *See also* BSA
Boxing South Africa. *See also* Boxing SA
Boyboy Mpulampula 179, 328, 331, 360, 414

Branco Milenkovic 135, 237, 283
Brian Mitchell 52, 185, 219, 221, 289, 325, 346, 347, 348
Brian Wysonke 53, 266
British occupation 147
BSA 87
Buffalo City 61, 62, 88, 148, 155, 157, 174, 178, 190, 299, 315, 324
  boxers and administrators 61, 62, 88, 148, 155, 157, 174, 178, 190, 193, 195, 196, 220, 223, 299, 312
Business
  acumen 50, 63, 86, 88, 135, 137, 152, 181, 188, 238, 280, 282, 292, 293, 304, 312, 321, 349, 352, 361, 362, 363

C

Cape Colony 145, 147, 148, 149, 223
Cape Province 61, 155, 156, 157, 160, 189, 221, 237, 241, 243, 277, 302, 326, 329, 331, 339, 357, 365, 415
Cape Times 146
Casino 326
Category. *See* Categories
Cedric Kushner 324
Character 131
Charles Sebe 156, 161, 163, 164, 198, 253
Chris Hani 158
Christian 308
Christianity 167, 414
Clive Sikhwebu 264, 265, 269, 355
Coach. *See also* Trainer
Coaches. *See also* Coach
Confidence 129
  in boxing 129
Corona. *See also* Covid-19
Covid-19 375
Cricket 291
Cyril Adams 174, 323
Cyril Groupe 234
Cyril Ramaphosa 376, 377

D

Daily Dispatch 239, 284, 305, 306, 307, 308, 318, 333, 354
Daily Sun 309
Danile Nzimela 193
Defence 127
Democratic Republic of Congo 239
Department
  of Sports Arts and Culture 96
Dieting 113
Dingaan Thobela 52, 219, 335, 349
Discipline 131
Don King 134, 135, 207, 239, 284
Duncan Village 175, 178
  Boxing Club 152, 153, 154, 165, 171, 174, 175, 178, 180, 182, 202, 214, 257, 272, 282, 287, 288, 289, 292, 293, 294, 296, 297, 332, 333
  Community Center 152, 153, 154, 165, 171, 174, 175, 178, 180, 182, 202, 214, 257, 272, 282, 287, 288, 289, 292, 293, 294, 296, 297, 332, 333
Dutch East India Company 149

E

Eastern Cape 44, 61, 85, 118, 134, 148, 155, 179, 185, 312, 323, 329, 338, 340, 357, 392
  boxing managers 63
  community 92
  Department of Sports Arts And Culture 92
  Government 44, 61, 86, 118, 134, 148, 155, 304, 312, 323, 329, 331, 338, 340, 357, 392
  Promoters Association 87
East London 49, 50, 52, 152, 163, 168, 170, 175, 190, 201, 252, 276, 304, 307, 314, 321, 328, 331, 339
East London Harbour 152, 153
EC. *See* Eastern Cape Province
EC Government. *See also* Eastern Cape Government
Egyptians 140
England 142
Ethics
  of Journalism 415
European countries 144
experienced trainer. *See also* Trainer

F

Father
  of boxing 143, 291, 295
Fighter 123. *See also* Boxer
Fight fixing 133, 135, 137
Fighting
  Skills 126
Fikile Mbalula 351
Financial
  challenges 48, 62, 68, 84, 85, 86, 88, 90, 94, 147, 192, 208, 235, 245, 247, 272, 274, 280, 283, 315, 359, 361
First World War 144
Floyd Mayweather 47, 137, 242, 415, 417
Flyweight 45, 91, 157, 184, 185, 187, 188, 191, 192, 194, 239, 249, 251, 269, 280, 328, 333, 340, 372
Foreign
  boxers 415
Fort Hare University 91, 180, 181, 254, 316, 317, 320, 328
France 144, 325, 348, 416
Frere Hospital 263, 264

G

Galelekile Botha 192
Gambling 141, 214, 239
garage gyms. *See also* boxing gym
Gauteng 50, 51, 52, 62, 239
  managers 65
  Province 61, 67
General Charles Sebe 163, 164
Germany 144, 242
Ginsberg 90, 152, 173, 199, 208, 223, 224, 327
Golden Gloves 65
Golden Gloves Promotions. *See also* Golden Gloves
Gold Reef City 299
Government 143
  funding 85, 88

Great Britain. *See also* England
Greek gladiators 141
Gym 118. *See also* Boxing Gym

H

Head butting 142
Heavyweight
  boxer 47
  championship 134
Heavyweights 135, 142, 151, 276
Higher Being. *See also* God
Home
  of boxing 61, 114, 135, 148, 166, 172, 187, 308, 332, 335, 345, 346, 348, 349, 350, 360, 369, 370, 376

I

IBF 45, 135, 159, 176, 185, 236, 237, 238, 240, 242, 246, 251, 328, 329, 379
International
  Boxing club 67, 135, 159, 171, 174, 175, 176, 180, 211, 235, 237, 246, 289, 346, 347, 349, 359, 366
Iraq 140, 141
IsiXhosa. *See also* Xhosa language
Italian 134, 218

J

Jeff Ellis 318, 320, 358
Joe Frazier 213
Junior
  Featherweight champion 46, 159, 177, 180, 195, 221, 224, 325, 328, 329, 335, 338, 340, 379
  Lightweight title 46, 159, 177, 180, 182, 184, 185, 192, 221, 289, 303, 324, 325, 328, 340, 379
Junior Lightweight Title. *See also* Junior Lightweight Champion

K

Kimberly 145, 148, 149, 169, 208, 284, 331
King. *See also* Don King

King Korn 84, 91, 235
King Williams Town 152, 153, 178, 204, 223
Knuckle City 288, 390
KwaZulu-Natal 292

L

Larry Holmes 135, 213
Last Born Promotions 65, 194, 243, 244, 245, 302, 303, 417
Las Vegas 214, 334, 391, 417
Leadership
  skills 87, 157, 170, 186, 197, 234, 292, 369
Legalisation
  of boxing 145
Lennox Lewis 212
Leonard Neil 317
Les Muller 154, 172, 192, 234, 263, 289, 302, 312, 320, 326, 328, 329
Lightweight 46, 157, 159, 177, 180, 188, 221, 249, 289, 299, 313, 314, 329
Lindi Memani 45
London Prize Ring Rules 147
Losing
  weight 119
Ludwig Japhet 145

M

Madison Square Garden 213
Makhenkesi Stofile 91
Mayweather. *See also* Floyd Mayweather
Mbali Zantsi 273, 274, 330
Mbulelo Botile 45, 176, 177, 182, 185, 237, 250, 313, 329, 417
Mdantsane 48, 53, 154, 155, 157, 158, 161, 163, 164, 169, 173, 174, 175, 177, 191, 214, 258, 355, 372, 392
  halls 209
Media ii, 302, 390, 394
Mesopotamia 141
Middleweight 45, 95, 113, 130, 158, 180, 182, 188, 193, 221, 239, 250, 273, 281, 282, 299, 335, 348, 349, 358
  boxing champion 113

412 | BOXING - THE STORY OF MONEY, BLOOD, SWEAT AND TEARS

Middleweights 151
Mike Donovan 113
Mike Tyson 417
Minister
   for Sports 91, 224, 272, 274, 285, 308, 319, 320, 327, 351, 353, 354, 376, 377, 378
   of Defence 91, 224, 272, 274, 285, 308, 319, 320, 327, 351, 353, 354, 376, 377, 378
   of Health 91, 224, 272, 274, 285, 308, 319, 320, 327, 351, 353, 354, 376, 377, 378, 417
   of Sports Arts and Culture 91, 224, 272, 274, 285, 308, 319, 320, 327, 351, 353, 354, 376, 377, 378, 417
Money 1
Muhammad Ali 47, 134, 135, 147, 213, 390, 392, 417
Mxolisi Ntshuca 239, 284, 308, 318
Mzimasi Mnguni 182, 185, 214, 324, 325, 329
Mzi Mnguni 193, 235, 236, 312, 321, 323

N

Natal. *See also* KwaZulu-Natal
Nathi Mthethwa 377
National
   Sports Council 48, 53, 67, 146, 148, 154, 174, 175, 178, 328, 351, 377
National Boxing Convention 352
National Party 162, 178
National Relief Fund 377
National title. *See also* Championship
NBA. *See* National Boxing Association
Nceba Gqaleni 182
Nelson Mandela 67, 158, 286, 287, 324, 393, 418
Netball 170, 177, 201, 259, 291
Newspapers 146
New York iii, 213, 218, 328, 347, 418
New Zealand 271
Ngconde Balfour 224, 272, 274, 327, 351, 352, 353
Nkosana Mgxaji 126, 153, 158, 164, 171, 174, 180, 201, 252, 260, 293, 294, 302, 313, 314, 325, 337, 339
Nkqubela Gwazela 157
Nofoti Tsenene 330, 362
Nomandithini Ndyambo 195, 273
Northwest
   Province 171, 239, 246, 365
Nosimo Balindlela 276
Nubian 140

O

Offensive Boxing. *See also* Fighting
Old Buck Belt 224
Old Buck Gin 235
Olympic Games 67, 181, 328, 368, 372, 418
   in Atlanta, Georgia 1996 67
Olympic Style Boxing 373
Open Boxing 372, 373
Orient Theatre 174, 186, 212, 215, 216, 217, 218, 219, 220, 242, 246, 286, 288, 391, 392, 418
OR Tambo 67, 148, 418
   Municipality 148
Oscar De La Hoya 137, 241

P

PAC 170, 334, 335
Patrice Motsepe 285
Patrick Quka 45
Peter Bacela 198, 204, 306
Peter Ngatane 87, 254, 267, 317, 319, 320, 321
Philip Ndou 286, 361
Phindile Ngingi 192
Physical
   Strength 125
Political 146
   party affiliations 146
Port Elizabeth 53
praise. *See also* Worship
Professional
   boxing in South Africa 146

Q

Queen Shabalala 273
Queenstown 152, 153

R

Rhodesian. *See also* Zimbabwe
Ring Magazine 137, 345
Ring Officials 289, 290, 300, 359
Roman Amphitheatres 141
Roman Empire 141
Rome 141, 345
Ron Jackson 147, 318
Rugby 125, 153, 154, 167, 170, 171, 186, 191, 198, 201, 202, 205, 208, 209, , 292, 294, 295, 299, 307, 327, 361
Rules
  of Boxing 142
Rules and Regulations 91, 312
Rumble in The Jungle 239

S

SA. *See* South Africa
Sanctioning
  fees 134, 136, 237, 239, 240, 289, 311, 312, 346, 348, 349, 365, 366
Sandi Kwaza 197
Sinethemba Mncane 157
Siphiwe Nonqayi 46
Sisa Dukashe stadium 48, 158, 173, 174, 201, 294, 320, 338, 339
Smuts Ngonyama 260, 276
South Africa 144
South African
  boxing 65
  Boxing Act 11 of 2001 90, 95
  boxing scene 94
  championships 48, 52, 65, 67, 90, 91, 92, 94, 95, 114, 130, 135, 138, 145, 146, 149, 365, 372, 395
  context boxers 48
  Flyweight champion 91
  Heavyweight Champions. *See also* South African Heavyweight Division
  history 48, 52, 65, 67, 90, 91, 92, 94, 95, 114, 130, 135, 138, 145, 146, 149, 155, 65, 367, 368, 369, 371, 372, 373, 375, 379, 392, 395
National Boxing Control Commission 48, 52, 65, 67, 90, 91, 92, 94, 95, 114, 130, 145, 354, 371, 392
South African Olympic 355
Sowetan Sunday World 309
Soweto 48, 148, 202, 207, 313, 314, 338, 347, 412, 419
Spokes Witbooi 161, 162, 164, 190, 199, 252, 296
Sponsors. *See also* Sponsorship
Sponsorship 50, 63, 65, 67, 87, 88, 94, 184, 192, 194, 197, 207, 235, 244, 300, 314, 361, 372
Sports Aid 304
Sports Leadership 304
Sportsmen 67
Stan Christodoulou 346, 348
Stanley Christodoulou 51, 311, 394
Steve Tshwete 276, 319, 351
Sugar Ray Leonard 137, 419
Sun City 392, 419
Sunday Times 307, 309, 389, 390, 392, 394

T

Tennis 209
Terror Lekota 276
Thabo Mbeki 67, 276, 419
The Act. *See also* South African Boxing Act 11 of 2001
The Government. *See* South African Government
The Sowetan 309
Trainers. *See also* Trainer
Transkei championship 156
Transvaal 145, 171, 199, 202, 251, 254, 353, 365
TV coverage 65

U

Ubuntu 166, 301
Uitenhage 162, 286, 327, 360, 361
UK 47, 208
United Kingdom. *See also* UK

United States of America. *See also* USA
USA 47, 140, 144, 208

V

Victories. *See also* Victory
Village boy 152
Vodacom 84, 90, 91, 328, 353
Vuyani Bungu 45, 185
Vuyani Gxashe 182
Vuyo Nomvethe 176

W

Walter Sisulu 67, 158
WBA 46, 49, 159, 185, 211, 237, 240, 241, 242, 250, 269, 282, 311, 312, 315, 330, 335, 339, 346, 348, 349, 360
  championship 46, 49, 159, 185, 211, 237, 240, 241, 242, 250, 269, 282, 311, 312, 315, 330, 335, 339, 346, 348, 349, 360
WBC 135, 237
WBC International 159, 282, 283
WBF Intercontinental 159
WBO 95
WBO African 159
Weight
  categories 121, 142, 420
  classifications 113, 114, 118, 121, 122, 189, 252, 268, 273, 299, 417
  division 122
  fluctuations 119
Weight-class. *See also* Weight classifications
Weight fluctuation 119
Weight management 113
Welcome Ncita 45, 126, 182, 206, 207, 208, 211, 237, 284, 319, 323, 324, 325, 328, 329, 340, 348, 349
West Bank 165, 205, 291
White
  boxers 48, 62, 84, 91, 153, 165, 172, 173, 190, 207, 215, 235, 239, 251, 289, 292, 318, 326, 327, 328, 331, 347
  promoters 48, 84, 135, 138, 143, 149, 167, 190, 199, 206, 328, 357, 358

Winnie Madikizela Mandela 67
World
  Bantamweight championship 135
  championship 66
  Heavyweight champion 212
  Junior Flyweight title 48, 51, 53, 65, 66, 68, 83, 164, 170, 175, 176, 177, 178, 182, 184, 205, 263, 265, 272, 354, 361, 366, 375, 392, 393

X

Xhosa 178
  language 149, 178, 198, 208, 217, 305, 308, 309
  roots 208
  speaking people 149, 178, 198, 208, 217, 305, 308, 309
Xhosaland 233
Xolani Mcotheli 186, 195, 218
Xolisani Ndongeni 46

Z

Zimbabwe 283, 293, 334, 389, 390
Zinzi Mandela 208
Zola Madyaka 171, 182
Zolani Petelo 45, 177, 182, 185, 214, 237, 313, 329, 421
Zolani Tete 46, 127, 193, 194, 218, 240, 243, 244, 251, 281, 285, 302, 303, 350, 361
Zolile Tete 183
Zweli Mkhize 376
Zwelitsha Township 198

redOystor

AN INVITATION FROM THE PUBLISHER

Join us at www.redoystor.com or connect with us on facebook, instagram and twitter @redOystor to be part of a community of people who love the very best in books and reading.

Whether you want to discover more about the author or the book, read more about upcoming events, interviews or watch trailers, or have a chance to win early limited editions, we think you will like what you are looking for.

And if you don't, let us know what's missing through our contact us page or email us at **theEditor@redoystor.com**

We love what we do, and we'd love you to be a part of it.

www.redoystor.com

www.ingramcontent.com/pod-product-compliance
Lightning Source LLC
Chambersburg PA
CBHW020827160426
43192CB00007B/550